SOCIAL RESEARCH

SOCIAL RESEARCH

Theory, Methods and Techniques

PIERGIORGIO CORBETTA

Translated from the Italian by Bernard Patrick

SAGE Publications

London • Thousand Oaks • New Delhi

© Piergiorgio Corbetta 2003

First published 2003

Apart from any fair dealing for the purposes of research or
private study, or criticism or review, as permitted under the
Copyright, Designs and Patents Act, 1988, this publication
may be reproduced, stored or transmitted in any form, or by
any means, only with the prior permission in writing of the
publishers, or in the case of reprographic reproduction, in
accordance with the terms of licences issued by the Copyright
Licensing Agency. Inquiries concerning reproduction outside
those terms should be sent to the publishers.

SAGE Publications Ltd
6 Bonhill Street
London EC2A 4PU

SAGE Publications Inc.
2455 Teller Road
Thousand Oaks, California 91320

SAGE Publications India Pvt Ltd
B-42, Panchsheel Enclave
Post Box 4109
New Delhi 110 017

British Library Cataloguing in Publication data

A catalogue record for this book is available from the British Library

ISBN 0 7619 7252 8
ISBN 0 7619 7253 6 (pbk)

Library of Congress Control Number 2002112356

Typeset by C&M Digitals (P) Ltd., Chennai, India
Printed in Great Britain by The Alden Press, Oxford

Contents

Introduction

One of the problems facing a teacher of social research methodology is the shortage of manuals of a general, introductory nature. Recent years have witnessed an ongoing process of fine-tuning of the techniques of collection and analysis of social data and a marked differentiation among research instruments. As regards the quantitative approach to research, these developments have involved both data collection (with the near hegemony of the survey, the growing importance of secondary analysis, centralized archives, panel studies, international comparative surveys) and data analysis (through the creation of increasingly sophisticated statistical techniques). At the same time, qualitative research has experienced a veritable boom in new methods and approaches which, under various labels (critical theory, semiotics, structuralism, deconstructionism, interpretive theory, biographical approach, etc.) have given fresh impetus to this way of tackling social research.

This process of fine-tuning and differentiation has been mirrored by the production of textbooks. Anyone who walks into a 'social research supermarket' will find the shelves stacked with manuals and handbooks, each one focusing on some particular subject or technique. If, however, the reader is looking for a complete general manual, a sort of 'first textbook' that explains what social research is, how it developed historically and how it can be undertaken today, in its various branches and different approaches, the search is likely to be an arduous one.

It is this need for a general synthesis that has given rise to the present volume. First of all, I believe that an introductory manual of social research must necessarily start out by illustrating the philosophical foundations on which the various research methods have been constructed. The empirical approach to the study of society sprang from the enthusiasm of the positivist illusion at a time when it seemed that the research methods that reigned in the natural sciences and in technology could be applied to the study of man and society. This perspective, however, was soon challenged by those who maintained that the human sciences could not be equated with the natural sciences and that research on people and society had to be conducted along alternative pathways which would safeguard the intrinsic individuality and irreproducibility of the human being. It was in these two opposing views, which became consolidated at the beginning of the twentieth century, that the methods and techniques of social research were rooted, and I am convinced that without an understanding of this fundamental philosophical dichotomy it is impossible for the student to understand fully the spirit that animates the techniques themselves.

With regard to the methods of quantitative research, it was my intention to write a manual that did not focus solely on the survey as a technique of social investigation. Although this subject has been given the attention it deserves – today it is the most important and widely used social research technique – I have also dealt with experimentation in depth. This decision was based not only on the importance of experimentation in social psychology but also, and especially, on the conviction that only a complete understanding of the logic underpinning experimentation enables us fully to understand the issue of causality and how it can be tackled in the social sciences. In addition, I have also examined an important and often neglected source of social information: official statistics. Modern society generates masses of social statistics, which constitute a source of knowledge and provide an empirical base for important studies that cannot be carried out with other means.

At the same time, it was my aim to analyse the logic of social research and to devote ample space to the delicate passage from theory to empirical research, from hypotheses to concepts, indicators and variables; in other words, to the question of so-called 'operationalization'. While all these issues constituted the core of methodology in the 1940s and 1950s – a flourishing period for social research, which saw the great contribution of American sociology and in particular of Paul Lazarsfeld – in recent times they have risked slipping into oblivion. Over the years, the term 'methodology' has gradually become synonymous with 'statistical techniques of data analysis'. This has partly been due to the introduction of information technology and the widespread use of personal computers and specialized social research software. While such developments have given an enormous boost to the techniques of data processing, they have also been accompanied by a critical decline in attention to the procedures through which the data themselves are constructed and gathered. The negligence with which this phase of research is carried out, the lack of control and, in general, the scant sensitivity towards the accuracy of data and the reliability of operational definitions engender the risk of carrying out sophisticated elaboration of flimsy data, thereby producing 'garbage research'. It can never be repeated too often that no technique of analysis can improve the quality of the data, and that this quality – which is established *before* the analysis is undertaken – therefore imposes precise constraints on the validity of the results yielded by statistical analysis.

If a social research manual aims to be 'complete', it must of course place proper emphasis on the qualitative approach. As the reader will see, I uphold the view that, although the quantitative and qualitative approaches to social research differ radically, they are nevertheless eminently complementary. According to whether we wish to access the 'world of facts' or the 'world of meanings', we will choose one approach or the other. Two different approaches to the same reality can both make significant contributions to our knowledge of that reality. Indeed, it is almost universally accepted that a painting by Raphael and a painting by Picasso are both works of art, and yet there is an enormous difference between the apparent naturalism and personal interpretivism of the two underlying artistic paradigms.

Nonetheless, the reader will notice that the greater space has been devoted to quantitative techniques. This does not mean that I consider the quantitative approach to be superior. Rather, the main reason behind this choice lies in the fact that the qualitative perspective, because of its very subjectivity, does not lend itself to formalization, and is therefore more difficult to transform into schematic procedures that can be communicated through a textbook. Unlike quantitative research, it does not possess a codified arsenal of techniques, and many of its procedures have to be worked out in the field, in the unique interaction between the observer and the observed. Furthermore, it should be borne in mind that in sociological experience (which constitutes the basic reference of this volume) the long tradition of quantitative research has, for at least 80 years, uninterruptedly accumulated an imposing array of tried and tested techniques. By contrast, the qualitative approach, after its rich and fruitful initial phase, became sidelined for the entire period (from the 1940s to the 1980s) in which neo-positivist sociology predominated, coming back into play only in recent years.

In discussing qualitative research, I have not only dealt with the best known and most commonly applied techniques, such as participant observation and qualitative interviews, but also with the 'analysis of documents', a heading under which I have grouped both personal documents (letters, diaries, etc.) and institutional documents (court sentences, company reports, mass media output, etc.). In modern society, individuals and institutions produce huge numbers of documents every day; these constitute a treasure chest of empirical material for the study of the most diverse social phenomena.

My long experience in teaching has convinced me of the difficulty of 'learning to do research' without actually 'doing research'. Indeed, only by applying the techniques directly to theoretical problems and to empirical material can one become fully aware of both the potential and the limitations of these tools, and therefore learn to choose the strategies that fit the individual cases. Naturally, reading a book (or teaching by means of theoretical lectures) is by no means the same as learning or teaching through 'doing' (in fact, it is the very opposite).

In an attempt to offset (to some degree) this intrinsic shortcoming of the 'book medium', I have included in the text, wherever possible, a range of examples drawn from actual research. The purpose of these examples is to visualize the context in which the illustrated technique has been used, the questions that the researcher was trying to answer, the efficacy of the technique and the conclusions reached. These examples have been taken from sociology, anthropology, social psychology, political science, education and history, in order to provide as complete a view as possible of social research and its basic unitary nature. Naturally, however, my own scientific background and experience as a researcher have prompted me to place the accent on sociology. The strategy of using examples to illustrate techniques has been adopted most frequently in the part of the book that deals with qualitative research; in the absence of standardized methods, it seems to me that the use of examples taken from actual research projects is the best way of getting across to the student the great variety of situations encountered in qualitative sociology and its creativity in terms of technical solutions, approaches and documentary sources.

This book is intended to be rigorous, complete, and simple. Completeness demands that a wide range of subjects be dealt with; the first chapter has a vaguely philosophical slant, while some sections of the book – such as those on experimentation, sampling and scaling – contain a few more formalized passages. Rigor demands a certain attention to terminology, and the reader is constantly reminded of the definitions of terms; while these may seem prolix, useless or pedantic, in my view they help to maintain conceptual clarity and terminological accuracy. As for simplicity, I have taken as my point of reference a student who has absolutely no knowledge of social research. Hence, nothing is ever taken for granted and each concept or new term is explained as it is introduced. Moreover, I have tried to maintain a measured pace when explaining, without worrying about repeating myself, and bearing in mind the ancient Latin motto *repetita juvant* (repetition is helpful). As a result, some passages may appear excessively lengthy; however, I feel that this is preferable to excessive concision.

Simple does not mean simplistic. If some parts seem particularly simple, this means that I have succeeded in my aim. Nevertheless, the reader should beware of such apparent simplicity. Doing empirical research in the social sciences is a difficult challenge and one that has been faced by generations of scholars. It should be remembered that today's apparently simple acquisitions are the result of decades of discussion and argument, that many problems remain to be solved, and that solutions are never definitive, but rather bound to evolve over time.

This book is no mere introduction, nor does it claim to provide an exhaustive treatment of the field. Needless to say, the philosophical foundations and the technicalities of social research have not been discussed in depth. Although important, certain issues have been dealt with fairly rapidly; others have deliberately been omitted. In any case, even with regard to those issues that are dealt with more completely, the reader will need to refer to more specialized texts containing empirical applications, in order to become fully conversant with that specific sector. In this respect, the present volume only aims to provide as complete an illustration as possible of the potential, the fields of application and the variety of social research. It can therefore be regarded as a starting point for further investigation of the various techniques; there is no shortage of high-quality specialized material.

This book has been written with three types of reader in mind. First, social science students. Even if they are not destined to become actual 'empirical researchers', in other words to do research in the field, only through learning the methodology and techniques of social research will they be able to learn what social science *is*. Indeed, research methodology stands at the very core of the social sciences; it constitutes the essence, or distinguishing characteristic, of social science; it is indeed what makes social science a 'science', as distinct from other kinds of intellectual activity, such as philosophical speculation. No one who is interested in exploring the nature of the social sciences can do so without some familiarity with social research methodology.

Second, the book is intended for those who want to learn how to 'do research'. Clearly, for anyone wishing to become a professional researcher, it can be no more than a 'first book' and will be followed by many others dealing with specific issues (starting with a good statistics handbook). The present text should be able to provide such readers with a general overview – a solid base on which to build up subsequent knowledge.

Finally, it aims to be of use to the ordinary 'consumer' of social research. In all sectors and at all levels of modern society, among policy-makers, social workers, journalists and so on, there is a growing need to keep track of social phenomena. Such information often takes the form of avalanches of data, percentages, tables and graphs, research reports, case studies, international comparisons and statistical simulations, all of which require skills for informed critical interpretation. It is my hope

that this book will be able to provide the critical tools needed.

Outline of the book

The book is divided into three parts. The *first part* (Chapters 1 and 2) illustrates the two basic paradigms – quantitative and qualitative – of social research, describes their origins in philosophical thought, and outlines their current interpretations. The first chapter reconstructs the philosophical foundations of the two approaches and their historical genesis, and traces their subsequent development. In the second chapter, concrete examples are used to illustrate what quantitative and qualitative research consist of today. In addition, the differences between the two approaches are analysed point by point, starting from the ideal types of each kind of research.

The *second part* (Chapters 3–8) is devoted to quantitative research. Chapter 3 deals with the delicate phase of operationalization – a veritable bridge between theory and research. The chapter therefore examines theory, hypotheses, concepts and variables, and introduces the *language of variables*, which constitutes the true distinguishing feature of quantitative social research – a completely new way of talking about social reality, which differs from the traditional language of concepts.

Chapter 4 tackles the problem of causality. The concept of cause is central to all sciences, but it is also highly problematic; in the social sciences in particular, this concept is enormously difficult to transfer into the empirical setting. It could not therefore be overlooked in a book of this kind. The concept is dealt with alongside what is the most coherent attempt at empirical corroboration of the causal relationship, the experiment (with particular reference to the experiments conducted in social psychology).

Chapter 5 looks at the survey. Though this is only one of the data-gathering tools available in social research, it is currently the most widely used technique of social investigation. The in-depth examination of the subject begins with the fundamental problems that arise when we attempt to study society by questioning its members, and then moves on to look at how questions are formulated and data are collected. Finally, an outline is provided of the current situation, in which large archives set up by national and international agencies provide data on which research can be carried out directly.

The subject of Chapter 6 is 'scaling' — that is to say, 'measuring' complex concepts. This issue is closely linked to those of the operationalization of concepts (Chapter 3) and the survey (Chapter 5), in that it largely involves 'measuring' opinions and attitudes, once again by questioning the subjects studied.

Chapter 7 focuses on official sources of statistics. Produced by governments (as in the case of the census) or by nationwide agencies, official statistics constitute a very important (and often under-exploited) source of information on society.

Finally, Chapter 8 concludes the part of the book devoted to quantitative research by exploring sampling issues, which are a prerequisite both for survey-based studies and for a great deal of research conducted through official statistics.

The *third part* of the book (Chapters 9–11) is devoted to qualitative research. Schematic analysis of this field is much more difficult than that of quantitative research, since the techniques used cannot easily be distinguished from one another and are often interwoven. The strategy adopted here has been to break down the analysis into three chapters according to whether the data-gathering operation is conducted through 'observing', 'questioning' or 'reading'.

Chapter 9 looks at the oldest and most classical of the qualitative techniques, that of participant observation. A certain amount of space is also devoted to more recent developments and other types of observation, such as those utilized in a broad range of ethnomethodological studies.

Chapter 10 deals with the qualitative interview, which may be regarded as the qualitative counterpart of the survey. While the distinctions made (among structured, semi-structured and unstructured interviews) may appear to be slightly contrived, they nevertheless meet the inevitable need to systematize the material for presentation in textbook form.

Finally, Chapter 11 discusses the analysis of 'documents'. This term covers a host of documentary material autonomously produced by individuals and institutions, which the social researcher can gather and 'read'.

To conclude this presentation, I wish to express my thanks to all those who have provided me with valuable advice, suggestions and ideas – in short, scientific dialogue. Various colleagues read parts of the book, and I discussed specific issues with others. In particular, I wish to thank Fabrizio Bernardi, Massimiano Bucchi, Sergio Brasini, Mario Callegaro, Giorgio Chiari, Antonio Cobalti, Asher Colombo, Giolo Fele, Pierangelo Peri, Marilena Pillati, Maurizio Pisati, Francesca Rodolfi, Raffaella Solaini, Marco Santoro and Antonio Strati. I am especially indebted to Alberto Marradi, with whom I discussed virtually every topic, and from whom I received precious intellectual stimuli. I would also like to thank my friends at the Istituto Cattaneo, Marzio Barbagli, Roberto Cartocci, Raimondo Catanzaro, Arturo Parisi, Hans Schadee and Giancarlo Gasperoni, with whom I shared many years of research and lively discussion, and who have surely left their mark on this book. I am also grateful to my friends at the Survey Research Center of Berkeley University – and to the directors Percy Tannenbaum, Mike Hout and Henry Brady – where I spent a sabbatical year and various subsequent study periods of full immersion in the American empirical research experience. Among my American colleagues at Berkeley, my special thanks go to Tom Piazza and Jim Wiley for their lengthy and substantive discussions and valuable suggestions. I am particularly grateful to Jon Stiles, whose help in adapting the chapter on Official Statistics to the American and British contexts was fundamental. Finally, I wish to thank Bernard Patrick, who tackled the arduous task of translating the text from Italian to English with creativity and competence.

Part One

The Logic of Social Research

1 Paradigms of Social Research

This chapter illustrates the philosophical bases of the two basic approaches to social research which gave rise to the families of quantitative and qualitative techniques. We will begin with the concept of paradigm – that is, the perspective that inspires and directs a given science. Then we shall examine the historical roots and the guiding principles of the positivist and the interpretive paradigms. The chapter ends with a few reflections concerning currents trends in social research.

1. KUHN AND THE PARADIGMS OF SCIENCES

The notion of 'paradigm' has ancient origins in the history of philosophical thought. It was utilized both by Plato (to mean 'model') and by Aristotle (to mean 'example'). In the social sciences its use has been inflated and confused by multiple and different meanings: these range from a synonym for theory to an internal subdivision of a theory, from a system of ideas of a pre-scientific nature to a school of thought, from an exemplary research procedure to the equivalent of

method. It seems useful therefore briefly to review the meaning given to the concept of the paradigm by the scholar who, in the 1960s, brought it once again to the attention of philosophers and sociologists of science. We are referring to Thomas Kuhn and his celebrated essay *The Structure of Scientific Revolutions* (1962).

Reflecting on the historical development of the sciences, Kuhn refuted the traditional understanding of the sciences as a cumulative and linear progression of new acquisitions. According to the traditional conception, single inventions and discoveries would be added to the previous body of knowledge in the same manner as bricks are placed one on top of another in the construction of a building. According to Kuhn, however, while this is the process of science in 'normal' times, there are also 'revolutionary' moments, in which the continuity with the past is broken and a new construction is begun, just as – to take up the building metaphor again – from time to time, an old brick building is blown up to make room for a structurally different one, for example a skyscraper made of glass and aluminium.

Kuhn illustrates his argument with a rich collection of examples from the natural sciences (especially from physics). For instance, he cites the development of optical physics, which is currently interpreted in quantum terms; according to this view, light is made up of photons, which display some of the features of waves and some of the properties of particles. Kuhn points out that, before quantum theory was developed by Planck, Einstein and others, light was believed to be a transversal wave movement. This latter theory was developed at the beginning of the nineteenth century. Still earlier, in the seventeenth century, the dominant view was that of Newtonian optics, according to which light was made up of material corpuscles.

The shift from one theoretical perspective to another is so pervasive and has such radical consequences for the discipline concerned that Kuhn does not hesitate to use the term 'scientific revolution'. What changes in a given discipline after one of these revolutions? It produces 'a shift in the problems available for scientific scrutiny and in the standards by which the profession determined what it should count as an admissible problem or as a legitimate problem-solution' (1962: 6). A reorientation in the discipline occurs that consists of 'a displacement of the conceptual network through which scientists view the world' (1962: 102). This 'conceptual network' is what Kuhn calls a 'paradigm',

and it is this aspect of his theorising, rather than his analysis of the developmental process in science, that interests us here.

Without a paradigm a science lacks orientations and criteria of choice: all problems, all methods, all techniques are equally legitimate. By contrast, the paradigm constitutes a guide: 'Paradigms' – recalls Kuhn – 'provide scientists not only with a map but also with some of the directions essential for map-making. In learning a paradigm the scientist acquires theory, methods, and standards together, usually in an inextricable mixture' (1962: 109).

Kuhn defines *normal science* as those phases in a scientific discipline during which a given paradigm, amply agreed to by the scientific community, predominates. During this phase, as long as the operating paradigm is not replaced by another in a 'revolutionary' manner, a scientific discipline does indeed develop in that linear and cumulative way that has been attributed to the whole of scientific development. 'No part of the aim of normal science is to call forth new sort of phenomena … Instead, normal-scientific research is directed to the articulation of those phenomena and theories that the paradigm already supplies' (Kuhn, 1962: 24).

Numerous examples of scientific paradigms are to be found in the history of the

---

BOX 1.1   PARADIGM

What does Thomas Kuhn mean by 'paradigm'? He means a theoretical perspective:

- accepted by the community of scientists of a given discipline
- founded on the previous acquisitions of that discipline
- that directs research through:

  o the specification and choice of what to study
  o the formulation of hypotheses to explain the phenomenon observed
  o the identification of the most suitable empirical research techniques.

natural sciences. Going back to our previous example, we can speak of corpuscular, wave, and quantum paradigms in optical physics. Likewise, as examples of alternative paradigms that have succeeded one another in time, we can quote Newtonian and Einsteinian mechanics, Ptolemaic and Copernican cosmology, and so on.

To what extent can we speak of paradigms in the social sciences? Kuhn notes that the paradigm is a characteristic feature of the 'mature' sciences. Before the corpuscular theory of light was introduced by Newton, no common paradigm existed among scientists in this sector; instead, various schools and sub-schools opposed and competed with one another, each with its own theory and point of view. Consequently, concludes Kuhn, 'The net result of their activity was something less than science' (1962: 13). In this perspective, because the social sciences lack a single paradigm broadly shared by the scientific community, they are in a pre-paradigmatic state, except perhaps for economics (according to Kuhn, 'economists agree on what economics is', while 'it remains an open question what parts of social science have yet acquired such paradigm at all' (1962: 14).

What has been said with regard to the social sciences also holds for sociology. Indeed, it is difficult to identify a paradigm that has been agreed upon, even for limited periods, by the community of sociologists. Nevertheless, there exists another interpretation of the thinking of Kuhn, which has been proposed in an attempt to apply his categories to sociology. This interpretation redefines the concept of the paradigm, maintaining all the elements of the original definition (theoretical perspective that defines the relevance of social phenomena, puts forward interpretative hypotheses and orients the techniques of empirical research) except one: that the paradigm is agreed upon by the members of the scientific community. This paves the way for the presence of multiple paradigms inside a given discipline; thus, instead of being a *pre-paradigmatic* discipline, sociology becomes a *multi-paradigmatic* one.

This is the interpretation of Friedrichs (1970) who, after highlighting the paradigm inspired by Parsons' structural-functionalism, sees in the Marxist dialectic approach the second paradigm of sociology, in which the concepts of system and consensus that are central to functionalism are replaced by that of conflict.

This interpretation of the concept of the paradigm in terms of an overall theoretical perspective which does not exclude other perspectives but rather is in open competition with them, is certainly the most widespread interpretation and corresponds to the current use of the term in the social sciences. Nevertheless, this less rigorous interpretation, which adapts Kuhn's original category to the status of the social sciences, must not be trivialized by equating a paradigm with a theory or a school of thought. Indeed, fundamental to the concept of the paradigm is its pre-theoretical and, in the final analysis, metaphysical character of a 'guiding vision', 'a view of the world', which shapes and organizes both theoretical reflection and empirical research and, as such, precedes both.

In this interpretation, the concept of the paradigm seems useful in analysing the various basic frames of reference that have been put forward, and which are still being evaluated in the field of social research methodology.

2. THREE BASIC QUESTIONS

Having defined and circumscribed the concept of a paradigm and briefly discussed its application to the social sciences, we will now abandon the slippery terrain of the paradigms of *sociological theory* (one paradigm? two paradigms? a hundred paradigms?) for more solid ground: the methodology of *social research*. We will not, however, go deeply into the complex epistemological problems of how many and which philosophical frameworks guide empirical research in the social sciences. Instead, we will confine ourselves to a historical review by briefly describing the fundamental perspectives that have been proposed and become accepted during the evolution of the discipline. Since this is a book on social research techniques, it seems natural and proper to begin by raising the question of *the founding paradigms of social research*, from which the first operative procedures emerged, and which subsequently guided the development of empirical research. Indeed, as has been said, one of the functions of a paradigm is to establish acceptable research methods and techniques in a discipline. As Hughes writes:

> Every research tool or procedure is inextricably embedded in commitments to particular versions of the world and ways of knowing that world made by researchers using them. To use a questionnaire, an attitude scale of behavior, take the role of a participant observer, select a random sample ... is to be involved in conceptions of the world which allow these instruments to be used for the purposes conceived. No technique or method of investigation ... is self validating: its effectiveness, its very status as a research instrument ... is dependent, ultimately, on philosophical justification. (Hughes, 1980: 13)

Within the philosophical perspectives that generated and have accompanied the growth of social research, can we identify visions that are sufficiently general, cohesive and operative to be characterized as paradigms? It seems so. Indeed, there is broad agreement among scholars that two general frames of reference have *historically oriented* social research since its inception: the 'empiricist' vision and the 'humanist' vision. Various labels have been used, including 'objectivism' and 'subjectivism'; here, we will utilize the canonical term 'positivism' and the less consolidated 'interpretivism'. As we will soon see, these are two organic and strongly opposed visions of social reality and how it should be understood; and they have generated two coherent and highly differentiated blocks of research techniques. Before describing

these techniques, however, it is essential to explore their philosophical origins, since only by doing so can we achieve a full understanding of them.

In order to adequately compare the two above-mentioned paradigms, we will attempt to understand how they respond to the fundamental interrogatives facing social research (and scientific research in general). These can be traced back to three basic questions: Does (social) reality exist? Is it knowable? How can we acquire knowledge about it? In other words: *Essence, Knowledge and Method*.[1]

The ontological question[2]   This is the question of 'what'. It regards the nature and form of social reality. It asks if the world of social phenomena is a real and objective world endowed with an autonomous existence outside the human mind and independent from the interpretation given to it by the subject. It asks, therefore, if social phenomena are 'things in their own right' or 'representations of things'. The problem is linked to the more general philosophical question of the existence of things and of the external world. Indeed, the existence of an idea in the mind tells us nothing about the existence of the object in reality, just as a painting of a unicorn does not prove the existence of unicorns.

The epistemological question[3]   This is the question of the relationship between the 'who' and the 'what' (and the outcome of this relationship). It regards the knowability of social reality and, above all, focuses on the relationship between the observer and the reality observed. Clearly, the answer to this question depends on the answer to the previous ontological question. If the social world exists in its own right, independently from human action, the aspiration to reach it and understand it in a detached, objective way, without fear of altering it during the course of the cognitive process, will be legitimate. Closely connected with the answer given to the epistemological question are the forms knowledge can take: these range from deterministic 'natural laws' dominated by the categories of cause and effect, to less cogent (probabilistic) laws, to various kinds of generalizations (e.g. Weberian ideal types), to the exclusion of generalizations (only specific and contingent knowledge being admissible).

The methodological question[4]   This is the question of 'how' (how can social reality be studied?). It therefore regards the technical instruments of the cognitive process. Here, too, the answers depend closely on the answers to the previous questions. A vision of social reality as an external object that is not influenced by the cognitive research procedures of the scientist will accept manipulative techniques (e.g. experimentation, the control of variables, etc.) more readily than a perspective that underlines the existence of interactive processes between the scholar and the object studied.

The three questions are therefore interrelated, not only because the answers to each are greatly influenced by the answers to the other two, but also because it is sometimes difficult to distinguish the boundaries between them (though, for the purpose of our exposition, we will try to do so). Indeed, it is difficult to separate conceptions of the nature of social reality from reflections on whether (and how) it may be understood and, in turn, to separate these from the techniques that can be used to understand it. Then again, these interrelations are implicit in the very definition of the scientific paradigm which, as we have seen, is both a theoretical perspective and a guide to research procedures.

3. POSITIVISM

Table 1.1 shows a synopsis of the different paradigms with regard to the fundamental questions introduced above. First of all, it will be noted that two versions of positivism are presented: the original nineteenth-century version, to which even the most tenacious empiricists no longer subscribe, and its twentieth-century reformulation, which was constructed to address the manifest limits of the original version. The original positivist paradigm is presented both for historical reasons – since it was the vision that accompanied the birth of the social sciences and, in particular, the birth of sociology – and because the character of the other two paradigms can be better understood by examining the criticisms levelled against it.

Sociology was born under the auspices of positivist thought. In the middle of the nineteenth century, when the investigation of social phenomena was evolving into a subject of scientific study, the paradigm of the natural sciences reigned supreme. Inevitably, the new discipline took this paradigm as its model. Indeed, the founders of the discipline, Auguste Comte and Herbert Spencer among them, shared a naïve faith in the methods of natural science. The positivist paradigm is no more than this: *the study of social reality utilizing the conceptual framework, the techniques of observation and measurement, the instruments of mathematical analysis, and the procedures of inference of the natural sciences.*

Let us look more closely at the distinctive elements of this definition. The conceptual framework: the categories of 'natural law', cause and effect, empirical verification, explanation, etc. The techniques of observation and measurement: the use of quantitative variables, even for qualitative phenomena; measurement procedures applied to ideological orientation, mental abilities and psychological states (attitude measurement, intelligence tests, etc.) Mathematical analysis: the use of statistics, mathematical models, etc. The procedures of inference: the inductive process, whereby hypotheses regarding the unknown are formed on the basis of what is known and specific observations give rise to general laws; the use of theory to predict outcomes; extrapolation from the sample to the whole population.

According to Comte, the prophet of nineteenth-century sociological positivism, the acquisition of the positivist viewpoint constituted, in all sciences, the end-point of a trend that had previously passed through theological and metaphysical stages. Such development

Table 1.1 *Characteristics of the basic paradigms of social research*

	Positivism	**Postpositivism**	**Interpretivism**
Ontology	Naïve realism: social reality is 'real' and knowable (as if it were a 'thing')	Critical realism: social reality is 'real' but knowable only in an imperfect and probabilistic manner	Constructivism: the knowable world is that of meanings attributed by individuals. Relativism (multiple realities): these constructed realities vary in form and content among individuals, groups, and cultures
Epistemology	Dualism-objectivity	Modified dualism-objectivity	Non-dualism; non-objectivity. Researcher and object of study are not separate, but interdependent
	True results	Results probabilistically true	
	Experimental science in search of laws	Experimental science in search of laws Multiplicity of theories for the same fact	Interpretive science in search of meaning
	Goal: explanation Generalizations: 'natural' immutable laws	Goal: explanation Generalizations: provisional laws, open to revision	Goal: comprehension Generalizations: opportunity structures; ideal types
Methodology	Experimental-manipulative	Modified experimental-manipulative	Empathetic interaction between scholar and object studied
	Observation Observer-observed detachment	Observation Observer-observed detachment	Interpretation Observer-observed interaction
	Mostly induction	Mostly deduction (disproof of hypotheses)	Inuction (knowledge emerges from the reality studied)
	Quantitative techniques	Quantitative techniques with some qualitative	Qualitative techniques.
	Analysis 'by variables'	Analysis 'by variables'	Analysis 'by cases'

Source: Partially adapted from Guba and Lincoln (1994: 109).

did not occur at the same time in all disciplines; it first took place in the inorganic sciences, such as astronomy, physics and chemistry, followed by the organic sciences, such as biology. It was therefore natural, in the progression from simple to complex material, that the positivist approach should be applied to the most complex material of all:

society. Thus, a new science would emerge: sociology, the positive science of society. According to this view, science is universal, and scientific method is unique. The social sciences do not differ from the natural sciences, and the positivist way of thinking that brought such great advances in the fields of astronomy, physics and biology is destined to triumph even when its focus shifts from natural objects to social objects, such as religion, politics and work.

The first attempt to apply this overall theoretical perspective to empirical research was made by Durkheim. Indeed, as Durkheim pointed out:

> Up to now sociology has dealt more or less exclusively not with things, but with concepts. It is true that Comte proclaimed that social phenomena are natural facts subject to natural laws. In so doing he implicitly recognized there are only things. Yet when, leaving behind these general philosophical statements, he tries to apply his principle and deduce from it the science it contained, it is ideas which he too takes as the object of study. (Durkheim, 1895: 63)

By contrast, Durkheim actually tried to translate the positivist principles of thought into empirical procedures; he was the first 'social scientist', the first true positivist sociologist. His empirical procedure is founded on the theory of 'social fact'. In his *Rules of Sociological Method*, he states at the outset that 'the first and most basic rule is to *consider social facts as things*' (1895: 60). For Durkheim, social facts are:

> Ways of acting, thinking and feeling which possess the remarkable property of existing outside of the consciousness of the individual ... When I perform the duties as a ... husband or a citizen ... I carry out the commitments I have entered into, I fulfil obligations which are defined in by law and custom and which are external to myself and my actions. Even when they conform to my sentiments and when I feel their reality within me, that reality does not cease to be objective, for it is not I who have prescribed these duties; I have received them through education ... Similarly the believer has discovered from birth, ready fashioned, the beliefs and practices of his religious life; if they existed before he did, it follows that they exist outside him ... (Likewise, for as far as) the system of signs that I employ to express my thoughts, the monetary system I use to pay my debts ... the practices I follow in my profession, etc., all function independently from the use I make of them. (Durkheim, 1895: 50–51)

These social facts, even if they are not material entities, nonetheless have the same properties as the 'things' of the natural world, and from this derive two consequences. On the one hand, social facts are not subject to human will; they are things that offer resistance to human intervention; they condition and limit it. On the other hand, just like the phenomena of the natural world, they function according to their own rules. They possess a deterministic structure that can be discovered through scientific research. Thus, notwithstanding their different objects, the natural world and the social world share a substantial *methodological unity* (they can both be studied through the same investigative logic and the same method, hence the name 'social physics' attributed to the study of society).

The first assertion is, therefore, that social reality exists outside the individual. The second is that this social reality is objectively understandable, and the third that it can be studied by means of the same methods as the natural sciences. As Durkheim states, 'Our rule implies no metaphysical conception, no speculation about the innermost depth of being. What it demands is that the sociologist should assume the state of mind of physicists, chemists or in physiologists, when they venture into an as yet unexplored area of their scientific field' (1895: 37). And again: 'Our main objective is to extend the scope of scientific rationalism to cover human behaviour ... What has been termed our positivism is merely a consequence of this rationalism.' (Durkheim, 1895: 33)

Let us now look at how this understanding is acquired. Positivism is fundamentally inductive, where *induction* means 'moving from the particular to the general'[5] the process by which generalizations or universal laws are derived from empirical observation, from the identification of regularities and recurrences in the fraction of reality that is empirically studied. Implicit in inductive procedures is

---

BOX 1.2   ANSWERS GIVEN BY POSITIVISM TO THE THREE BASIC QUESTIONS

Ontology: naïve realism   This position stems from everything that has been said regarding the 'codification' of social reality, and can be succinctly expressed by two propositions: (a) there exists an objective social reality that is external to human beings, whether they are studying or performing social acts; (b) this reality is knowable in its true essence.[6]

Epistemology: dualist and objectivist; natural law   The assertion that knowledge is attainable is based on two assumptions: (a) that the scholar and the object studied are independent entities (dualism); (b) that the scholar can study the object without influencing it or being influenced by it (objectivity). Investigation is carried out as if through a 'one-way mirror'. Knowledge assumes the form of 'laws' based on the categories of cause and effect. These laws are part of an external reality that is independent of the observer ('natural laws'); the scientist's task is to 'discover them'. There is no fear that the researcher's values might distort her reading of social reality, or vice versa. This position, which excludes values in favour of facts, necessarily derives from the vision of social fact as *given* and unmodifiable.

Methodology: experimental and manipulative   The methods and techniques of positivist research – like its basic conception – draw heavily on the classical empiricist approach to the natural sciences. Two features of the experimental method are taken up: (a) its use of inductive procedures, whereby general formulations are derived from particular observations; and (b) its mathematical formulation which, though not always attainable, is the final goal of the positivist scientist. The ideal technique remains – even though its applicability to social reality is limited – that of experiment, founded on manipulation and control of the variables involved and the detachment of the observer from what is observed.

---

the assumption of order and uniformity in nature, that universal organizing principles exist. The task of the scientist is, of course, to discover these. This vision has long dominated the natural sciences and has even been identified with the scientific method. In assuming that social life, like all other phenomena, is subject to immutable natural laws, the positivist conception of society fully adopts this vision. According to Durkheim, the social scientist is an explorer 'Conscious that he is penetrating into the unknown. He must feel himself in the presence of facts governed by laws as unsuspected as those of life before the science of biology was evolved. He must hold himself ready to make discoveries which will surprise and disconcert him.' (1895: 37)

Finally, with regard to the 'form' of this knowledge, there is no doubt that these laws of nature will eventually be identified, formulated, demonstrated and 'proved'; in their most complete form, they are laws that link cause and effect:

Since the law of causality has been verified in the other domains of nature and has progressively extended its authority from the physical and chemical world to the biological world, and from the latter to the psychological world, one may justifiably grant that it is likewise true for the social world. Today it is possible to add that the research undertaken on the basis of this postulate tends to confirm this. (Durkheim, 1895: 159).

In the positivist paradigm, the elements that we have called 'naïve faith' in the methods of the natural sciences are all too evident. Underlying the various manifestations of positivism there is always, in fact, a sort of enthusiasm for 'positive' scientific knowledge, whereby the 'scientific method' is viewed as the only valid means of achieving true knowledge in all fields of human endeavour.

4. NEOPOSITIVISM AND POSTPOSITIVISM

Throughout the twentieth century, the positivist approach was continually revised and adjusted in attempts to overcome its intrinsic limits. The reassuring clarity and linearity of nineteenth-century positivism gave way to a twentieth-century version that was much more complex and detailed and, in some respects, contradictory and unclear. However, some basic assumptions were maintained, such as ontological realism ('the world exists independently of our awareness of it') and the pre-eminent role of empirical observation in understanding this world. We will not enter into the details of this development, or the various phases of its history; rather, we will mention only 'neopositivism', the term used

to denote the approach that dominated in the period from the 1930s to the 1960s, and 'postpositivism', which is used to identify its further evolution from the end of the 1960s onwards.[7] We will therefore outline the principal shifts in perspective that occurred – over time and with differing degrees of intensity – with respect to the positivist orthodoxy presented in the previous section.

One of the first revisions of nineteenth-century positivism was made by the school known as *logical positivism*, which gave rise to neopositivism. The movement formed around the discussions of a group of scholars of different disciplinary origins who, in the second half of the 1920s, constituted the so-called 'Vienna Circle'. Among its principal exponents were the philosophers Schlick and Carnap, the mathematician Hahn, the economist Neurath, and the physicist Frank. A few years later, a group of like-minded thinkers (Reichenbach, Herzberg, Lewin, Hempel and others) was formed in Berlin. In the wake of Nazi persecution, some notable representatives of this school emigrated to the United States, where the affinity between their views and American pragmatism contributed considerably to the spread of neopositivist thought. This influenced other disciplines, including sociology, which had been developing a very rich tradition of empirical research in the United States throughout the 1930s.

The new point of view assigned a central role to the criticism of science and redefined the task of philosophy, which was to abandon its broad theorization in order to undertake critical analysis of the theories elaborated within single disciplines (Schlick hoped to see a time when there would be no more books on philosophy, but all books would be written in a 'philosophical way'). This led to the rejection of the 'great questions' and of all metaphysical issues that could not be demonstrated ('pseudo-problems'), and which were therefore branded as meaningless. Instead, the utmost attention was devoted to methodological problems in every science, to the logical analysis of their language and their theoretical output, to the criticism of their assumptions, and – not least – to the procedures by which conceptual elaboration could be empirically verified.

From what has been said, it is evident that epistemological questions are central to this movement of thought, and the influence it had on the methodology of the sciences, including the social sciences, is comprehensible. It must be remembered that one of the postulates of neopositivism is the widespread conviction that the meaning of a statement derives from its empirical verifiability. The formula 'the meaning of a proposition is the method of its verification' neatly summarizes this point of view.

What did this conception of science and scientific knowledge mean for social research? What were the repercussions on operational procedures and research techniques? The main consequence was the development of a completely new way of speaking about social reality, using a language borrowed from mathematics and statistics. Paul F. Lazarsfeld, the principal exponent of neopositivist empirical methodology in sociology, called this the *language of variables*. Every social object, beginning with the individual, was analytically defined on the basis of a range of attributes and properties ('variables'), and was reduced to these; and social phenomena were analysed in terms of relationships among variables. The variable, with its neutral character and objectivity, thus became the protagonist of social analysis; there was no longer any need to recompose the original object or individual as a whole again. In this way social research became 'depersonalized', and the language of variables, with the measurement of concepts, the distinction between dependent and independent variables, the quantification of their interrelations and the formulation of causal models, provided a formal instrument that allowed social scientists to go beyond 'the notoriously vague everyday language (in a process of) clarification and purification of discourse (that is)

very important for the social scientist; ... we must sort out this knowledge and organize it in some manageable form; we must reformulate common sense statements so that they can be subjected to empirical test' (Lazarsfeld and Rosenberg, 1955: 2,11). In this way, all social phenomena could be surveyed, measured, correlated, elaborated and formalized and the theories either confirmed or disproved in an objective manner without ambiguity.

But nothing would ever be the same again. The twentieth-century conception of science was by now far removed from the solid certainties of nineteenth-century positivism, in which a 'mechanical' conception of reality dominated, together with a reassuring belief in immutable laws and faith in the irresistible progress of science. This new philosophic-scientific atmosphere arose first of all out of developments in the natural sciences and, in particular, in physics, during the early years of the new century. Quantum mechanics, Einstein's special and general theories of relativity, Heisenberg's principle of uncertainty – to cite only a few of the cornerstones of the new physics – introduced elements of probability and uncertainty to crucial areas such as the concept of causal law, the objectivity of the external world, and even the classical categories of space and time.

Theories were no longer expressed in terms of deterministic laws, but of probability. The crucial moment in this change was the shift from classical physics (Newtonian approach) to quantum physics. According to quantum mechanics, there are processes in elementary physics – so-called quantum jumps – that are not analyzable in terms of traditional causal mechanisms, but are absolutely unpredictable single facts governed by probabilistic laws. Scientific theories would no longer explain social phenomena through models characterized by logical necessity, and deterministic laws were replaced by probabilistic laws that implied the existence of haphazard elements and the presence of disturbances and fluctuations. If this notion of probabilistic indeterminism was valid for the natural world, then it would be even more valid for the social world, the world of language, thought, and human interaction.

An element introduced into scientific methodology by this evolution of positivism is the concept of falsification, which was taken up as a criterion for the empirical validation of a theory or a theoretical hypothesis. This states that a theory cannot be positively confirmed by data, and that empirical validation can take place only in the negative, through the 'non-confutation' of the theory by the data – that is to say, by demonstrating that the data do not contradict the hypothesis and, therefore, that the theory and the data are merely compatible. Positive proof is impossible, since the same data could be compatible with other theoretical hypotheses.

This position gives rise to a sense of the provisional nature of any theoretical statement, since it is *never definitively proven* and always exposed to the axe of possible disproof. As Popper writes, the idol of certainty crumbles: 'The old scientific ideal of *episteme* – of absolutely certain, demonstrable knowledge – has proved to be an idol. The demand for scientific objectivity makes it inevitable that every scientific statement must remain *tentative for ever*' (1934, English translation 1992: 280). Man cannot know but only conjecture. This point is also illustrated by a statement attributed to Einstein: 'to the degree that our propositions are certain, they say nothing about reality; to the degree that they say something, they are uncertain'.

Lastly, and this brings us to the most recent development of the postpositivist approach, it has become a widespread conviction that empirical observation, the very perception of reality, is not an objective picture, but is *theory-laden*,[8] in the sense that even the simple recording of reality depends on the researcher's frame of mind, and on social and cultural conditioning. In other words, despite the assumption that reality exists independently

from the cognitive and perceptive activity of humans, the act of understanding remains conditioned by the social circumstances and the theoretical framework in which it takes place. The thesis of the theory-laden nature of empirical observations – that is to say, the claim that no clear distinction exists between theoretical concepts and observed data – brings down the last positivist certainty: that of the objectivity of the data collected and of the neutrality and inter-subjectivity of the language of observation.

It must be said, nonetheless, that this process of moving away from the original positivist orthodoxy, first through neopositivism and then postpositivism, did not mean that the empiricist spirit was abandoned. Modern positivism, when its states that laws (both natural and social) are probabilistic and open to revision, when it affirms the conjectural nature of scientific knowledge and in the end, the theoretical conditioning of the observation itself, has come a long way from the naïve interpretation of the deterministic laws of the original positivism. It has lost its certainties, but does not repudiate its empiricist foundations. The new positivism redefines the initial presuppositions and the objectives of social research; but the empirical approach, though much amended and reinterpreted, still utilizes the original observational language, which was founded on the cornerstones of operationalization, quantification and generalization. And, since we are dealing with research techniques, it is this point that interests us here. The operational procedures, the ways of collecting data, the measurement operations and the statistical analyses have not fundamentally changed. Conclusions are more cautious, but the (quantitative) techniques utilized in reaching them are still the same.

At this point, we will conclude our brief excursus on the developments of the positivist paradigm by filling out the column in Table 1.1 regarding the positions of modern postpositivism on the three fundamental questions.

BOX 1.3 ANSWERS GIVEN BY NEO- AND POST-POSITIVISM TO THE THREE BASIC QUESTIONS

Ontology: critical realism As in the case of positivism, the existence of a reality external to human beings is assumed; but – contrary to what is upheld in the positivist paradigm – this reality is only imperfectly knowable, both because of the inevitable imperfection of human knowledge and because of the very nature of its laws, which are probabilistic. This point of view has also been called 'critical realism': realism, in that it assumes that cause-effect relationships exist in reality outside the human mind; critical, in that it underlines the view that the scientist must always be prepared to question every scientific acquisition.

Epistemology: modified dualism-objectivity; middle range, probabilistic and conjectural laws With regard to the question of the relationship between the scholar and the object studied, dualism, in the sense of separation and non-interference between the two realities, is no longer sustained. It is recognized that the subject conducting the study may exert a disturbing effect on the object of study, and that a reaction effect may ensue. The objectivity of knowledge remains the ideal goal and the reference criterion, but this can only be achieved approximately. In the cognitive process, deductive procedures are emphasized, through the mechanism of falsifying hypotheses. The intent remains that of formulating generalizations in the form of laws, even if limited in scope, probabilistic and provisional.

Methodology: modified experimental-manipulative The operational phases of research remain fundamentally inspired by a substantial detachment between the researcher and the object studied (experiments, manipulation of variables, quantitative interviews, statistical analysis, etc.). Nevertheless, qualitative methods are admitted. The scientific community is important as it critically analyses new hypotheses, and can confirm results by means of new experiments (repeated results are more likely to be true).

---

5. INTERPRETIVISM

5.1 Beginnings

Two versions of the positivist paradigm have been presented: the initial nineteenth-century perspective and its critical revision, carried out in the 1930s and again in the 1970s. The paradigm presented in this section underwent an almost symmetrical development. If we wished to stress the analogy between the two paradigms, we would introduce the initial vision of 'interpretive sociology', which owed both its methodological elaboration and its first attempts at empirical research, at the beginning of the twentieth century, to Max Weber (his role was symmetrical to that played by Durkheim in positivism). This would then be followed by the 1960s reinterpretation of the original approach, above all in American sociology. This, in turn, gave rise to the various lines of thought found in symbolic interactionism, phenomenological sociology and ethnomethodology, which, in spite of their differences, are unified by a common emphasis on individual interaction.

However, we prefer not to proceed in this manner, since there is no discontinuity between the original Weberian vision and subsequent developments, as there was in the shift from nineteenth to twentieth-century positivism. Instead, we will put these two historical blocks of approaches to social research together under the same heading and utilize the general term 'interpretivism' for all the theoretical visions in which reality is not simply to be observed, but rather 'interpreted'.

How did this new vision of social science arise? While positivism originated in nineteenth-century French and English cultures (we need mention only Auguste Comte, John Stuart Mill and Herbert Spencer) and owed its sociological development chiefly to the French culture (we are, of course, referring to Durkheim), its most radical and organic criticism emerged in the context of German historicism.

In general, the German philosopher Wilhelm Dilthey is credited with the first critical attack on Comtean scientism in the name of the autonomy of the human sciences – in the sense that they are non-homologous to the natural sciences. In his *Introduction to the Human Sciences* (1883), Dilthey draws a famous distinction between 'sciences of nature' and 'sciences of the spirit', basing the difference between them precisely on the relationship that is established between the researcher and the reality studied. Indeed, in the natural sciences the object studied consists of a reality that is external to the researcher and remains so during the course of the study; thus, knowledge takes the form of *explanation* (cause-effect laws, etc.). In the human sciences, by contrast, since there is no such detachment between the observer and what is observed, knowledge can be obtained only through a totally different process, that of *comprehension* (*Verstehen*). According to Dilthey, we *explain* nature, whereas we *understand* the life of the mind.

5.2 Max Weber: objectivity and orientation towards individuality

But it is only with Max Weber that this new perspective enters fully into the field of sociology. Indeed, Dilthey had spoken generically of 'sciences of the spirit', among which he singled out historiography. Weber brought the concept of *Verstehen* into sociology, and revised Dilthey's original position. While adopting the principle of *Verstehen*, Weber did not want to fall into subjectivist individualism or psychologism; he wanted to preserve the objectivity of social science both in terms of its being independent of value judgements, and in terms of the possibility of formulating statements of a general nature, even when an 'orientation towards individuality' is adopted.

Regarding the first point, throughout his life Weber reiterated the need for the historical and social sciences to be free from any value judgement whatsoever. However, his awareness of the problem (sharpened by his intense involvement in politics and, later, by the ethical questions arising from the imminent threat of world war) exceeded his ability to provide an unequivocal answer. Nonetheless, he never abandoned his conviction that the historical and social sciences must be *value-free*. 'The distinction between knowledge and judgement – that is to say, between fulfilling the scientific responsibility of seeing factual reality and the fulfilling the practical responsibility of defending one's own ideals – this is the principle to which we must adhere most firmly' (Weber, 1904).

While value judgements must be kept out of the historical and social sciences, values will, according to Weber, inevitably influence the choice of the objects of study, thus taking on a guiding role for the researcher. Even if they play no role in forming judgements, values are still involved in what could be called a 'selective function'; they serve to decide upon a field of research in which the study proceeds in an objective manner in order to reach causal explanations of phenomena.

Freedom from values was therefore the first condition for objectivity in the social sciences. The terms of the second condition, understood as the ability to produce statements which would be to some extent *general*, remained to be defined. According to Weber, the social sciences are to be distinguished from the natural sciences not on the basis of their object (as in Dilthey's contraposition of human sciences with the sciences of the spirit), nor because their goal is to study social phenomena in their individuality, since the social sciences also aim at formulating generalizations; rather, the distinction lies in their 'orientation towards individuality'.

This orientation is primarily one of method. For Weber the method is that of 'Verstehen'. However, in defining what he means by this, Weber rejects any form of psychologism. *Verstehen* is neither psychological perspicacity nor sudden illumination; it is the rational comprehension of the motivations underlying behaviour. It is not intuition, but 'interpretation': understanding the purpose of the action and grasping the intentional element in human behaviour. The ability to identify with others, which is inherent in *Verstehen*, is also channelled towards rational interpretation: putting oneself into the other person's position so as to 'understand'. This involves understanding the motivations of actions, the subjective meaning that individuals attribute to their own behaviour: because every action, even the most apparently illogical, has its own inner rationality, its own interior 'sense'. As Boudon writes:

> For Weber, to understand an individual action is to acquire sufficient means of obtaining information to understand the motives behind it. In his view, observers *understand* the action of an observed subject as soon as they can conclude that in the same situation it is quite probable that they too would act in the same way. ... As can be seen, *understanding* in the Weberian sense implies the ability of the observer *to put him or herself in the actor's place*, but does not in any way imply that actor's

subjectivity is immediately transparent. ... Indeed, the Weberian notion of *comprehension* designates a procedure which is very close to what textbooks of logic call 'ampliative induction' and which consists of reconstructing motives not directly accessible by cross-checking facts. (Boudon, 1984: 31, 51)

How can this orientation towards individuality yield objectivity? If we start with the individual and the subjective sense of his action, how can we attain objective knowledge that has general characteristics? Here we are faced with the second condition for objectivity in the historical and social sciences.

The answer is provided by the Weberian concept of the *ideal type*. For Weber, ideal types are forms of social action that are seen to recur in human behaviour, the typical uniformity of behaviour constituted through an abstractive process which, after isolating some elements within the multiplicity of empirical fact, proceeds to coordinate them into a coherent picture that is free from contradiction. The ideal type, then, is *an abstraction that comes from empirically observed regularities*.

The Weberian ideal type impinges upon all fields of social science and can be found at different levels of generality, ranging from the single individual to society as a whole. Weber exemplified ideal types with reference to social structures (for example capitalism), institutions (e.g. bureaucracy, church and sect, forms of power) and individual behaviour (e.g. rational behaviour).

These 'ideal types', writes Weber, are not to be 'confused with reality ... they were constructed in an ideal heuristic manner' (Weber, 1922a); they are 'ideal' in that they are mental constructs; they carry out a 'heuristic' function in that they direct knowledge. They are empty shells, 'fictions lacking life' as Schutz has described them; they have no concrete counterpart in reality, but are theoretical models that help the researcher to interpret reality. For example, probably none of the three ideal types of power Weber distinguishes – charismatic power, traditional power, and rational-legal power – has ever existed in its pure form. The ideal type is a clear, coherent, rational, unambiguous construct. Reality, however, is much more complex, contradictory and disorderly. No form of charismatic power that has ever existed has been wholly and exclusively charismatic; though globally identifiable with this Weberian 'type', the actual form will doubtless contain elements of the other two forms of power.

The regularities that the researcher pursues and identifies in order to interpret social reality are not 'laws' in the positivist sense. For Weber, 'the number and type of causes that have determined any individual event whatever, are in fact, always *infinite* … and the causal question, when treating the *individuality* of a phenomenon is not a question of laws but rather a question of concrete causal *connections* … the possibility of a selection within the infinity of determining elements' (Weber 1922b). Instead of laws, then, we have causal connections, or rather, to use Boudon's expressions, *mere possibilities or opportunity structures* ('If A, then most frequently B', Boudon, 1984: 75). It is therefore impossible to establish the factors that determine a certain social event or individual behaviour, but one can trace the conditions that make it possible.

Thus, in contraposition to the causal laws of the positivist approach, which are *general and deterministic* (though less so in the more probabilistic neopositivist interpretation), we have statements and connections characterized by *specificity* and *probability*.

5.3 Further developments

Weber has been discussed at some length because the work of the great German sociologist anticipated practically all the themes that would be subsequently developed in the rich vein of sociological theory and research that gave rise to approaches such as phenomenological sociology (Husserl and Schutz), symbolic interactionism (Mead and Blumer) and ethnomethodology (Garfinkel and Cicourel), which became established in American sociology from the 1960s onwards. All these perspectives share fundamental characteristics

of the Weberian approach: a strong anti-deterministic conviction; opposition to all philosophies of history and all forms of evolutionism; the fundamental 'ontological' difference between natural sciences and social sciences, and the irreducibility of the latter to the former's methods of research; and the criticism of any attempt to explain human action by starting from social systems and the conditioning factors within them. Finally, all of these approaches share – this time in positive terms – a strong conviction that 'individual action endowed with meaning' must be seen as the core of every social phenomenon and of the sociologist's work.

Weber, however, did not push his methodological approach to extreme consequences. While he elaborated these concepts in his methodological writings, in his theoretical reflections and empirical research he constantly operated on a macrosociological level, adopting the perspective of comparative history, in an effort to understand macrostructural phenomena such as the economy, the state, power, religion, and the bureaucracy. By contrast, the movement that arose in the United States in the 1960s developed the Weberian perspective in its natural direction, that is, in a 'micro' perspective. If society is built on the interpretations of individuals, and if it is their interaction that creates structures, then it is the interaction of individuals that one must study in order to understand society. This conviction opened up a completely new area of sociological research, the study of everyday life, which had formerly been disregarded as non-scientific.

It is clear that the interpretivist paradigm differs radically from the positivist frame of reference. The 'subjectivist' view is first of all a reaction to the 'objectivist' positivist position. By treating social reality and human action as something that could be studied objectively, the positivist approach overlooked the individual dimension: all those aspects that distinguish the world of human beings from the world of things. The very elements that disturbed the 'scientific'

BOX 1.4 ANSWERS GIVEN BY INTERPRETIVISM TO THE THREE BASIC QUESTIONS

Ontology: constructivism and relativism (multiple realities) 'Constructivism': the knowable world is that of the meanings attributed by individuals. The radical constructivist position virtually excludes the existence of an objective world (each individual produces his own reality). The moderate position does not ask whether a reality external to individual constructions exists, since it claims that only the latter can be known. 'Relativism': these meanings, or mental constructions, vary among individuals; and even when they are not strictly individual in that they are shared by the individuals within a group, they vary among cultures. A universal social reality valid for all persons, an absolute reality, does not exist; rather, there are multiple realities in that there are multiple and different perspectives from which people perceive and interpret social facts.

Epistemology: non-dualism and non-objectivity; ideal types, possibilities, opportunity structures The separation between the researcher and the object of study tends to disappear, just like that between ontology and epistemology. In contrast to the positivist vision, social research is defined as 'not an experimental science in search of law, but an interpretive one in search of meaning' (Geertz, 1973: 5), in which the central categories are those of value, meaning and purpose. In pursuing its objective, which is to understand individual behaviour, social science can utilize abstractions and generalizations: ideal types and possibilities or opportunity structures.

Methodology: empathetic interaction between the researcher and the object of study The interaction between the researcher and the object of study during the empirical phase of research is no longer judged negatively but constitutes, instead, the basis of the cognitive process. If the aim is to understand the meanings that subjects attribute to their own actions, the research techniques cannot be anything but qualitative and subjective, meaning that they will vary from case to case depending on the form taken by the interaction between the researcher and the object studied. Knowledge is obtained through a process of induction; it is 'discovered in reality' by the researcher who approaches it without prejudices or preconceived theories.

---

research of the positivist approach and were therefore excluded – individual, motivations and intentions, values, free will, in short, the subjective dimension that cannot be perceived by quantitative tools – become the primary object of interpretive research. It is on this fundamental difference between the objects studied that the interpretive point of view bases its alleged superiority over the positivist approach. The convinced supporter of the interpretive paradigm affirms not only the autonomy and diversity of the historical and social sciences from the natural sciences, but also their superiority, since only an approach that adopts the principle of *Verstehen* can achieve that understanding from the inside which is the basis of the knowledge of behaviour and of the social world.

These fundamental differences inevitably imply different techniques and research procedures. And it is this aspect that most interests us here. Indeed, if the essence of human life differs from that of the natural world, then it should be studied by means of different methods from those of the positivist approach. The subjectivist position cannot adopt 'the language of variables'. It cannot adopt it in the phase of empirical observation on account of the centrality of intentional and subjective components which, by definition, escape objective quantification and can be seized only through empathy. It cannot adopt it during the phase of data analysis because it cannot imagine analysing human behaviour in terms of the interaction of separate components (variables), as the human being is a whole that cannot be reduced to the sum of its parts. The subjectivist position has therefore developed its own research procedures, its own observation techniques and its own ways of analysing empirical reality, which form the body of so-called 'qualitative research'. This will be discussed in greater detail later. For now, we will conclude our presentation of the interpretive paradigm by summarizing this approach according to the scheme shown in Table 1.1.

6. A FINAL NOTE: RADICALIZATION, CRITICISM AND NEW TENDENCIES

In the previous sections we have described – with reference to their fundamental concepts and their founding fathers – the two paradigms which have guided social research and shaped its strategies and techniques since its inception. We will now mention the criticisms levelled at these two approaches and a few instances of their radicalization.

For what concerns the positivist paradigm, we have seen that great attention was focused, especially in the period of neopositivism, on formulating and developing empirical procedures. The radicalization of this trend gave rise to a sort of anti-speculative empiricism in which 'the method', and subsequently 'the data', reigned supreme; the task of the social scientist was no longer to formulate theories and then to test them empirically, but to collect and describe data under the naïve illusion that 'the data speak for themselves'.

This was a process of progressive reduction (hence the accusation of 'reductionism') that went through various phases. First, the boundaries of theoretical exploration were shrunk; questions of verification, or confirmation of hypotheses (*ars probandi*), were stressed at the expense of discovery (*ars inveniendi*). Subsequently, attention was shifted from the content to the method. This emphasis on empirical validation meant that questions which could not be translated immediately and simply into empirically verifiable procedures were excluded from theoretical considerations. Theoretical complexity was therefore gradually reduced to banality. Finally, attention was shifted from the method to the data, from the operationalization of concepts to the practical problems of collection and analysis of data (perhaps even statistically sophisticated) – data which by now were bereft of theoretical and methodological background. As Luciano Gallino points out, 'The immediate results of the research were what the critics of sociological neopositivism might have expected: a huge mass of data, meticulously recorded, measured and classified, but uncoordinated, lacking significant connections, and unable to yield adequate knowledge of the object to which they nominally refer' (Gallino, 1978: 457).

Interpretivism was no less exposed to criticism. It was not so much Weber's original model as its subsequent interpretations that came under fire; as we have seen, these took to the extreme the original concept of 'orientation towards the individual'. Weber himself strove to go beyond subjectivity. He did not rule out the possibility of reaching forms of cognitive generalization (ideal types); moreover, a considerable number of his methodological treatise deal with his attempt to reconcile causality and comprehension. In addition, although he started out by focusing on the individual, he did not neglect the great systemic issues or the institutional dimension of society.

By contrast, the new schools of sociological thought that developed from the 1960s onwards accentuated the subjective character of Weber's original model and shifted their attention to the world of everyday life and to inter-subject interaction. Again, this occurred through a process of reduction, though in this case it was the breadth of reflection that was reduced, while in the case of neopositivism the reduction was in the depth of reflection. This shift gave even greater impetus to the two basic criticisms levelled at the interpretive paradigm.

The first of these holds that extreme subjectivity rules out the very existence of science, and of social science in particular. If human action always has a unique dimension or if reality is merely a subjective construction, then generalizations above the individual level cannot be made and knowledge cannot be objective. Moreover, the objectivity of knowledge is also denied by the very mechanism through which knowledge is pursued, since this involves the non-separation of the researcher from the object studied. In addition, the fact that the researcher cannot transcend the object studied also excludes the possibility of inter-subject verification, which is a fundamental principle of science (that is to say, that another researcher can obtain the same result by elaborating the same or other data).

Second, the interpretive approach – again on account of its focus on the individual – is accused of ignoring those objects that should stand at the centre of sociological reflection: institutions. Thus, it allegedly neglects aspects of society which, though stemming from individual interaction, have become independent of individuals and their choices. This same basic criticism is also levelled at phenomenological sociology, ethnomethodology and symbolic interactionism, which are accused of limiting their interests to interaction and interpersonal relationships, in that they are unwilling or unable to address problems that transcend the minutiae of everyday life.

Up to now we've discussed these issues against the backdrop of the major currents of sociological thought, on which the discipline of sociology was founded, which have shaped its research techniques and dominated social enquiry from its very beginnings up to the mid-1970s. The last quarter of the twentieth century has challenged the preceding history of social research. The 1960s – featuring the civil rights movement, student protests, racial conflicts in urban settings, struggles against poverty and inequality, and the rise of feminism – were an extremely lively period in Western societies. Sociological theory and research played a central role and achieved a great degree of popularity in such a context, and sociology seemed to uncover a new 'mission' in its reflections on that decade's social changes. There emerged new theoretical perspectives, such as the neo-Marxian and neo-Weberian approaches, critical theory and other new radical perspectives which openly contested the comfortable alliance between neopositivism and functionalism that had previously dominated social theory and research.

In those same years these new macro-perspectives were accompanied by novel developments in the field of so-called 'micro-sociology', an umbrella term grouping different schools of thought and theoretical outlooks, that resembled each other in their interest for the 'minor' facts of everyday life, micro-interactions among individuals, interpersonal dynamics (rather than great historical transformations and major social processes).

This abandonment of comprehensive theoretical perspectives and wide-ranging explanations eventually led to a generalized critique of any theoretical explanation and questioned sociology's status as a science. This tendency has assumed particularly radical traits in recent years (in the 1990s, roughly speaking) in a heterogeneous (and sometimes confusing) intellectual movement that has been labelled 'post-modernism'.

In extremely simplified terms, one could define this movement in terms of what it challenges: modernism, i.e. the consequences of the Enlightenment, including the critical use of reason over humanity, nature, and society, and confidence in science, based on order, rationality, simplicity of scientific explanations and the cumulative nature of knowledge. 'Post'-modernism transcends (and disputes) modernity's achievements, with a critique which can be summed up in four points: (a) *rejection of general theories*, which stands accused of totalitarianism, cultural imperialism, negation and repression of differences among societies in order to perpetuate the hegemonic goals of Western culture; promotion of multiple theoretical approaches and languages; defence of the fragmentary and non-unitary nature of scientific explanation; (b) *rejection of rationality*, linearity, and scientific knowledge's simplicity; praise for paradoxes, contradictions, opacity, alternative and incompatible multi-faceted outlooks; (c) *exaltation of differences*, multiplicity of local and contextual truths, rejection of the cumulative nature of science; and (d) *exaltation of the 'Other'*, differences, minorities; identification with the oppressed, assumption of 'power' as an explanatory category at the basis of all social relationships and structures.

This overview of recent tendencies and potential paradigms in contemporary social science is too simple and brief, but we will not further develop the issue. Our primary interest is to describe the basic social science paradigms which have influenced and shaped empirical research strategies, methods and techniques. The new perspectives which have emerged in the last quarter-century have not had revolutionary effects on social research techniques, except for promoting the full legitimacy and actual use of qualitative research techniques (but without innovating them in any appreciable way).

SUMMARY

1. Any 'mature' science is accompanied by, in any given moment in history, its own paradigm. Each science's paradigm is its 'guiding vision', a theoretical perspective accepted by the community of scientists that directs research effort by specifying what to study and formulating hypotheses to explain observed phenomena.

2. In the social sciences, the two paradigms that have historically oriented social research since its inception have been 'positivism' and 'interpretivism'. In order to compare them, we have attempted to understand how they deal with the three fundamental questions facing social research: the ontological question (does social reality exist?); the epistemological question (is it knowable?); and the epistemological question (how can we acquire knowledge about it?).

3. The positivist paradigm started to take root in social research in the second half of the nineteenth century, due to the great success achieved by the natural sciences. Positivism applied to social research maintained that social reality should be studied through the same investigative logic and the same method of the natural sciences, hence the name 'social physics' attributed to the study of society.

4. Over the twentieth century the original positivist outlook has been adapted to overcome its intrinsic limits. According to the neopositivist and postpositivist paradigm, social theories are no longer expressed in terms of deterministic laws, but of probability. Any theoretical statement has a provisional nature, is never definitively proven and always remains

exposed to possible disproof. Moreover, the research community grew increasingly convinced that any empirical observation is not an objective depiction, but is rather *theory-laden*, in the sense that even the simple recording of reality depends on the mental framework employed by the researcher. This revised form of positivism, however, does not repudiate its empiricist foundations nor its faith in quantification and generalization; and it promoted a further development of quantitative empirical research methods, the so-called 'language of variables', a language borrowed from mathematics and statistics.

5. According to interpretivism, there exists a fundamental 'epistemological' difference between social and natural sciences. This perspective holds that social reality cannot simply be observed, but rather needs to be 'interpreted'. In the natural sciences the object of study consists of a reality that is external to the researcher and remains so during the course of research; thus, knowledge takes the form of explanation. In the human sciences there is no such detachment between the observer and what is observed; and knowledge can be obtained only through a totally different process, that of comprehension (*Verstehen*). These fundamental differences inevitably imply different techniques and research procedures. The subjectivist position cannot adopt the 'language of variables' and has therefore developed its own observation techniques and its own ways of analysing empirical reality, which form the body of so-called 'qualitative research'.

FURTHER READING

A useful collection of essays that explore the theoretical perspectives that have shaped social research methods is the reader edited by G. Ritzer and B. Smart, *Handbook of Social Theory* (Sage, 2001, pp. 552). The issues addressed in this chapter are further examined in M. Gane, *Durkheim's Project for a Sociological Science*; P. Halfpenny, *Positivism in Twentieth Century*; S. Whimster, *Max Weber: Work and Interpretation*; K.L. Sanstrom, D.D. Martin and G.A. Fine, *Symbolic Interactionism at the End of the Century*; S. Crook, *Social Theory and the Postmodern*.

An introductory discussion about the paradigmatic divisions between quantitative and qualitative research traditions is given in the first chapter of A. Tashakkori and C. Teddlie, *Mixed Methodology: Combining Qualitative and Quantitative Approaches* (Sage, 1998, pp. 185). A more comprehensive guide to the different answers given to fundamental social research dilemmas by classical and contemporary schools of thought can be found in N. Blaikie, *Approaches to Social Inquiry* (Polity Press, 1993, pp. 238).

An attempt to place current approaches to qualitative research in a theoretical perspective can be found in an essay by Y.S. Lincoln and E.G. Guba, *Paradigmatic Controversies, Contradictions, and Emerging Confluences*, in Denzin and Lincoln (2000). Another, more detailed attempt, is the book by J.F. Gubrium and J.M. Holstein, *The New Language of Qualitative Method* (Sage, 1997, pp. 244): the authors identify four 'idioms' (naturalism, social constructionism, emotionalism, postmodernism) which inspire recent qualitative research. A discussion of current trends in social research from a quantitative standpoint can be found in J.H. Goldthorpe, *On Sociology: Numbers, Narratives, and the Integration of Research and Theory* (Oxford University Press, 2000, pp. 337).

NOTES

1. The treatment illustrated in the following pages borrows heavily from Guba and Lincoln (1994), which deals with the topics more extensively.

2. Ontology: that part of philosophy that studies the essence of 'being'; from the Greek óntos (to be, being) and lógos (discourse, reflection).

3. Epistemology: reflection on scientific knowledge, from the Greek epistéme (certain knowledge).

4. Methodology: from the Greek méthodos (pathway to, method). The methodological question has to do with 'methods' of social research, meaning an organic body of techniques. It could also be called (perhaps more correctly) 'technological question', in that it focuses on techniques; this term has been avoided as it has taken on a different meaning in the common language.

5. Stuart Mill states that induction is 'that operation of the mind by which we infer what we know to be true in a particular case or cases, will be true in all cases which resemble the former in certain assessable respects' (Mill, 1843: 288).

6. Some epistemological questions (regarding the knowability of reality) are introduced into our discussion of the ontological issue (the essence of reality) in order to facilitate understanding for the reader new to these concepts. Moreover, as will be seen in the section on the interpretive paradigm, the two issues are inseparable.

7. The criticisms of neopositivism that gave rise to what is now called postpositivism are generally attributed to Kuhn, Lakatos and Feyerabend.

8. The expression comes from Hanson (1958).

2   Quantitative and Qualitative Research

This chapter examines two typical examples of quantitative and qualitative research in order to supply a general overview of the two approaches. The specific stages of social research are outlined, and special emphasis is placed on how quantitative and qualitative procedures deal with each stage. The final part of the chapter describes how the two types of research techniques are both sources of social knowledge and complement each other.

1.   NEOPOSITIVIST PARADIGM: *CRIME IN THE MAKING* BY SAMPSON AND LAUB

Over the years, the debate between the quantitative and the qualitative approaches to sociological research has seen both ebb and flow. The lively and fruitful clashes of the 1920s and 1930s gave rise to valuable outputs on both sides of the divide and contributed significantly to the advancement of the discipline (with particular regard to the qualitative perspective, we can quote the so-called 'Chicago School'). In the 1940s and 1950s, and in the first half of the 1960s, the discussion went through a quiet phase, in which the quantitative perspective dominated. In those years qualitative research was considered a

sort of stepchild of social research. And the image of the ethnographer wasn't very dissimilar from that of the good newsreporter, to whom the status of social scientist was denied.

The controversy re-emerged in the 1960s as a result of a series of important theoretical works (Blumer, 1969; Goffman, 1959, 1967; Glaser and Strauss, 1967; Schutz, 1967). But it was only in the 1980s (in a process that continued throughout the 1990s and continues yet today) that qualitative research experienced a lively development, which has sparked methodological debates, given rise to new journals expressly devoted to qualitative research and stimulated an unprecedented production of reflections, proposals, studies and manuals.

In Chapter 1, we discussed what were defined as the 'basic paradigms' of social research. In the present chapter, we will illustrate the results that they have produced in terms of empirical research. This chapter can therefore be seen as an expansion of the last third of Table 1.1.

We will begin by describing two studies, one inspired by the neopositivist paradigm and the other by the interpretive paradigm. In order to highlight the differences between the two approaches, we have chosen two studies conducted on the same theme – juvenile delinquency – and tackling many of the same questions. We will then analyse the differences between these two approaches in detail.

The first study that we will examine can easily be traced back to the inspiration and the techniques of the neopositivist current. This is *Crime in the Making: Pathways and Turning Points Through Life* by Robert J. Sampson and John H. Laub, published in 1993 in the United States.

This research sprang from a curious coincidence: the discovery of some 60 'dusty cartons of data in the basement of the Harvard Law School Library'. The cartons contained the original material from an impressive longitudinal study conducted over 24 years, from 1939 to 1963, by Sheldon and Eleanor Glueck, and only partly utilized in their publications (including the classic *Unraveling Juvenile Delinquency,* published in 1950). This lucky find prompted Sampson and Laub to re-analyse the data (through what is commonly called *secondary analysis*) in an attempt to answer the new questions that developments in theory and research had in the meantime laid before scholars of juvenile deviance.

1.1 Hypothesis

The authors lamented the fact that criminal sociology tended to focus on adolescence to the exclusion of other ages. While this emphasis stems from the observation that a disproportionately high number of crimes are committed by adolescents, it also leads to neglect both of childhood, in which some claim that anti-social behaviour is rooted, and of adulthood, in which crucial events, such as marriage or starting work, can induce radical changes in the individual's social attitudes. According to this view, 'cross-sectional studies', which provide a picture of a group of individuals at a particular moment in time, should give way to 'longitudinal studies', in which subjects are followed up for a certain period of time and data are recorded at successive points during their lives.

Sampson and Laub therefore examined the theses put forward by those who had investigated criminal behaviour in the perspective of the life cycle. Before turning their attention to

the data, they roughly outlined a possible 'age-graded theory of informal social control', in which both the fundamental variables traditionally regarded as the causes of deviant behaviour (poverty, family breakdown, anti-social childhood, etc.) and the informal mechanisms of social control operating at each stage of the life cycle were discussed. The aim was to achieve a global vision that would go beyond the 'narrow sociological and psychological perspectives, coupled with a strong tradition of research using cross-sectional data on adolescents' (Sampson and Laub, 1993) which had dominated the field of criminology up to that time; in short, to integrate criminology into a life-course perspective.

1.2 Research design

As has already been said, Sampson and Laub's research was a secondary analysis of data assembled by the Gluecks more than 30 years earlier. The Gluecks had collected data on 500 young white males convicted of crimes, aged between 10 and 17 years at the beginning of the study in 1939, and on 500 youths without a criminal record. The former were located in two houses of correction in Massachusetts. The latter were 'public school' pupils from the same area, selected on the basis of a very thorough matching design; the 500 officially defined delinquents and the 500 non-delinquents were matched case by case on age, race/ethnicity, neighbourhood, and intelligence quotient. The subjects were followed up systematically from 1939 to 1948 through interviews with the individuals themselves, their families and teachers (or employers). Information was also gathered from neighbours, social workers, police officers and judges, and official judicial records were consulted with a view to recording any other possible crimes committed.

1.3 Empirical recording and results of analysis

An example of the quantification procedure followed by the authors can be seen in their construction of an 'unofficial delinquency' index. In addition to illegal acts (pick-pocketing, theft, gambling, vandalism, etc.), they recorded episodes of simple 'bad behaviour' (smoking, drinking, running away, bunking off, truancy, etc.) reported by the subjects themselves, their parents and teachers. The information gathered from the various sources was pooled into an overall deviance index (with a score from 1 to 26). This index represented 'unofficial' delinquency, while 'official' delinquency, defined on the basis of crimes actually reported to the judicial authority, was represented by the dichotomous variable (delinquents, non-delinquents) on which the sampling design of the 500 + 500 subjects was based. In the final analysis, these two indicators of delinquency constituted the dependent variables in the study.

Sampson and Laub presented the results of their research in five chapters of their book, on the subjects of the family context of juvenile delinquency, the role of school, peers and siblings, continuity in behaviour over time, adult social bonds and change in criminal behaviour. Each chapter is constructed in the same strictly linear fashion: (a) theoretical framework; (b) empirical recording; (c) results of analysis; and (d) return to the theory.

To illustrate the procedures used in analysing the data, we will look at the first of these chapters. In this chapter, as in all the others, the authors draw a distinction between *structural background variables* and *processual variables*. The former are the classic variables (poverty, family breakdown, parental crime, etc.) normally invoked in studies of this kind. The latter refer to those 'informal bonds' (with the family in this chapter, and with school, work, etc. in those that follow) to which Sampson and Laub imputed a fundamental role in the process that leads to delinquency. Thus, the authors hypothesize a theoretical model set out in two stages; the structural background variables are claimed to influence deviant behaviour only indirectly, through the mediation of the 'intervening' variables constituted by the family bond/control.

Having reviewed the literature and drawn up the theoretical framework, the authors move on to the *variables*. They identify nine structural background variables: 'household crowding', classified in three categories (comfortable, average and overcrowded); 'family disruption', classified dichotomically (i.e. in two categories), the value 1 being assigned when one or both parents are absent following divorce, separation, desertion or death; 'family size', determined by the number of children; 'family socio-economic status', classified in three categories (comfortable, marginal, dependent on outside help); followed by 'foreign born', 'residential mobility', 'mother's employment', 'father's criminality/ drinking', 'mother's criminality/drinking'. Likewise, they pick out five 'family processual variables'; these have to do with the affective relationship with parents, the use or otherwise of corporal punishment, the presence/absence of maternal supervision, and rejection, abandonment and hostility on the part of the parents. The dependent variable is, of course, constituted by delinquent behaviour; this may be 'official' or 'unofficial', as described above.

We will now look at the *results of the analysis*. In their statistical analysis, the authors used multiple regression. Having drawn up the variables in three blocks – structural background, family processual and the two dependent variables (delinquent behaviour) – they correlated the blocks two by two. Strong correlations were found between background variables and processual variables (a correlation that can be interpreted as meaning that the structural conditions of the family influence the affective bonds and the pedagogical relationship); between background variables and delinquency (family instability, poverty, etc., foster deviant behaviour); between processual variables and delinquency (weakened family bonds also foster it). All of this is to be expected. What is interesting, however, is that when the complete model is analysed (structural background variables and family processual variables are taken together as independent variables and deviant behaviour is taken as the dependent variable), the effect of the background variables almost disappears. What does this mean? It means that the structural variables do not have a *direct* effect on deviant behaviour, but that their action is mediated by the processual variables. For example family disruption favours abandonment by the parents (absence of control, etc.) and this in turn facilitates the onset of deviant behaviour. However, when there is no difference in terms of parental care and control, the influence of family disruption ceases. The authors estimate that 73% of the effect of the structural variables is mediated by the processual variables.

On completion of the empirical phase, the authors *return to the theory*. They conclude that 'the data suggest that family processes of informal social control have important inhibitory effects on adolescent delinquency … Given the overall nature of our results, it is troubling that many sociological explanations of crime ignore the family. This neglect has generated a marked divergence between both empirical findings and the conventional wisdom of the general public – especially parents – and the views of social scientists who study criminal behavior' (Sampson and Laub, 1993: 85, 97). These results support their 'integrated theory of informal social control' with regard to the family context.

In later chapters, Sampson and Laub apply a similar scheme of analysis to the role of school, the peer group, siblings, work and marriage, and conclude by reformulating their initial summary model in a detailed (and this time empirically corroborated) manner. The result is what they call their 'dynamic theoretical model of crime, deviance and informal social control over the life course', in which they divide the first 45 years of life into five ages (childhood, 0–10 years; adolescence, 10–17; transition to young adulthood, 17–25; young adulthood, 25–32; and transition to middle age, 32–45) and highlight the role of the factors that facilitate or inhibit the onset (or maintenance) of deviant behaviour in each phase. This model provides answers to the questions raised during elaboration of the hypotheses. From their investigation of both 'structural' and 'processual' variables, it emerges that the latter are those which ultimately explain most of the variation seen both in juvenile delinquency and in the subsequent abandonment of delinquency at a later stage in life.

2. INTERPRETIVE PARADIGM: *ISLANDS IN THE STREET* BY SÁNCHEZ-JANKOWSKI

In the conclusion to their book, Sampson and Laub state, 'This book has been driven by the following challenge: can we develop and test a theoretical model that *accounts for* crime and deviance in childhood, adolescence and adulthood?' (Sampson and Laub, 1993: 243). By contrast, the book that we are about to look at (*Islands in the Street: Gangs and American Urban Society*, by Martín Sánchez-Jankowski, published in 1991 in the United States) contains the concluding remark that 'We, in the social science and public policy communities have not fully *understood* gangs. To begin with, we have failed adequately to *understand* the individuals who are in gangs … The fact that gangs have not been *understood* as organizations has crucially impaired our *understanding* of their behavior' (Sánchez-Jankowski, 1991: 311, 314).

The lexical difference between these two passages, which make reference to the objectives of 'accounting for' and 'understanding' respectively (the italics in the quotations are mine), eloquently expresses the difference between the methodological approaches adopted in these two studies.

2.1 Research design and data collection

Sánchez-Jankowski's research is an example of 'participant observation'. Unlike most studies conducted through participant observation, which focus on a specific group or a single organization, Sánchez-Jankowski's research was conceived right from the outset as a comparative study aimed at understanding what gangs have in common and what is specific to each of them. The author therefore studied gangs of different sizes, with different racial features and in different cities (metropolitan areas of Los Angeles, New York and Boston). Over a 10-year period, he studied some 37 gangs; he participated fully in the life of the gangs, got involved in what they did, and shared their everyday business, so much so that he got hurt in fights with rival gangs and was repeatedly stopped by the police. In order to study such a large number of groups, his participation had to be rigidly planned (unlike what usually happens in participant observation). At first, he spent an entire month with a new gang, once he had been accepted; subsequently, he spent another five or ten days, and in the last three years of the study, he again spent from three to six days with each one.

As is usual in participant observation, information was recorded in a notebook during the course of the observation, and was filled out, summarized and commented on both daily and weekly (this procedure will be dealt with more fully in Chapter 9). In addition, the author also occasionally tape-recorded conversations.

2.2 Hypothesis

Unlike Sampson and Laub, Sánchez-Jankowski did not go through that phase of systematic theoretical reflection that leads to the elaboration of hypotheses to be tested empirically. In his first chapter, he does not review the literature in order to compare the various theses, nor put forward hypotheses. Instead, he draws exhaustively on the research conducted and sets out the conclusions to which his experience has led him. This structure does not stem from the author's personal choice, but from the very characteristics of the interpretive approach, which – as has already been pointed out – proceeds in an essentially inductive manner and deliberately avoids being conditioned by the theory at the outset; indeed, the theory

has to be 'discovered' during the course of the investigation.

What is original in Sánchez-Jankowski's approach is that he does not look upon the gang as a pathological deviation from social norms; rather, he interprets gang membership as a rational choice. He claims that 'Nearly all theories of gangs emerge from the assumptions associated with theories of social disorganization ... the lack of social controls leads to gang formation and involvement because young people in low income neighborhoods (slums) seek the social order (and security) that a gang can provide' (1991: 22). On the other end, according to Sánchez-Jankowski, 'Low-income areas in American cities are, in fact, organized, but they are organized around an intense competition for, and conflict over, the scarce resources that exist in these areas. They comprise an alternative social order ... and the gang emerges as one organizational response ... seeking to improve the competitive advantage of its members' (1991: 22).

Sánchez-Jankowski develops three themes: the individual and his relationship with the gang, the gang as an organization, and the gang and the community. With regard to the individual, he works out the concept of the 'defiant individualistic character'. This is seen as embodying an acute sense of competition, which often turns to physical aggression and is present in all patterns of behaviour. It is imbued with mistrust of others, and thus gives rise to individualism, social isolation and the need for self-reliance; finally, it is associated with a worldview that the author calls 'Darwinian', according to which life is a struggle in which only the fittest survive, and which engenders a strong survival instinct. In this brief description, the reader will discern the characters of Weber's 'ideal type'.

The gang provides a possible means of meeting the demands that this individual makes of society. Sánchez-Jankowski defines the gang (and this is another ideal type) as a social system that is quasi-private (not open to all) and quasi-secret (only the members are fully aware of its activities), governed by a leadership structure with clearly defined roles whose authority is conferred through a mechanism of legitimization. The gang aims not only to serve the social and economic interest of its members, but also to ensure its own survival as an organization. It pursues its aims without worrying whether or not they are legal, and has no bureaucracy (there is no administrative staff apart from the leadership). The subject endowed with 'defiant individualism' asks to join the gang because he believes that it is in his interest, that he can gain advantages in terms of wealth, status and power. The gang will take him in if its own needs (prestige, efficiency, services provided) will be met by doing so.

The author goes on to analyse the gang as an organization: the strategies utilized to involve and to keep members, the leadership structure its mechanisms of legitimization, the incentives offered and sanctions imposed in order to ensure the obedience of its members.

Finally, Sánchez-Jankowski examines the gang's relationship with the wider community. Indeed, tight internal cohesion is not sufficient to guarantee survival; this can only be ensured if the gang is integrated into the local community. The local residents must accept the gang as an integral part of the neighbourhood, and will expect services from it. In exchange, the gang will gain the support of the local community in terms of protection from the police and from 'rival predators' (other gangs). The ability to establish such links is one of the main factors that will determine the long-term survival of the gang.

2.3 Interpretation of the empirical material

All the above themes are dealt with in successive chapters – five covering the internal dynamics of the gang and its relationships with the local community, and three concerning its relationships with the outside world (public institutions, the judicial system and the mass media) – in which the author interprets the data with the aid of the categories introduced in the

chapter on theory. In order to illustrate the procedure used, we will look briefly at the first chapter, entitled *Gang Involvement*, in which the author tries to answer the basic questions of who joins a gang and why.

Sánchez-Jankowski rejects the four answers provided by the specialist literature: that adolescents join gangs because they come from broken homes where the father is absent, and they seek to identify with other males and with male figures of authority; that they join because the gang is a surrogate family – a motivation closely linked to the previous point; that they have dropped out of the school system and, unqualified for any sort of job, can find nothing better to do than join a gang; or else that they join in order to emulate older youths. As the author says, 'I found no evidence for these propositions. What I did find was that individuals who live in low-income neighborhoods join gangs for a variety of reasons, basing their decisions on a rational calculation of what is best for them at that particular time' (1991: 40). He then goes on to list some of the motivations that he came across:

Material incentives   The individual joins the gang in order to obtain money in a more regular and less risky manner than engaging in illegal activity on his own, in order to have an income in times of emergency (the gang generally promotes a sort of mutual assistance among its members), and in the hope of future money-making opportunities (e.g. getting into the drug trade). The author illustrates the various cases by means of extracts from interviews, as reported below:

> Hey, the club (the gang) has been there when I needed help. There were times when there just wasn't enough food for me to get filled up with. My family was hard up and they couldn't manage all of their bills and such, so there was some lean meals! ... They (the gang) was there to help. I could see that (they would help) before I joined, that's why I joined. They are there when you need them and they'll continue to be. (Street Dog, Puerto Rican, aged 15, a member of a New York gang for two years) (1991: 42)

Recreation The gang also provides opportunities for enjoyment; it often has a sort of club with a bar, video games, cards and slot machines; it organizes parties and offers a chance to meet girls:

> I joined originally because all the action was happening with the Bats (gang's name). I mean, all the foxy ladies were going to their parties and hanging with them. Plus their parties were great. They had good music and the herb (marijuana) was so smooth ... Hell, they were the kings of the community so I wanted to get in on some of the action. (Fox, aged 23, a member of a New York gang for seven years) (1991: 43)

Refuge and camouflage The gang provides anonymity for anyone who needs it on account of his activities in a highly competitive context:

> I been thinking about joining the gang because the gang gives you a cover, you know what I mean? Like when me or anybody does a business deal and we're members of the gang, it's difficult to track us down 'cause people will say, 'Oh, it was just one of those guys in the gang'. You get my point? The gang is going to provide me with some cover. (Junior J., aged 17, New York) (1991: 44)

In like manner, through interview extracts, Sánchez-Jankowski goes on to illustrate the other reasons that he recorded for joining a gang. The final result is a radically different kind of knowledge from that gleaned by Sampson and Laub. The objective is no longer to discern 'causal models', in which variables are connected through cause-effect relationships, but rather to draw up classifications and typologies based on first-hand experience, in a clear application of the interpretive paradigm.

3. QUANTITATIVE AND QUALITATIVE RESEARCH: A COMPARISON

We will now compare quantitative and qualitative research techniques analytically. To this end, the two studies illustrated above will be used (as far as possible) by way of example. The differences between the two approaches – no longer in terms of their philosophical and epistemological premises, but of their concrete application to research – will be made clear by the following analysis. To facilitate comparison, the four phases of each technique – planning, data collection, analysis and results – are summarized in Table 2.1. This is merely an enlargement of the third part ('methodology') of Table 1.1 (some repetition is therefore inevitable).

3.1 Research planning

If we had to pick out a single overall feature to differentiate concisely between these two types of research, we would probably point to the structuring of the various phases that lead from the initial query to the final report. The research conducted by Sampson and Laub displays a strikingly geometrical pattern: exposition of the theory, its formulation in terms of an empirically testable 'model', research planning (the so-called 'research design'), data collection, data analysis and return to the theory. This circular pattern is repeated in each chapter. It should be noted that this format is no mere 'orderly' presentation of the material; rather, it is the expression of a conceptual order which guides the authors through their work and which springs from a vision of research as a rational, linear process.

Sánchez-Jankowski proceeds in a totally different way. His book does not open with a discussion of the literature findings, nor sets out theories and empirically testable hypotheses. His conclusions are already woven into the fabric of the initial theoretical chapter; there is never a distinct separation between theory and empirical findings. His way of working is distinctly different from that of Sampson and Laub; he does not start off with clear hypotheses in mind, but constructs them as he goes along. For example when he rejects the traditional psychosocial explanations for why a youth joins a gang (identity-seeking,

TABLE 2.1   *Comparison between quantitative and qualitative research*

	Quantitative research	**Qualitative research**
Research planning		
Theory-research relationship	Structured; logically sequential phases	Open, interactive
	Deduction (theory precedes observation)	Induction (theory emerges from observation)
Function of the literature	Fundamental in defining theory and hypotheses	Auxiliary
Concepts	Operationalized	Orientative, open, under construction
Relationship with the environment	Manipulative approach	Naturalistic approach
Psychological researcher-subject interaction	Neutral, detached, scientific observation	Empathetic identification with the perspective of the subject studied
Physical researcher-subject interaction	Distance, detachment	Proximity, contact
Role of subject studied	Passive	Active
Data collection		
Research design	Structured, closed, precedes research	Unstructured, open, constructed in the course of research
Representativeness	Statistically representative sample	Single cases not statistically representative
Recording instrument	Standardized for all subjects. Objective: data-matrix	Varies according to subjects' interests. Tends not to be standardized
Nature of the data	'Hard', objective and standardized (objectivity vs. subjectivity)	'Soft', rich and deep (depth vs. superficiality)
Data analysis		
Object of the analysis	The variable (analysis by variables, impersonal)	The individual (analysis by subjects)
Aim of the analysis	Explain variation ('variance') in variables	Understand the subjects
Mathematical and statistical techniques	Used intensely	Not used
Production of results		
Data presentation	Tables (relationship perspective)	Extracts from interviews and texts (narrative perspective)
Generalizations	Correlations. Causal models. Laws. Logic of causation	Classifications and typologies. Ideal types. Logic of classification
Scope of results	Generalizability	Specificity

etc.) in favour of a detailed list of rational motivations, we can plainly see that this conclusion is based on the interviews conducted, and not on theoretical prejudice. Indeed, this is a case of 'theory emerging from the data'.

In these two approaches, the relationship between *theory* and *research* (the first point in Table 2.1) is radically different. In the case of quantitative research inspired by the neopositivist paradigm, this relationship is structured in logically sequential phases, according to a substantially deductive approach (theory precedes observation) that strives to 'justify', that is to say, to support the previously formulated theory with empirical data. Within this framework, systematic analysis of the *literature* takes on a crucial role, since it is this that provides the theoretical hypotheses on which fieldwork will be based.

In qualitative research, which springs from the interpretive paradigm, there is an open, interactive relationship between theory and research. The researcher often deliberately avoids formulating theories before fieldwork begins, on the grounds that this might hinder his capacity to 'comprehend' the point of view of the subject studied. Theoretical elaboration and empirical research are therefore intertwined. As the theories accumulated within the scientific community lose their importance, it follows that analysis of the literature takes on a minor role.

These two approaches to research also differ in their use of *concepts*. The concepts are the constituent elements of the theory and, at the same time, they allow the theory to be tested empirically through their operationalization, that is, their transformation into empirically observable variables. In the neopositivist approach, the concepts are clarified and operationalized into variables even before the research begins. Let us take the concept of 'family disruption' in the research by Sampson and Laub. As we have seen, the authors operationalized this concept by assigning a value of 1 (disruption) when one or both parents were absent owing to divorce, separation, desertion or death, and a value of 0 in all other cases. This definition (to be precise, 'operational definition') of the concept of family disruption offers the advantage that the concept can be gauged empirically. However, it considerably limits and impoverishes the concept itself. Moreover, it engenders

the risk of reifying the indicator used. In the empirical transformation of the theory, this indicator comes to embody the concept of family disruption itself and, as the analysis proceeds, we may lose sight of the fact that the initial definition is restrictive.[1]

This approach would never have been adopted in qualitative research. Instead of transforming the concept into a variable at the outset (that is, into a clearly defined entity that can be recorded empirically), the researcher would have utilized 'family disruption' as a *sensitizing concept*, to use Blumer's definition: a guiding concept that remains to be refined during the course of the research, not only in operational terms, but also in theoretical terms:

> A definitive concept refers precisely to what is common to a class of objects, by the aid of a clear definition in terms of attributes or fixed benchmarks ... A sensitizing concept lacks such specification of attributes or benchmarks ... Instead, it gives the user a general sense of reference and guidance in approaching empirical instances. Whereas definitive concepts provide prescriptions of what to see, sensitizing concepts merely suggest directions along which to look ... (in a) self-correcting relation with its empirical world so that its proposals about that world can be tested, refined and enriched by the data of the world (Blumer, 1969: 147–148).

Moreover, as Blumer adds, these concepts should be sensitizing rather than definitive not because social science is immature or lacks scientific sophistication, but because of the very nature of the natural world, in which 'every object of our consideration – whether a person, group, institution, practice or what-not – has a distinctive, particular or unique character and lies in a context of a similar distinctive character. I think that it is this distinctive character of the empirical instance and of its setting which explains why our concepts are sensitizing and not definitive' (1969: 148).

Another set of differences between quantitative and qualitative research can be seen in the personal relationship between the researcher and the object studied. Let us look first at what may be called the general *relationship with the environment studied*. Needless to say, one of the main problems facing the social researcher is that of the 'reactivity' of the object under investigation. The mere fact of examining human behaviour may induce changes in the behaviour itself. Studying people is not like studying ants or atoms; if people know they are being observed, they are very likely to behave in an unnatural way.

The neopositivist approach does not seem to be particularly concerned about this. Not that the social researcher working within this paradigm is unaware of the fundamental difference between the objects studied in the natural sciences and those studied in the social sciences. Nevertheless, she maintains that the problem of subject reactivity does not constitute a fundamental obstacle, or at least believes that a certain margin of 'controlled manipulation' is acceptable. By contrast, qualitative research sees the *naturalistic approach* as a basic requisite to empirical study. When we say 'naturalistic approach', we mean that the researcher refrains from any form of manipulation, stimulation, interference or disturbance, and that the object is studied in its natural setting.

These two opposing ways of conducting research can best be illustrated by the techniques of experimentation and participant observation. In carrying out an experiment, the researcher manipulates social reality extensively, even to the extent of constructing an artificial situation (for instance, by showing students in a laboratory a film on political propaganda). Before and after exposure to the stimulus, subjects are tested (again an artificial situation); moreover, the initial subdivision of the subjects into an experimental group and a control group (on the basis of abstract, unnatural criteria) also involves an artificial operation. The situation is therefore totally unnatural and the researcher's manipulation is all-pervading. By contrast, in participant observation, the researcher's role is restricted to observing what happens in the social reality under investigation, and the

researcher may sometimes even refrain from interviewing or questioning the subjects observed.

Obviously, these are two extreme cases, between which a whole range of situations may be encountered. Participant observation itself is only rarely perfectly 'naturalistic', in the sense that the mere presence of an outside observer is likely to have some effect on the subjects (except in particular cases, such as the observation of small children, etc.) It therefore follows that all instruments of qualitative analysis other than observation (e.g. in-depth interviews, life stories, etc.) will necessarily involve some degree of intervention in the reality studied, even if this means no more than prompting subjects to speak and to communicate. By the same token, quantitative research is not always as manipulative as it is in the case of the experiment, and again various degrees can be discerned. For example, a questionnaire that uses open questions respects the natural context more than one that uses closed questions. Moreover, there are quantitative techniques that do not impinge directly on subjects, but involve statistical sources or 'non-reactive' variables; in such cases, the problem of reactivity does not arise.

So far, reference has been made to the researcher's relationship with the study environment as a whole. A further aspect concerns the relationship between the researcher and the individual subjects studied. As we have already seen, one of the fundamental differences between the neopositivist paradigm and the interpretive paradigm lies in how they define their research objectives; in the former case, the objective can be summarized as 'empirical validation of the hypotheses', while in the latter case it is 'to discover the social actor's point of view'. This dual perspective gives rise to two issues, one of a psychological-cultural nature and the other of what could be called a physical-spatial nature.

The first of these concerns the *psychological interaction between the researcher and the subject studied*. In quantitative research, observation is carried out from a position that is external to the subject studied, just as the 'scientific' observer adopts a neutral, detached stance. Moreover, the researcher focuses on what he (or the scientific community) considers to be important. By contrast, the qualitative researcher tries to get as deep inside the subject as possible, in an attempt to see social reality 'through the eyes of the subject studied'. To do so, he can never remain neutral or indifferent, but instead will tend to identify empathetically with the subject. As Sánchez-Jankowski points out in the preface to his book:

> The ten years and five months that I have spent on this research project have indeed been a journey.[2] A journey not only through time but also into the lives of gang members and various other individuals who live in the low-income areas of New York, Boston, and Los Angeles. Ironically, it has also been a journey back into my youth ... throughout this journey I have met some wonderful people, whom I shall always remember with fondness, and I have met some not-so-wonderful people, whom I shall also not forget. (Sánchez-Jankowski, 1991: xi)

Clearly, this psychological involvement raises the question of the objectivity of qualitative research. It is a problem that also arises in quantitative research, in that what the researcher sees must pass through the filter of his own perspective, experience of life, culture and values. In the social sciences at least, the ideal of absolute scientific objectivity is unattainable. However, it is in qualitative research that this problem is most acutely felt, in that empathetic interaction with the subject studied engenders a risk of emotional involvement, which in turn may give rise to heavily one-sided interpretations.

The second issue, which is directly linked to the first, concerns the *physical interaction between the researcher and the subject*. Quantitative research does not envision any physical contact between the researcher and the subject. We need only think of a questionnaire survey on a sample of the population, in which interviews are conducted by a data-collection agency; or of

a laboratory experiment in which the researcher simply observes the behaviour of the subjects. Another example is that of secondary analysis, like the study conducted by Sampson and Laub (1993), in which the researcher never physically meets the subjects.

Obviously, the opposite is true in the case of qualitative research, in which contact – and even close interaction – between the researcher and the subject is a prerequisite to comprehension. In describing his interaction with the subjects studied, Sánchez-Jankowski writes that during his ten-year study 'I participated in nearly all the things they did. I ate where they ate, I slept where they slept, I stayed with their families, I traveled where they went, and in certain situations where I could not remain neutral, I fought with them' (1991: 13). Once again, it is participant observation that exemplifies the interpretive approach most aptly. However, the need for physical-spatial proximity to the object studied is seen in all qualitative research techniques (such as, e.g. in-depth interviews, life stories, analyses of group dynamics, etc.).

From what has been said, it will be evident that the two approaches also differ in terms of the *role of the subject studied*. From the quantitative standpoint, the subject studied is regarded as being *passive*, and even when he cannot be regarded as such, every effort is made to reduce his interaction with the researcher to a minimum. Research is conceived of as 'observation' and 'recording', and this implies looking at the individuals studied as objects (this takes us back to the original positivist conception of social facts as 'things'). On the qualitative side, by contrast, research is conceived of as 'interaction', which naturally implies an active role on the part of the subject studied. The subject's direct, creative participation in the research process, far from being shunned, is actively sought, as is clearly shown by the two extracts from Sánchez-Jankowski's book quoted earlier.

3.2 Data collection

One of the principal differences between the two approaches has to do with the *research design* – that is to say, all those operational decisions concerning where, how and when to gather the data; this means deciding what data-collection tools are to be used (interview or participant observation, questionnaire or experiment, etc.), where data collection is to be carried out, how many and which subjects or organizations are to be studied, etc. Again, the difference lies in the degree to which the procedures are structured. The quantitative design, which is drawn up on paper before data collection begins, is rigidly structured and closed, while the qualitative design is unstructured, open, shaped during the course of data collection, and able to capture the unforeseen.

In the case of Sampson and Laub's research, for instance, once the sample of 500 delinquents and 500 non-delinquents had been drawn up, these were rigidly taken as the subjects to be studied. By contrast, in Sánchez-Jankowski's research, once a few basic criteria had been defined (the number of gangs from each of the three cities, plus some constraints on gang size and race), the researcher was free to choose those gangs most suited to his purposes. Moreover, he also had the freedom to interview whomever he wished, to lengthen or shorten the observation as he thought fit, etc. From this point of view, the two studies illustrated are not among the most typical. Indeed, the Gluecks' research, from which Sampson and Laub took their data, envisioned using various sources of information (regarding, for instance, the criminal activities of the subjects) at the discretion of the researcher. Likewise, Sánchez-Jankowski bore in mind the objective of representativeness-comparability, and therefore selected the gangs according to a plan that was to some extent predetermined. Generally speaking, quantitative research has a highly rigid design (as in the case of a questionnaire survey with closed questions conducted on a random sample, or of an experiment), while qualitative research is totally free of constraints (the researcher decides in the field which subjects to study and which data-collection tools to use).

This difference in research design – closed or open, established in advance or during the course of the research – is linked to two further distinguishing features. The first of these is the *representativeness* of the subjects studied. The quantitative researcher is concerned with the generalizability of the results (we will return to this issue later), and the use of a statistically representative sample is the most evident manifestation of this concern; indeed, we might say that the researcher is more concerned with the representativeness of the slice of society that he is studying than with his ability to comprehend it. The opposite is true of the qualitative researcher, who gives priority to comprehension, even at the cost of pursuing atypical situations and non-generalizable mechanisms. Statistical representativeness is of no interest to the qualitative researcher. What may be of interest is a sort of substantive, sociological representativeness, which will be decided on the basis not of mathematical formulae but the researcher's own judgement. Indeed, the cases to be studied in depth will be chosen not because they are typical, or even common in the population, but on the basis of the interest that they seem to hold. Moreover, this interest may be modified during the course of the research itself; thus, as one qualitative research manual states, 'sampling (must be performed) on the basis of the evolving theoretical relevance of concepts' (Strauss and Corbin, 1990: 179).

An example can be seen in the research on 'Communists and Catholics' conducted in a neighbourhood of Bologna at the end of the 1970s by the American anthropologist David Kertzer (1980). Following the classical 'community study' approach, he basically used the technique of participant observation, but supplemented this with a series of interviews with 'key informants'. Both unstructured in-depth interviews and structured interviews were used. However, not all the interview subjects had been selected in advance. The author began data collection with the aim of interviewing all political activists and social workers in both the Communist and Catholic spheres: local Communist Party committee members, activists in the UDI (Union of Italian Women) and FGCI (Communist Party Youth Federation), priests working in the parishes, lay workers in Catholic associations, etc. During the course of the research, however, Kertzer realized that this objective was unattainable (some Communist Party activists did not trust the 'American' and declined to be interviewed, as did some of the priests). At the same time, some individuals who had not been previously counted among those to be interviewed turned out to be precious informants (one of the richest sources of information on the interaction between Communists and Catholics being a local barmaid).

The second of the two above-mentioned distinguishing features concerns the standardization of the *data-collection tool*. In quantitative research, all subjects receive the same treatment. The data-collection tool is the same for all cases (e.g. a questionnaire) or at least strives for uniformity (e.g. a code-book to harmonize open questions or information gathered from different sources, as was partly the case in Sampson and Laub's research). The reason for this is that the information gathered will be used to create the 'data-matrix', a rectangular matrix of numbers in which the same information is coded for all the cases.

Qualitative research does not aim for this standardization. On the contrary, the heterogeneity of information, as we have seen, is a constituent element of this type of research, since the researcher records different information according to the cases, and at different levels of depth according to his judgement. Once again, the difference in approach stems from the difference in the cognitive objective; in the one case, it is to cover the uniformities of the world of human beings, while in the other, it is to understand its individual manifestations.

The final point to be mentioned under the heading of 'data collection' concerns the *nature of the data*. In quantitative research, the data are (or, at any rate, are expected to be) reliable, precise, rigorous and unequivocal: in a word, *hard*. They ought to be 'objective' in the sense that they should lend themselves

neither to subjective interpretations by the researcher (in the sense that two investigators applying the same techniques should obtain the same results), nor to the expressive subjectivity of the individual studied (in the sense that two people with similar states should give similar answers). They should also be 'standardized', in the sense that data recorded on different subjects (even by different researchers) must be able to be compared. This can easily be achieved when dealing with some basic structural variables (gender, age, educational qualification) or behavioural variables (such as religious observance or voting), but becomes more difficult in the case of multi-faceted concepts (such as social class or intelligence), and even more so when attitudes are involved (e.g. authoritarianism, political conservatism, etc.). In any case, quantitative research always strives to produce *hard* data; for instance, to assess attitudes towards some political personality, respondents might be asked to give the person a score from 0 to 100 (to gauge the warmth of approval by means of a sort of 'feelings thermometer').

In qualitative research, by contrast, the issue of the objectivity and standardization of data does not arise; what counts is their wealth and depth. Data produced by qualitative research are termed *soft*, as opposed to the hard data mentioned earlier. Thus, to return to our previous example, a politician's popularity may be assessed by recording the various opinions expressed by the respondents; according to the point of view, culture, way of thinking, depth of analysis and mode of expression of each individual, judgements may run from the simple and sober to the complex and colourful.

3.3 Data analysis

Data analysis is perhaps the phase in which the difference between the quantitative and qualitative approaches is most visible, not least from the purely graphic point of view. Quantitative research makes ample use of mathematical and statistical tools, together with a whole array of tables, graphs, statistical tests, etc., as well as the full set of technological equipment (computers, files, data banks, software, etc.). The impact of this weaponry contrasts starkly with the sobriety of a qualitative analysis, in which there is no statistical-mathematical apparatus and the contribution of information technology (if any) is limited to the organization of empirical material.

The most fundamental difference, however, lies not so much in the technological tools of data analysis or the different presentation of results as in the logic that underlies the analysis itself. Let us look first at the *object of the analysis*. By way of example, we will go back again to Sampson and Laub's research into juvenile delinquency.

On the basis of correlations between the dependent variable and the independent variables, these authors reach the conclusion that 'family and school processes of informal social control provide the key causal explanation of delinquency in childhood and adolescence' (Sampson and Laub, 1993: 246). What was the logical and operational pathway that led them to these conclusions? First of all, the research team collected the data *per subject* (as is done in all studies, both quantitative and qualitative), in the sense that all those individual properties that we call 'variables' in the data-analysis phase (acts of violence committed, composition of the family, occupation of the parents, family environment in which the child was brought up, progress at school, etc.) were recorded on the 500 + 500 subjects. Each subject was then described analytically on the basis of all these characteristics. We could say that the unity of the individual is broken down into the same number of elements as the variables that describe him. From this point on, the subject is no longer reassembled into a whole person. Indeed, *data analysis is always carried out on variables*, in an *impersonal* manner. Reference is made to the means of *variables* (mean number of crimes committed, mean number of children per family, mean income, etc.), to the percentages of *variables* (percentage of subjects with previous convictions in the family, with a violent,

authoritarian father, etc.), to relationships among *variables* (correlation between family disruption and youth violence, etc.). Moreover, the *objective of the analysis* is to 'explain the variance' of the dependent variables – that is to say, to pick out the causes of the variation in the dependent variable among the subjects: the factors that 'explain' why some youths become delinquents while others do not. For example, if *all* the delinquents have violent fathers and *all* the non-delinquents have non-violent fathers, then we have found a 'statistical explanation' for the variance of the variable 'delinquency'; we can therefore claim to have found the 'cause' of the variable 'delinquency' (in this case identified as the father's behaviour).

It should be noted that this is the approach adopted in the natural sciences. For instance, the causal relationship between smoking and lung cancer was deduced by observing a statistical connection between the variations in these two variables on thousands of subjects and isolating the trends in these two variables within the array of variables that vary with them.

The interpretive approach criticizes this way of working on the grounds that it constitutes a misappropriation of the scientific model used in the natural sciences (this criticism has not only been put forward in the social sciences; in medicine too, the cause-effect relationship between single variables has come under fire from those who uphold the mental and physical unity of the human being). This accusation is based on the conviction that the integral human being cannot be broken down into a series of distinct and separate variables, and that analysis of human behaviour therefore has to be carried out within a global perspective or, more precisely, a *holistic perspective*.[3] According to this view, the complex interdependence among the parts that make up the whole individual cannot be reduced to the relationships among a few variables, and the comparison of subjects through variables distorts the nature of the subjects themselves.

Qualitative research thus adopts a completely different approach to the analysis of data. *The object of the analysis is not the variable, but the entire individual*. While quantitative research is *variable-based*, qualitative research is *case-based*. To illustrate the point, we will again turn to Sánchez-Jankowski's research. During the course of his work, Sánchez-Jankowski investigated the causes of violent behaviour among members of gangs. Sánchez-Jankowski began by picking out four factors that trigger violence: fear, ambition, frustration and exhibitionism. At this point, a quantitative researcher would try to record the dependent variable 'violence' (e.g. by assigning a score to individuals according to the degree of violence displayed in their behaviour) and then pick out suitable indicators (no easy task) through which to gauge the four independent variables (fear, ambition, frustration and exhibitionism). By means of statistical techniques, he would then attempt to 'explain the variance' of the dependent variable 'violence', starting from the variations observed in the independent variables; in other words, he would try to spot the correlations between the independent variables and the dependent variable.

Sánchez-Jankowski did not do this. His analysis was not conducted on variables, but on subjects. Rather than breaking the subject down into variables, he classified the subjects in their entirety into types. The classification was the pattern linking the subjects, just as in quantititive research the causal model links the variables.

Sánchez-Jankowski separated incidents of violence into two classes according to whether the violence was individual or collective. He then identified six contexts in which the violence took place (violence against members of the same gang, against members of other gangs, against local residents, against outsiders, against property inside the community, and outside the community). In this way, he drew up a classification composed of 12 situations, within each of which he identified four cases corresponding to the four abovementioned triggering factors (fear, ambition, frustration, exhibitionism). This gave rise to a typology of 48 types, within which he classified the acts of violence sometimes with more

than one subject-incident per type. For example with regard to the type 'individual violence, against members of the same gang, due to ambition', he describes the case of Shoes. Shoes was a 16-year-old member of a New York gang who wanted to become one of the gang leaders, in spite of the fact that he was considered too young and had not been in the gang long. One day, during a gang fight with a rival gang, he noticed that two members of his own gang were hanging back from the fray for fear of getting hurt. At the next gang meeting, Shoes physically attacked one of the two. After being separated by the other members, he justified his behaviour by accusing his two companions of cowardice and claiming that they should be expelled from the gang. The purpose behind all this was to raise his own status within the group.

In this study, the *objective of the analysis* was in line with the perspective of the interpretive paradigm, the aim being to 'understand people', to interpret the social actor's point of view (in the example, to understand the motives behind violent behaviour), just as the objective in the quantitative approach was to 'explain the variation in the variables'.

Finally, it will be all too obvious to the reader that quantitative and qualitative research have different relationships with *mathematical and statistical techniques*. In the quantitative paradigm, the language of mathematics is taken purely and simply to be *the* language of science. Consequently, every effort is made to operationalize concepts in mathematically treatable terms (even to the extent of creating actual 'measurements'); likewise, the greatest possible use is made of statistical techniques of data analysis in order to extrapolate generalizations from the sample to the population. From the qualitative standpoint, by contrast, mathematical formulation is considered not only useless, but also harmful (reductive, pointless aping of the natural sciences), and is completely disregarded.

3.4 Production of results

Given that the two ways of conducting research differ in terms of planning, recording

TABLE. 2.2 *Party activists' vision of social reality*

	Christian Democrats	Communists	Total
Absolutely dichotomous	5.6	31.5	18.5
Predominantly dichotomous	25.9	38.9	32.4
Sees reality as a struggle between opposing positions but has a more balanced view of the alternatives	51.8	25.9	38.9
Not at all dichotomous	16.7	3.7	10.2
Total	100	100	100
(N)	(54)	(54)	(108)

and data analysis, it is natural that they will also differ in terms of the type of results obtained. We will look first at the most obvious difference: *how the data are presented*. The two classical (and also the simplest) forms of data presentation in the quantitative and qualitative traditions, respectively, are the 'table' and the 'account'.

By way of example, we will look at a study conducted in Italy in the middle of the 1960s on grassroots militants in the Christian Democratic Party and the Communist Party (Alberoni et al., 1967). Interviews were conducted with 108 activists (54 Christian Democrats and 54 Communists) according to a common framework. The interviews, which lasted from six to seven hours on average and were subdivided into various sessions (from three to six), were recorded and transcribed verbatim. They were subsequently coded by classifying the respondents' comments on each theme into categories and assigning a numerical value to each category (the technical details of this operation will be dealt with in Chapter 10). One of the variables so obtained was defined as 'dichotomous vision of reality' – that is to say, the tendency to interpret the forces operating in the social field in terms of 'opposing fronts ... two sides, one of which is good and is identified with, and the other of which is the enemy to be fought and, if possible, defeated and destroyed' (1967: 381). This tendency towards a dichotomous vision of reality naturally varied among the subjects, who were classified according to the four levels shown in Table 2.2

(from 'absolutely dichotomous' to 'not at all dichotomous').

What does Table 2.2 tell us? First of all, if we look at the column corresponding to the total number of interviewees, we can see that the activists studied are split almost perfectly between 'dichotomous' and 'non-dichotomous' (about 50% per group if we combine the first two categories and the last two categories). However, if we consider the Communist and Christian Democrat activists separately, the picture changes completely; while the dichotomous view is in the minority (less than a third) among the former, it is prevalent (more than two-thirds) among the latter. The quantitative information provided by the table is succinct, economical and compact; in just a few numbers, an important feature of the ideology of party activists is illustrated, as is the relationship between party membership and ideological orientation. This is the *relationship perspective* that we mentioned in Table 2.1.

However, such data have two drawbacks. First of all, 'dichotomous vision of reality' is a conceptual category created by the researchers and is interposed like a screen between the person who reads the table and the true mental categories of the interviewee. Moreover, behind this elementary concept there lies a wealth of information that is difficult to imagine for anyone who only reads the table. Interview extracts are less vulnerable to these two limitations. In the first place, the very fact that the interviewee's exact words are reported better enables the reader to 'see reality through the eyes of the subjects studied'.[4] Second, the verbatim report provides a pictorial dimension that lies beyond the scope of the simple table, thus enabling the reader to 'visualize' the interviewees, much in the same way as a photograph of a person gives us a very different and much more complete image than a simple physical description ever could. This is the *narrative perspective* mentioned in Table 2.1.

The following interview extract refers to the 'dichotomous vision of reality' and reveals that this is a highly synthetic concept made up of numerous specific components. For instance, it involves a clear-cut view of international politics which, in the case of this Communist activist, is expressed as an uncritical idealization of the Soviet Union:

> I've always liked the Soviet Union, ever since I was young. Now of course I know it better still. I'm convinced that Russia has the right policy. I'm sure Russia does everything it can to avoid war. Russia doesn't want war; Russia's war is the propaganda it spreads throughout the world. That's what wins popularity in other countries and attracts the commercial market from countries all over the world. This system has turned a profit, and sooner or later socialism will have to be all over the world and in those states they'll bring them to their knees without having to go to war because she'll strangle them with her action … In Russia they don't have to go on strike at all; they work for the people there … they work for them … There's socialism, and with socialism there's no need to strike … they're way ahead there … I don't know if it was last year or a few years ago, everyone got their bread free … When people get to that stage, it means they don't need to go on strike. (Alberoni et al., 1967: 479)

While the table and the account are the two typical modes of presenting results in quantitative and qualitative research, their use is not restricted to one or the other research type. Indeed, we very often come across quantitative studies in which accounts are used for the purpose of illustration, in much the same way as a photograph accompanies a newspaper article. In such cases, data analysis is conducted by means of quantitative instruments, on numerical variables through tables and multivariate analysis. The account serves to exemplify the results, to give the reader a clearer understanding of the world that lies behind the numerical data. For example, in the study quoted earlier, the researchers used multivariate analysis to pick out the variables that best characterized the different types of party activist (in this case, age, education, commitment to political activism, dichotomous attitude, striving for personal advantage); they then identified some interviewees who displayed this specific set of characteristics, and reported extracts taken from their interviews.

The opposite case is far rarer. A researcher who adopts the interpretive approach is very unlikely to depict relevant variables[5] in table form. Since his objective is to report the subject's vision of reality rather than to pick out generalizable features, he will be reluctant to apply his own categorizations to the responses and attitudes of the subjects studied.

We will now look at the question of *generalization*. The table and the account are two forms of elementary, and in a sense fragmentary, presentation of data. The conclusion of a study has to go beyond the simple exposition of the distributions of variables or a mere illustration of cases; it must be able to establish relationships among the variables or connections among the cases. Indeed, the objective of research is not just to describe aspects of reality, but to systematize them and to provide higher-order *syntheses* (be they explanations or interpretations). Only in this way can research be linked to theory, which is a form of synthetic rational abstraction of reality.

The pathway leading to these syntheses is clear in quantitative research; through the study of the relationships among variables, it brings the researcher to the enunciation of causal relationships among the variables themselves. After breaking down the individual into variables, quantitative analysis reaches a preliminary synthesis by correlating these variables (which can be synthesized into

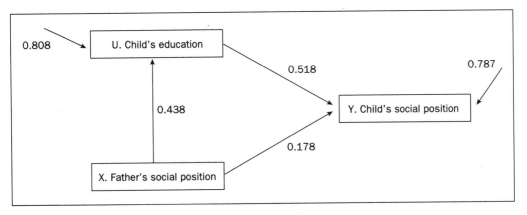

FIGURE 2.1   *Causal model of the links among father's social position, child's education and child's social position (Blau and Duncan, 1967)*

numerical indexes such as the correlation coefficient). It then achieves a higher level of conceptualization in the causal model (constituted by a network of cause-effect relationships among variables) and, in the most successful cases, in the formulation of synthetic expressions that come close to the 'laws' of the natural sciences.

To illustrate this point, we will look at a well-known study of the processes of social stratification conducted in the United States in the 1960s (Blau and Duncan, 1967). One of the tasks undertaken by the authors was to gauge how far an individual's social position was influenced by 'ascribed' status (in this case, the social position of the father) and how far by 'acquired' status (acquired during life, in this case through education). To put it bluntly, they wanted to find out whether it was more important to have a rich father or a good academic curriculum in order to be socially successful. The authors were well aware of the difficulty of separating the action of the two factors, given that the two 'causal' variables are interrelated (as the father's social position also influences the child's success at school). The model reported in Figure 2.1 shows the causal links (represented by arrows) hypothesized among the variables: a direct influence of 'child's education' on 'child's social position' (U → Y); a direct

influence of 'father's social position' on 'child's social position' (X → Y); and, finally, an indirect influence of 'father's social position' on 'child's social position' operating through 'education' (X → U → Y: a father with a good social position can help his child to achieve a high level of education, which in turn acts favourably on social position). Through the statistical technique of *path analysis* (which we will not dwell upon here) the relative weights of these different causal factors can be quantified (cf. the coefficients assigned to the arrows in the figure). The values reported reveal that the influence of education is greater than that of the father's social position. Moreover – going deeper into the analysis – it can be shown that even when the indirect influence of the father's social position is taken into account, the overall action (direct + indirect effect) of this variable does not reach the level of influence of education. Therefore the study was able to quantify the separate effects of the variables' 'ascribed' and 'acquired' status, and to demonstrate that the latter plays a more important role than the former.

This type of procedure is fairly common in quantitative research. In qualitative research, however, it is more difficult to pick out generally agreed-upon methods of synthesizing information. Nevertheless, many authors (including Lofland, 1971; Hammersley and

Atkinson, 1983; Spradley, 1980) maintain that the best way to achieve this kind of synthesis is by identifying 'types'. Then again, this is the approach proposed by Weber, who formulated the concept of the 'ideal type'.

As mentioned in Chapter 1, the ideal type is a conceptual category that does not have a genuine counterpart in reality. Although arising out of the observation of actual cases, it is a construction. It distils out the essence of the actual cases by purging them of the details and haphazard features of reality. In this way, it raises them to a higher plane of abstraction, so that the 'model' thus obtained can be used as a limit-concept to illuminate and interpret reality itself.

The use of the ideal type to guide the interpretation of reality is exemplified by the study *Lads, Citizens and Ordinary Kids*, conducted at the end of the 1970s by Jenkins (1983) on a group of working-class, Belfast adolescents (53 boys and 33 girls). Through in-depth interviews and participant observation, the author was able to identify three synthetic conceptual categories: 'lads' (boys whose behaviour and reference values are characterized by certain male-chauvinist, anti-bourgeois traits traditionally found in the working class), 'citizens' (who embody the respectable bourgeois values of sobriety, hard work, independence and aspiration to social betterment), and 'ordinary kids'. These he used to re-examine, order and analytically interpret the whole of his empirical material.

Through these categories, the author was able to interpret lifestyles (spending, clothing, pastimes, etc.), interaction with the opposite sex, relationships with the Church and with sport, views of the family and marriage, school careers, early work experience, etc. Classification into the three types provided a very good framework within which to interpret the subjects' various views of, for instance, marriage and the family. According to the 'lads' and the 'ordinary kids', a woman's place is in the home and, as a general rule, she will give up her job shortly after getting married, in order to have children. The 'citizens', on the other hand, hold the

view that a wife should continue to work, in order to save up to buy a house, and put off having children until later. The 'citizens' also see public courtship, engagement and a Church wedding as the 'respectable' pathway to marriage; sex before marriage is acceptable, but only within the context of a steady relationship. The other two types express various degrees of dissent from these views. Likewise, this typology is used to interpret the differences in the sample over the whole range of issues raised.

It should be stressed that, in all such cases, reality is not simply described; on the basis of the categories or ideal types identified, it is read, interpreted, analysed and finally *recomposed and synthesized*. Indeed, Jenkins re-examines the cases, reassesses their attributes and reinterprets the data in the light of the three types proposed. To return to an example quoted earlier, Sánchez-Jankowski (1991) used his four emotional triggers of violence in the same way (and these were also ideal types: fear, ambition, frustration and exhibitionism) in order to interpret the various episodes of violence that he had witnessed.

We will conclude this section with a reminder of the difference between the quantitative and qualitative approaches in terms of the two mechanisms of 'explanation' and 'interpretation'. In the qualitative studies illustrated here, no attempt is made to investigate the causal mechanisms that lead to the differences in attitudes, behaviours and lifestyles observed among the subjects during the course of data analysis. Jenkins does not ask why the 'lads' have a different view of marriage from the 'citizens'; rather, he seeks to describe these differences by interpreting them in the light of the general characteristics of the two ideal types. To put it simply, while quantitative research asks *why*, qualitative research asks *how*. Denzin, a staunch supporter of the interpretive approach, affirms, 'In my study on "Alcoholics Anonymous", I did not ask why individuals became alcoholics; I asked instead, how they came to see themselves as alcoholics. This way of asking the question led to a focus on social process, and not to a preoccupation with antecedent causal variables … My preference is to always focus on how an event or process is produced and created, and not to ask only why it happened or what caused it' (Denzin, 1989: 26).

At the other extreme, the ultimate aim of quantitative research is to identify the causal mechanism. While it will not always be possible to formalize a 'causal model' in which independent and dependent variables are linked by a precise network of causal relationships (as in the example of Blau and Duncan's 1967 study), the quantitative researcher will nevertheless be guided by the logic of the cause-effect mechanism. An example of this has already been seen in Sampson and Laub's research, in which the variables can basically be grouped under the three headings of 'causes', 'effects' and 'conditions', and the researchers' inquiries are always driven by the question of 'what causes what' and on what conditions.[6]

Recalling what has been said about the different focus – on variables or on subjects – of quantitative and qualitative analyses, we may add that the causal model binds *variables* together (in the logic of 'causation'), while the typology represents the theoretical scheme that links *subjects* (in the logic of 'classification').

Finally, a question that subsumes many of the themes treated is that of the *scope of findings*. This issue has already been touched upon with regard to sampling and the representativeness of the cases studied. As qualitative research necessitates in-depth investigation and identification with the object studied, it cannot handle large numbers of cases. The research carried out by Sánchez-Jankowski, who took part in the lives of the members of 37 gangs, is not so much rare as unique. Indeed, his observation in the field lasted some 10 years, which is in itself exceptional. Normally, research is conducted on few, or even very few, units. A very frequent occurrence is that of the 'case study', which focuses on a single specific situation (a gang, a neighbourhood, a factory, an organization, an event, etc.)

But in situations that are so specific (even if they are chosen in such a way as to be as representative as possible), how can we make observations or draw conclusions that have general validity? Research conducted on few cases can certainly go into greater depth, but this will necessarily be at the expense of the generalizability of its findings. As Michael Patton points out:

> It is possible to study a single individual over an extended period of time – for example the study, in depth, of one week in the life of one child. This necessitates gathering detailed information about every occurrence in that child's life and every interaction involving that child during some time period. With a more narrow research question we might study several children during a more limited period of time. With a still more limited focused question, or an interview of a half hour, we could interview yet a larger number of children on a smaller number of issues. The extreme case would be to spend all of our resources and time asking a single question of as many children as we could interview given the resource constraints (Patton, 1990: 166).

Depth and breadth are therefore inversely correlated; the more deeply the study penetrates, the fewer cases it can take in. However, the number of cases is linked to the generalizability of the findings. The broader the research – that is, the greater the number of subjects it covers – the better the sample will be able to represent the multifarious nature of reality, and the more legitimately the research results (provided no systematic bias arises) can be extended to the entire population.[7] In sum, quantitative research findings are undoubtedly more generalizable than those of qualitative research.

4. A FINAL NOTE: TWO DIFFERENT MODES OF INVESTIGATING SOCIAL REALITY

We will conclude this chapter with a naïve question: Is it better – scientifically more correct, cognitively more fruitful – to adopt the quantitative or the qualitative approach to research? Can it be claimed that one is superior to the other from a 'scientific' point of view? Three positions on the issue can be discerned. The first is that the quantitative and qualitative approaches, the neopositivist and interpretive paradigms, represent two incompatible points of view, in that they are epistemologically incommensurable and are based on contrasting philosophical foundations. The supporters of each perspective claim that theirs is the right one and that the other is wrong. According to the advocates of the quantitative approach, the qualitative approach is simply not science, while adherents to the latter maintain that aping the natural sciences is no way to grasp the true essence of social reality.

A second point of view is widely held among social scientists of the quantitative persuasion. Though having opted for the neopositivist paradigm, these researchers do not deny that worthwhile outputs can be yielded by qualitative techniques. Nevertheless, such techniques are seen as belonging to a pre-scientific exploratory phase, their function being to stimulate thinking in a kind of brainstorming that precedes the truly scientific phase. This ancillary role of qualitative research is aptly illustrated in the following extract by Blalock:

> In general, techniques of participant observation are extremely useful in providing initial insights and hunches that can lead to more careful formulations of the problem and explicit hypotheses. But they are open to the charge that findings may be idiosyncratic and difficult to replicate. Therefore, many social scientists prefer to think of participant observation as being useful at a certain stage of the research process rather than being an approach that yields a finished piece of research. (Blalock, 1970: 45–46)

Finally, the third view upholds the legitimacy, utility and equal dignity of the two methods, and expresses the hope that social research will adopt whichever approach best suits the circumstances (and this may mean both). This is a stance that has been consolidated in recent years, and one which has emerged not so much from new philosophical and epistemological reflections as from the pragmatic realization that valuable contributions have been made to sociology and social research by both quantitative and qualitative techniques. On this point, Bryman states explicitly that 'the distinction between quantitative and qualitative research is really a technical matter whereby the choice between them has to do with their suitability in answering particular research questions ... (not unlike other technical decisions) such as when it is appropriate to use a postal questionnaire, or to construct a stratified random sample' (Bryman, 1988: 109). This same viewpoint is expressed in the manual of qualitative research methodology entitled *Two Styles of Research, One Logic of Inference*, in which the authors claim that 'the same underlying logic provides the framework for each research approach ... the differences between the quantitative and qualitative traditions are only stylistic and are methodologically and substantively unimportant' (King et al., 1994: 3–4).

My own position is closest to this third view, but with some important differences. I do not agree that quantitative and qualitative methods are simply two different technical manifestations of what is substantially the same vision of the social world and of the purposes of research. In my view, these two ways of conducting research do not differ merely in terms of procedure, as Bryman claims. Rather, they are the direct and logically consequential expression of two different epistemological visions, the methodological manifestations of two different paradigms which imply alternative conceptions of social reality, research objectives, the role of the researcher and technological instruments.

But if the two approaches are different, does this necessarily mean that one is right and one is wrong? My personal answer is 'No'. Surely, two different visual perspectives of the same reality can both contribute significantly to our knowledge of that reality, just as a city might be illustrated both by a

> ### BOX 2.1 THE NEOPOSITIVIST AND INTERPRETIVE APPROACHES
>
> The quantitative and qualitative techniques yield different kinds of knowledge. Far from being a handicap, this is actually an advantage. Only a multi-faceted, differentiated approach can provide a complete vision of social reality, just as a statue in a square reveals the completeness of its form only when viewed from different angles. Social research is like painting a portrait. A perspective is chosen. However, innumerable other perspectives exist, and not only in terms of visual angle (the subject being seen full-face or in profile, close up or at a distance) but also in terms of fidelity to the formal appearance or otherwise (psychological traits may be brought out through colour or through lines that deform; the person may be portrayed in a surreal context). There is no absolute portrait, just as there is no absolute 'true' representation of reality.

panoramic photograph and by a photograph of one of its most characteristic streets.

Let's consider Sampson and Laub's research, which aims to test a precise theoretical model of the pathway that leads the individual into crime and consolidates illegal behaviour, analyses this process in terms of dependent and independent variables by utilizing the categories of cause and effect and recording quantitative data on a sample of 1000 subjects. And let's consider, by contrast, Sánchez-Jankowski's research, which strives from within to understand the motivations that prompt a youth to join a gang and to engage in acts of violence, involves close participation in the daily life of city gangs. Of the two perspectives that are illustrated by these two different methods of conducting research, can we say that one is right and the other is wrong? Can it be claimed that one enriches our knowledge of juvenile delinquency while the other paints a distorted and deceptive picture? Such a thesis would be difficult to sustain, as both studies clearly make their own significant contribution to our knowledge of this social phenomenon.

Nevertheless, I feel that it is difficult, if not impossible, to harness the two approaches within the same research design; the procedures and the instruments used are too different.

Indeed, those studies that are quoted as having adopted both approaches have, in reality, been substantially oriented towards one of the two perspectives, and have made purely ancillary use of techniques taken from the other. Moreover, I believe that the same researcher is unlikely to be able to conduct studies by means of the two different approaches (obviously at different times) and achieve equally good results. His training as a scholar, indeed the very structure of his scientific mind-set, will probably preclude this kind of flexibility.

To conclude, neopositivist and interpretive approaches, quantitative and qualitative research, yield different results, but both are rich of social knowledge.

SUMMARY

1. Sampson and Laub's secondary analysis of survey data concerning juvenile delinquency is an example of quantitative research based on the neopositivist paradigm. It features a systematic working method, in which each chapter follows a four-step path: theoretical framework, empirical recording, results of analysis,

return to theory. Data analysis is performed on variables with quantitative statistical tools in order to produce 'causal models', in which variables are connected through cause-effect relationships.

2. Sánchez-Jankowski's study, a typical case of participant observation, is a good example of qualitative research based on the interpretivist paradigm. Even though the topic is similar to Sampson and Lamb's study, the working method is very different. The author participated fully in the life of the gangs which were the object of his investigation, got involved in what they did, and recorded data by writing notes in his notebook during the course of observation. His overall goal is not to discern cause-effect relationships between variables, but rather to understand the motivations underlying gang members' behaviour and to draw up classifications and typologies.

3. The differences between quantitative and qualitative research – no longer in terms of their philosophical and epistemological premises, but of their concrete application to research – can be understood by examining how they develop the four basic stages of empirical research: planning, data collection, data analysis and scope of findings.

3.1 *Research planning* The difference between quantitative and qualitative research hinges on the fact that the first relies on a pre-defined, structured design based on hypotheses drawn from theory; whereas the second rests on an open, interactive work plan, in which specific procedures emerge and change as the research proceeds. Moreover, in quantitative research the researcher's attitude toward her subjects is neutral and detached, whereas in qualitative research it features empathy and identification.

3.2 *Data collection* Quantitative research usually deals with a representative sample of the target universe and aims to build a 'data matrix', i.e. gather the collected data in a standard format which is the same for all cases. Qualitative research does not address issues of standardization and representativeness, and prefers treating selected cases in a differential manner, according to their perceived relevance.

3.3 *Data analysis* In quantitative research data analysis focuses on variables, i.e. on the characteristics of cases, which are examined with mathematical procedures and statistical tools. In qualitative research, on the other hand, analysis focuses on subjects considered in their entirety and attempts to achieve an understanding of these subjects rather than identify relationships among variables.

3.4 *Scope of findings* The goal of quantitative research is to produce generalizations, i.e. syntheses that apply at a higher, abstract, conceptual level (such as cause-effect relationships among variables) and in a wider field (such as other societies, different from the one actually studied). In general, qualitative research is less interested in generalization of findings and pays more attention to the specific features of social situations in which research is carried out.

FURTHER READING

A. Bryman, *Quantity and Quality in Social Research* (Routledge, 1988, pp. 198) is a good introductory text which explores the distinction between qualitative and quantitative research. Another introductory text, which will help the would-be researcher to choose between the two approaches, is J.W. Creswell, *Qualitative and Quantitative Approaches* (Sage, 1994, pp. 227).

Two volumes are recommended for all those who wish to reconcile qualitative and quantitative approaches and make the most of their differences: I. Newman and C.R. Benz, *Qualitative-Quantitative Research Methodology: Exploring* the *Interactive Continuum* (Southern Illinois University Press, 1998, pp. 218); A. Tashakkori and C. Teddlie, *Mixed Methodology: Combining Qualitative and Quantitative Approaches* (Sage, 1998, pp. 185).

The basic text on qualitative research is the vast collection of materials and discussion gathered by N.K. Denzin and Y.S. Lincoln, *Handbook of Qualitative Research* (Sage, 2000, pp. 1065); it offers a large number of essays (41) that trace the history of qualitative methods (see A.J. Vidich and M.L. Stanford, *Qualitative Methods: Their History in Sociology and Anthropology*), the underlying paradigms, the different strategies of inquiry and methods of collecting, analyzing and interpreting empirical materials.

Two volumes can be recommended for further study of quantitative methods. The first – P.S. Maxim, *Quantitative Research Methods in the Social Sciences* (Cambridge University Press, 1999, pp. 405) – adopts a more methodological approach and addresses the philosophical bases of scientific research, the issues of statistical inference, measurement, scaling, research design, and sampling. The second volume – T.R. Black, *Doing Quantitative Research in The Social Sciences: An Integrated Approach to Research Design, Measurement and Statistics* (Sage, 1999, pp. 751) – is more technical and devotes over half its pages to procedures of statistical transformation of information into data and their analysis.

NOTES

1. A much debated example of this kind of reification was that of the intelligence quotient; in many situations, the instrument (IQ) used to measure intelligence became synonymous with the concept of intelligence itself. The highly restrictive and culturally biased nature of the instrument gave rise to serious consequences.

2. The author had previously noted that one of the meanings given for the word 'gang' in Webster's *New American Dictionary* was that of 'journey'.

3. The 'holistic perspective' (from the Greek *hólos* = whole, entire) is also taken to mean an approach in which social objects (organizations, institutions, groups, etc.) are studied in their entirety as complex systems, on the supposition that a system cannot be divided into distinct, independent parts on account of the systemic interaction of all its parts.

4. This does not mean that the simple use of quotations can convey to the reader the vision of reality held by the individuals studied. What is conveyed by the research report will always be the researcher's interpretation: the choice of which subjects to quote, emphasis on one snippet of conversation rather than another, and the logical thread that ties the various quotations together. Nevertheless, the fact remains that the interviewee's response is reported in its original form, while the data reported in the table are subject to a further mediating element, which is the coding of responses within categories pre-established by the researcher.

5. Tables may, of course, be used to depict secondary and descriptive variables, such as basic sociographic variables.

6. For illustrative purposes, the comparison between quantitative and qualitative methods has highlighted the opposition between explanation and interpretation, the question of why and the question of how, causation and classification, analysis by variables and analysis by subjects. In reality, of course, these distinctions are never so clear-cut. For instance, quantitative research also makes ample use of typologies. What is even more important, however, is that the causal mechanism is evident in many interpretive approaches; Weber, for example, even admits the existence of 'laws', though he regards them only as instruments for understanding the behaviour of the individual, and not as the objective of social research (cf. Kaplan, 1964: 115).

7. The argument that few cases, if carefully selected (so as to be 'typical'), can represent the range of variations present in the population is unconvincing. Indeed, how can we ensure that the cases selected are 'typical' of the host of possibilities occurring in reality, when the very purpose of the research is to discover that reality? Moreover, sometimes it is those very cases that deviate from the norm which are the most illuminating.

Part Two

Quantitative Techniques

In the six chapters that follow, we will leave behind more general methodological considerations in order to deal with the specific techniques of research, beginning with the quantitative approach. In reality, the first of these chapters, which looks at how theory is transformed into empirical research, discusses issues that are still very general in nature. These issues fit into a context that could be defined as pre-technical and which is not limited to quantitative research. However, there are two reasons for dealing with this subject within the sphere of the quantitative approach.

First of all, in qualitative research there is no equivalent of the operationalization of concepts, a notion which, in quantitative research, lies at the core of the transformation of theoretical hypotheses into empirically testable propositions. As has already been pointed out, the concepts used in qualitative research are, to use Blumer's expression, 'sensitizing concepts' – that is to say, they are inchoate, open frames of reference, whose purpose is to point the way and to heighten the researcher's sensitivity to particular themes during the course of the interview. They therefore lack the detail, precision and definition demanded by quantitative research, in which concepts are to be operationalized.

Second, the assumption that theory precedes research is implicit in the very title of the chapter 'From theory to empirical research', an assumption that is rejected by a great deal of qualitative research. Indeed, *grounded theory* holds that concepts and hypotheses should not precede the gathering of information, in that theory is 'rooted' in the reality observed and it is the researcher's task to discover it. According to the advocates of this point of view, theory should be generated by empirical observation (they use the term 'generate' as opposed to 'verify') – that is, the concepts and hypotheses should be extracted from reality, rather than imposing preconceived theoretical schemes on reality. They argue that this approach yields theories that fit the data better and work better, in that the categories are discovered by examining the data themselves; moreover, such theories are easier for the ordinary person to understand, as they are deduced from his own way of thinking. Thus, 'grounded theory can help to forestall the opportunistic use of theories that have dubious fit and working capacity', and which are often adopted by researchers out of intellectual laziness and acquiescence to the dominant fashion (Glaser and Strauss, 1967: 3–4).

Clearly, such approach excludes the sequence 'theory – hypotheses – data-gathering – analysis – return to theory' which, as we will see, constitutes the typical structure of classical quantitative research.

It is for these reasons that we have preferred to place such general issues as the passage from theory to research under the umbrella of quantitative research. It should, however, be added that the first part of this chapter, in which the notions of theory, hypothesis and concepts are discussed, goes beyond the pure and simple quantitative approach to deal more generally with the whole context of theory and social research.

3 From Theory to Empirical Research

The central topic of this chapter is operationalization – that is, the transformation of theoretical hypotheses into empirical research operations. The meaning of 'theory', 'hypothesis' and 'concept' are clarified. Then the notion of variable – a key theme in empirical social research – is introduced, and the various types of variable are described. Finally, the chapter addresses the general issue of errors which inevitably occur along the road from theory to empirical research.

1. THE 'TYPICAL' STRUCTURE OF QUANTITATIVE RESEARCH

Before going into the details of the individual research techniques, it is advisable to provide a general picture of the logical structure of the entire process of empirical research and the stages into which it is broken down. First all, we can begin by saying that:

- scientific research is a creative process of discovery,
- which is developed according to a pre-established itinerary and according to predetermined procedures,
- that have become consolidated within the scientific community.

The juxtaposition of the terms 'creative' and 'predetermined procedures' in this statement should not be seen as contradictory. The adjective 'creative' is important in this definition as it evokes the researcher's personal capability, perspicacity and insight. But this is only one aspect, and not the most important, of the process of scientific research. Reichenbach made a well-known distinction between the moment in which a new idea is conceived and the phase in which it is presented, justified, defended and tested; these he called *context of discovery and context of justification*, respectively. With regard to the former, Reichenbach claims that it is not possible to establish rules or procedures: 'The act of discovery escapes logical analysis; there are no logical rules in terms of which a "discovery machine" could be constructed that would take over the creative function of the genius' (Reichenbach, 1951: 231). However, the scientist's work consists not only of producing theories, but also of testing them. And this phase, whether it involves logical-formal examination of the theory or verification of its consistency with reality (and this brings us to empirical research), must follow precise rules.

The first fundamental rule of empirical research is that it must be carried out within a framework that is collectively agreed upon. Unlike art, scientific research is a collective process. As Merton (1968) points out, 'Science is public, not private'. This collective-public aspect of science has a dual connotation and stems from a dual necessity. On the one hand, it implies *control*: 'The concepts and the procedures adopted by even the most intuitive of sociologists must be standardized, and the results of their intuitions must be able to be verified also by others' (Merton, 1968). On the other hand, it implies *cumulativeness*: 'If I have seen farther, it is by standing on the shoulders of giants' goes the famous aphorism commonly ascribed to Isaac Newton, around which Robert Merton constructed a brilliant and erudite essay on the sociology of science (Merton, 1965). Moreover, one of the most common definitions of science is that of 'systematic accumulation of knowledge'.

The collective frame of reference that the social scientist must bear in mind when carrying out research – especially within the quantitative approach, which is much more formalized than the qualitative approach – is made up of two components: the logical structure of the research pathway and the technical instruments to be used. We will begin with the first of these.

1.1 The five stages of the research process

The *'typical'* itinerary followed in social research consists of a loop, which begins with the theory, runs through the phases of data collection and analysis, and returns to the theory. This pathway is traced in more or less

the same forms in all empirical research manuals; it is illustrated in Figure 3.1, which shows five phases and the five processes that link them.

The first phase is that of the *theory*.

The second is that of the *hypotheses*, and the passage between the two involves a process of *deduction*. The hypothesis constitutes a partial articulation of the theory and, in relation to the theory, is located on a lower level of generality.[1] The theory is 'general', while the hypothesis is 'specific'. For example, from the general theoretical proposition (which will form part of a broader theoretical system of propositions regarding political involvement) that 'there is a positive correlation between political participation and the centrality of one's social position', three specific hypotheses (among others) can be deduced: that voting will be higher among men, among adults (than among the young or the elderly), and among the professionally more successful. In this example, the concept of political participation has been limited to voter turnout, and that of social centrality to the three aspects mentioned.

The third phase is that of empirical observation, or rather, *data collection*. This is reached through the process of *operationalization* – that is to say, the transformation of hypotheses into empirically observable statements. This process is very complex and can be broken down into two stages. The first of these concerns the operationalization of concepts; this involves transforming the concepts into variables – that is, entities that can be assessed. For example, the concept of professional success can be gauged through income, or by comparing the individual's occupation with that of his father, etc. The second stage regards the *choice of the tool* and of the procedures for data collection. In the example concerning political involvement, the researcher may decide to work on aggregate data provided by official statistics on voting, by investigating whether voting varies with gender and age; alternatively, he might use survey data, or in-depth interviews conducted on a sample of citizens. Such decisions will lead to the construction of the *research design* – that is

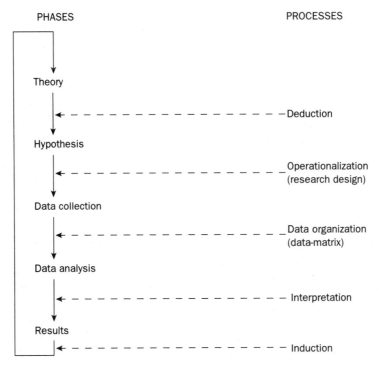

PHASES   PROCESSES

Theory

— — — — — — — — — — — — — — —Deduction

Hypothesis

— — — — — — — — — — — — — — Operationalization
                                                  (research design)

Data collection

— — — — — — — — — — — — — — Data organization
                                                  (data-matrix)

Data analysis

— — — — — — — — — — — — — — Interpretation

Results

— — — — — — — — — — — — — — Induction

FIGURE 3.1   *The 'typical' structure of quantitative research*

Source: Adapted from Bryman (1988: 20).

to say, a 'fieldwork plan' in which the various phases of empirical observation will be established (e.g. *n* subjects will be interviewed, located in the following geographical areas…, selected according to the following criteria…, utilizing the following questionnaire…, etc.)

Once the empirical material has been gathered, one proceeds to the fourth phase, or *data analysis* phase, which will be preceded by the organization of the data. In general, the term *information* is applied to the raw empirical material that has not yet been systematized, while the term *data* is used to indicate the same material once it has been organized into a form that can be analyzed. For instance, a set of questionnaires or tape recordings of interviews constitute information, while the same questionnaires or recordings will become 'data' once they have been transformed into sequences of numbers that can be compared with one another. In quantitative research, the

process of data organization usually involves transforming information into a rectangular matrix of numbers. This *data matrix* – which is also called the 'cases by variables' (C × V) matrix – will be obtained, for example, by systematically coding questionnaire responses, by standardizing the answers given in open interviews, by normalizing statistical sources, by submitting texts to a content-analysis grid, etc. The resulting data matrix forms the basis for the data analysis, which normally involves computer-aided statistical elaboration.

Results are presented in the fifth phase, which is reached through a process of *interpretation* of the statistical analyses carried out in the previous phase.

Finally, the researcher returns to the starting point of the whole procedure – that is to say, the *theory*. The process involved here is one of *induction*; the empirical results will be compared with the theoretical hypotheses and, more generally, with the initial theory. In this way, the theory will either be confirmed or reformulated.

As shown in Figure 3.1, the research process can be represented as a loop that begins with the theory and returns to the theory. However, a closer analogy might be that of a spiral, in which theory and research are linked in an endless process of accumulation of sociological knowledge. It should be added that what has been described is the 'ideal' pathway of quantitative research, and that this basic sequence may vary, even considerably, in actual practice. For instance, with respect to the theory, the equilibrium between deduction and induction may be different. Although the basic scheme envisions beginning the research only after a thorough review of the theory and the formulation of clearly defined hypotheses, some research projects begin with an embryonic theory, which develops and takes shape only in the data analysis phase. On other occasions, the entire data-collection phase – including the processes of operationalization and data organization – is omitted, in that the research is conducted on data already collected. Nevertheless, the scheme illustrated in Figure 3.1 can be regarded as the reference model.

In this chapter, we will deal with everything that takes place between theory and data collection – that is to say, the two processes labelled as deduction and operationalization in our figure. The first of these processes is dealt with in Section 2. The rest of the chapter is devoted entirely to the operationalization of concepts. That ample space has been given over to this issue is evidence of both its complexity and its importance within the research pathway.

2. FROM THEORY TO HYPOTHESES

2.1 Theory
A theory can be defined as:

- a set of organically connected propositions,
- that are located at a higher level of abstraction and generalization than empirical reality,

- and which are derived from empirical patterns,
- and from which empirical forecasts can be derived.

In order to illustrate what we mean by a theory, we will look at the classic example of Durkheim's suicide theory. As is well known, Durkheim identified three 'ideal types' of suicide: egoistic, altruistic and anomic. Within his theory, we will focus on – from among its many statements – the following causal proposition, which also represents the theoretical foundation of egoistic suicide: 'The higher the level of individualism in a given social group, the higher the suicide rate in that group'. Here, individualism refers to a social and cultural situation in which the individual is completely free (and substantially alone) when making decisions concerning his own life, and therefore must rely solely on his own personal morality; the opposite situation is that of social cohesion, in which the individual's actions are constantly subjected to social controls, and choices are largely determined by collective norms. The theoretical proposition stated, which links individualism and suicide, is a *causal proposition*. It displays the feature of *abstraction*, in that the concepts of individualism, social cohesion and suicide are abstract constructs, and the feature of *generalization*, in that the proposed connection is thought to be valid for a whole range of societies (if not for all human societies). It is *derived from empirical patterns*, in that Durkheim deduced and empirically tested his theory by analysing the statistical sources of his day. It gives rise to *empirical forecasts*, in that it enables us to predict, for example, a lower suicide rate in Ireland than in England, although Durkheim did not investigate the Irish situation.

2.2 Hypotheses
A theoretical proposition must be able to be broken down into specific hypotheses. By hypothesis, we mean:

- a proposition that implies a relationship between two or more concepts,
- which is located on a lower level of abstraction and generality than the theory,
- and which enables the theory to be transformed into terms that can be tested empirically.

The hypothesis has two distinguishing features. First, it is less abstract (or more concrete) than the theory in conceptual terms, and less general (or more specific) in terms of extension. Second, it is provisional in nature; it is a statement that has yet to be proved, which is derived from the theory but awaits empirical confirmation.

A series of specific hypotheses can be deduced from Durkheim's general theory. For example, a higher suicide rate can be expected in Protestant societies than in Catholic ones (as Protestantism allows greater scope for the free will of the individual, while Catholicism is more prescriptive and normative). Similarly, the suicide rate should be lower among married people with children (on account of the demands, bonds, duties and controls imposed by the family situation), at times when a society is going through a political crisis or a war (owing to the strengthening of social bonds among citizens in the face of common danger), and so on.

These hypotheses can be *tested empirically*[2] through the application of suitable operational definitions. For example, the concept of 'family integration' will be defined operationally by considering the highest degree of integration to be that of married people with children, and the lowest that of persons who live alone (and by establishing the intermediate degrees); the data will then be examined to see whether there is an association between this variable and suicide. Alternatively, we can look for a relationship between the suicide rate and the type of dominant religion in different societies (all other conditions being equal), as Durkheim did.

The validity of a theory depends on whether it can be transformed into empirically testable hypotheses. *The criterion of empirical testability is the very criterion of its 'scientificness'.* If a theory is vague and confused, it is very unlikely that it will be able to be transformed into testable statements; lacking empirical corroboration, it will remain in the pre-scientific sphere of supposition. In the social sciences, the risk that theories will be too vague and confused to be operationalized is particularly acute. From this point of view, we cannot but endorse the statement that 'an erroneous theory is better than a vague theory'.

2.3 Turning theories into hypotheses

We will now look at some examples of how theories have been transformed into specific hypotheses.

The first case involves the theory formulated by Inglehart in the middle of the 1970s with regard to the change in values seen in Western countries. According to this theory, the values of the generations that grew up in the post-war period are different from those of the preceding generations. This change is claimed to be marked by a shift in emphasis from issues of physical and economic security to themes of quality of life, self-fulfilment and intellectual and aesthetic satisfaction – that is to say, from a chiefly materialistic orientation to one that has been called 'post-materialistic'. This shift is explained by various factors, one of which (perhaps the most important) is the improved living conditions enjoyed by members of the post-war generations during their formative years. Unlike their predecessors, who grew up between the two world wars and in the period of the Great Depression, the younger generations did not have to cope with economic crises. Moreover, in the post-war period, Western societies enjoyed unprecedented prosperity, which enabled the basic needs of almost the whole population to be met. A further aspect is that of physical safety; the newer generations had not experienced war, as their fathers and grandfathers had. According to the theory of needs, people begin to focus on non-material objectives only when their physical and economic security is ensured.

Some specific hypotheses can be derived from this general theory (cf. Inglehart, 1977).

First, and most obviously, we should find a marked difference between young and old in all Western countries in terms of their scales of values. This is the result of the fact that (as has been repeatedly demonstrated by social psychology) value orientation is established during the subject's formative years and tends to remain fixed throughout life, even if social and environmental conditions change.

The second hypothesis is that this generation gap will differ from one nation to another. If the theory is valid, the gap should be wider in countries where the increase in living standards from the pre- to the post-war period is greatest. The gap should therefore be widest in Germany, since it is the country in which post-war prosperity and social stability contrast most starkly with the famine, bloodshed, runaway inflation, economic depression, internal strife and destruction suffered in two world wars and in the interwar period. By the same reasoning, the narrowest gap should be seen in Britain. The wealthiest nation in Europe before World War II, Britain was not ravaged by fighting within her own borders nor did she suffer an enemy invasion. Moreover, the country went through a prolonged post-war period of economic stagnation that held down living standards below those of many other European countries, and certainly below the levels reached during the first half of the century.

A further hypothesis again concerns the differences among nations, but this time refers not so much to the generation gap as to the total proportion of those who embrace post-materialistic values. These numbers should be greater in wealthier countries such as Belgium, the Netherlands and Switzerland (to remain within the European context) than in less prosperous ones such as Spain, Greece and Italy. All these hypotheses can easily be transformed into operational terms and therefore subjected to empirical testing.

With regard to the sequence linking theory and hypotheses, it should be pointed out that research practice does not always follow the pathway described above: first, the theory is worked out; then the hypotheses are drawn up and, on the basis of these, the 'research design' is established – that is to say, the data-collection is organized. Often, hypotheses are drawn up *after* the data have been collected and are compared with the data *a posteriori*.

Let us take the case of a study conducted in Italy on decisions taken by individuals with regard to their education. The author analysed how subjects decide whether or not to carry on with their education after finishing middle school or high school. To this end, he compared three different ways of looking at an individual's actions: the 'structuralist' view, which 'considers man's action as channelled by external constraints which do not leave any substantial room for choice'; the 'pushed-from-behind view', which again sees the individual as being conditioned, though this time not so much by external structural factors as by internal psychological factors, most of which are unconscious; and the the 'pulled-from-the-front view', which assumes that individuals act purposively in accordance with their intentions. Individuals here are viewed not so much as pushed from behind as attracted from the front (Gambetta, 1987: 8, 16).

This is a classic expression of the theory of individual action. What is of interest to us here, however, is that, in searching for empirical answers to these questions, the author utilized the data – *already gathered* (secondary analysis) – from two surveys carried out for somewhat general purposes (to investigate the political and cultural orientation of young people). Thus, the author started out from three specific hypotheses of behaviour, and analyzed the data available to see which of them might be confirmed empirically. In this case, although the theoretical elaboration took place after the data had been collected, it preceded their analysis.

On other occasions, the theory is constructed after the data have been analysed, in order to explain some anomalous feature or unexpected result. For example, in a study on abstention from voting conducted in Italy in the 1980s (Corbetta and Parisi, 1987), the authors empirically tested two hypotheses.

One hypothesis was that abstentions reflected political *apathy* due to the inability of the parties' organizational network to mobilize the electorate; the other was that abstentions constituted a *protest* on the part of voters, who wanted to signal their discontent and resentment by staying away from the ballot-box. In investigating the first hypothesis, the authors expected to find more absenteeism among the peripheral sectors of society, those least likely to be reached by the parties' propaganda machinery (the extreme case being that of elderly women living in rural areas of the south, who fall into the most marginal category on all four variables: gender, age, rural-urban, north-south). In testing the second hypothesis, the authors expected to see more abstentions among young males living in large northern cities: mainstream social categories exposed to the flow of new ideas and apt to signal a split between the more modern sectors of society and traditional politics.

Surprisingly, however, the data clashed with both hypotheses. The greatest proportion of abstentions was seen among women living in large provincial cities; a marginal chracteristic – traditionally, women are less involved in politics than men – was therefore unexpectedly combined with a feature of centrality, i.e. city residence. Closer analysis revealed that a large number of these women had previously voted for the Christian Democrats. To explain this unforeseen result, the authors turned to the theory of 'cross-pressures', which asserts that when a voter is exposed simultaneously to stimuli of equal intensity but opposite direction, he will probably opt out of the dilemma and abstain from voting. The authors therefore interpreted this result in the light of several factors: the weakened rallying-cry of religion in a secularized society, the fact that the Catholic Church had intentionally distanced itself from the political arena, and the groundswell of new values propagated particularly by the mass media. According to the authors, that part of the female electorate that had traditionally been receptive to the message of the Church was caught in a dilemma between old and new values; this produced uncertainty, which led to abstention. This process began in the large cities, which classically respond to change more promptly than other areas. In this case, when confronted with an unexpected result, the authors turned to a different theory, which had already been used on other occasions to interpret voting trends.

A new theory may sometimes be discovered during the empirical phase. A well-known example is that of the experiments conducted in the 1920s at the Western Electric factory in Hawthorne, near Chicago (Mayo, 1966). These experiments were designed to investigate a very simple question: what effect changes in lighting might have on worker output. At first, it was found that productivity rose when the lighting was increased. Subsequently, however, when the lighting was restored to its original intensity, productivity remained high. Nor were the researchers' expectations met when the workers were divided into two groups, an experimental group (working under various conditions of lighting) and a control group (for which the lighting remained constant); the output of both groups was higher than the average and displayed no light-related variation. Baffled, the researchers called in a team of sociologists from the organization led by Elton Mayo, who broadened the focus of their observation to factors other than purely environmental ones. Using various techniques, including participant observation and interviews, they discovered that the variable responsible for the higher productivity was not the lighting (nor any other variable of a technical or organizational kind, such as the length of the coffee break, etc.); it was simply the fact that the workers realized they were being observed. These experiments gave rise to a whole new theoretical current in the sociology of work, which was dubbed 'human relations'. Thus, among the conditions required to ensure good productivity, emphasis was placed on psychological variables such as work-group cohesion, a feeling of belonging, a sense of the worth of one's own work, etc.

With regard to changes in the canonical sequence theory-hypothesis-observation, it should be said that data collection sometimes precedes hypotheses for reasons of necessity. This is the case of 'secondary analysis', for instance, in which data gathered previously by other researchers is analysed further (examples being Gambetta's study and *Crime in the Making* by Sampson and Laub, which was extensively covered in Chapter 2). It should also be added that the theory is often insufficiently well defined to enable clear hypotheses to be made. Sometimes the issue is new and unknown, and research therefore has to be predominantly descriptive. On other occasions, data collection does not spring from a specific theory, in that the intention is to cover a wide range of issues, in order to enable subsequent diverse analyses to be made (as in periodic investigations like Eurobarometer, General Social Survey, National Election Studies, etc.).

3. FROM CONCEPTS TO VARIABLES

The term 'concept' refers to the *semantic content* (the meaning) *of linguistic signs and mental images*. Its etymological meaning (from the Latin *cum capio* = take together) indicates both the action of ordering the multifarious within a single thought and the act of abstracting a universal meaning from immediate sense impressions and from manifestations of the particular. It is the means by which human beings are able to know and to think; it is also the basis of all scientific disciplines, which consist of knowing by universals.

From this definition, it follows that 'the term has a very general meaning and may include any kind of sign or semantic procedure, whatever object it refers to, whether abstract or concrete, near or far, universal or individual, etc. We can therefore have a concept of table or of the number three, of man or God, of genus or species … of a historical period or of a historical institution (the Renaissance or feudalism)' (Abbagnano,

1971: 146). Furthermore, concepts can refer to abstract mental constructions that are impossible to observe directly, such as power, happiness or social class, or else to immediately observable concrete entities, such as flower or worker.

In Section 2, a *hypothesis* was defined as *a proposition that implies a relationship between two or more concepts*; in other words, it is *an interconnection among concepts*. The hypothesis that the rate of suicide is higher among the better educated or in Protestant societies is constituted by a connection between the concept of suicide and that of education or religion. Similarly, the hypothesis that post-materialistic values are more commonly found among middle-class young people than working-class young people sets up a relationship between the concepts of value and social class.

We can therefore say that the concepts are the 'building blocks of the theory', and that it is through the operationalization of the concepts that the theory is transformed into empirical terms. Thus, the concept bridges the gap between theory and the observable empirical world. As Blumer points out, 'Theory is of value in empirical science only to the extent to which it connects fruitfully with the empirical world. Concepts are the means … of establishing such connection' (Blumer, 1969: 143).

If the theory is a network of connections among abstract entities represented by concepts, then once these abstract entities become concrete, the whole theoretical network will become concrete. It will therefore be possible to establish the same connections among the concepts made concrete – that is, transformed into empirically observable entities. If the theoretical hypothesis is that post-materialistic values are more widely held in wealthy societies, then as soon as we are able to empirically gauge both wealth and the presence of such values in different societies, we will also be able to test the validity of the theory empirically, simply by observing whether the two operationalized concepts are positively correlated in the data recorded.

How, then, is a concept operationalized? Think about some typical social science concepts, such as power, social class, authoritarianism, political participation, deviance, underdevelopment, etc. How can these concepts be transformed into empirically assessable entities?

The first step in the empirical transformation of concepts consists of applying the concepts to concrete objects. This is done by *causing the concepts to become* attributes or *properties of* the specific objects studied, which are called *units of analysis* (or simply units). For example, the concept of power may be a property of units constituted by corporate roles, or by political roles (city councillor, party functionary, Member of Parliament, etc.); the concepts of social class and authoritarianism may be properties of individuals; the concepts of political participation and deviance may characterize both individuals and geographic areas. The concept of underdevelopment may be a property of nations. Moreover, it should be noted that the concepts-properties used in social analysis do not necessarily have to be complex concepts; even simple, easily observed concepts, such as gender, age, place of residence and the time spent getting to work, can be numbered among our examples.

On the objects to which they appertain, these properties assume different *states* – that is to say, they vary among the units of analysis. For example, some corporate posts have more power than others; social class varies among individuals, as does authoritarianism; political participation and crime vary from one geographic area to another.

The second step in the process is to make the concept-property operational. This involves giving it an *operational definition* – that is to say, *establishing the rules for its transformation into empirical operations*. For instance, the power of a corporate post may be defined operationally in terms of the number of posts subordinate to it; authoritarianism may be operationalized by means of a set of questions, with a score being assigned on a scale from 0 to 5; political participation and crime in a municipality may be operationalized on

the basis of the percentage of the electorate that turns out to vote in an election and the number of crimes committed per 1000 members of the population.

The third step is to *apply the* above-mentioned *rules to the concrete cases studied*; this is the phase of *operationalization* in the narrow sense. The operational definition is drawn up on paper, while operationalization is its practical implementation. The operational definition is a 'text'; operationalization is an 'action'.

The property so operationalized is called a *variable*. The operationalized 'states' of the property are called *categories*, each of which is assigned a different symbolic *value*, which is normally constituted by a number. For example, the concept 'cultural level' may be assessed through the property 'educational qualification', which assumes different states in the various individuals studied; these states could be recorded in the four categories, 'elementary-school', 'middle-school', 'high school' and 'university degree', to which the *values* 1, 2, 3, 4, respectively, are assigned.

At this point, a specification needs to be made with regard to the term 'operationalization', which we have used to denote the passage from property to variable. The current language uses the term 'measurement' to refer to the process of assigning numerical values to the states of the property. The definition of 'measurement' reported in the methodology manuals was originally formulated in the 1940s by Stevens, according to whom 'Measurement is the assignment of numbers to objects or events according to rules' (Stevens, 1946). In reality however, as Marradi has pointed out, it is improper to use the term measurement when no unit of measure is available (Marradi, 1981: 602 ff.). Thus, the passage from property to variable often involves an operation which is something other than *measurement*. For instance, while we can measure age (in terms of the unit of measure 'year'), we cannot measure nationality (which is a classification). By the same token, the operation may consist of *ordering* (e.g. professions on the basis of their social prestige) or *counting* (e.g. the number of children a person has). However, no single term has been agreed upon to define this operation of measuring-ordering-counting-classifying. The intrusiveness of the natural sciences – in which a unit of measure can almost always be established – has prompted the use of the term 'measure' even when it is improper. We have called the process 'operationalization'. This term is sometimes used in a broad sense to mean 'translatation from theoretical language to empirical language'. However, strictly speaking, it refers to the *passage from properties to variables*. On the broader pathway from theory to research, operationalization constitutes a crucial bridge from one side of the divide to the other, illustrated as follows:

Concept ———— Property ————▶ Variable
Operationalization
(classifying
ordering
measuring
counting)

4. UNITS OF ANALYSIS

In empirical research, the unit of analysis is the social object to which the properties investigated appertain. A theoretical reflection does not need precisely defined units of analysis. We may think, for example, of the interpretation of social revolt and political radicalism in terms of 'relative deprivation'. According to this theory, 'Dissatisfaction with the system of privileges and rewards in a society is never felt in an even proportion to the degree of inequality to which its various members are subject' (Runciman, 1966: 3); rather, it depends on the sense of deprivation perceived by its members. This, in turn, stems from the 'reference groups' and from the communities with which individuals compare themselves, and from the expectations that arise within them. Thus, 'Historians of various times and places ... have noticed the

tendency for overt discontent to be relatively rare in stable hardship and to rise alike in frequency, magnitude and intensity as opportunity is seen to increase ... (and) revolutions are apt to occur at times of rising prosperity' (Runciman, 1966: 21). A similar theory of social rebellion can be amply developed at the level of philosophical, historical, social and psychological reflection, and applied to various contexts, problem areas and historical events.

However, if we wish to test this theory empirically through specific quantitative research, we will first have to establish the unit of analysis; this will be done during the planning phase of the research, when the 'research design' is drawn up. The unit of analysis might be constituted by the *episode* of social revolt, as in the research carried out by Gurr and co-workers (Gurr, 1972: 92–8). These researchers systematically gathered data on incidents of political violence and social protest in 38 nations from 1961 to 1965. On the basis of news reports of each episode, they recorded a range of information (the 'properties' of the units of analysis), such as the number of people involved, the number of killed and injured, the duration of the rioting, the type of people involved, the reasons for the unrest, the methods of protest, and the characteristics of the social context (type of political regime, economic variables, civil liberties, etc.). In this way, they were able to record ('code') more than 1000 episodes (i.e. 'cases', to use a technical term that will be illustrated later). The aim of the research was to ascertain whether these outbreaks of violent conflict really were linked to situations of social change that had triggered unfulfilled expectations and, more generally, to situations of relative deprivation rather than absolute deprivation.

Research designed to test a theory may also use a *geographic area* as its unit of analysis. According to Tocqueville, the French Revolution arose in the more prosperous areas of France: 'Thus, it was precisely in those parts of France where there had been most improvement that popular discontent ran highest' (de Tocqueville, 1856: 176). This observation might well prompt us to take the geographical area as our unit of analysis. In the case of France at the time of the revolution, this would involve looking for indicators of economic well-being and of the intensity of revolutionary fervour in the various regions of the country, and investigating the relationship between the two variables.

The theory of relative deprivation applied to political unrest could also be tested empirically by taking the *individual* as the unit of analysis. In 1962, Runciman interviewed about 1400 citizens in England and Wales. Using both open and closed questions, he tried to identify the subjects' reference groups, self-attributed social class, degree of satisfaction with their own social position, and unfulfilled aspirations – in short, the components of relative deprivation – together with their political leanings, in order to see to what extent these two variables might be correlated.

As mentioned earlier, a concept (which is by definition abstract) is transformed into empirical terms by assigning it as a property to a concrete social object ('unit of analysis'). In the three examples reported, the concepts of relative deprivation and political radicalism (which the hypothesis links in a causal relationship) were associated to three different units of analysis: the episode of rioting, the geographical area, and the individual, respectively. Roughly speaking, the following types of unit of analysis can be found in sociological research: *the individual, the aggregate of individuals, the group-organization-institution, the event, and the cultural product.*

4.1 Different types of unit of analysis

From the examples quoted earlier, it will have become clear that in social research – and particularly in sociology – by far the most common unit of analysis is the *individual*. Then again, as Galtung points out, 'Sociology is often defined as the science of social interaction, from which it should follow that the unit of sociological analysis should be a social actor. In most sociological analyses this will be the case, and in the majority of them the choice will fall on the prototype of the social actor, the human individual' (Galtung, 1967).

Another frequently adopted unit of analysis is the *collective*. These 'collectives' may be constituted by an aggregate of individuals or by a group-organization-institution. The most common example of an *aggregate of individuals* is seen in official statistical sources based on 'territorial' aggregates of individuals (municipalities, counties, etc.). In this case, the variables are mainly derived from mathematical operations carried out on variables recorded at the individual level (e.g. mean income, unemployment rates, etc.).

On the other hand, we speak of *group-organization-institution* when the variables are recorded at the group level. This would be the case, for example, of a study conducted on educational institutions in which the variables concern the type of management (private/public), the implementation of experimental syllabi, the social catchment area of the school, the number of classes, the number of students, the proportion of women on the teaching staff, the rate of promotion, etc. Although some variables (e.g. the last two quoted) refer to underlying individual levels of recording, the data are gathered at the collective level (e.g. by interviewing the head teacher or consulting school archives).

This kind of unit of analysis is encountered fairly often in social research. We need only think of such *groups* as families, associations, religious sects, ethnic groups, youth groups and gangs, or of *organizations-institutions* such as trade unions, political parties, work organizations (hospitals, factories, etc.), local administrative bodies (such as municipalities), public institutions, whole societies and even nations.

The fourth type of unit of analysis mentioned is the *event*. The research conducted by Ted Gurr on episodes of political unrest is a case in point. Another case in which the unit of analysis is an event is seen in political elections. In a study of the elections held in the European democracies between 1885 and

1995, Bartolini and Mair (1990) examined the issues of electoral volatility, class voting, voter turnout, etc; each of these variables constitutes a property of the unit of analysis 'electoral event'. Other such events include strikes, wars, coups d'état, judicial trials, religious ceremonies, election campaigns, and so on.

A further type of unit of analysis is what we might call *symbolic representation* or *cultural product*. This concerns the field of content analysis, in which the unit of analysis, in the vast majority of cases, is constituted by the written, oral or audio-visual output of the media of mass communication: newspaper articles, literary texts, electoral propaganda, political speeches, photographs, television programmes, films and plays.

We will conclude this section with a note on terminology. The specimens of a given unit of analysis that are included in a particular study are called *cases*. The 'unit of analysis' is an abstract definition, which denotes the type of social object to which the properties appertain (e.g. the voter or the episode of rioting). This unit is localized in time and space by defining the 'reference population' of the research (for instance, British voters in the 1966 elections, or the episodes of political unrest that occurred in Italy between 1966 and 1973). The reference population as a whole may be the object of the study (such as all governments holding office from 1945 to 1979) or, as is much more often the case, only a part of this population may be studied. Often, a sample of the population is randomly chosen; on other occasions, different selection criteria may be adopted (see Chapter 8). The cases are the specimens of the given unit of analysis, and it is on these that the data are recorded. While the unit of analysis is singular and abstract, the cases are multiple and concrete, and constitute the specific objects of empirical research.

5. VARIABLES

A *variable* is an *operationalized concept*. More precisely, it is the *operationalized property* of an object, in that the concept, in order to be operationalized, has to be applied to an object and to become a property of that object. The difference between concept, property and variable is the same as the difference between weight (concept), the weight of an object (property) and the weight of the object measured by means of a weighing-scale (variable) (cf. Figure 3.2). There is no unique correspondence between 'concept' and 'variable', in that a concept can be operationalized in different ways. For example, as a property, it can be associated with different units of analysis; as we have seen, the concept 'power' may be a property of an individual, a corporate role, a political role, an institution, etc. As a property, it can give rise to different variables. For instance, the property 'cultural level' of an individual can be defined operationally through (a) educational qualifications; (b) the number of books read in a year; (c) daily consumption of cultural material (newspapers, films, plays); (d) a general knowledge test, and so on.

A variable can 'vary' (hence the name) among different categories (each of which is identified by a value), which correspond to the different states of the property. Gender, for example, is a variable, in that it can take on the states of male and female. It should be noted that a property, though variable (in the sense that it 'can vary') in principle, may prove to be unvarying in the specific subset of objects studied. For instance, while nationality is a property that can vary among individuals, in a study conducted on the British population, it is unvarying. In such a case, in its operationalized form, it is no longer called a variable, but a *constant*.

In the examples quoted so far, reference has been made to variables that vary among the objects (units of analysis) studied (e.g. gender, which varies among individuals, or power, which varies among different corporate roles). However, it is important to point out that the variation of a variable may occur in two ways: *over time*, on the same case; or, *among cases*, at the same time. This can be illustrated by two examples taken from the

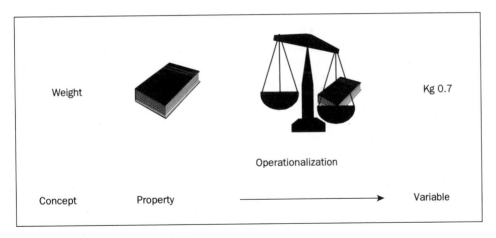

Weight

Kg 0.7

Operationalization

Concept   Property   Variable

FIGURE 3.2   *From concepts to variables*

field of medicine. Let us suppose that we wish to study a patient's reaction to a particular drug, for instance by examining the relationship between the administration of a certain chemotherapy drug and the variation in the concentration of the patient's white blood cells. To do so, we will vary the drug dose (e.g. by administering progressively increasing doses) and observe the ensuing variations in the concentration of white cells in the blood. In this case, the two variables *vary over time* on the same subject.

A different procedure will be adopted to test the hypothesis that lung cancer correlates with cigarette smoking. For example, a group of cancer patients may be compared with a group of healthy subjects, in order to ascertain whether the different states of disease/health correspond to different levels of cigarette smoking. In this case, the variables considered – disease and smoking – *vary among the subjects*. In both cases, that of variation over time and that of variation among subjects, we are dealing with variables. In the first case, we are conducting a *longitudinal study* (sometimes called diachronic study), while in the second case it is a *cross-sectional study* (sometimes called synchronic study).

Longitudinal studies are frequently undertaken in the natural sciences. Indeed, the pre-eminent technique used in the natural

sciences to study causal relationships – experimentation – is based on variations in variables over time ('vary x and see how y varies'). In the social sciences, however, cross-sectional studies, in which variables vary among the units of analysis, are far more common. The reason for this is that the majority of social variables cannot be manipulated; for example, we cannot bring about variations in the age or religious affiliation of an individual and then observe whether his inclination towards post-materialistic values also varies.

By now, the reader will be fully aware of the central role played by the 'variable' in empirical social research. Just as the concepts are the building blocks of the theory, the variables are the core element of empirical analysis. The variables are the essential terms, the fundamental elements, the 'vocabulary' of the social sciences. As Lazarsfeld and Rosenberg (1955: 6) point out, 'The formation of variables, the study of their interrelation, and the analysis of their change through time form the backbone of all social research'. It therefore comes as no surprise that Lazarsfeld defined the language of social research as 'the language of variables' (though, as we know, this definition is only applicable to quantitative research).

As we have already said, operationalization is the passage from concepts to variables. In order to visualize this crucial step in empirical research more clearly, we will now return to an example quoted earlier. In Inglehart's research, the problem arose of how to operationalize the concept of materialistic or post-materialistic value orientation (the other concepts mentioned – age, gender and nationality – being easy to operationalize). This concept was operationalized through a battery of questions. Starting out from Maslow's hierarchy of needs, the author selected two areas of material needs (sustenance and security) and two areas of post-materialistic needs (belonging and esteem, and aesthetic and intellectual self-fulfilment). For each of the four areas, he formulated a statement in terms of national political objectives (e.g. maintaining a high economic growth rate, guaranteeing a strong military defence, giving the people greater decision-making, etc.), and interviewees were asked to choose the objective that they considered most important. The answers were then combined so as to produce a score ranging from 0 (greatest materialism) to 5 (greatest post-materialism), taking into account both the choices made and the rank-order of the choices.

This illustration reveals the extreme arbitrariness of any operational definition. The way in which the author operationalized the concept of value orientation is highly controversial. In this regard, it should be borne in mind that there is no right or wrong way to operationalize a concept. The decision is left entirely to the discretion of the researcher, who can only be asked (a) to explain and (b) to justify the choices made. In any case, a gap will always remain between the variable and the concept. It can therefore be claimed that an operational definition is never perfectly adequate. It is a necessary step, but it is rarely sufficient to grasp the entire complexity of the theoretical concept.

The operational definition therefore limits and impoverishes the concept. The danger does not, however, lie so much in its inevitably reductive nature as in its 'reification'. The fact, for instance, that a set of responses to a battery of questions is labelled as being indicative of post-materialism, and that the name of the concept is used even when dealing with relationships that concern its operationalized form (variable), may make us forget that we are not talking about value orientation in the true sense, but about a very particular and arbitrary interpretation and operationalization. By way of example, we need only mention the damage done over the years by equating intelligence with its culturally biased operationalization through IQ (intelligence quotient).

Thus, the operational definition is an arbitrary and subjective act. Paradoxically, however, it is also the foundation on which the scientific and objective nature of social research stand.[3] Indeed, we may go so far as to say that it is the very *criterion of scientificness*, in that the operational definition of the properties studied is the surest discriminator between scientific research and other forms of activity, such as philosophical speculation. Moreover, it should be added that the arbitrariness and subjectivity of the operational definition will decline as the discipline matures and techniques are fine-tuned; within the scientific community, consensus will form to give rise to widely agreed-upon conventional definitions.

The operational definition also constitutes the *criterion of objectivity* in scientific research, in that it provides directives that enable the same assessments to be carried out by different researchers. In this way, the subjectivity of the researcher's claims is reduced; they are no longer opinions, but empirically supported statements. Claiming that someone is authoritarian is an opinion; if, however, the claim is based on that person's responses to a given battery of questions, it becomes a justifiable and testable assertion. While the operational definition does not eliminate arbitrariness, it does make it explicit and therefore assessable.

6. NOMINAL, ORDINAL AND INTERVAL VARIABLES

Variables are classified according to the operations that can be carried out on them.

TABLE. 3.1 *Types of variable*

States of the property	Operationalization procedure	Type of variable	Characteristics of the values	Operations applicable to the values
Non-orderable discrete	Classification	Nominal	Names	$= \neq$
Orderable discrete	Ordering	Ordinal	Numbers with only ordinal properties	$= \neq$ $> <$
Countable discrete	Counting	Interval	Numbers with cardinal properties	$= \neq$ $> <$ $+ - \times \div$
Continuous	Measuring	Interval	Numbers with cardinal properties	$= \neq$ $> <$ $+ - \times \div$

This classification is based on the logical-mathematical characteristics of the variable, which refer to the logical operations (e.g. operations of equality and inequality) or the mathematical operations (e.g. the four arithmetical operations) that its values can undergo.

This classification is of fundamental importance, in that it establishes which statistical procedures can be applied to the variable. Even the most common statistics, such as the mean or an association index, depend on the logical-mathematical characteristics of the variable (e.g. we can calculate the mean age of a sample of individuals, but not the mean nationality; and yet both age and nationality are variables).

Variables are grouped into three classes (nominal, ordinal and interval; see Table 3.1). Although this classification chiefly refers to the *analysis of the data*, it nevertheless depends heavily on the nature of the empirical operations carried out in order to *gather the data* – that is to say, to operationalize the states of the property when it is transformed into a variable. This brings us back to the question of operationalization procedures which, as we have already seen, can be grouped into four classes (classification, ordering, measurement and counting).[4]

6.1 Nominal variables

We have a nominal variable when the property to be recorded takes on non-orderable

discrete states. 'Discrete states' means that the property takes on a range of finite states; in everyday language, we could say that the property 'jumps' from one state to another, and that intermediate states are not possible (for instance, a person may be a Catholic or a Muslim, but not halfway between the two; similarly, gender has only two states: male and female). By 'non-orderable', we mean that no order or hierarchy can be established among the states. Thus, a person's nationality may be French, Swedish or Chinese, but we cannot place these states in a hierarchical sequence. Similarly, we cannot establish an order between the states of male and female, or among those of Catholic, Protestant, Muslim, Jewish, atheist, etc. (we cannot say that the Catholic has a 'higher' religion than a Protestant, while we can say that a university graduate has a higher educational qualification than someone with a high-school diploma, or that a temperature of 18°C is lower than a temperature of 20°C). The only relationships that we can establish among the categories of a nominal variable are those of 'equality' and 'inequality' (in terms of religion, one Catholic is the same as another Catholic and different from a Protestant).

The operationalized states of the variable are called *categories*, and the symbols assigned to the categories are called *values*.

In the case of nominal variables, the operationalization procedure – which enables us to pass from the property to the variable – is *classification*. As mentioned earlier, this operation is located at the lowest level of mathematical formalization; indeed, classification is the first and simplest operation that can be carried out in any science. The categories into which the states of the property are classified must be (a) *exhaustive*, in the sense that each case we examine must be able to fit into one of the categories provided and (b) *mutually exclusive*, in the sense that a case cannot be classified in more than one category. From this latter requisite, it follows that there must be *only one classification criterion*; for example, nationality cannot be classified by using such mixed categories as Italian, French, Protestant, Nordic, English-speaking, European, etc.

A symbol is assigned to each category. Known as a *value*, this symbol serves no other purpose than that of indicating the category. Though the symbol is generally a number, it has no numerical significance; for instance, when dealing with the variable 'religion', we might assign the numbers 1–6 to the categories Catholic, Protestant, Jewish, Muslim, other religions and atheist, in that order or in any other; indeed, we could use any six numbers (as long as they were all different), or six letters, or any other six symbols. Subdividing a property into non-ordered categories quite simply involves giving each category a *name* – any name. That is why this type of variable is called 'nominal'.

A particular case of nominal variables is that in which there are only two categories: male and female, employed and unemployed, married and unmarried, favourable and unfavourable, etc. Such variables are called *dichotomous* and have the distinctive feature of being amenable to treatment with statistical techniques that cannot normally be applied to nominal variables, but only to variables located at a higher level of operationalization.

6.2 Ordinal variables
In this case, the property to be recorded assumes *orderable discrete states*. We need only think of educational qualifications (elementary-school diploma, middle-school diploma,

high-school diploma, university degree), army hierarchies (lieutenant, captain, major, colonel), or social classes (upper middle-class, middle-class, lower middle-class, working-class). This is also the case of a questionnaire in which the interviewee is asked to choose responses from among ordered categories, such as 'very, somewhat, a little, not at all' (interested in politics, in agreement with a statement, etc.).

What distinguishes this level of variable from the previous one is the existence of an order, which enables us to establish not only relationships of equality and inequality among the categories (a university degree and a high-school diploma are different), but also relationships of order – that is, 'greater than' and 'less than' (a degree is a higher qualification than a school diploma; cf. Table 3.1). It should, however, be pointed out that, in an ordinal variable, the distance between one category and the next is not known. We know that an industrial worker occupies a higher position in the occupational hierarchy than a seasonal farm worker, but we do not know how much higher; nor can we say whether the gap between the two is greater than, less than or equal to the gap between an industrial worker and an office worker.

In this case, the procedure used to operationalize the properties is 'assignment to ordered categories', or *ordering*, which takes into account the requirement that the states of the property must be orderable. Values can therefore no longer be assigned to the single categories in random fashion; instead, a criterion must be used which preserves the order among the states. A series of natural numbers is nearly always used for this purpose; these numbers have the ordinal, but *not* the cardinal, properties of numbers. If we assign the values 1–5 to the categories 'no educational qualification, elementary-school diploma, middle-school diploma, high-school diploma and university degree', respectively, these numbers are understood as indicating that sequence; they do not, however, indicate a numerical score. We cannot, for example, say that the distance between a university degree and a high-school diploma is the same as the distance between an elementary-school diploma and no qualification (though in each case the gap is of one unit in our sequence), or that a high-school diploma (to which we have assigned the value 4) is twice as high as an elementary-school diploma (which has the value 2).

Since these numbers have a purely ordinal meaning, they are assigned to the categories in such a way as to indicate the sequence, and nothing else. It therefore follows that the sequence proposed above (1–5) could be replaced by any other ascending sequence of numbers, such as 12, 25, 32, 43, 55. It is, however, common practice either to adopt the criterion of the series of natural numbers in simple sequence (1, 2, 3, …) or else to adopt a criterion based on an estimate, albeit approximate and subjective, of the distances among the categories. Given that the simple sequence is just as arbitrary as any other ordered series of numbers, it is reasonable to utilize a sequence based on whatever knowledge we have of the distances between the categories.[5]

6.3 Interval variables

When the distances between the categories are known – that is, the interval between categories 1 and 2 , 2 and 3, etc. are equal – we have the so-called interval variables. In this case the numbers identifying the categories (the 'values' of the variable) are not simply labels; these values have a 'full' numerical meaning, in that they possess not only ordinal but also cardinal properties of numbers. The distances between the categories can be determined because we have a reference unit (which, as we will see, may be a unit of measurement or a unit of counting); this enables us to apply to these distances the four operations that are applied to numbers; we can therefore carry out on the variables all the most sophisticated mathematical operations and statistical procedures.[6] Age, income, number of children and so on are variables of this kind.

Interval variables can be obtained by applying two basic operationalization procedures to the property: measurement and counting. *Measurement* takes place when the following conditions are fulfilled: (a) the property to be measured is *continuous* – that is to say, it can take on an infinite number of intermediate states in a given range between any two states; and (b) we possess a pre-established *unit of measurement* that enables us to compare the magnitude to be measured with a reference magnitude. The example that springs to mind is that of length measured by means of a conventional unit of measurement (for instance, the metre), but we can imagine numerous others. In the process of measuring, the real number corresponding to the state measured will be rounded off to the nearest figure compatible with the approximation that we have established for our measurement (e.g. a person's height may be measured in centimetres as 167 cm, where the last figure has been rounded off).

By contrast, *counting* takes place when: (a) the property to be recorded is *discrete* – that is, it can take on a finite number of indivisible states; and (b) a *counting unit* exists – that is to say, an elementary unit which is contained a certain finite number of times in the property of the object. In this case, operationalization consists of 'counting' how many units are included in the total amount of the property possessed by the object. This is what happens when we count the number of children that a person has, the number of rooms in a house, the number of employees in a company, the number of times a person goes to church in a month, or the number of newspapers read in a week. The counting unit is 'natural', unlike the unit of measurement, which is 'conventional'. In the examples mentioned, the counting unit is constituted by the child, the room, the employee, the visit to church and the newspaper, respectively. As the properties are discrete (the counting unit is indivisible), decimals do not occur in the counting phase (a person may have 2 children, but not 2.3); nor are the figures rounded off. However, in subsequent statistical elaboration, the variable may give rise to decimals as a result of mathematical operations; for instance, we may find a mean of 0.7 rooms per person, or a fertility rate of 1.2 children per woman in a nation.

In physics, a distinction is made between *fundamental* variables and *derived* variables. Examples of fundamental variables are length, mass, time and temperature, while derived variables include density (given by the mass to volume ratio), velocity (length to time ratio), and so on. Derived variables are mathematical functions of fundamental variables. In the social sciences, too, many interval variables are derived from operations carried out on other interval variables. In a family, the number of square metres of living space per person is obtained by dividing one interval variable, which refers to a continuous property (the surface area), by another interval variable, which refers to a discrete property (the number of family members). Derived variables are frequently encountered when the unit of analysis is constituted by a geographic aggregate of individuals. The percentage of votes obtained by a particular political party, of university graduates, of unemployed members of the workforce, etc. are all properties that are derived from ratios among interval variables counted on discrete states.

It should be noted that the characteristics of the three types of variable mentioned are *cumulative*, in that each level includes the properties of the levels below it. Thus, only relationships of equality and inequality can be established among the values of nominal variables, while among the values of ordinal variables, relationships of order can be established *in addition* to those of equality and inequality; finally, among the values of interval variables, relationships regarding the distances among the values can be established *in addition* to the other two types of relationship. Consequently, analysis can shift downwards from a higher level to a lower one. For example the values of the interval variable 'age' can be grouped within the three ordered categories 'young', 'adult' and 'elderly' (ordinal variable). Likewise, the various degrees of 'religious observance', ordered in categories ranging from 'go to church every day' to 'never go', can be grouped into a nominal variable that distinguishes between 'practising' and 'non-practising'.

A sub-set of the interval variables is constituted by the *quasi-interval variables*. We have already discussed interval variables that are obtained from continuous properties by means of measurement, and interval variables obtained from discrete properties by means of counting. Variables of the first type, especially, are rare in the social sciences. Apart from time-based variables (such as age, the duration of a particular learning process, the time taken to perform a certain action, etc.) we could cite income and distance, but not many others. Moreover, these variables are all derived from properties that are typical of the natural sciences. And yet, the properties that are most characteristic of the social sciences, from religious observance to political orientation, authoritarianism, depression, social cohesion, prejudices, value orientation, etc., can all be imagined as continuous properties that vary among individuals in a gradual manner (indeed, social scientists refer to a 'continuum' underlying a certain variable). However, they cannot be operationalized from continuous property to interval variable, on account of the difficulty of applying a unit of measurement to human attitudes.

Numerous efforts have been made to overcome this obstacle. As early as the 1920s, the technique known as *scaling* was proposed in order to measure opinions, attitudes and values ('attitude measurement' is the name by which this branch of the discipline is known) and, more generally, to assess continuous properties appertaining to the psychological make-up and value structure of the individual. Even simple techniques, such as 'self-anchoring' scales, 'the feelings thermometer' and the 'left-right' placement scales of political orientation, move in that direction (these techniques will be dealt in Chapter 6). The objective is to obtain 'measurements' in the true sense of the term – that is, variables in which the distance between two values is known (which is tantamount to saying that we have a unit of measurement and therefore we have an interval variable). It seems perfectly legitimate to apply to variables produced by these techniques the same mathematical-statistical procedures used on interval variables. To highlight the plausibility of doing so, while at the same time underlining the epistemological difference between these variables and interval variables, we call them *quasi-interval variables*.

The statistical techniques that can be applied to variables can be divided into two broad groups: those used on interval variables and those used on nominal variables. Techniques specifically designed for ordinal variables are available only in rare cases. Strictly speaking, ordinal variables should only be handled by means of statistical techniques designed for nominal variables. However, this issue has given rise to a long-running controversy among social science methodologists, and ordinal variables are often analysed with techniques that were developed for interval variables.

7. CONCEPTS, INDICATORS AND INDEXES

In this section, we will discuss in greater depth an issue raised in Section 3, that of the passage from concepts to variables. As we said then, in the process of empirical transformation, a concept is 'anchored' to an object (unit of analysis), becomes a property of that object and is then operationalized – that is, recorded in the form of a variable. Thus, the concept of religious observance is defined as a property of human subjects, and is operationalized in terms of, for example, the number of times per month that a person goes to church (variable). But if, instead of religious observance, the concept to be operationalized is the more general one of religious sentiment, it will be more difficult to give it an operational definition. Religious observance may be one aspect of it, but there is certainly much more to it. In other words, some concepts cannot easily be transformed into properties of the units of analysis.

Concepts can be classified on the basis of a continuum embracing varying degrees of generality-specificity. With regard to religion,

for example, we can imagine five conceptual formulations graded in order of decreasing generality (and therefore increasing specificity): 1) believing in the existence of a divinity; 2) believing in the Christian God; 3) belonging to a specific Church; 4) acting in accordance with Church doctrine; and 5) going to services every Sunday. This scale of generality correlates (though does not coincide) with a 'scale of abstraction' (in which the poles are abstract-concrete), which refers to the empirically observable nature of a concept. It is correlated in the sense that a specific concept is generally easier to observe from an empirical standpoint than a general concept. For example, faith in God is not observable, but practice of religious rites is.[7]

The majority of sociological concepts are located on a high level of generality (e.g. alienation, socialization, power, conflict, etc.). Nevertheless, since our objective is to submit theory to empirical corroboration, we have to define even these concepts empirically. But how can we transform an abstract concept like alienation into observational terms?

This is where the *indicators* come in. These are simpler, 'specific' concepts that can be translated into observational terms. They are linked to the 'general' concepts by what is defined as a *relation of indication*, or semantic representation (representation of meaning). What we are in fact doing is stepping down on the above-mentioned generality scale, from general concepts to specific concepts that are linked to them by affinity of meaning. To return to our previous example, even if we cannot observe religious sentiment empirically, we can observe a specific form of it: observance of selected religious practices. The problem with this will be all too obvious to the reader: the relationship between the concept and the indicator is a partial one. On the one hand, a (general) concept cannot be covered by a single (specific) indicator. On the other hand, an indicator may only partially overlap with the concept for which it has been chosen, and depend for the rest on some other concept.

Let us take the first point first. Precisely because they are specific, indicators are able to reveal only one aspect of the complexity of a general concept. for example, religious observance may be an indicator of the ritualistic component of religious sentiment (and not even the only one, but together with other indicators such as prayer, reading the scriptures, etc.). But the concept of religious sentiment also includes other aspects. As well as the ritualistic aspect, Glock mentions the aspect of experience (religious devotion), the ideological aspect (beliefs guided by religion) and the consequential aspect (behaviour inspired by religious conviction) (Glock, 1959). For instance, indicators of the consequential component might include charitable deeds, political behaviour and sexual morality inspired by religious convictions, etc. Hence the *need for several indicators* to get at the same concept. Lazarsfeld suggests using the expression originally coined by Guttman 'the universe of indicators' (Lazarsfeld, 1959: 48). Another proposal by Lazarsfeld was to call the various aspects of a concept 'dimensions', in order to identify the indicators of these aspects (in the previous example, the four aspects mentioned – rituality, experience, ideology and consequentiality – are dimensions of religious devotion).

The second point concerns the fact that an indicator may be linked to several concepts, each with a profoundly different content. For example, in societies that are culturally and politically dominated by ecclesiastical institutions, participation in religious rites may be an indicator of social conformity rather than of religious sentiment. Marradi (1980: 36) distinguishes the *indicating portion* of an indicator from the *extraneous portion*, the former being that element of semantic content that the indicator has in common with the concept (where there is an overlap of meaning), and the latter being that part which is extraneous to the concept. Of course, indicators having a large indicating portion and a small extraneous portion are to be preferred.

A further question concerns the arbitrariness of the choice of indicator. As has been said, an indicator is a partial representation of a concept and there may be – and normally there are – several indicators of the same concept. The choice of indicators will be left to the researcher's discretion (unless there are practical constraints, such as the availability of data), the only obligation towards the scientific community being that the researcher should explain this choice (not 'demonstrate' its correctness, of course, which would be impossible).

To sum up, we can say that the empirical recording of a concept that is not directly observable goes through four successive stages:

1. the concept is broken down into dimensions;
2. the indicators are selected;
3. the indicators are operationalized; and
4. the indexes are formed.

The first stage consists of pure theoretical reflection; here, the concept is broken down into its main semantic components ('dimensions'). In our example of religious sentiment, the four components mentioned earlier (rituality, etc.) are identified during this phase. In the case of intelligence, the various skills and abilities would be identified.

The second stage involves selecting indicators pertaining to each dimension. Although we are still in a phase of conceptual formulation (the indicators are still concepts), this operation will be carried out with empirical observation in mind; that is to say, specific concepts amenable to empirical observation – to use the expression coined by Geertz (1973), 'experience-near' – will be chosen. Given the partial nature of the indicator, the researcher will pick out more than one indicator for the same conceptual dimension. For example, with regard to the ritual dimension of religious sentiment, we have already mentioned participation in collective rites, private prayer, and reading of the scriptures. Similarly, knowledge of vocabulary, writing ability and verbal fluency might be taken as indicators of language capability.

In the third phase, the indicators are operationalized – that is, they are transformed into

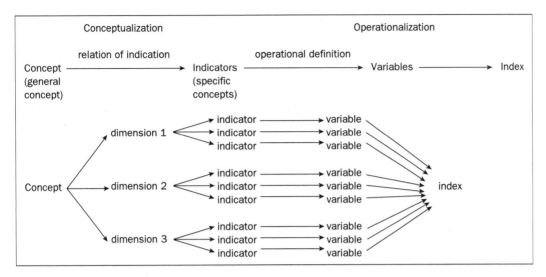

FIGURE 3.3 *Schematic representation of the process of empirical transformation of a complex concept*

variables. Thus, religious observance may be operationalized in terms of the number of times a person goes to church in a month, or by quantifying the time that a person spends praying or reading the scriptures. Similarly, some sort of test could be devised to operationalize intellectual capacity as a score.

The fourth and final phase involves the construction of *indexes*. When a concept is broken down into dimensions and gauged by means of several indicators, it is often necessary to synthesize the array of variables produced into a single index. Thus, after having assessed religious sentiment by means of variables that operationalize its dimensions of rituality, experience, ideology and consequentiality, we may wish to reconstitute the original unit into what we may call a (global) *index* of religious sentiment. This might be a unidimensional index that 'orders' religious sentiment according to a score with ordinal characteristics, or 'measures' it as a quasi-interval score; then again, it might be a typological index that 'classifies' religious sentiment into distinct types that cannot be graded, such as 'devout', 'practising', 'conformist' and 'non-religious'.

The process that we have described is depicted schematically in Figure 3.3.[8] An example of this process has already been discussed with regard to religious sentiment. A further illustration was also provided when we looked at how the concept of materialistic and post-materialistic value orientation was transformed into operational terms. In that case, the concept was broken down into four dimensions relating to the needs of sustenance, security, belonging-esteem, and self-fulfilment. These dimensions gave rise to indicators regarding opinions on 'fighting crime', 'freedom of speech', 'protection of the environment', etc. Inglehart (1977) maintained, for example, that attaching greater importance to protecting the environment than to fighting crime was indicative of a post-materialistic orientation. These indicators were operationalized by means of a questionnaire, and the author finally synthesized the answers to the questions into an index of materialism/post-materialism (with a score ranging from 0 to 5).

In conclusion, it should be pointed out that the process of transforming a concept into empirical operations does not always take place in the chronological sequence outlined above (breakdown into dimensions, followed by selection of the indicators and by their empirical recording). For instance, when the researcher does not record the data directly, but instead uses data that have already been collected by others (secondary analysis or studies conducted on official statistics), it is impossible to plan empirical recording of the indicators on the basis of conceptual analysis, in that the data already exist. This problem becomes particularly relevant when the research techniques involve the analysis of official statistics, in which the unit of analysis is a geographic area (municipality, province, nation, etc.).

To illustrate the point, we will return once again to the issue of religious sentiment. In an Italian study which utilized statistics compiled at the provincial level, this concept was operationalized through the use of the following indicators: number of Catholic Church weddings, and readership of the Catholic weekly *Famiglia Cristiana* (operationalized through such variables as 'Church weddings as a percentage of total weddings', and 'number of copies of the magazine distributed per 1000 inhabitants') (Cartocci, 1993). By combining these two indicators, the author was able to produce a typological index of religious sentiment, according to which the provinces were classified into four types (practising, conformist, in transition, and secularized). In addition to the two indicators used, the author used other indicators of religious sentiment, again taking the province as the unit of analysis; these were birth rate; the number of babies born to unmarried women; the number of divorces, separations and abortions; and the number of taxpayers opting to allocate a fraction of their tax payments to Church-run charities rather than to state-run programmes. In this example, the study was based not so much on the author's own reflections on the dimensions of the concept of religious sentiment as on the availability of the data.

In such situations, there is a particularly high risk that the 'extraneous portion' of the indicators will be considerable; in other words, the indicators are likely to be linked semantically to concepts that have nothing whatever to do with the concept under investigation. For instance the circulation of the magazine *Famiglia Cristiana* may be an indicator of weekly reading habits rather than of religious sentiment. Likewise, the allocation of a fraction of one's tax payments to the Church may indicate mistrust in state institutions rather than genuine religious sentiment. In adopting indicators for complex concepts, particular caution should therefore be exercised when the choice of the indicators takes place after data collection rather than orienting it – that is to say, when the relation of indication and the operational definition are established in the opposite sequence to that shown in Figure 3.3. Unfortunately, however, such caution is often lacking. Indeed, when faced with complex concepts and inadequate data, researchers may well be tempted to make do with what they have. Forcing the indicators to fit the concept and using indicators that have an extremely modest indicating portion can only yield groundless analyses and unjustified conclusions.

8. TOTAL ERROR

In our discussion of the process that leads from the domain of concepts and theories to the world of sense experience, due importance must be given to what psychometricians call 'measurement error' and, to broaden its meaning, what we will call 'total error'. Indeed, this error constitutes the gap between the (theoretical) concept and the (empirical) variable.

This error is usually split into two components: systematic error and random error. Thus, we can say that the *observed value* – that is to say, the value of the empirical variable as it is recorded – is the sum of three parts: the *true value* (which is neither observed nor observable) of the concept that the variable is intended to gauge and the two components of the error. This can be written as follows:[9]

Observed value =
  (variable)
True value + Systematic error + Random error
  (concept)

Which is the same as:

  Error = Observed value − True value
      = Systematic error + Random error

A *systematic error* ('bias') is a consistent error, in the sense that it is present in all the data, whether they are recorded on different individuals or on the same individuals at different times. Its mean value on the total of the cases observed is not equal to zero, but is either positive or negative in the sense that the 'observed value' tends systematically to over-estimate or underestimate the 'true value'. For example, if we interview a sample of citizens to find out how many of them voted in the last election, we can expect to obtain in all our recordings an 'observed' mean rate of voting that is systematically higher than the 'true' mean rate, since we know that there is a wide-spread tendency on the part of interviewees to overstate their voting participation.

A *random* error is a *variable* error, in that it varies both from one sample of individuals to another and in repeated observations on the same individual. On all possible repetitions of the observation and on all possible samples, such oscillations tend towards a mean (expected value) that is equal to zero.

In a nutshell, systematic error is the portion of error that is common to all observations, while random error is the portion that is specific to each single observation.

In which phases of the process leading from concepts to variables do these errors arise? As we have seen, this process is made up of two phases (Figure 3.4): a *theoretical* or *indication* phase, in which the indicators are selected, and an *empirical* or *operationalization* phase, in which recording of the indicators takes place. Errors may arise in both phases; an indicator may be badly chosen or badly operationalized.

An error in the *indication* phase – that is, in the choice of indicators to represent a given concept, is a *systematic* error. For example if

trade union membership is taken as an indicator of a person's political involvement, this choice may be subject to systematic error; indeed, trade union membership may reflect a certain social conformity, a desire to protect one's own interests or a behaviour that is repeated automatically each year, rather than genuine political involvement. In this case, the indicator 'covers' the concept inadequately (or too partially) and we therefore have a faulty indication relationship. As already mentioned, an indicator has an 'indicating portion' and an 'extraneous portion' with respect to the variable that it is intended to represent, the indicating portion being that part which overlaps semantically with the concept. The greater the indicating portion and the less the extraneous portion, the greater the *validity* of the indicator will be. In the above case of trade union membership, if the part of the indicator that is extraneous to the concept of political involvement (e.g. social conformity) outweighs the indicating portion, the indicator is affected by a systematic error.

An error arising during the *operationalization* phase may be either *systematic* or *random*. In classical social research, for example a study conducted by means of interviewing a sample of subjects, the operationalization process is made up of three different stages:[10] (a) *selection* of the study units; (b) *data collection* which we will call *observation*; and (c) *data processing*. Errors can arise in each of these states.

Selection errors   These cover a range of errors that arise when the research is carried out on a sample of subjects rather than an entire population. Three types of selection error can be distinguished. *Coverage errors* arise when the population list from which the sample of cases is drawn is incomplete. This happens, e.g. when telephone interviews are conducted in order to study the voting orientation of the electorate; all those who do not have a tele-phone are excluded from the sample a priori, which results in error. The second type of selection error is *sampling error*; the fact that the research is conducted on a sample, and not on the whole population, involves error,

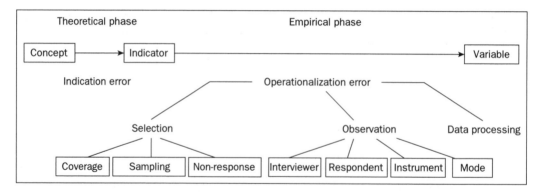

FIGURE 3.4   *Types of error and their location on the pathway from concept to variable*

which will vary from one sample to another. The third type is *non-response error*, which is due to the fact that some subjects included in the sample either cannot be traced by the interviewer or refuse to respond.

Observation errors   These can be ascribed to four sources. *Interviewer-related* errors occur when the interviewer unwittingly influences the interviewee's responses, wrongly records responses, and so on. *Respondent-related* errors include the misunderstanding of questions, lying (for instance, in order to make a good impression), memory lapses when answering questions that refer to the past, etc. *Instrument-related* errors are caused by the use of questions that are badly worded, tendentious, affected by the so-called social desirability bias (see Chapter 5), etc. Errors may also be due to the *administration mode*; for instance, telephone interviews are conducted more rapidly than face-to-face interviews and may therefore prompt the respondent to answer too hastily, while the mail questionnaire involves other types of error, etc.

Data-processing errors   These occur after the data have been collected, and include errors in coding, transcription, data entry, analysis, etc.

All these errors can be either systematic or random. For example, with regard to the instrument used, a question on income will engender a consistent underestimation of the true income (systematic error); similarly, a question may give rise to varying degrees of misunderstanding or incomplete understanding on the part of different respondents (random error).

This brief outline, which is summarized graphically in Figure 3.4, should serve to illustrate how varied the types and sources of error are. This analytical way of looking at error is also called the 'total survey error' approach (cf. Groves, 1989: 14–15). The total survey error cannot be estimated, since too many of its components lie beyond our control. Attempts to overcome, or at least attenuate, this problem have involved looking upon a particular survey as one of the possible repetitions of the same research design. However, this approach can take into account only random error (which is variable from one recording to another). It is powerless to deal with systematic error, which by definition is present in all possible repetitions of the survey, and therefore eludes detection.

One component of total error, however, can be calculated: sampling error. Precise statistical techniques have been worked out to estimate the range of probable error caused by the fact that the data are collected on a sample rather than on the entire population. But this is only one component of the total error and, in the majority of studies, probably not the most important.

Nevertheless, since sampling error is the only quantifiable component, it is often reported as the total error. Indeed, whether in a simple newspaper summary of the results of a survey or in the most sophisticated methodological appendix to a research report intended for a specialist readership, we often come across such statements as 'The estimates presented here are subject to an error of *n* (e.g. ± 3) percentage points'. Such statements are erroneous in that they suggest that this is the total error of the estimate, when really it is only the part of the error due to sampling. In order to obtain the true total error affecting the data, we would have to add a number – indeed unknown – of additional percentage points.

9. A FINAL NOTE: RELIABILITY AND VALIDITY

What we have called the 'observation' phase (Figure 3.4), which therefore excludes the issues of sample selection and data processing, is called the measurement phase by psychometricians (hence the term 'measurement error'). With regard to this phase, psychometricians have developed two notions that we will discuss here: reliability and validity.

Reliability has to do with the 'reproducibility' of the result, and marks *the degree to which a given procedure for transforming a concept into a variable produces the same results in tests repeated with the same empirical tools (stability) or equivalent ones (equivalence).* If we weigh an object on a weighing-scale, and then re-weigh the same object, either on the same scale or on another, and obtain the same result, the first scale can be regarded as reliable. Likewise, if an individual gets a score of 110 on an aptitude test and, the following day, gets a score of 80 on the same test or on an equivalent test (to avoid memory or learning effects), we can conclude that the test is not reliable.

Validity, on the other hand, refers to *the degree to which a given procedure for transforming a concept into a variable actually operationalizes* the concept that it is intended to. Whether IQ (intelligence quotient) actually gauges intelligence, whether GNP (gross national product) measures the wealth of a nation, or whether the F scale actually registers a person's degree of authoritarianism are all questions that have to do with the validity of these operational definitions. Clearly, in this case, repeating the test does not enable us to pick up this kind of error. A certain operational procedure may be perfectly stable in successive applications (that is, reliable), but that does not mean it is valid. If, for example, we measure a person's intelligence by means of his shoe size, the datum we obtain is reliable, but obviously has no validity.

In general, reliability is associated with *random* error, and validity with *systematic* error. For this reason, reliability is easier to ascertain than validity, in that the random error can be detected by repeating the recording on the same subject (variations among the values being due to random error). Validity, on the other hand, is more difficult to evaluate, as the underlying systematic error impinges on every recording, thus preventing us from knowing the real state of the property being studied.

9.1 Reliability

In the social sciences – as in the natural sciences – the first aspect of *reliability* to be studied was the *stability* of the recording over time. This can be assessed by means of the so-called *test-retest* technique, which involves repeating the recording (on the same subjects) and calculating the correlation between the two results. This technique is, however, difficult to apply in the social sciences for two reasons: the reactivity of the human subject (the first test may alter the property that we wish to assess, in that memory or learning effects may influence performance on the second test) and the change that may take place in the subject between the two tests. Moreover, although this repetition over time enables us to detect random factors that vary from one test administration to the next, it does not reveal the two other types of random variation mentioned earlier, which are attributable to the instrument and to the recording mode.

A second approach has therefore been proposed, according to which reliability is defined in terms of *equivalence* and is assessed by means of the correlation between two distinct, albeit very similar, procedures. One such technique is that of the so-called *split-half*, whereby reliability is indicated by the correlation between two halves of the same test (a battery of test questions is split into two halves, for example odd- and even-numbered questions, and scores are calculated separately and then correlated). A similar procedure is that of parallel forms; two tests are said to be '*parallel*' when they are assumed to gauge the same underlying 'true value' and to differ only in terms of random error. The two tests are generally of the same length and contain questions on the same theme, worded in the same way, etc. For example, the procedure might involve administering two intelligence tests in which mathematical ability is assessed by means of two sets of very similar questions requiring the same type of knowledge and logical operations, or in which verbal ability is tested through the recognition of 40 words that simply differ between the two tests, etc.

A further means of assessing reliability is based on the assumption that random errors vary not only from test to test, but also from question to question within the same test. Assessments of the *internal consistency* of the test (e.g. Cronbach's alpha, see box 6.4 in Chapter 6) have therefore been proposed in which reliability is estimated by correlating the answers to each question with the answers to all the other questions.

All these techniques were conceived within the sphere of psychometrics and are oriented towards a specific procedure, the psychological test, involving a 'battery' of questions – that is, a set of questions relevant to the same objective (as in an intelligence test in which the individual undergoes a variety of tests and the final score is obtained by combining the scores of the single tests). However, it is more difficult to estimate the reliability in other situations, for example when an individual's specific behaviour (such as voting or religious observance) is being investigated, or when the unit of analysis is not the individual but for instance, a geographic area such as a municipality or a region. Given the difficulty (if not the impossibility) of repeating the recording, an approach that remains fundamentally valid is that of assessing reliability through multiple operationalizations carried out by means of different instruments. For example, religious observance may be investigated by means of one direct and one indirect question about how the subject spent Sunday morning; similarly, the reading of newspapers might be probed both by means of a direct question and by means of an indirect question regarding the subject's knowledge of topical issues, etc.

9.2 Validity

Validity testing is a much more arduous task. It is also a very important one. If systematic error exists, it will be very difficult to detect, as it is reproduced consistently in all recordings. Validity errors generally arise in the passage from the concept to the indicator and stem from an 'indication error', as seen earlier (Figure 3.4). Indeed, the validity of a given indicator is extremely difficult to establish, much less measure.

Psychometricians have broken down the concept of validity into a wide variety of aspects and have proposed a corresponding number of validation procedures. In our view, however, the concept of validity can, in the final analysis, be split into two aspects, content validity and criterion-related validity, each of which has its own validation procedure. *Content validity* is a theoretical notion, and concerns the question of whether the indicator or indicators selected to reveal a certain concept actually cover the entire domain of meaning of that concept. Validation can only take place at a purely logical level (and indeed some authors use the term 'logical validation'); this consists of breaking down the concept into its constituent parts, just as it was subdivided into dimensions in the procedure referred to earlier, with a view to ensuring that all the dimensions are covered by the indicators selected.

In the case of *criterion-related validity*, as the name suggests, validation is not based on the analysis of the internal correspondence between the indicator and its concept, but rather on the correspondence between the indicator and an external criterion that, for some reason, is deemed to be correlated with the concept. This criterion may be constituted either by another indicator that is already regarded as valid, or by an objective fact, generally of a behavioural nature. As it is possible to quantify this correspondence (for instance, through a correlation coefficient), it has been proposed that this type of validity should be called 'empirical validity', as opposed to the 'theoretical validity' mentioned earlier (Lord and Novick, 1968: 261). Nevertheless, in spite of the name, we should not be led to believe that this type of validity is empirically measurable. Indeed, what this procedure measures is the correlation between two indicators, not the correspondence between the indicator and its concept.

Various types of criterion-related validity have been distinguished. One of these is *predictive validity*, which consists of correlating the datum yielded by the indicator with a subsequent event that is linked to it. For example, the results of a university entrance test may be correlated with the marks obtained by the students in subsequent examinations, in order to see how well the test has been able to predict student performance. Likewise, an aptitude test for a certain occupation may be validated by comparing its results with the individual's subsequent performance on the job. By contrast, *concurrent validity* involves correlating the indicator with another indicator recorded at the same moment in time. For example, an indicator of political conservatism may be correlated with a question on how the subject has voted. An important type of concurrent validity is 'validity for known groups', in which the indicator is applied to subjects whose position is known with regard to the property under investigation. For instance, an indicator of religious sentiment may be applied to subjects belonging to religious groups and regular churchgoers to see whether, as one would expect, it registers particularly high values of religious sentiment among these individuals. Similarly, a scale rating democratic/anti-democratic leanings could be validated through administration to subjects belonging to anti-democratic associations (e.g. neo-fascist groups).

In addition to content validity and criterion-related validity, psychometrics manuals report a third type of validity, called *construct validity*. In my view, however, this is ultimately a combination of the two previous types of validity. Construct validity is judged on the basis of whether an indicator corresponds to theoretical expectations in terms of relationships with other variables. For instance, numerous studies have demonstrated that there is an inverse correlation between educational level and racial prejudice. If we draw up a new indicator of racial prejudice, its construct validity can be judged on the basis of these expectations; if the expectations are not confirmed (e.g. subjects with high values on this indicator are also the most highly educated), we can conclude that this indicator is not a valid indicator of racial prejudice, but is probably recording something else. Clearly, this procedure is based on theoretical considerations and on relationships to other indicators that are already accepted as valid; for this reason, it can be regarded as a combination of the two validation criteria illustrated above.[11]

We will conclude this lengthy discussion of error by underlining the importance of this issue and by stressing the need for vigilance on the part of the researcher. Errors that arise during the phase of transformation of concepts into variables are extremely damaging, in that they adversely impact the entire development of the empirical phase. The subsequent collection of data may be impeccable; sampling procedures may be very accurate, and sophisticated statistical techniques may be utilized. If, however, our variables do not correctly reflect the concept, all will be in vain. Moreover, such errors are particularly insidious, as they may easily escape detection by the less attentive analyst (we have already mentioned the fact that an operational definition often reifies a concept and, unbeknown to the reader and sometimes even to the analyst, may replace that concept; in this regard, we should bear in mind the case of IQ taken purely and simply as a synonym for intelligence).

SUMMARY

1. The 'typical' itinerary followed in social research consists of a loop, which begins with theory and returns to *theory*. The first phase is that of theory. The second phase involves *hypotheses*, which are derived from theory through a process of *deduction*. *Data collection* comprises the third phase, which requires *operationalization* – that is to say, the transformation of hypotheses into empirically observable statements. The next phase involves *data analysis*, which is usually preceded by *data organization*. In the fifth phase the researcher presents his *results*, which are obtained through a process of *interpretation* of the statistical analyses carried out in the previous phase. Finally, the researcher returns to theory by engaging in a process of *induction*.

2. A *theory* can be defined as a set of organically connected propositions that are located at a higher level of abstraction and generalization than empirical reality, and which are derived from empirical patterns and from which empirical forecasts can be derived. A *hypothesis* is a proposition that implies a relationship between two or more concepts, and is located at a lower level of abstraction and generality than theory. Hypotheses enable theory to be transformed into terms that can be tested empirically.

3. Since a theory is an interconnection between concepts, once these abstract entities become concrete, the whole theoretical network will become concrete. The concepts can be transformed into empirically observable entities by causing them to become attributes or properties of the specific objects studied, which are called units of analysis (or simply 'units'). Operational definitions then establish the rules for empirical recording of these properties. The operationalized 'states' of properties are called *categories*, each of which is assigned a different symbolic value, which is normally coded as a number.

4. The unit of analysis is the social object to which the investigated properties appertain. In social research, the following types of analysis unit are most common: the individual, the aggregate of individuals, the group-organization-institution, the event, and the cultural product.

5. A variable is an operationalized concept. More precisely, it is the operationalized property of an object, in that the concept, in order to be operationalized, has to be referred to an object and become a property of that object. The difference between concept, property and variable is the same as the difference between weight (concept), the weight of an object (property) and the weight of the object measured by means of a weighing-scale (variable). Just as concepts are the building blocks of theory, variables are the core elements of empirical analysis.

6. Variables are grouped into three classes: nominal, ordinal and interval. When the property to be recorded takes on non-orderable discrete states, we have *nominal variables*. In this case the operationalization, which enables us to pass from the property to the variable, is based on *classification*. The only relationships that we can establish among the categories of a nominal variable are those of equality and inequality.

When the property assumes orderable discrete states, we have *ordinal variables*; the procedure used to operationalize the properties is based on assignment to ordered categories, *or ordering*. The existence of an order enables us to establish not only relationships of equality and inequality among the categories, but also relationships of order ('greater than' and 'less than').

Interval variables can be obtained by applying two basic operationalization procedures to the property: measurement and counting. *Measurement* takes place when the property to be measured is continuous and we possess a pre-established unit of measurement. *Counting* takes place when the property to be recorded is discrete, and a counting unit exists. In the case of interval variables the distances between the categories are known; the numbers identifying the categories (the 'values' of the variable) have a full numerical meaning in that they possess not only ordinal features, but cardinal ones as well. The distances between categories can be determined because there is a reference unit, and this enables us to apply to such distances the four basic arithmetical operations.

7. When concepts are located at a high level of generality, it may be difficult to operationalize them. In this case we use indicators, which are simpler, specific concepts that can be more easily translated into observational terms and are linked to general concepts by affinity of meaning. Since they are specific, indicators reveal only one aspect of the complexity of a general concept, and it may be necessary to identify several indicators for the same concept, one for each of the concept's different dimensions. Operationalization of such indicators produces variables, the combination of which into indexes allows the researcher to return to the original concept.

8. In the process that leads from concepts to variables, various forms of error (measurement error or total error) may occur; these errors constitute the gap between the (theoretical) concept and the (empirical) variable. Such errors may be systematic (bias) or random. They may arise in the *theoretical* phase, in which indicators are selected (indication error), or in the *empirical* phase, when recording of indicators takes place (operationalization error).

FURTHER READING

A classic text on the logic of scientific inference and the connections between theory, hypotheses and concepts is A.L. Stinchcombe, *Constructing Social Theories* (Harcourt, Brace & World, 1968, pp. 303), especially Chapter 2. For an in-depth introduction to the relationship between theory and research in the context of current social theories, see D. Layder, *Sociological Practice*: *Linking Theory and Social Research* (Sage, 1998, pp. 191).

O.D. Duncan, *Notes on Social Measurement*: *Historical and Critical* (Russell Sage Foundation, 1984, pp. 256) is a classic essay on the problem of measurement, and includes a historical overview and timely reflections. Measurement and the theory-hypothesis-concepts transition are well addressed in Parts I and II of the voluminous work of E.J. Pedhazur and L. Pedhazur Schmelkin, *Measurement Design and Analysis*: *An Integrated Approach* (Lawrence Erlbaum, 1991, pp. 819). On the critical relationship between social indicators and social theories, see M. Carley, Social Measurement and Social Indicators (Allen & Unwin, 1981, pp. 195). On validity and reliability E.G. Carmines and R.A. Zeller, *Reliability and Validity Assessment* (Sage, 1983, pp. 70) is recommended.

'Measurement error' in social research (and especially in surveys) are dealt with by R.M Groves, *Survey Errors and Survey Costs* (Wiley, 1989, pp. 590), a comprehensive treatment of survey errors due to sampling, non-response, non-coverage, and inadequate measurement, and by P.P. Biemer, R.M. Groves, L.E. Lyberg, N.A. Mathiowetz and S. Sudman (eds), *Measurement Errors in Surveys* (Wiley, 1991, pp. 760), a collection of papers on measurement errors due to questionnaire design and interviewing, and how to estimate those errors.

NOTES

1. And sometimes of ambit, meaning the geographical area or period of time to which the hypothesis refers.

2. The reader is reminded that here – as in the rest of the text – the terms 'test' and 'testing' are used rather than 'verify' and 'verification'. Indeed, it should be borne in mind that *verify* means 'show to be true' (and *falsify* is taken to mean 'show to be false'), while *test* has a more general meaning that does not imply the outcome. According to Karl Popper, science can never demonstrate the definitive truth of alternative theories (verify), but only confute ('falsify') them. As he pointed out, 'No matter how many instances of white swans we may have observed, this does not justify the conclusion that *all* swans are white' (Popper, 1934: 27). Indeed, conclusions of this kind are valid only with regard to the past (as is the claim that 'all US Presidents are men'); not being valid for the future (the possibility of seeing a black swan or a woman President remains open), they do not display the universality demanded by scientific law. According to this point of view (which is fairly generally accepted), the term 'verify' should be replaced in scientific language by other terms (such as 'test' or 'corroborate'), which refer only to the operation of 'submitting to empirical testing' without giving any indication of the outcome of that operation.

3. On this point, we endorse Marradi's analysis (1980: 25).

4. Except for minor variations, the present treatment closely follows the methodological proposal put forward by Alberto Marradi (in particular, Marradi, 1980).

5. In the case of educational qualifications, for example, it could be claimed that individuals with no qualification find themselves in a marginal situation that distances them from all the others, and that the gap between them and those who have an elementary-school diploma is, in any case, greater than the gap between the elementary-school diploma and the middle-school diploma. It could also be claimed that the high-school diploma and the university degree are fairly close in that the holders of both share a common level of higher education; thus, the five positions could be assigned the numerical sequence 1, 4, 6, 8, 9.

6. Measurement can produce variables that have either a conventional zero or an absolute zero (a 'physical' zero which stands for the total absence of the property); we may think of temperatures expressed in centigrade degrees and in Kelvin degrees. Counting produces variables that have an absolute zero (Stevens, 1946, called variables with a conventional zero 'interval' scales and those with an absolute zero 'ratio' scales). For variables that have a conventional zero, operations of addition and subtraction can be carried out among the categories of the variables (we can calculate the difference between 20 and 22 degrees or between 40 and 44 degrees). The four arithmetical operations can be applied to the *differences* among the values; e.g. we can say that the difference between 10 and 30 degrees is twice that between 0 and 10 degrees. This can be done regardless of the unit of measurement adopted; since 0°C corresponds to 32°F, and 10°C = 50°F, 20°C = 68°F, 30°C = 86°F, it will be seen that, on the Fahrenheit scale, the corresponding difference between 86°F and 50°F (= 36°F) is twice as great as the difference between 50°F and 32°F (= 18°F), just as it is on the centigrade scale. The fact that all four arithmetical operations are applicable to the differences among the values (the intervals) enables us to apply the vast majority of statistical procedures to these variables. For the sake of simplicity, we will not introduce the distinction between variables with a conventional zero and those with an absolute zero, in view of the fact that the most common statistical techniques can be applied equally to both types of variable.

7. Concepts are always abstract, but they may have references that are concrete (e.g. tree) or abstract (e.g. freedom).

8. For the sake of simplicity, the distinction between concept and property has not been included in this diagram, as the two notions are almost the same (as we know, a property is a concept assigned to a unit of analysis).

9. We will use the terms 'true value' and 'observed value' for what are called 'true score' and 'observed score' in psychometric terminology. While the field of psychometric testing does actually deal with scores, this is not generally the case in the social sciences, in which the variable is often nominal or ordinal. For this reason, the term 'score' will be avoided.

10. The empirical research model referred to in the following pages is the survey. This involves working on a sample of the study population, using the individual as the unit of analysis, and recording the data by questioning the subjects (e.g. by

means of a questionnaire). Nevertheless, the comments made have a general validity and are applicable to other empirical models (when adapted accordingly; for instance, sampling error cannot arise in the case of a census, nor is interviewer-related error applicable to a mail questionnaire).

11. Experimental psychologists also use the notion of *internal* and *external validity*. However, this is a very different concept of validity from that which has been presented so far. It does not refer specifically to the passage from concepts to variables, but to the more general issue of the meaning that should be attached to the results of a study, and in particular to the correspondence between the relationship between two variables, as seen in the study data, and the relationship that actually exists in the real world.

Internal validity means that the relationship found between X and Y actually exists in the data and is not, for instance, 'spurious' – that is, apparent. External validity means that this relationship also exists outside the specific context (in terms of subjects studied, experimental conditions, etc.) in which the research has been carried out. Internal validity therefore concerns the correctness of the research and of the analysis conducted within it, while external validity has to do with whether the results obtained can be generalized to different situations from those considered in the study. Clearly, this is an application of the concept of validity that lies outside the specific sphere of the relationship between concept and variable. As it is of little use here and may be a source of confusion, it will not be used.

4 Causality and Experimentation

The chapter begins with a discussion of the concept of cause, which is both crucial in all scientific reasoning and extremely difficult to translate into empirical terms. Next, we describe 'experiments', the main tool, developed by the physical sciences, to ascertain cause and effect relationships and how they may (or may not) be applied in the field of social science. The remaining parts of the chapter illustrate the various experimental designs used in social research.

1. THE CONCEPT OF CAUSE

Since ancient times, humans have wondered about the causes of what happens in the world. Whether it be the influence of the stars on terrestrial events, or the effect of rain on the growth of grain, people have always tried to understand how one phenomenon influences another. Although the concept of cause lies at the very heart of science, it is one of the most controversial notions from a philosophical standpoint and one of the most difficult to translate into operational terms; in other words, the concept of cause is particularly exposed to that 'gap between the languages of theory and research which can never be bridged in a completely satisfactory way' (Blalock, 1961: 5). The problem that this raises in all sciences, and particularly in the social sciences, is that only very rarely – as we shall see – can one use the main instrument for empirically controlling a causal relationship, i.e. the *experiment*.

This book will not enter into the philosophical debate on the *concept of cause*. Philosophers have wrestled with this concept for centuries: in the Aristotelian doctrine, the notion of cause constitutes the very foundation of science and its principle of intelligibility, to the point that 'knowledge and science consist of understanding causes, and are nothing outside of this' (Abbagnano 1971: 118); in the eighteenth century, Hume pondered the impossibility of demonstrating a necessary causal connection, the non-deducibility of effects from causes, and the arbitrary nature of any prediction; in recent years the concepts of function and probability have replaced the traditional concept of deterministic cause.

In general, 'one admits that causal thinking belongs completely on the theoretical level and that causal laws can never be demonstrated empirically' (Blalock, 1961: 6). As Mario Bunge (1959) puts it, in order to express the idea of causation, the following statement is not sufficient:

If C, then E

In that this affirmation indicates that the relationship between C (cause) and E (effect) can be true both 'sometimes' and 'always', while the causal principle must assert the occurrence of E every single time that C happens. Bunge therefore considers the following statement:

If C, then (and only then) E always

This formulation expresses some characteristics of the causal link (conditionality, succession, constancy, univocity), but it is still insufficient. Indeed, according to Bunge, 'what we need is a statement expressing the idea ... that causation, far more than a relation, is a category of genetic connection ... a way of *producing* things, new if only in number, out of other things' (Bunge, 1959: 46). For this reason, the statement that Bunge proposes to express the causal link is the following:

If C, then (and only then) E always produced by C

The key element that this statement adds to the preceding ones is the idea of *production*: it is not enough, in order to have causation, to ascertain that there exists a 'constant conjunction' between two phenomena; it must be shown that 'the effect is not merely *accompanied* by the cause, but is *engendered* by it' (Bunge, 1959: 47).[1]

Nevertheless, as Blalock writes (1961: 10):

'"producing" refers to an ontological process ... it has a reality apart from the observer and his perceptions ... We cannot possibly observe or measure such forcings. Perhaps the best we can do is to note covariations together with temporal sequences. But the mere fact that X and Y vary together in a predictable way, and that a change in X always precedes the change in Y, can never assure us that X had produced a change in Y.'

This is why – according to Blalock – the concept of 'prediction' (instead of causation) is often used, especially by statisticians, in order to avoid the empiricist objection to the very idea of cause. To sum up, the notion of cause must remain confined to the field of theory, and we must come to terms with the impossibility of empirically verifying causal laws.

Although the existence of a causal law can never be 'proved' empirically, hypothesizing a causal relationship at the theoretical level implies observing facts. In other words, the theoretical existence of a causal mechanism implies observable consequences at the empirical level. While empirical observation of such consequences cannot provide definitive evidence of the existence of a causal link, it can 'corroborate' our theoretical hypotheses. In other words, we can never state, *at the empirical level* (although we can hypothesize it at the theoretical level) that the variation in X 'produces' the variation in Y. But *if we empirically observe that a variation in X is regularly followed by a variation in Y – when all other possible causes of Y are kept constant – then we have strong corroborating evidence of the hypothesis that X is the cause of Y.*

Before discussing these issues, however, we should first clarify the distinction between *dependent variables* and *independent variables*. In an asymmetrical relationship – that is to say, when one variable influences another – the variable that exerts the influence is called the independent variable, while that which is influenced is called the dependent variable. Thus, in the relationship between social class and political orientation, e.g., social class is the independent variable and political orientation is the dependent variable. If the relationship is of a causal type, *the cause is the independent variable and the effect is the dependent variable.*[2] In a bivariate relationship, X indicates the independent variable and Y the dependent.

2. EMPIRICAL CORROBORATION OF THE CAUSAL RELATIONSHIP

In order to empirically corroborate the hypothesis of a causal relationship between two variables, three empirical elements are needed: covariation[3] between independent and dependent variables, direction of causality, and control of other possible causes.

2.1 Covariation between independent and dependent variables

The researcher must, *in the first place*, be able to observe *variations in the independent variable* – that is to say, in what is hypothesized to be the 'cause'. For example, if the researcher wants to collect empirical evidence to support the theoretical statement that social individualism produces a high rate of suicides, he or she must be able to observe situations (societies, social groups) which show differing degrees of individualism (e.g. Protestant and Catholic societies, people involved to a greater or lesser extent in social networks, married couples with children and singles, etc.). Empirical evidence of the influence of social cohesion on suicide rates cannot be gathered by observing only situations in which the independent variable (social cohesion) is constant. Moreover, *at the same time* as the independent variable varies, the researcher must be able to observe *variations in the dependent variable*. In statistical terms, a 'covariation' between the two variables must be observed: when one varies, the other must also vary. If the theory affirms the existence of a causal link between social individualism and suicide rates, one must be able to observe higher rates of suicide in societies with higher degrees of individualism (and vice versa).

2.2 Causal direction

One must be able to ascertain that a variation in the independent variable is followed, and not preceded, by a variation in the dependent variable. This can be empirically established in two ways. The first is by *manipulation of the independent variable*: if the researcher brings about a variation in the variable X, and subsequently observes a variation in the variable Y, then there is no doubt that – *if* a causal link exists – its direction is from X to Y and not vice versa.

This approach can only be adopted in the case of experiments which, as we shall see, involve the artificial variation (i.e. manipulation) of one of the two variables. When this is impossible, the direction of the causal link can be established through the criterion of *temporal succession*, which stems from the observation that the variation in the independent variable X precedes the variation in the dependent variable Y. If we state that a religious upbringing (X) leads to a more intolerant attitude towards different ideologies in adult life (Y), the fact that the first variable precedes the second establishes the direction of the causal link. Similarly, the correlation between educational level and earnings, if observed and interpreted in a causal sense, necessarily points to the conclusion that the level of education attained influences the salary subsequently earned, and not vice versa.

In addition, some causal directions can be excluded on the grounds of *logical impossibility*. If we claim that there is a causal link between social class and political orientation, this can only run from the former to the latter (as a change in political opinions cannot push an individual from one social class into another).

2.3 Control of extraneous variables

When we vary the independent variable, we must be able to exclude the variation of other variables that are correlated with it, as these may themselves cause the dependent variable to vary. For instance, if the rate of suicide is higher in Protestant regions than Catholic ones, but if all the Protestant regions analysed are German and all the Catholic ones are French, then we cannot establish whether the cause of the different suicide rates is religion or nationality.

It is therefore essential to control extraneous variables if we are to achieve empirical control (even in the sense of corroboration and not of proof) of causal relationships. Empirical observation of the first aspect alone (i.e. covariation) is not sufficient to have causation. In social research there is a familiar slogan that states, 'covariation is not causation'. The two concepts are very different in terms of their context: the concept of causation is theoretical, whereas covariation is empirical. Moreover, and this is the point that most interests us here: covariation alone can *never* be taken as empirical proof of the existence of a causal relationship. This is the point that was raised earlier when Bunge was quoted regarding the fact that the notion of causality includes the idea of production and not mere 'constant conjunction', or recurrent association. In other words: *there can be covariation even without causation*.

On this point it is worth reading the ironic observations by George Bernard Shaw in the preface to his play, *The Doctor's Dilemma*, concerning what he calls the statistical illusions: 'It is easy to prove that the wearing of tall hats and the carrying of umbrellas enlarges the chest, prolongs life, and confers comparative immunity from disease; for the statistics show that classes which use these articles are bigger, healthier, and live longer than the class which never dreams of possessing such things' (Shaw, 1941: 54). In a similar vein, one can cite the correlation between the consumption of ice cream and support for the Radical Party in Italy (i.e. in areas where ice cream consumption is high, the Radical Party wins more votes, and vice versa), but nobody would seriously think that a causal link exists between these two variables.[4]

To sum up, if the theoretical statement 'X causes Y' is true, then we should be able to observe, at the empirical level, that a variation in X – when all other possible causes of Y are kept constant – is accompanied by a variation in Y. But how can we empirically achieve the so-called *ceteris paribus* ('all other things being equal') condition? The answer depends on whether we adopt the logic of *covariation analysis* or that of *experimentation*.

3. COVARIATION ANALYSIS AND EXPERIMENTATION

In order to control a causal statement empirically, scientists can adopt two basic techniques: *covariation analysis* in the natural setting, or *experimentation* in an artificial situation. The adjectives 'natural' and 'artificial' should immediately be stressed, though their meanings will become clearer in the following pages. With regard to covariation analysis, *natural* means that covariations are examined just as they occur in social situations, without any manipulation by the researcher; *artificial* pertains to experimentation, which – in its ideal form – takes place in a laboratory, and in which variations in the independent variable are produced by the researcher. Two examples, involving the same research issue (the impact of television propaganda on citizens' political views) will clarify the differences between the two approaches.

Let us imagine that two candidates for the presidency of a nation, A and B, use television propaganda to promote their election campaigns. We know that voting is influenced by a great number of 'independent' variables such as age, gender, education, social class, religion, family traditions, etc. However, let us suppose that we are not interested in the impact of these variables, but only in the influence of television propaganda. If, therefore, X is the variable 'exposure to television propaganda' (which, for simplicity's sake, we can imagine as having only two states: 'followed/did not follow the election campaign on TV') and Y is the dependent variable 'vote' (split into 'votes for candidate A/votes for candidate B'), the researcher's goal is to compare the variations in the two variables X and Y, to see whether exposure to television propaganda (X) leads to changes in voting behaviour (Y).

3.1 Covariation analysis

A research design constructed according to the logic of covariation analysis will involve interviewing a sample of subjects, asking a few questions concerning basic socio-demographic characteristics (e.g. the variables mentioned above: age, gender, education, etc.) and asking if (and how closely) they followed the campaign on TV and which candidate they voted for. If we find a correlation between the two variables, in the sense that more of those who were exposed to the television propaganda voted for conservative candidate A, can we conclude that television worked in favour of this candidate, that it influenced voting in this direction?

Certainly *not*! In fact, the two groups of citizens – those that watched television and those that did not – do not differ only in terms of this variable: those who watch more television probably spend more time at home and tend to be women rather than men, senior citizens rather than young people, etc. If, for example, people who watch more television are older than the average, the correlation between exposure to television and votes for A cannot tell us whether the real determinant of voter preference is age or exposure to television propaganda. The two variables are, in fact, 'confused', as those who watch more television are also older. Did they vote for A because they were older or because they watched more TV? Although the data reveal a correlation between X (exposure to television propaganda) and Y (vote), the real causal factor could be age, which influences both variables: older people watch more television, and older people are more conservative. This is a classic example of what, in sociology, is called a *spurious relationship*. A spurious relationship is a correlation between two variables, X and Y, that does not derive from a causal link between them, but from the fact that they are both influenced by a third variable Z (in this case age). Variations in Z bring about simultaneous variations in X and Y (through a causal mechanism) without there being a causal link between X and Y.

When this happens, the researcher has two ways of establishing whether or not the relationship between X and Y is due to the external action of Z on the two variables: a) *subset comparison*, achieved by transforming the external variables into constants, and b) *mathematical estimation*, through the statistical analysis and control of the effects of such external variables.

The first procedure involves a sort of *mechanical control* of the variables that may cause interference. If the people who watch more television are, on average, older than those who do not, the variable Z (age) is likely to interfere with the relationship between X (exposure to TV) and Y (voter preference). In order to eliminate this interference, we need only transform the variable Z into a constant. This can be done by analysing the correlation between X and Y in groups of the same age. For example, the people interviewed can be classified into groups – such as youths, adults, and senior citizens; the correlation between television propaganda and voter preference within each of these groups can then be ascertained. If the relationship persists (i.e. in all three groups a correlation is seen between television propaganda and voter preference), we need no longer suspect that this is due to the age factor, in that our observations involve groups in which age has been held constant. Of course, this procedure becomes somewhat complicated when many variables have to be controlled simultaneously, in that the subjects participating in the study will have to be classified into ever smaller groups.

This problem can be overcome through what we can call *statistical control* – that is to say, by computing the net correlation between X and Y through mathematical estimation. Without going into the details of multivariate statistics, let it suffice to say that in order to control third variables it is not necessary to keep them physically constant. Indeed, if we know how the third variables are related to one another and to the dependent variable (and this can be calculated from the data), we can take these effects into account when we calculate the correlation between X and Y; this mathematical technique yields the net correlation between X and Y – that is to say, the correlation that remains once the effects due to extraneous variables have been filtered out. The statistical techniques used are partial correlation, if only one extraneous variable is to be controlled, and multiple regression (or other multivariate techniques) when there is more than one extraneous variable.

Experimentation   There is, however, another way of solving the problem based on a different way not of analysing data, but of producing them. Let us look again at the same theoretical question ('Does television propaganda influence voter preference?'). This time, we will suppose that the researcher chooses a sample of, say, 200 citizens, and assigns them *at random*[5] (e.g. by drawing lots) to one of two groups, each containing 100 people. The members of one group are asked to follow the election campaign on television, and the members of the other to avoid watching altogether. After the election, the 200 citizens are interviewed in order to find out who they voted for. If there is a correlation between having watched the television campaign (X) and voting behaviour (Y) – for example, many more votes for candidate A were cast by subjects exposed to the TV campaign than by non-exposed subjects – this correlation cannot be 'spurious', as it was in the previous example. In the present example, the group exposed to the TV campaign is not, on average, older, nor does it contain more women, nor is it less educated than the non-exposed group. The assignment of individuals to the two groups was, in fact, deliberately performed in a random manner, in order to ensure that the groups were, *on average*, equal in terms of the characteristics of their members. Thus, the mean difference in voter preference (the dependent variable, Y) between the two groups can be reasonably attributed to the only element that differentiates them: exposure to television propaganda (the independent variable, X).

The first example is one of *covariation analysis*; the second is one of *experimentation*. What is the difference? In both cases the researcher studies a covariation between a hypothesized causal variable, X (independent), and a hypothesized effect variable, Y (dependent). In the first case, he *observes* and analyses how the variations in X relate to the variations in Y in a *natural setting*. In the second case, she *produces* a variation in X in a *controlled situation* and measures how much Y subsequently varies. The researcher 'produces' a variation in that he manipulates the independent variable from the outside – that is, he causes it to vary (in the example, by deciding to expose or not to expose a group to television propaganda). This occurs in a 'controlled situation', in that the random assignment of the subjects to one of the two groups provides a way of controlling all[6] other variables: it guarantees that the two groups differ (except for incidental fluctuations) only with regard to the independent variable (exposure to television propaganda).

In the first case, the researcher intervenes *after* collection of the data, which he only analyzes. In the second case, he controls the very production of data, which takes place in an artificial situation that he himself has set up. The basic idea underpinning the experiment, therefore, is that, given the hypothesis 'X causes Y', if we *produce* a variation in the value of X on a certain number of subjects and *keep constant* all other possible causes of variations in Y, we should be able to observe variations in Y in those same subjects. *Manipulation* of the independent variable and *control* of third variables are, therefore, the two features of experimentation that distinguish it from covariation analysis.

It should be noted that by randomly assigning subjects to the experimental and control groups, *all* possible variables that may cause interference are controlled, including those unrecorded or even unknown to the researcher. The two groups therefore differ only with regard to the experimental variable. By contrast, the statistical control procedures used in the case of covariation analysis are applicable only to a *finite and explicitly recorded* number of variables – that is to say, variables pre-selected by the researcher and recorded during the data collection stage.

Although experimentation is the most rigorous approach to the problem of empirical identification of causal relationships, the vast majority of social research projects involve observing correlations rather than conducting experiments. *Most social variables cannot be manipulated*, and therefore the researcher is rarely able to bring about variations in the independent variable. If we want to study the causal relationship between social individualism (expressed, for example, by the indicator 'dominant religion') and suicide rates, we cannot take a Catholic society, convert the whole society to Protestantism, and then re-measure suicide rates.

There are, however, a number of situations – especially in psychology research settings – in which such manipulation is possible, and thus experiments can be carried out. The rest of this chapter deals with these research situations.

4. EXPERIMENTS IN THE SOCIAL SCIENCES

An *experiment* can be defined as *a form of experience of natural facts that occurs following deliberate human intervention to produce change; as such it distinguishes itself from the form of experience involving the observation of facts in their natural settings.*

The philosophical roots and the first scientific applications of experimentation date back to the seventeenth century. At the beginning of that century, Bacon distinguished between *observed experience* and *experience produced* by manipulative human intervention, and Galileo placed experimentation at the very foundation of modern scientific knowledge. Experimentation has its epistemological setting in the natural sciences; its application to the social sciences requires some adaptation, or at least the creation of specific forms. An experiment that can be carried out in the realm of physics, for example on a sample of undifferentiated gas molecules, cannot be transposed in an identical form into the social sciences, in which the units of analysis are individuals who differ from one another. This section deals with the specific type of experiment that can be performed in the social sciences.[7]

Imagine a population composed of units of analysis called *u*; let *X* be the independent variable and *Y* the dependent variable. For simplicity's sake, suppose that *X* has only two values: $X = c$ (control) or $X = t$ (treatment).[8]

Returning to our previous example, let us suppose that *X* is exposure to political propaganda on television and *Y* is voter preference. Now let us imagine that we can record the value of *Y* *on the same unit*, both in the case of $X = c$ and in the case of $X = t$ (which is, of course, impossible). In other words, in our example, imagine being able to record the vote of the same individual both after exposure to the television propaganda ($X = t$) and after non-exposure ($X = c$), as if we had a time machine that could re-run history with only one variation. If Y_t is the vote after exposure to the campaign and Y_c the vote in the case of no exposure to the campaign, the causal effect of the campaign is measured in terms of the difference in behaviour between the two situations:

$$\text{Causal effect } t = Y_t(u) - Y_c(u) \text{ on the same unit } u, \text{ at the same point in time}$$

As it is impossible to observe the values Y_t and Y_c on the same unit and at the same time (an individual is either exposed or not exposed to election propaganda), it is impossible to observe the effect of *X* on *Y*. This is called *the fundamental problem of causal inference*.[9] From the impossibility of a simultaneous observation of Y_c and Y_t on the same unit stems the impossibility of observing the effect of *X* on *Y* and therefore of controlling empirically the presence of a causal link. And there is no solution to the problem: whether in the social sciences or in the natural sciences, there is no research design, unit of analysis, type of data, or type of variable that enables us to overcome this obstacle. Not even in the more 'objective' science of physics is the researcher able to solve the fundamental problem of causal inference. This is the basic reason why a causal inference cannot be verified empirically.

Nevertheless, although no definitive empirical solution to the problem of causal inference exists, partial solutions can be found. There are two practical solutions, which Holland calls the *scientific solution* and the *statistical solution* (1986).

4.1 Scientific solution

The *scientific solution* is possible if one of the following (*undemonstrable*) assumptions can be adopted: *the assumption of invariance* or *the assumption of equivalence*.

The assumption of invariance involves supposing:

- temporal stability: the value of Y_c can be substituted by a measure of the same Y_c recorded earlier;
- non-influence of the measuring procedure: the value of Y_t is not affected by the preceding measurement of Y_c on the same unit.

At this point, Y_c and Y_t no longer need to be measured simultaneously on the same unit (which is impossible): Y_c can be measured at an earlier time. In other words, Y_c is recorded first, X is made to vary, and Y_t is then recorded. The difference between the two values of Y reveals the causal effect.

This approach is common in the natural sciences. Take the following example. In 1850 the English physicist James Prescott Joule, in order to empirically verify the principle of the conservation of energy – which states that heat and work are equivalent forms of energy – built a device in which descending weights caused fan blades to rotate in a tank of water. He hypothesized that the mechanical work produced by the fan blades would raise the temperature of the water. The experiment enabled Joule not only to establish this causal connection, but also to determine quantitatively the relationship ('law') between heat and energy, and to establish that 1 calorie corresponds to 4.186 joules (the unit of measure of energy named after him).[10]

If Y_c is the temperature of the water before the 'treatment' (i.e. before the input of mechanical energy), Y_t the temperature after

the treatment, and u the unit on which the experiment is performed (in this case, the mass of water subjected to the variation in energy; in the social sciences an individual, an institution, etc.), we can say that the causal effect, on a given unit u, is represented by the algebraic difference:[11]

$$\text{Causal effect } t = Y_t(u) - Y_c(u) \text{ on the same unit } u, \text{ at different times}$$

The conclusion that the difference between the two values of the dependent variable Y represents the causal effect is based on the assumption of invariance, which is *undemonstrable*. In Joule's experiment this assumption is plausible, in terms of both temporal stability and the non-influence of the first measurement. The *temporal stability* of Y_c is plausible, since energy variations other than the variation in X do not occur in the laboratory situation. The value of Y_c (the temperature of the water before the movement of the fan blades) is kept stable (if X does not vary) in the short interval of time between the beginning and the end of the experiment. For this reason, the temperature of the water before the rotation of the fan blades can be assumed to be identical to the temperature that would have been recorded *if* the fan blades had not moved. It is also plausible to assume *the non-influence of the first measurement,* in as much as the first measurement of the temperature does not influence the second measurement.

The assumption of equivalence states that two units u and v are *equivalent* – that is, equal in all relevant aspects. So much so that $Y_c(u) = Y_c(v)$ and $Y_t(u) = Y_t(v)$. In this case, the measurement of Y_c (value of Y when $X = c$) is performed on one unit (v) and the measurement of Y_t (value of Y when $X = t$) is performed on the other unit (u). The causal effect will be seen as $Y_t(u) - Y_c(v)$.

Let us suppose that the researcher wants to ascertain the effect of a certain fertilizer on agricultural production. The logic of the preceding experiment – that is, of the assumption of invariance – would suggest taking a piece of land, cultivating it for one year without treatment (fertilizer) and measuring its yield $Y_c(u)$; and the next year using fertilizer and re-measuring its yield $Y_t(u)$. Obviously, in such an experiment the condition of temporal stability of $Y_c(u)$ is implausible; from one year to the next, other factors will alter the productivity of the field (e.g. the weather conditions), and therefore $Y_c(u)$ in the first year (yield without fertilizer) cannot be assumed to be the same as in the second year (the yield that would have been obtained in the second year had fertilizer not been used) for purposes of comparison with $Y_t(u)$.

In this case, then, the assumption of invariance cannot be adopted, but the assumption of equivalence can, if we take two equivalent units that are equal for all relevant purposes. Let us imagine two adjacent fields in which the variables relevant to productivity are equal (same environmental conditions, same soil, same irrigation, etc.): unit v is not exposed to treatment (no fertilizer is used), and here we measure $Y_c(v)$; the other unit (u) is exposed to treatment, and here we measure $Y_t(u)$. The causal effect will be taken as:

$$\text{Causal effect } t = Y_t(u) - Y_c(v) \text{ on the two units } u \text{ and } v, \text{ at the same point in time}$$

In this case, too, the assumption of equivalence is undemonstrable.

4.2 Statistical solution
The assumptions of both invariance and equivalence are normally implausible in the social sciences. Let us again take the example of the effect of television propaganda on voter preference. If the researcher adopts the assumption of invariance, he will first ask individuals which way they intend to vote (thus measuring Y_c, i.e. the dependent variable 'voter preference' before treatment), then expose them to the televised debate between the candidates, and finally re-record their intentions (Y_t). However, the temporal stability of Y_c is

somewhat implausible; in the time between the two measurements, the subjects may have changed their minds for reasons that have nothing to do with the television debate, such as discussion with a spouse, reading the newspapers, or other concomitant political events. The non-influence of the first measurement is also difficult to sustain; remembering the answer given in the first interview, a subject might respond in the same way in the second interview, even if he has changed his mind, in order to avoid seeming inconsistent.[12]

Even the assumption of equivalence of the units is implausible in the social sciences, in that it is impossible to find two units that are exactly equivalent. In the agriculture example, it is relatively safe to presume that two contiguous fields derived from the division of one piece of land will be equal in terms of all the variables related to production, such as soil composition, irrigation, weather, exposure to the sun, etc. But even if they are not exactly similar, in the natural sciences it is possible to identify which properties of a certain unit can influence a certain dependent variable Y and to make the two units equivalent with regard to these. If, for example, we want to measure the effects of corrosion by two different acids on a metal sheet, we can find out which properties of the metal influence corrosion (e.g. surface texture, shape, the microcrystalline structure of the metal, etc.) and design an experiment in which two sheets of absolutely identical metal, under the same experimental conditions, are subjected to corrosion by the two acids.

In the social sciences it is impossible to find absolutely identical units: their intrinsic irreproducibility – whether individuals, institutions, groups of individuals, etc. – is one of the fundamental epistemological differences between the social sciences and the natural sciences (all carbon atoms are the same, whereas no two individuals are identical). Moreover, it is impossible to establish unequivocally which variables influence a given dependent variable Y, in such a way as to find two units which can be considered equivalent at least from this limited point of view. In the example of the cultivation of grain, once we have identified the type of soil, seed, irrigation procedures, weather conditions and so on, we can reasonably claim to have identified the main variables influencing productivity; in the case of human subjects, however, the number of variables that may influence behaviour is almost infinite.

How can this problem be overcome? The answer lies in the *statistical solution*. Although it is impossible to find two identical individuals, it is possible to obtain two *groups of individuals* that are *statistically equivalent* (i.e. different only with regard to incidental aspects). Each group can be exposed to a different value of X, and the variations in Y can then be measured. Groups with these characteristics are obtained through the so-called process of *randomization*: the initial sample of experimental subjects is subdivided into two groups by assigning the subjects 'randomly' (e.g. by drawing lots) to one group or the other. The two groups will be equivalent *on average*, with regard to *all* variables (whether overt, like gender and age, covert, or even unconscious), except for incidental differences (which are slight and haphazard). By subjecting each of the groups to a different value (c or t) of the variable X, and observing the average results of the variable Y in each group, we will be able to quantify the causal effect, which will now be the *mean* causal effect:

Mean causal effect $T = E(Y_t) - E(Y_c)$ on the two 'randomized' groups

where E is the 'expected value', or 'mean value' (thus, $E(Y_t)$ is the mean of Y_t values in the group of subjects exposed to $X = t$).

In experimental psychology, the group exposed to a certain treatment (value $X = t$ of the independent variable) is called the *experimental group*, while the group that is not exposed to treatment (value $X = c$) is called the *control group*.[13]

At this point, the differences between experimentation in the natural sciences and experimentation in the social sciences should be clear, as should the specific features of the latter (although, admittedly, the randomization

procedure that has been presented here as typical of social science experiments can also be applied – and may sometimes be the only procedure applicable – in the natural sciences). Moreover, it should also be clear why, in the example dealing with the influence of television propaganda on voter preference, we used a research design which may not have been immediately comprehensible (random assignment of subjects to two groups, exposure of only one group to television propaganda, etc.).

Finally, it must be stated that the essential prerequisite for experimentation is the ability to control (*manipulate*) the independent variable. After assigning the subjects to groups, the researcher must be able to assign different values of X to those groups: in other words, he must be able to determine the action of the independent variable X. If this is not possible, a 'true experiment' cannot be conducted. Moreover, it should be noted that, for the sake of simplicity, we have so far hypothesized that the variable X assumes only two values (presence/absence), thus giving rise to only two groups (the experimental group and the control group). As we shall see, the logic of experimentation does not change substantially when the variable X assumes more than two values (if there are three, the subjects will be assigned to three groups, and so on), nor when more than one independent variable is involved (this point will be discussed further in the section on factorial design).

5. LABORATORY EXPERIMENTS AND FIELD EXPERIMENTS

In this section and the following, we will take a closer look at experimentation in the social sciences. We will also outline a few studies in order to illustrate the ways in which this important method is applied. We will not, however, go into the technical details of the individual experiments or the numerous types of various possible experimental designs; rather, we will confine our attention to two basic types. Indeed, this area of social research has developed enormously, giving rise to an almost autonomous branch of the discipline, and for a detailed analysis the reader should consult specialized manuals.

Our presentation will be organized on the basis of a two-fold subdivision which distinguishes between laboratory experiments and field experiments on the one hand, and which differentiates experiments (or 'true experiments') from 'quasi-experiments' on the other. The first distinction does not concern the methodological set-up of the experiment, but rather refers to the setting in which the experiment is conducted. The second distinction focuses on how the experiment is carried out and separates 'true' experiments – those which fulfil all criteria of the method – from those cases in which some basic requisite of the experimental method cannot be satisfied.

5.1 Laboratory experiments

The difference between laboratory experiments and field experiments is simple: it is the distinction between an experiment conducted in an artificial situation and an experiment carried out in a real-life setting. This distinction will readily be grasped if we imagine two experiments aimed at studying the effect of noise on mental concentration. One experiment is conducted in a laboratory, in which tasks requiring mental concentration are performed by subjects in conditions that are disturbed by a variety of artificially produced noises; the other is carried out in a school and assesses, for example, the performance in a test of classes that are disturbed by traffic noise and classes that are not exposed to this disturbance.

The characteristic feature of the laboratory is *control*, meaning both (a) that unwanted variables and external influences can be kept out of the experimental environment, and (b) that the researcher can establish the experimental conditions down to the smallest details.

With regard to the first point, the laboratory pursues the objective of *isolating* the experimental environment in the social sciences, just as it does in the natural sciences (through such operations as sterilization, sound-proofing, thermal insulation, the creation of a vacuum, etc.), in order to minimize the effect of external factors, such as the interference of everyday life, the influence of social roles and network relationships, etc.

With regard to the second point, in the laboratory the researcher is able to 'construct' the experiment by establishing in detail exactly how each procedure is to be carried out. From this point of view, the laboratory offers great *flexibility*, in that it enables the researcher to produce (and – importantly – to reproduce) experimental situations which vary only in terms of one small particular. For instance, in the above-mentioned experiment on noise disturbance, the researcher can test whether the effect of a noise produced at regular intervals differs from the effect of a noise produced at irregular intervals or of a continuous noise, and so on.

In short, the social science laboratory – not unlike the natural science laboratory – enables the researcher to isolate specific phenomena from the social setting in which they occur, and to analyse them in conditions that are free from accidental interference. The researcher can therefore *create situations* and *make observations* that are impossible in the natural setting; for instance, particular group dynamics may be created or mechanisms of interaction may be analysed by means of a video camera or a one-way mirror.

Our analysis of laboratory situations will start from the classification proposed by Aronson et al. (1985). This classification divides experiments into three categories on the basis of the task assigned to the subjects: studies requiring the involvement of the subjects studied (*impact studies*), those in which they are asked to make a judgement (*judgement studies*), and those in which the subjects are observed (*observational studies*).

In *impact studies* the researcher's intervention acts on the subjects themselves, who may be prompted by the train of events of the experiment to indulge in behaviour that is different from that which they would adopt in a spontaneous situation. A famous series of experiments that fall into this category was carried out in the 1960s at Yale University by Stanley Milgram on the question of obedience to authority (Milgram, 1974). The aim of the experiment was to shed light on the mechanism of obedience. In order to do so, subjects were prompted by a figure of authority – in this case a university researcher – to carry out actions which increasingly clashed with their consciences.

In this instance, two people were invited into the psychology laboratory to take part in a study on 'memory and learning' and the researcher leading the test explained that it was a study on the effects of punishment on learning. One of the subjects was assigned to the role of 'teacher', while the other was to take the part of the 'pupil'. The pupil was led into a room, where he was strapped to a chair and an electrode was attached to his wrist; he had to memorize a list of word associations, and every time he made a mistake, he was to be punished by the teacher – supposedly to assess the effect of punishment on learning – who had to administer electric shocks of increasing intensity by pressing buttons which were labelled from 'slight shock' to 'danger: severe shock'. In reality, the 'pupil' was one of the researcher's assistants and never received any shocks (but merely pretended to do so), while the 'teacher', who was convinced that he was really taking part in a learning experiment, was the true subject of the study. The experiment was designed to reveal how far a person would be willing to obey authority (the university researcher who insisted that the experiment should be completed) even in the face of increasingly painful scenes (going as far as agonized wheezing followed by a sinister silence) and insistent pleas by the pupil to stop the experiment.

The experiment was repeated with numerous subjects (over 100) of different ages, types and social background, and with various experimental modalities (physical contact, verbal contact or no contact between teacher and pupil; presence or absence of mock assistants, who either urged the teacher to go on with the experiment or else protested that it should be stopped, etc.). This series of experiments was able to clarify some of the mechanisms of obedience to authority. What amazed the researchers themselves was 'the extreme willingness of adults to go almost any length on the command of an authority, (and this not on the part of) sadistic fringe of society ... but on the part of ordinary people drawn from working, managerial and professional classes ... (so) ordinary people simply doing their jobs, and without any particular hostility on their part, can become agents in a terrible destructive process' (Milgram, 1974: 5–6).

With regard to *judgement studies*, we can quote a study by Pheterson et al. (1971) on prejudice against women. According to these authors, one of the reasons why women achieve less social success than men lies in a negative prejudice towards women on the part of women themselves. In this experiment, 120 women were shown eight paintings; two independent variables were introduced in this case: the gender of the artist (half the women were told that the painter was a man, and half that the painter was a woman) and the success of the painting (half the women were told that the painting had won a prize, and the other half that it had merely competed for a prize). The women taking part in the experiment were led one by one into a room equipped with a projector; first, they were asked to read a short biographical note on the artist, then they were shown a slide of the painting, and finally they were asked to evaluate the painting by filling in a 5-item questionnaire. The results of the questionnaires revealed that the women rated the same paintings more positively when they were attributed to male artists, but only if the painting had not won a prize; in the case of paintings said to have won prizes, no such negative prejudice towards female artists emerged. This showed that 'the work of women in competition is devalued by other women ... Even work that is equivalent to the work of a man will be judged inferior until it receives special distinction'. Women therefore harbour a negative prejudice towards other women unless the latter have already achieved success, even to the extent that, as the authors state, 'a woman who has succeeded may be overevaluated ... perhaps if the artists had been identified as famous and really superior, women would have been rated more highly than men' (Pheterson et al., 1971: 117–118).

Finally, with regard to *observational studies*, an example is provided by the research conducted by Albert Bandura in the 1960s on the imitative aggressive effects induced in children following exposure to scenes of violence on television. One of his many studies had both the general aim of studying the imitation of aggressive models and that of assessing the impact of the various ways of communicating violence (Bandura et al., 1963). The violence was variously represented through live scenes played by actors, videotapes of the same live scenes, and cartoons, in order to test the hypothesis that the further such representations are from reality, the weaker their impact will be.

The experiment involved 96 children between the ages of three and five years, who were subdivided into four groups of 24. Assignment to the groups was random, except for the fact that each group was to be made up of equal numbers of males and females and that each should contain equal numbers of aggressive and non-aggressive children (a score on a scale of aggressiveness had previously been assigned to each child on the basis of observation of behaviour). One group acted as a control group and was not exposed to any aggressive stimulus. The other three groups were exposed to the three different stimuli (live scene, videotape, cartoon). The first of these groups watched the live scene, in which an actor performed a series of violent acts on an inflatable rubber doll (punching, kicking, hammering it on the nose, throwing it in the air, etc. – acts which a child would be unlikely to perform except by imitation). The second group was shown a videotape of the same scene, while the third group watched a cartoon of a similar scene in which the doll's aggressor was a character

commonly seen in children's cartoons (a cat) and the setting contained elements that reinforced the unreality of the scene (background features that were obviously drawn, brightly-coloured fanciful houses, trees and birds, typical cartoon music, etc.). Each child was then exposed individually to a frustrating experience (walking through a room full of attractive toys without being allowed to touch them) before being led into a room in which various opportunities for play were offered; half of these involved aggressive games (the inflatable rubber doll seen earlier, a punch-ball, guns that fired rubber bullets, etc.) while the other half involved non-aggressive games. The child's behaviour was observed through a one-way mirror, and subdivided into units of a few seconds; any aggressive behaviour was further subdivided into imitative (repetition of the aggressive acts shown in the previous scenes) and non-imitative.

The results revealed a marked tendency to imitate; the children who had been exposed to the violent scenes displayed twice as many aggressive reactions as the control group. Moreover, it became clear that the prior exposure to scenes of aggression not only increased the likelihood of aggressive behaviour, but also influenced the form that it took, in that most of the children's aggressive actions mimicked those shown in the earlier scenes. On the other hand, the hypothesis that aggressive behaviour might be linked to the degree of realism of the scene was only partly confirmed; though the children exposed to the live scenes displayed more aggressiveness than those exposed to the cartoons, the difference only bordered on statistical significance. The researchers also investigated the influence of the child's gender (males showing a clearly greater propensity for aggressiveness than females), the relationship between the behaviour observed and the child's predisposition to aggressiveness (measured by the score attributed to previous behaviour), and further aspects which need not be detailed here. From this experiment, and from others conducted with the same kind of instruments, Bandura gleaned important findings regarding the influence of filmed (and especially televised) representations of violence, not only from the point of view of their reinforcement of aggressive tendencies, but also in the light of their ability to construct social behaviour, in that they are capable of suggesting ways of acting that human subjects would not otherwise adopt spontaneously.

5.2 Field experiments

Two examples of field experiments are reported here. The first concerns the studies carried out by Sherif (1967) on group dynamics, and in particular on the ways in which the notions of 'us' and 'them' are developed – that is to say, the mechanisms that lead to the formation of a feeling of solidarity towards members of one's own group (in-group) and hostility towards those who are outside the group (out-group).

Sherif's experiments lasted about three weeks and were conducted within the setting of a summer camp; the subjects were American children of 11–12 years of age, who did not know each other before the experiment. The period of the summer camp was subdivided into four phases. In the first phase, the children were left to interact freely and to form groupings spontaneously. In the second phase, the children were subdivided into two groups, lodged in different dormitories some distance apart, and engaged in separate activities that required them to work together and to overcome common difficulties. The new situation led to the development of close bonds of friendship, so much so that, although the groups had been drawn up in such a way as to split up the small groups of friends that had formed in the first phase, in the second phase 90% of the children chose their friends from within the new group (thus repudiating the previous friendships). In the third phase, the two groups were brought into contact through a range of competitive games structured in such a way as to create a conflict of interest between the two groups (with attractive prizes for the winning group). The relationship between the groups rapidly

changed from one of friendly rivalry to one of open hostility. Finally, in the fourth phase, the two groups in conflict were set objectives that could not be achieved by one group alone, but which required the cooperation of the other group. In short, the two groups began to interact again, hostility subsided, and bonds were formed which crossed the borders of the old groups. In this study, the independent variable was constituted by the group's objectives, and the dependent variable by the type of interpersonal relationships. The experiment shows that interpersonal relationships are conditioned by the structural setting in which the individuals are placed and have to act.

The second field experiment reported here is taken from the famous series of studies conducted by Rosenthal and Jacobson in the 1960s on the 'self- fulfilling prophecy', meaning that A's expectations regarding B's behaviour may actually prompt B to enact the expected behaviour (Rosenthal and Jacobson, 1968). These two authors applied this principle to the teacher-pupil relationship, and claimed that the underprivileged children of the American ethnic minorities often perform badly at school because that is precisely what is expected of them. For ethical reasons, in their experiment these researchers aroused positive (rather than negative) expectations in teachers with regard to some pupils, and showed that such enhanced expectations led to a real improvement in the performance of those pupils.

The experiment was structured as follows: at the end of the school year, the researchers administered an intelligence test to all the pupils of an American elementary school in a poor, immigrant neighbourhood, without revealing the true results to the teachers. At the beginning of the new school year, the researchers pointed out to the teachers 20% of the pupils – on average five per class – as pupils in whom a marked improvement could be expected. In reality, however, these children were not the ones who had obtained the highest scores on the test, but had been selected at random. During the school year, the test was again administered on various occasions, and the results demonstrated conclusively that the children from whom the teachers expected the greatest progress did indeed make such progress. This result can be attributed to some form of unconscious interaction between the teacher and the pupil: 'Her tone of voice, facial expression, touch and posture, may be the means by which – probably quite unwittingly – she communicates her expectations to the pupils. Such communication might help the child by changing his conception of himself ... his motivation or his cognitive skills' (Rosenthal and Jacobson, 1968: 23).

6. EXPERIMENTS AND QUASI-EXPERIMENTS

The distinction that has been drawn between laboratory and field experiments is based on the setting in which the experiment is conducted, regardless of the *experimental design*. The experimental design concerns the technical and organizational features which define the experiment: the number of experimental groups, the way in which the groups are made up, the number and types of independent variables, any repetition of observations, etc. Such characteristics may vary greatly and, when combined, give rise to a multitude of possible experimental designs. In the following pages, we will outline the most common types of design. Before doing so, however, we will examine the two basic aspects of the experimental design: the *assignment of subjects to groups* and the *manipulation of the independent variable*.

Assignment of subjects to groups. The best method of ensuring that groups will be homogeneous over the whole range of variables, except for slight haphazard differences, is *randomization*.[14] This yields so-called *equivalent* groups. If random assignment is not possible, an alternative method that can be adopted is *matching*. This consists of forming pairs[15] of subjects who are identical in terms of the

characteristics thought to be relevant to the issue that is being examined; one member of the pair is then assigned to the first group, and the other to the second group. This was the method adopted by Sampson and Laub in the research described in Chapter 2 (which actually was not an experiment). The sample studied by these authors was made up of 500 convicted criminals and 500 subjects without a criminal record; the members of the second group were chosen in such a way that each matched one subject in the first group in terms of socio-demographic features.

The superiority of random assignment over matching stems from the fact that the latter guarantees the equivalence of the two (or more) groups only with regard to the variables on which the formation of the pairs is based (the 'controlled' variables); we do not know, therefore, whether the subjects who make up the pairs differ in terms of other important features. Moreover, matching may be difficult to implement when formation of the pairs is based on several variables, in that some subjects may be left without a counterpart. Nevertheless, matching can be profitably used when, for any reason, randomization cannot be carried out, or when the groups taking part in the experiment are numerically small. Indeed, it should be remembered that randomization produces groups that differ only in terms of haphazard fluctuations. Such fluctuations are inversely proportional to the size of the groups, and may therefore be considerable if the groups are small. In such cases, it may be preferable to aim for complete control over a few important variables (matching) rather than having to deal with somewhat marked haphazard fluctuations in all the variables (randomization).

Randomization and matching are very often combined. This involves forming pairs of subjects that are identical in terms of a few basic variables, and then randomly assigning the members of each pair to the two groups. This ensures that the groups are identical in terms of the variables on which the formation of the pairs is based, while with regard to the other variables only haphazard fluctuations between the groups will be encountered. This procedure was followed by Bandura in drawing up the groups for his experiment on aggressiveness; the children assigned to the four groups were randomly selected from quartets of subjects of the same gender and attitude (aggressive/non-aggressive), so that these two variables were 'controlled' in the four groups (each 24-member group therefore contained 6 aggressive males and 6 non-aggressive males, 6 aggressive females and 6 non-aggressive females) (Bandura et al., 1963).

Manipulation of the independent variable. In experiments in the social sciences, the independent variable is normally (though not necessarily) a categorical variable; its variation among the experimental groups lies in the fact that each group displays a different value of this variable. For instance, mathematics may be taught to one class of pupils by means of an innovative method, and to another class by a traditional method; one group of subjects may be told that a certain picture has been painted by a man, and another that it has been painted by a woman; a particular film may be shown to one group and not to another; different working conditions may be imposed in three different departments of a factory, and so on.

It should be noted that the independent variable X may vary *among groups* or may vary over time within the *same group*, in that the different categories of X may be imposed on different groups at the same time or on the same group at different moments in time. A comparison between Bandura's study on the influence of televised violence and Sherif's study on group dynamics will illustrate the point.

In the former case, *different groups* of children were exposed to different values of the independent variable X: one group was not exposed to scenes of violence (X_1) while the other three groups were exposed to different modes of communication of scenes of violence (X_2, X_3 and X_4). In the latter case, the *same group* of children was exposed to four successive values of the variable X (structure of the relationship between the groups): the

subjects were first exposed to X_1 (no formal groupings), then to X_2 (separate groups involved in activities to reinforce internal cohesion), subsequently to X_3 (separate groups in competition), and finally to X_4 (cooperation between groups). In Bandura's experiment, the variable X differed among the groups (at the same time, since the experiment was conducted on all groups simultaneously); in Sherif's experiment, it varied within the same group (at different times, since the same group was exposed sequentially to different values of the variable X). Changing the independent variable within the same group of subjects – followed by recording of the dependent variable – may be regarded as a surrogate for randomization (instead of exposing equivalent groups to different values of X, the same group is exposed at different points in time).[16] Nevertheless, as we will see, this procedure is not risk-free, owing to the distortions that may arise when the same test is repeated, and to the time-lag between one test and the next.

In conclusion, the experiment must have two fundamental features: manipulation of the independent variable and random assignment of subjects to groups. If the first of these two is lacking, the study is to be regarded as research based on the analysis of covariation (although some authors classify particular cases of this situation as so-called *ex post facto* experiments). If the second condition is lacking, we have a so-called *quasi-experiment*. On the basis of this distinction, we will outline the principal types of experimental design, following the classic approach adopted by Campbell and Stanley (1963) who first introduced the distinction between experiments and quasi-experiments.

6.1. True experiments
In describing the various types of experimental design, we will use Campbell and Stanley's graphic representation, in which:

- R is the randomization of subjects to groups;

- *X* is the independent variable ('treatment' or 'stimulus' in the terminology of experimental psychology); and
- *Y* is the dependent variable ('observation' or 'response').

6.1.1 'Only-after', two (or more)-group design

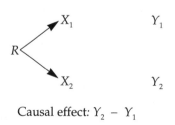

Causal effect: $Y_2 - Y_1$

The experiment is structured in three stages, which are graphically represented in the above figure by the sequence of the three letters *R*, *X* and *Y*: (a) the subjects are randomly assigned to two groups; (b) the independent variable is manipulated in such a way as to have the value X_1 in one group and X_2 in the other; and (c) the *mean value* of the dependent variable *Y* is recorded in the two groups. The causal effect brought about by the variation in *X* is measured as the difference $(Y_2 - Y_1)$. This experimental design is called 'only-after' because the dependent variable *Y* is measured *only-after* exposure to the experimental stimulus, rather than *before and after* exposure, as is the case of other experimental designs, which will be illustrated shortly.

This is the simplest of the designs that can be classified as a 'true experiment'. Nevertheless, it contains all the essential elements: random assignment, exposure to a stimulus, and recording of the dependent variable after exposure. Randomization ensures that the groups are *equivalent* before exposure to the stimulus – that is to say, they display the same *mean values* (except for haphazard fluctuations) over the whole range of variables. Thus, after exposure to the different values of the independent variable *X*, the two groups will differ only in terms of the value of this

variable. The difference between the mean values of the dependent variable $(Y_2 - Y_1)$ recorded in each group after the change in *X* can therefore be attributed to this manipulation.

In the simplest case, the two modes of the independent variable *X* are represented by 'presence/absence' – that is to say, exposure to the experimental stimulus (experimental group) or no exposure to the stimulus (control group). An application of this design would be obtained if we were to simplify Bandura's experiment on the influence of televised violence by reducing the number of groups to two (from the four actually used in the experiment described earlier). This would involve: (a) randomly assigning the children to two groups; (b) exposing only one of these groups to the televised scenes of violence; and (c) recording the behaviour of the children in the subsequent play session. The mean differences in behaviour between the two groups would, in this case, be attributable to exposure to the televised scenes, which is the only variable that differs between the two groups.

A variant of this design is *multiple-group design*, in which more than two values of the variable *X* are set. This was the design of Bandura's experiment, as described earlier, in which the variable *X* was given four values (absence of exposure, live scenes, filmed scenes, cartoons). The structure of the experiment is illustrated schematically below:

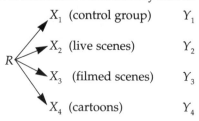

6.1.2 'Before-after', two (or more)-group design

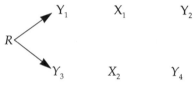

Causal effect: $(Y_4 - Y_3) - (Y_2 - Y_1)$

Unlike the previous experimental design, this design involves recording the dependent variable before, as well as after, exposure to the stimulus (hence the term 'before-after'). The two measurements of the dependent variable are also called *pre-test* and *post-test*. In this experimental design, variation in the independent variable *between groups* (when we compare the post-tests of the two groups) is combined with variation *over time within groups* (when we compare the pre-test and post-test of the same group).

This type of design is very often used in assessment studies, in order to evaluate the effectiveness of a programme aimed at producing modifications in the subjects targeted. For instance, we may wish to assess the effectiveness of a campaign to increase literacy by testing the language skills of the subjects before and after implementation of the programme, or the effectiveness of a political propaganda campaign by recording the subjects' political leanings before and after the campaign.

Strictly speaking, these objectives could also be achieved by means of the 'only-after, two-group design' illustrated earlier. If, for example, we wished to assess the influence of a televised debate between the leaders of two opposing political factions on voter orientation, we could proceed as follows: select a certain number of voters, assign them randomly to two groups, expose only one of these groups to the televised debate, and record voter orientation among the subjects the day after the debate. Since the subjects have been randomly assigned to the two groups, the political orientation of the groups should be the same, with the exception of slight haphazard variations. If, after exposure of only one of the two groups to the debate, differences emerge that are too great to be regarded as incidental, these can be attributed to the influence of the debate itself. The causal effect is therefore indicated by the difference between the mean orientations of the two groups $(Y_2 - Y_1)$.

The 'before-after, two-group' design adds a further measurement to this scheme: voter orientation before exposure to the televised debate (pre-test). In this case, the variation in orientation of the experimental group $(Y_4 - Y_3)$ minus the variation in orientation of the control group $(Y_2 - Y_1)$ represents the causal effect.

What advantage does this experimental design have over the previous one, or – in other words – what does the pre-test add? Indeed, *pre-testing is not essential in true experiments*, since randomization guarantees the initial equivalence of the two groups. Nevertheless, pre-testing does verify this equivalence. In the above example, the random assignment of subjects to the groups should result in two groups which have an equivalent mean political orientation before exposure to the experimental stimulus. However, the haphazard differences between the two groups may still be fairly great, especially if the groups are small. Consequently, the difference $Y_4 - Y_2$ between the two post-tests might be due to initial differences between the two groups (without the researcher's being able to ascertain this) rather than to the effect of the stimulus. Pre-testing therefore provides a means of ascertaining the real initial equivalence of the groups with regard to the dependent variable. Moreover, it enables the causal impact of the stimulus to be assessed even if the groups are not equivalent, given that it compares the *variation* in the orientation of the two groups rather than the absolute values of this orientation.[17]

There are, however, disadvantages to pre-testing; it may influence post-test responses, especially if the two tests are administered within a fairly short space of time. Let us suppose that we wish to study the influence on racial prejudice of a documentary film on the condition of black people by means of the following procedure: a pre-test conducted on an experimental group and a control group, exposure of the experimental group to the film, and a post-test on both groups. The post-test responses may be influenced by those of the pre-test, in that the respondent may realize, from being insistently asked what he thinks of black people, that the test is about racial prejudice, and therefore give a socially desirable response rather than expressing his true opinions. It may, however, be maintained that this distortion will be the same for both groups (since both have been pre- and post-tested) and will not therefore influence the differences between the two groups. Nevertheless, we cannot be sure that the pre-test will not influence the two groups in different ways, thereby introducing effects that are indistinguishable from the differences produced by exposure to the stimulus. For instance, those who see the film about black people may connect it with the pre-test questions, realize that the test is about racial prejudice, and give a distorted response to the post-test; the control group subjects, on the other hand, who are not exposed to the film, may not come to this realization. We are therefore faced with an *interaction effect* between the pre-test and the stimulus which may considerably distort the experiment. The experimental design outlined below was worked out to control just such an effect.

6.1.3 Solomon four-group design

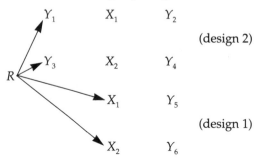

(design 2)

(design 1)

This experimental design combines the two previous designs, adding the advantages of the first (no interference by the pre-test) to those of the second (availability of the pre-test as a starting point before exposure to the stimulus). By means of simple differences (which we will not dwell upon here) among the six pre- and post-test values (Y_1 ..., Y_6), the effect of the stimulus can be separated from that of the interaction between pre-test and stimulus. This design is, however, more complex and

costly, since four groups are required to study the effect of only two values of the independent variable.

6.1.4 Factorial design

So far, we have considered only one independent variable (or stimulus) X, and our examples have dealt mainly with cases in which it assumes only two values (X_1 and X_2), often corresponding to absence/presence. It has, however, been pointed out that what has been said holds true when X_1 and X_2 stand for any values of the variable X; furthermore, it can easily be extended to cases involving more than two values of X (multiple-group design).

We have not yet looked at experimental designs involving more than one independent variable – so-called *factorial designs*. Nevertheless, in our exposition, we have already come across experiments with these characteristics. For example, the above-mentioned experiment on prejudice against women involved two independent variables: the gender of the artist and the success of the painting (and the experiment revealed that these two variables interacted, in that prejudice was manifested against unsuccessful women, but not against successful women).

An experiment on a similar theme was carried out by Costrich et al. (1975). These authors assembled four discussion groups, each made up of 5–8 subjects. In each group, they planted one individual who pretended to be an experimental subject like the others, but who was really playing a role assigned by the researchers. Two of these 'actors' were male and two were female; two (one male and one female) assumed a dominant role in the group, while the other two played a submissive role. After the discussion, the experimental subjects were asked to score the other members of the group, including the bogus subject, in terms of popularity-likableness. The experimenters hypothesized that these scores would be heavily influenced by the social stereotypes of behaviour deemed to be appropriate for men and for women.

In this experiment, two independent variables were used: the actor's gender X and behaviour Z. These variables are dichotomous (X_1 male, X_2 female, Z_1 dominant, Z_2 submissive) and give rise to what we call a 2×2 factorial design (this means that we have two independent variables or *factors*, each of which assumes two values). This design can be represented as follows:

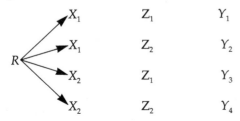

The above scheme shows that the subjects have been randomly assigned to four groups: in the first group, the variables X and Z have both been given a value of 1 (male actor, dominant behaviour); in the second group, the values are X_1 and Z_2 (male actor, submissive behaviour), and so on. If, however, the independent variable Z is given three values (e.g. dominant, submissive and neutral), the design will become 2×3 and require six groups (and therefore six actors). Similarly, if we wish to add to the initial 2×2 design a third independent variable (e.g. age, again dichotomized into 'young' and 'old'), the design becomes $2 \times 2 \times 2$ and there will be eight groups. Clearly, the experimental design rapidly becomes complicated as the number of independent variables increases.

The main advantage of the factorial design lies in the fact that it enables the researcher to study not only the isolated effect of the independent variables on the dependent variable (which could also be done through a sequence of simple experiments in which the independent variable is changed each time), but also the effect of the interaction between the independent variables. For instance, in the above-mentioned study by Costrich and co-workers, the popularity scores showed no significant difference between male and female actors, or between dominant and submissive behaviour. In other words, the variables gender and behaviour, when taken separately, did not influence popularity. However, this outcome

was the result of two opposing trends: the dominant woman and the submissive man proved to be highly unpopular, while the dominant man and the submissive woman enjoyed considerable popularity. In other words, both male and female were rejected by the group when they violated gender-linked stereotypes. In statistical terms, we can say that the two variables 'gender' and 'behaviour' showed a non-significant *main effect*, while their *interaction* proved to be highly significant. This finding would not have emerged from two separate experiments with a single independent variable; only a factorial design like the one described above can yield such a result.

6.2 Quasi-experiments

As already mentioned, and as Cook and Campbell pointed out in their classic treatise, quasi-experiments are 'experiments that have treatments, outcome measures, and experimental units (like true experiments), but do not use random assignment to create the comparisons from which treatment-caused change is inferred. Instead the comparisons depend on non-equivalent groups that differ from each other in many ways other than the presence of a treatment whose effects are being tested' (Cook and Campbell, 1979: 6).

The fact that the groups cannot be assumed to be equivalent before exposure to the stimulus clearly places a serious handicap on the logic of the experiment. Indeed, if the groups are not equivalent at the outset, the researcher cannot know whether the differences observed among the groups with regard to the values of the dependent variable are due to the initial non-equivalence or to the effect of the stimulus. Given the impossibility of separating the effect of the experimental stimulus from all the other effects, the researcher cannot draw causal inferences regarding the effect of the independent variable on the dependent variable. Consequently, some authors have gone so far as to deny legitimacy to the very existence of the category of quasi-experiments, claiming that it is a hybrid and confused classification.

In practice, however, it is often impossible in social research to assign subjects randomly to groups, particularly when the groups are pre-constituted (e.g. school classes, work departments, etc.). Nevertheless, experimental designs can be applied which are very close to the logic of 'true experiments', and which produce interesting results that cannot be obtained through research based on covariation analysis.

6.2.1 One-group, pre-test – post-test design

$$Y_1 \qquad X \qquad Y_2$$

Measured effect: $Y_2 - Y_1$

By definition, a true experiment is impossible to conduct on only one group. Nevertheless, the present experimental design is an important surrogate for the 'only-after', two (or more)-group design (cf. Subsection 6.1.1), in which one of the two groups is exposed to the stimulus while the other is not, and the dependent variable is subsequently recorded. In the present case, too, the dependent variable is observed both without exposure to the stimulus (Y_1) and after exposure (Y_2); the difference being that this time the two observations are carried out on the same group. The variation in X therefore occurs over time within the same group rather than between groups.

In other words, with regard to the two assumptions presented in Section 4, instead of the assumption of equivalence (between groups), we apply the assumption of invariance (of the same group). However, the assumption of invariance presupposes stability over time and non-interference on the part of the first measurement. We must therefore ensure that nothing – apart from the variation in X – occurs between the two observations Y_1 and Y_2 that might itself influence Y, thus contaminating the effect of the stimulus. At the same time, the pre-test must not influence the post-test.

Let us go back to our previous example on the effect of political propaganda on voter orientation. If we record which way a group of people intend to vote, expose them to the stimulus of a televised debate between candidates, and then re-record their intention to vote, we cannot be sure that any change in the mean orientation of the group is due to exposure to the televised debate. In the time between the two measurements, the orientation of the experimental subjects may have been decisively influenced by uncontrolled external events (reading political commentary in the newspapers, discussion with other members of the family, news of the economic situation, etc.).

For these reasons, we should ensure that the time-lag between the pre-test and the post-test is not too long. In doing so, however, we encounter the other risk; if only a short time elapses between the two tests, it is quite plausible that the post-test may be influenced by the pre-test. Thus, Y_2 may differ from Y_1 not as a result of the stimulus X, but on account of learning effects or memory effects (or other effects due to the fact that Y_2 is preceded by Y_1).

It should be noted that, among the 'true experiments' examined earlier, these two sources of distortion are null. They are absent from experimental design 1 (only after two (or more)-group), since it involves only one test, and consequently neither the problem of the inter-test interval nor that of the influence of the pre-test on the post-test arises; while in experimental design 2, the before-after two (or more)-group design, both sources are present, but are annulled by the use of the control group (both effects being present to the same degree in both the experimental and control groups).

To sum up, in spite of its severe shortcomings, this type of quasi-experimental design can still provide us with useful information. Indeed, researchers are frequently called upon to assess the impact of a given programme in situations in which no control group is available. Nevertheless, this design should only be adopted when other experimental or quasi-experimental designs cannot be applied.

6.2.2 Interrupted time-series design

$$Y_1 \qquad Y_2 \qquad Y_3 \qquad X \qquad Y_4 \qquad Y_5 \qquad Y_6$$

Again, this is a one-group design. It differs from the previous design, however, in one important respect; in order to avoid the risk that the difference in the value of Y before and after exposure to the stimulus may be due to an ongoing trend in Y rather than to the effect of the stimulus itself, this design compares not the mean values of Y but its *trend* over time before and after the stimulus.

The design involves serial recording of the dependent variable Y; at some point in the series, a variation in the independent variable X is introduced with a view to ascertaining whether this produces a variation in the trend of Y. Let us take the example of a school in which indicators of indiscipline among students are steadily rising. If at some point a radical change is made in the life of the school (new code of discipline, change of head teacher, student self-management, etc.), we can observe the effect that this might have on the indicators of discipline.

Compared with the previous design (only two measurements of Y), this design offers two advantages: first, any influence of the pre-test on the post-test will be slight (since this influence is present in all observations of Y except the first); and second, little interference can be expected from uncontrolled external events that take place between two successive measurements (since such events may occur during any of the intervals – between Y_1 and Y_2, Y_2 and Y_3, etc. – and not only in concomitance with the change in X). Thus, if a variation in the trend of Y is recorded between Y_3 and Y_4 in concomitance with the change in X, it is unlikely that this will be due to the effect of the pre-test Y_3 or to the intervention of other unknown factors. It can therefore be plausibly attributed to a causal action of X.

Clearly, this design is applicable only in particular cases such as, for example, in assessing the effects of a change in legislation. A design of this kind was used to study the controversial effect of pornography on sex crimes. In Denmark in the middle of the 1960s, liberalization of the law led to an increase in the publication of pornographic material. A simple 'before-after' analysis (rate of sex crimes after enactment of the law minus the previous rate) would have been misleading in this case, as the rate of sex crimes had been declining since 1956. The availability of a time series of data regarding the dependent variable (rate of sex crimes) enabled an 'interrupted time-series design' to be applied. This revealed that the new legislation had indeed contributed positively to this falling trend (Kutchinsky, 1973). The same method was used by Wagenaar (1981) in Michigan to assess the effect of raising the age limit for the purchase of alcohol on the rate of drink-related road accidents.

6.2.3 'Before-after' two-group design without randomization

$$\begin{array}{ccc} Y_1 & X_1 & Y_2 \\ \hline Y_3 & X_2 & Y_4 \end{array}$$

Measured effect: $(Y_4 - Y_3) - (Y_2 - Y_1)$

The scheme that illustrates this quasi-experimental design is similar to that of the 'before-after' two (or more)-group experimental design (cf. Subsection 6.1.2), with the difference that the letter R (for 'randomization') and the arrows pointing to the two groups have been replaced by a horizontal line between the groups; this indicates their separate origin and non-equivalence.

This quasi-experimental design is frequently used and is a very good surrogate for true experiments when random assignment to groups is impossible. The method involves taking two groups, pre-testing both, exposing only one of the groups to the stimulus, and then post-testing both. The presence of a control group eliminates the distortions due to events taking place between the two tests and to the influence of the pre-test on the post-test, since such effects will be present in both groups and will not therefore influence the differences between them. Naturally, the fact remains that the two groups are not equivalent, as they have not been randomized. However, the pre-test provides information on the pre-existing differences between the groups, thereby enabling the researcher to work not with the absolute values of the dependent variable, but rather with the post-test/pre-test variation, which will be only partly influenced by the pre-test level.

For example, if we wish to assess the efficacy of a new teaching method at school (e.g. the use of audio-visual aids in foreign language teaching), we can compare two classes, one of which is exposed to the new method and the other to the traditional method, and measure the increases in student performance from the beginning to the end of the experiment. Such increases should be only modestly affected by the different initial levels of the two classes (especially if care is taken to choose classes with similar levels of performance).

6.2.4 'Ex post facto' design

$$\frac{X_1}{X_2} \quad \text{Matching} \quad \frac{Y_1}{Y_2}$$

The name quasi-experiment has been given to those situations in which the experimenter cannot randomly assign subjects to experimental groups, but can still manipulate the independent variable. However, when even such manipulation is impossible – that is to say, when the stimulus is also beyond the control of the researcher – we can no longer speak of experimentation; what we have is, purely and simply, an analysis of covariation. Nevertheless, there are research situations which, although lacking both features of experimentation (i.e. randomization and manipulation), involve a design that closely resembles that of experimentation. Such designs are called *ex post facto* (as they are drawn up after the fact). While they cannot be classified as true experiments or quasi-experiments, they are usually dealt with in chapters on experimentation in methodology manuals, in that they are based on the logic of experimentation in terms of both research design and data analysis.

They are generally structured as follows. After an event has already taken place – that is to say, a group of subjects has already been exposed to a given stimulus – another group is formed comprising subjects with characteristics as similar as possible to those of the first group, but who have not been exposed to the stimulus. The means of the dependent variable are then compared between the two groups. The above scheme illustrates this procedure: one group of subjects has been exposed to X_1 (which may also mean non-exposure to the stimulus), and another has been exposed to X_2; the subjects are then 'matched' – that is to say, pairs are formed by selecting subjects (one from each group) who are identical in terms of a range of characteristics established by the researcher; the dependent variable Y is then recorded in the two groups thus formed.

An example of an *ex post facto* design can be seen in a study conducted by Goldfarb (1945) on the effects of institutionalization in children (independent variable X). On comparing 40 children who had spent two years in an orphanage before being adopted with 40 children brought up since birth in families with the same characteristics as those of the adoptive families, he found a higher incidence of personality disorders among the children who had been institutionalized. A similar design has been adopted in numerous studies on twins brought up separately; in such cases, the subjects are assumed to be extremely similar – being twins – over a range of base characteristics, while their experiences (independent variable X) differ.

A further example of this approach, though in a completely different setting, is provided by studies on the effects of earthquakes on the mental state of victims. Such studies have compared villages hit by earthquakes with similar villages that have not been hit. For instance, in a study conducted in South America, the population of some villages totally destroyed by an earthquake was compared with that of other villages that had the same economic and cultural conditions but which had emerged unscathed, in spite of being situated in the same valley.

7. A FINAL NOTE: ADVANTAGES AND LIMITATIONS OF EXPERIMENTATION

Experimentation in the social sciences offers two basic advantages. First, it is the research method that best enables us to tackle the problem of the causal relationship. Second, it allows us to isolate specific phenomena which could not be studied equally systematically in their natural setting, owing to the presence of other factors that hide, confuse and distort them, or on account of the background 'noise' of everyday life, which would mask the signal of the less evident phenomena.

Clearly, however, this approach is only applicable to certain phenomena and certain social situations. An experiment cannot be conducted if the independent variable cannot be manipulated, whether owing to intrinsic difficulties or for ethical reasons. Moreover, the method is generally applicable to 'micro' issues (involving interpersonal relationships) rather than to 'macro' situations (on account of the difficulty of manipulating institutions or social groups).

Experimentation consists of observing an artificial situation, the characteristics of which are established by the researcher himself. The causes of disturbance are reduced to a minimum, those which directly produce the phenomenon are studied by means of gradual variations, and the experiment is repeatable. However, it is this very flexibility in establishing the conditions that constitutes the principal limitation of the experiment. Broadly speaking, the disadvantages of the experimental method as applied to the social sciences can be summarized under two headings: *artificiality* and *non-representativeness*.

7.1 Artificiality

The problem of artificiality can be subdivided into two areas: *artificiality of the setting* and *reactivity of the experimental subjects*. With regard to artificiality of the setting, we may think back to the example of Milgram's (1974) experiments on submission to authority. These were conducted in a laboratory and simulated a relationship to authority that was somewhat unnatural and very different from the situations of authority-submission encountered in real life. Similarly, in Bandura's experiment (Bandura et al., 1963), the effects produced on the children by exposure to televised scenes of violence in the artificial setting created by the researcher may have been different from the effects produced in a reassuring domestic environment. Obviously this problem is more acutely felt in laboratory experiments than in field experiments.

The second point concerns the reaction of the human subject to the feeling of being observed. Unlike the chemist or physicist handling inanimate matter, the researcher who deals with living beings is faced with the risk that the experiment itself may elicit unforeseen effects on the phenomenon under examination. A person who knows that she is being observed, no less than an animal that is caged or immobilized, may behave differently from how she would behave in the natural environment. Returning again to the famous Hawthorne experiments mentioned in Chapter 3 (subsection 2.3) it should be remembered that the awareness of being under observation prompted the workers to increase their productivity regardless of the change in working conditions.

One form of reactivity is the so-called *experimenter effect*, whereby the experimenter's expectations are unconsciously transferred to the experimental subjects, thus influencing their behaviour. As we have seen, Rosenthal and Jacobson's experiment revealed that expectations (in that case, the teachers) are able to influence the behaviour of the individuals who are the focus of those expectations (in that case, the pupils). However, Rosenthal (1966) obtained similar results even on animals. In an experiment involving rats, he told the experimenters (in this case, students) that some rats were 'lively' and that others were 'stupid' (in reality, the rats had been randomly assigned to the two groups). The experimenters who worked with the so-called lively rats obtained better results (it turned out that the students working with these rats treated them in a friendly way, stimulated them gently and encouraged them verbally more than the other students had done with the so-called stupid rats).

The problem of reactivity arises more forcefully in laboratory experiments, in which it is difficult, if not impossible, to conceal from the subjects the fact that they are taking part in an experiment. However, it may also constitute a considerable source of interference in many field experiments.

7.2 Non-representativeness

The second disadvantage is *non-representativeness*, meaning that the results of an experiment often cannot be generalized to an entire population or to sectors of the population which differ from that of the study population. There are two reasons for this: the *sample size* and *selection criteria* of the experimental subjects.

The first problem stems from the fact that experiments can normally be conducted only on very limited samples. In the examples we have quoted, the experimental groups were made up of small numbers of subjects (on average about 20, but frequently fewer). While this restriction is clear with regard to laboratory experiments, it also affects field experiments, in that it is not possible to alter the independent variable and control all the other variables when the sample is very large. This limitation undermines the representativeness of the sample. Indeed, sampling errors are inversely proportional to sample size; consequently, a small sample will have a large sampling error and will therefore be poorly representative of the population from which it has been extracted. Thus, the results obtained will be difficult to generalize (this issue will be dealt with specifically in Chapter 8).

The second problem concerns the selection of subjects. Precisely because experimental groups cannot be deemed to be representative samples of an entire population, the experimenter often fails to tackle the question of what criteria to apply in selecting subjects for the experiment. As a result, instead of representing a certain – albeit limited – social group, the subjects may be chosen, for reasons of convenience, from

within a single social environment. Very often, for example, the experimental subjects are university students – clearly a very particular segment of the population and certainly somewhat unrepresentative of the public at large.

It should, however, be added that the aim of experimentation is not to describe how a given phenomenon is manifested in society (there are much more effective techniques for doing this in social research), but rather to analyse cause-effect relationships. And such relationships can in fact be studied even in specific situations and in particular segments of the population.

These criticisms and limitations should not conceal the fact that the experimental method has yielded valuable results throughout the history of social research. Moreover, there are issues that can be studied only by this method. Leslie Kish tells the story of a man who drank too much on four separate occasions. Once he drank Scotch and soda; the second time Bourbon and soda; then rum and soda, and finally wine and soda. Each time he ended up drunk. With rigorous scientific logic, he concluded, 'I'll never touch another drop of soda' (Kish, 1959: 333). And indeed it is difficult to avoid attributing the man's drunkenness to the effect of the soda if we apply covariation analysis. It is precisely in situations of this kind that experimentation comes to our aid; the flexibility of this method and the possibility of constructing experiments that differ from one another with regard to one single element (which, in this case, would involve administering soda alone) enable us to discover a truth that covariation analysis would not reveal.

In conclusion, experimentation is a social research technique that is very well suited to specific, circumscribed issues: group analysis, the dynamics of interaction among individuals, and all those phenomena that occur in limited segments of space, time and number of persons involved. Hence its development – in sociology – at the so-called 'micro' level and, especially, its success in psychology and social psychology.

SUMMARY

1. Although the cause-effect relationship is the very basis of scientific reasoning, it is one of the most difficult to translate into operational terms. However, even though the existence of a causal law can never be empirically proven, hypothesizing a causal relationship at the theoretical level implies observing facts. Such empirical observations cannot provide definitive evidence of a causal link, but they can corroborate the hypothetical existence.

2. In order to empirically corroborate the hypothesis of a causal relationship between two variables, three empirical elements are needed: covariation between the independent and dependent variables, direction of causality, and control of extraneous variables.

3. Scientists may use two different techniques of empirical testing of causal statements: *covariation analyses* or *experimentation*. In the first case, the researcher *observes* and analyses how the variations in X relate to the variations in Y in a natural setting, and through subset comparison or statistical control he may exclude the influence of all extraneous variables. In the second case he produces a variation in X in a controlled situation (the random assignment of subjects to one of two groups provides a way of controlling all other variables), and measures how much Y subsequently varies.

4. The experiment is a form of experiencing natural facts in which deliberate human intervention produces change; as such it distinguishes itself from forms of experience involving the observation of facts in their natural settings.

   If we wish to assess the effect of variable X on variable Y – that is, record states on Y when $X = t$ (treatment) and $X = c$ (control), we cannot do so on the same unit at the same point in time. This is the 'fundamental problem of causal inference'. Nevertheless, there are two practical solutions to this problem. The *scientific solution* is possible if we can adopt either the assumption of invariance (the value of Y_c can be substituted by a measure of the same Y_c recorded earlier) or the assumption of equivalence (the value of Y_c is substituted by a measure of the same Y_c recorded on a different but equivalent unit). The scientific solution usually isn't applicable in social science, unlike the *statistical solution*, which resembles the scientific solution based on the assumption of equivalence, but differs from it in that it deals with groups of individuals that are statistically equivalent, rather than with two identical units. Such groups are obtained through *randomization*: the initial sample of experimental subjects is subdivided into two groups by randomly assigning the subjects to one group or the other.

5. In the social sciences, experiments can be subdivided into laboratory experiments and field experiments: in the first case the experiment is carried out in an artificial situation, whereas in the second a real-life setting is used. Laboratory experiments can be classified into impact studies, judgement studies and observational studies.

6. An experiment must have two fundamental features: manipulation of the independent variable and random assignment of subjects to groups (randomization). If the first feature is lacking, we no longer have an experiment, but a study based on covariation analysis. If the second condition is lacking, we have a so-called 'quasi-experiment'. Therefore we can classify experimental designs into two groups: 'true' experiments and quasi-experiments.

FURTHER READING

For a brief discussion of causation, its application in sociological research and the use of statistics, see J.H. Goldthorpe, *Causation, Statistics, and Sociology*, in Goldthorpe (2000). To explore the analysis of cause-effect relationships when experimental designs are infeasible, see the statistically oriented review by C. Winship and S. Morgan, 'The Estimation of Causal Effects from Observational Data', *Annual Review of Sociology* 1999.

A classic description of experimental and quasi-experimental designs is the 'old' essay by D.T. Campbell and J.C. Stanley, *Experimental and Quasi-experimental Designs for Research* (Rand McNally 1963, pp. 84). A more detailed treatment is offered by T.D. Cook and D.T. Campbell, *Quasi-experimentation: Design and Analysis Issues for Field Settings* (Houghton Mifflin, 1979, pp. 405).

R. Pawson and N. Tilley, in *Realistic Evaluation* (Sage, 1997, pp. 235), develop a critique of the classical approach to experiments and place special emphasis on their applications in the field of evaluation.

Novel applications of experimental logic are set forth by P.M. Sniderman and D.B. Grob, 'Innovations in Experimental Design in Attitude Surveys', *Annual Review of Sociology* 1996).

NOTES

1. In this brief treatment, we have adopted Bunge's definition, which attributes the features of *necessity, sufficiency*, and *universality* to the concept of cause. It is a rigorous but restrictive vision; however, it is not the task of the present work to debate this point.

2. In experimental psychology, the terms *stimulus* and *response* are used to indicate the variables involved in the causal relationship. Again the formal causal models (such as path analysis or structural equation models) use the econometric terminology, which splits the variables into *exogenous* (external to the model, only independent) and *endogenous* (inside the model; these may be independent in some relationships and dependent in others). However, these differences are almost entirely terminological and reflect only slightly differing views of the causal relationship. For the sake of simplicity, the terms 'dependent' and 'independent' will be used almost exclusively in the following pages.

3. 'Covariation' means, literally, that two variables co-vary, i.e. vary together. This type of association is also called 'correlation'. The two terms should be kept separate, however: 'covariation' refers to the conceptual level, whereas 'correlation' has to do with statistical operations (correlation indices, correlation coefficients) performed on data.

4. This is a typical case of a so-called 'spurious' relationship: a third variable – in this case the degree of urbanization – influences both ice cream consumption and support for the Radical Party.

5. In scientific terms, the meaning of 'chance' or 'random' differs from that used in everyday language (e.g. 'haphazard', 'taking the first thing that comes along', etc.); here, it refers to a specific procedure that implies a drawing of lots (or an equivalent, like the use of random number tables). This issue will be discussed further in Chapter 8.

6. In the text we refer to an ideal situation. In fact one is never certain – not even in the experiments of the physical sciences – that *all* other possible causes of variation of the dependent variable are under control.

7. The origins of the application of experimentation to the social sciences and the modern concept of experimental design are attributed to Sir Ronald Fisher (1935). In 1920s England, at the Rothamstead Experimental Station, he planned agricultural experiments in which he used randomization to control extraneous variables and formulated the procedures of factorial design, thus working out its statistical underpinnings and laying down the bases of the 'statistical' application (opposed, as we shall see, to the 'scientific' application in physics) of the experimental method, which rapidly extended to the field of psychology.

8. In the following pages, we will use the terminology of experimental psychology and thus call the two values of X 'treatment' (t) and 'control' (c). 'Treatment' means exposure of a unit of analysis to a certain value of X; 'control' means exposure to another value which serves as a term of reference. In many cases this reference consists of 'absence of treatment', but not always (it may mean a different treatment). For example, we may have individuals exposed ($X = t$) and not exposed ($X = c$) to television propaganda; or individuals to whom mathematics is taught as set theory ($X = t$) or in a traditional way ($X = c$).

9. This part of the chapter adopts the approach developed by the statistical school which follows the so-called 'Rubin model' (Rubin 1974); in particular, I am indebted to Holland's contribution (1986).

10. This is due to the fact that, in this experiment, the descending weights perform a known quantity of work, and the rise in the temperature is also known (measurable). In Joule's experiment the independent variable, X, is mechanical energy, and the dependent variable, Y, is the temperature: by varying the mechanical energy, he produced a variation in temperature, and this variation represents the causal effect.

11. For the sake of simplicity, we have ignored measurement errors; in reality the experiment will involve numerous repetitions of trials, and the 'causal effect' will be the average of the various temperature differences recorded.

12. 'Memory effects' (as in this case) and 'learning effects' (e.g. in a test of ability repeated after exposure to some treatment) are among the most common sources of interference that may arise when a measurement is repeated on the same subjects. This issue will be taken up again in Section 6, with regard to 'before-after' experiments.

13. Randomization ensures the equivalence of the groups; thus, the logic illustrated earlier under the heading *assumption of equivalence* (in that case applied to two units) is applied to groups. Randomization can also be used to apply the logic underlying the *assumption of invariance* – again with regard to groups and therefore in a 'statistical' perspective.

In the first case, Y_c and Y_t are recorded in two groups, and randomization serves to ensure the equivalence of the two groups. In the second case, Y_c and Y_t are recorded in the same subjects (one measures Y_c, changes X and then measures Y_t), and randomization serves to control the group's invariance over time. If, for example, we record voter preference (Y_c) in a group of citizens, expose them to a television debate and then re-record their preference (Y_t), the mean difference $Y_t - Y_c$ can be attributed to the effect of exposure to the debate *plus* the influence of other variables that have intervened in the time between the two measurements (e.g. the disclosure of good news about the country's economy, which raises the popularity of the incumbent candidate). However, if we record the preferences of a control group (which is not exposed to the television debate) at the same time as we record those of the experimental group, we will be able to establish the mean effect of such extraneous variables, since the control group will only be affected by these variables, *not* by the television debate. Subtracting this mean effect from the mean variation in the voter preference of the experimental group enables us to ascertain the effect of the television debate *alone*.

The 'statistical solution' can therefore be applied, at the statistical and therefore group level, to solve problems raised by the implausibility – at the level of the single unit – of the assumptions of equivalence *and* invariance.

14. It should be pointed out that randomization does not necessarily involve separating the subjects physically. It can be done covertly. For example, to study the effectiveness of a propaganda campaign to increase voter turnout in political elections, one could randomly select half the names registered in the electoral rolls of a given constituency, expose these voters to propaganda (door-to-door canvassing, hand-bills in the letterbox, etc.) and, after the election, check the electoral rolls to see if voter turnout was higher among those exposed to the propaganda than among the other half.

15. In the following presentation, for the sake of simplicity, we will refer to 'pairs' of subjects, assuming that the experiment involves only two groups (ideally: the experimental group and control group). In practice, however, the number of groups depends on the number of values of the independent variable X; when there are more than two groups (as is often the case), the matching procedure will involve forming triplets, quartets, etc. of subjects who are identical in terms of the controlled variables.

16. The reader is reminded of the distinction introduced in Section 4 (particularly Note 13) between the assumption of equivalence and the assumption of invariance: variation between groups is linked to the assumption of equivalence, while variation within the same group is linked to the assumption of invariance.

17. Let us return to what was said in Section 4 (particularly Note 13). In this design, the control group serves to control – at the statistical level – both the assumption of equivalence

(between the two groups) and the assumption of invariance (in the experimental group between pre-test and post-test). Indeed:

$(Y_4 - Y_2)$: causal effect + effect of any non-equivalence equal to $(Y_3 - Y_1)$

$(Y_4 - Y_2) - (Y_3 - Y_1)$: causal effect purged of non-equivalence

$(Y_4 - Y_3)$: causal effect + effect of any non-invariance equal to $(Y_2 - Y_1)$

$(Y_4 - Y_3) - (Y_2 - Y_1)$: causal effect purged of non-invariance.

Note that $(Y_4 - Y_2) - (Y_3 - Y_1) = (Y_4 - Y_3) - (Y_2 - Y_1)$.

5   The Survey

The survey – the most widespread quantitative social research technique – is the object of this chapter, which discusses its theoretical and practical features. First we examine the basic issues one faces when collecting data by asking questions (standardization of procedures and reliability of verbal behaviour); then we address practical problems which occur when conducting a survey: question wording, questionnaire administration, data entry and so on. The main data sets and archives available in the US and the UK are also mentioned.

1.   SURVEYS IN SOCIAL RESEARCH

In everyday life, if we wish to examine a given social phenomenon, whether it be individual (such as the doctor-patient relationship) or collective (such as crowd behaviour in a sports stadium), we basically have two ways of gathering information: observing and asking. While observation is the most direct and immediate way of studying openly manifested behaviours, the only way we can explore motivation, attitudes, beliefs, feelings, perceptions and expectations is by asking.

The situations in which information is gathered through direct questioning of the subjects involved in the social phenomena under investigation vary enormously, ranging from journalistic inquiry to market research, public opinion polls, censuses, etc. The specific data-collection tool dealt with in this chapter is the *survey*. By the term 'survey', we mean a technique of gathering information:

- by questioning,
- those individuals who are the object of the research,
- belonging to a representative sample,
- through a standardized questioning procedure,
- with the aim of studying the relationships among the variables.

Let us analyse the five ingredients of this complex definition. First of all, conducting a survey involves asking questions, either orally (as is most often the case) or in writing. This may take the form of a face-to-face conversation, a telephone interview or the completion of a questionnaire; in all cases, questions are asked and answered.

These questions are addressed directly to those individuals who constitute the object of research. Thus, in a study on the social conditions of prison inmates, it is the inmates themselves who are interviewed; if the study involves soccer fans, then the fans themselves will be questioned, and so on. From this point of view, the survey approach differs from that of research conducted through interviews with so-called 'key informants'. For example, the same research into prison conditions could be carried out by interviewing persons whose professional role endows them with in-depth knowledge of the issue (prison governors, probation officers, social workers, psychologists, etc.), instead of the prisoners themselves. Likewise, with regard to football supporters, we could interview sports journalists or hardcore fans. But we would not be conducting 'surveys' in the sense we intend here.

Since the population under investigation is normally made up of a large number of individuals, the practical impossibility of questioning all of them demands that a sample of subjects be picked out for interview. In the above definition, this sample is described as being 'representative'; this means that the sample must be able to reproduce, on a small scale, the characteristics of the entire population under examination (so that the results obtained on the sample can be generalized to the whole population). The sample subjects must therefore be selected according to precise rules established by statistics (Chapter 8 is entirely devoted to this issue), and the sample itself has to be of considerable size (exploratory studies conducted on small numbers of subjects are not therefore classed as surveys).

According to our definition, the sample subjects must be questioned by means of a standardized procedure. This means that all subjects are asked the same questions in the same manner. Standardization of the stimulus is a fundamental feature of the survey and is aimed at ensuring that the answers can be compared and analysed statistically. If some members of a sample of young people are asked what feelings their national anthem arouses in them, while others are asked about the feelings aroused by the nation's flag, it will be impossible to say whether any differences recorded are due to real differences among the respondents or to some difference between the stimuli (questions). Similarly, if we know the religious practice of some subjects, but not of others, we will not be able to determine, on the total number of cases, whether or not there is a relationship between religious practice and political orientation, for example.

A survey is made up of two parts: the question and the answer. Both of these may be formulated in a standard way; alternatively, they may be freely expressed. Let us imagine an interview situation in which the same question is asked with the same wording (e.g. 'Are you interested in politics?') and the interviewee is required to answer by choosing one of four pre-established options (e.g. 'very, somewhat, a little, not at all'). In this case, both the question and the answer are standardized. In another situation, the subject may be asked the same standardized question, but this time be allowed to answer freely (e.g. the answer to the question above might be, 'It depends. I take an interest during election campaigns because everyone talks about it and I've got to decide which way to vote, but apart from that, I don't bother at all'). The third case is one in which the question is not standardized. For instance, the interviewer knows that she has to bring up the issue of interest in politics during the interview, but is free to formulate the questions in the way she thinks fit, according to the characteristics of the interviewee and how the interview itself progresses.

BOX 5.1   DATA MATRIX

In order to analyze the data by means of statistical techniques, not only the questions, but also the answers, will have to be standardized – that is to say, organized on the basis of a classification scheme that is common to all subjects. Once the data have been collected, the *data-matrix* will be produced; this constitutes the basis of all subsequent statistical elaboration. Since the same information is recorded on all the cases studied, this information can be organized in the form of a rectangular matrix of numbers, the so-called 'cases by variables' (C × V) matrix. This matrix reports the variables in columns and the cases in rows; in each cell created (where a row intersects a column) a single datum is reported – that is to say, the value of a particular variable in a particular case. For example, a matrix of 200 (rows) × 50 (columns) presupposes 200 cases (for instance, individuals) in which the same 50 variables have been recorded (one individual – the same – for each row; one variable – the same – for each column of the matrix).

Combining the features of standardization/ freedom of question/answers produces the structure illustrated in Figure 5.1, which gives rise to three different data-gathering tools (the fourth possibility does not exist in practice):

- the *questionnaire*, when the question and answer are standardized;
- the *structured interview*, when only the question is standardized and the answer is expressed freely; and
- the *unstructured interview*, when neither questions nor answers are standardized.

In the first case, the interviewer refers to a written text, which reports the exact wording of the questions and lists the possible answers. In the second case, the interviewer again uses a written text specifying the wording and the order of the questions. In the third case, only a checklist of the items to be covered is provided, and the order and formulation of questions is left to the interviewer's discretion. In this chapter, we will only deal with the first technique: the questionnaire. Structured and unstructured interviews will be dealt with later (Chapter 10)

in our discussion of the techniques of qualitative research.

The survey has a long history in social research. The idea of gathering information by questioning the subjects studied was applied long ago by Marx and also by Weber. In 1880, Marx sent out 25,000 copies of a questionnaire to the readers of 'Revue socialiste', asking them to comment on their living conditions (this forerunner of the mail questionnaire met with such a modest response that the data were not even analysed, cf. Bottomore and Rubel, 1956). On several occasions between 1880 and 1910, Weber also used questionnaires to study such social issues as working conditions in the rural areas of Eastern Prussia (questionnaires were mailed to farm owners and Protestant pastors) and the effects of working in large factories on the personality and lifestyle of the workers (by means of questionnaires submitted both to key informants and to a sample of the workers themselves, cf. Lazarsfeld and Oberschall, 1965). We might also mention the great investigations carried out in England a century ago under the impetus of the social reform movements, whose objective was to gather

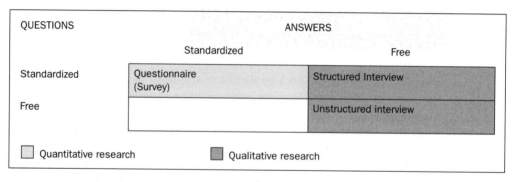

FIGURE 5.1 *Techniques of data collection through questioning*

information on the living conditions of the poor, the workers and the underprivileged. The underlying conviction of these early studies was that, until the nature and extent of these problems had been gauged, very little could be done to tackle them.

The real breakthrough in the field of survey techniques took place when the concept of representativeness became established and sampling procedures were introduced. This stemmed from the realization that, in order to ascertain the distribution of a certain number of characteristics in a given population, it was not necessary to study the entire population, and that a study conducted on a properly selected sample could produce equally accurate results (indeed, more accurate, in that the resources saved by reducing the breadth of data collection could be channelled into improving its quality). This principle, which was theoretically systematized in the middle of the 1930s in the writings of the Polish statistician Jerzy Neyman, rapidly took root and paved the way for the extraordinary success of the survey.

In more recent times (since the 1980s) two technological developments have given the survey a great boost. On the one hand, the increased availability of personal computers has enabled individual researchers to handle masses of data rapidly and directly; on the other hand, the diffusion of the telephone (among Western populations) has given rise to the widespread use of telephone interviews,

thus drastically reducing interview costs, which have always been an obstacle to the diffusion of the survey method.

2.   STANDARDIZATION, OR THE INVARIANCE OF THE STIMULUS

A researcher who attempts to investigate reality by questioning the social actors themselves is faced with some fundamental problems. In the final analysis, these can be traced back to the basic distinctions (ontological, epistemological and methodological) that separate and contrast what we defined in Chapter 1 as being the two base paradigms of social research: the contrast between the approach based on the positivist tradition (including its 'neo-' and 'post-' versions) and the approach which derives from *Verstehen*, and which we have called interpretivism. Two dilemmas appear to be particularly relevant.

2.1 Objectivist versus constructivist approach

The first dilemma concerns the contrast between the view that social reality exists outside the researcher and is fully and objectively knowable, and the view that the very act of knowing alters reality, which means that knowable reality can only be that which is generated by the interaction between the subject who studies and the subject that is studied. Thus, in the two extreme statements of these views, we find, on the one hand, a position that could be defined as *objectivist* (social data can be recorded objectively through a process not unlike that of 'observation' in the natural sciences) and, on the other, a position that could be defined as *constructivist* (according to which social data are not observed, collected or recorded, but 'constructed' or 'generated' in the interaction between the subject studied and the subject studying).

In the field of the survey, this dilemma opens up the problem of the *relationship between the interviewer and the interviewee*, contrasting detached impersonal recording versus empathetic interaction. The objectivist approach holds that the interviewer-interviewee relationship should be completely impersonal. The interviewer's main concern should be to avoid altering the subject studied. Interaction with the subject, which not even the most ardent advocate of the objectivist position would deny, is seen as a necessary evil, a negative factor to be kept to the minimum. Consequently, the interviewer is obliged to comply with codes of behaviour designed to achieve total neutrality and uniformity. The following recommendation is taken from an old edition of the 'interviewer's manual' of the best-known survey institute in the US, which for decades was a leading light in the field:

> Be careful that nothing in your words or manner implies criticism, surprise, approval or disapproval … have a normal tone of voice, an attentive way of listening, and a nonjudgmental manner … If the respondent asks for an explanation of a word or phrase, you should refrain from offering help and return the responsibility for the definition to the respondent … If for example the question asks 'Do you feel you personally have been discriminated against?' and the respondent inquires, 'Do you mean discriminated against socially or in my job?' you should say something such as 'Just whatever it means to you'. If the respondent … says, 'I don't understand the question', do not try to … explain it but go on to the next question'. (ISR, 1976: 11–13)

According to the advocates of this approach, which is clearly expressed in some of the classical social research manuals of the 1950s and 1960s, this does not mean that the interviewer has to be cold or remote. On the contrary, 'Through a variety of signals, you can indicate to the respondent that he is doing a good job of answering the questions' (ISR: 13); and again, the interviewer must show a 'sympathetic interest in the problems of the person himself … and approach the interview with some confidence' (Goode and Hatt, 1952: 190). But at the same time, excessive familiarity should be avoided: 'a certain degree of business formality, of social detachment, may be preferable. When rapport transcends a certain point, the relationship may be too intimate, and the respondent may be eager to defer to the interviewer's sentiments … especially the case when the respondent has little real involvement in the task … or has no strong views of his own' (Hyman, 1954: 48).

The criticism levelled at this kind of 'railway compartment etiquette' is easy to imagine. This detachment is seen as a myth on both sides of the relationship. The researcher is 'in this world and of this world'; he has his reactions, perceptions, angle of vision and mind-set, which will necessarily condition him and prevent him from playing the role of a neutral 'recorder'. Similarly, the interviewee will inevitably be reactive; as soon as he becomes the focus of investigation, he undergoes a change, is no longer himself, feels under scrutiny, wants to make a good impression, is nervous or put out, irritated or gratified and so on. The cognitive relationship can therefore no longer be one of observation-recording, but inevitably becomes one of interaction. The interviewer does not restrict himself to recording the interviewee's reply, but actually contributes to its production.

2.2 Uniformist versus individualist approach

The second dilemma contrasts what could be called the *uniformist* and the *individualist* positions. According to the uniformist view, there exist, if not exactly laws as in the physical world, empirical uniformities or regularities in social phenomena and human behaviour, which can therefore be classified and standardized to some degree. By contrast, the individualist perspective emphasizes the notion that inter-individual differences cannot be eliminated, that human beings cannot be reduced to any form of generalization or standardization, and that social reality becomes comprehensible to the researcher only insofar as the researcher is able to establish an empathetic relationship with single individuals. In short, the first of these positions holds that the actions of individual subjects can be traced back to uniform patterns, while the second maintains that each case or social action is a unique event.

This dilemma ushers in the problem of *standardization of the data-collection technique*. The questionnaire is binding not only on the interviewer, who has to ask every subject the same question in the same way, but also on the interviewee, who is forced to choose among sets of prefabricated answers. The manual quoted earlier warns, 'Since exactly the same questions must be asked of each respondent, you should not make changes in their phrasing. Avoid not only deliberate word changes, but also inadvertent ones ... experiments show that even a slight change in wording can distort results' (ISR, 1976: 11).

According to the critics of this approach, a standardized scheme of recording, which is what the questionnaire is, has two major drawbacks. First, the questionnaire is the same for everyone and is administered to everyone in the same way, as if all subjects were endowed with the same degree of sensitivity, maturity and presence of mind; it grossly ignores the fact that society is not homogeneous. Second, the questionnaire constrains the subject within a given level; above or below the level permitted by the questionnaire, the subject cannot testify to the reality in which he lives. In other words, it compresses the subject to the level of the average individual. Moreover, as Galtung points out, the survey leaves out those on the fringe

of society: 'the illiterates, the aged, the non-participants, the destitute, the vagabonds, the geographically-isolated periphery, etc.' (Galtung, 1967: 154). We might also add immigrants, those in hiding, etc. They are left out because their names do not appear in the population lists, because they refuse to be interviewed, because they do not understand the questions, or because they cannot fit into categories of answers designed for the average citizen.

2.3 Reducing investigation to a lowest common denominator

The fundamental goal of the *objectivist-uniformist* position is all too clear. The solutions proposed to the first dilemma (depersonalize the interviewer-interviewee relationship) and to the second (standardize the questions and answers) lead to the same point: the neutrality of the recording tool (of which the interviewer is also a part) or, to use behaviourist terminology, the *invariance of the stimulus*. The aim, of course, is to obtain answers that can be compared, and the answers are claimed to be open to comparison on the grounds that all interviewees are asked the same questions in nearly uniform interview situations.

But is this formal invariance of the stimulus – presuming that it is achievable – really matched by a corresponding parity in the condition of all interviewees when they are called upon to answer? The authors of one of the most widely read methodology manuals in the US in the 1970s state:

The impersonal nature of a questionnaire ... might lead one to conclude that it offers some uniformity from one measurement situation to another. From a psychological point of view, however, this uniformity may be more apparent than real; a question with standard wording may have diverse meanings for different people, may be comprehensible to some and incomprehensible to others'. (Selltiz et al., 1976: 295)

To put it bluntly, who can guarantee that *uniformity of the stimulus* corresponds to *uniformity of meaning*? This raises the problem of how different individuals may interpret the same question, or even the same word. The problem has been amply studied in cognitive psychology, and we will mention it only briefly here. The interviewer's question does not fall on neutral ground that is common to all subjects; the interviewee's background, culture and previous experiences will all influence how the question is interpreted, and these features will vary from subject to subject. Moreover, the meaning of a single expression may vary markedly according to the circumstances in which the interview takes place and how the interviewer is perceived by the subject. Each individual has his own frame of reference and, on receiving a stimulus, will interpret that stimulus in the light of his own experience. That the wording of the question is standardized does not ensure that it will have the same meaning for all interviewees. As Cicourel (1964: 108) writes, 'standardized questions with fixed-choice answers provide a solution to the problem of meaning by simply avoiding it.'

What, then, is the solution? The dilemma facing the researcher who is about to embark upon a survey is deeply rooted in the opposition between the two basic paradigms that inspire social research. In practical terms, this translates into a choice between a technique of questioning that puts a premium on standardization and one that gives free rein to the individuality of the subject and of the relationship with the researcher: in short, between the questionnaire and the unstructured interview.

When the researcher chooses to adopt the questionnaire, and therefore the survey, he makes a tactical decision: that of striving for uniformity rather than pursuing individuality; he looks for what individuals have in common rather than what distinguishes them. This choice involves limiting the study to that lowest common denominator of human behaviour that can be standardized, classified and compared in spite of the individuality of the subjects, and which can be recorded in spite of the variability of the

interviewer-interviewee relationship. Restricting the investigation to a *lowest* common denominator may appear to severely limit the objective of reaching a full understanding of human behaviour. It does. And this is the shortcoming of quantitative research, which consciously opts to work superficially on large numbers rather than in depth on small numbers.

3.   THE RELIABILITY OF VERBAL BEHAVIOUR

There is another basic objection to the survey. This is less radical than the first, in that it is not aimed at the epistemological foundations of the technique but rather at its empirical practicability. Nevertheless, in its extreme form, it casts doubt on the survey's very reason to exist. It can be summed up by the question 'Is verbal behaviour a reliable source for the exploration of social reality?'

Many social scientists have expressed pessimism with regard to the possibility of achieving a full understanding of social reality through the replies that subjects make to questions. Indeed, anthropologists have long since abandoned the idea that replies to questions can provide coherent and definitive information on human behaviour, in that what people say they have done or will do does not reflect their true behaviour. We will examine the question of the reliability of verbal behaviour from two points of view. The first concerns the so-called *social desirability of the answer*. The second has to do with *non-attitudes* (or *pseudo-opinions*).

Social desirability regards the commonly held evaluation of a certain attitude or behaviour of the individual within a given culture. Certain attributes or behaviours of an individual are disapproved of according to the collective norms of the society involved (e.g. poverty, alcoholism, drug abuse, extra-marital sex, etc.), while others (such as honesty, diligence, church attendance, etc.) meet with approval. If an attitude (or behaviour) has a strong positive or negative connotation in a certain culture, questions concerning such an issue may elicit a biased response. In other words, the respondent may be tempted to be less than truthful.

Sociological literature contains many examples of systematic bias caused by the social desirability factor. Sudman and Bradburn (1982) report four instances in which the researcher was able to check the truth of respondents' statements against official records. The following types of behaviour were considered: voting in the previous election, frequenting a library, being convicted of bankruptcy and being fined for drunken driving.[1] For the first two types of behaviour, which are socially desirable, affirmative replies given by interviewees were, respectively, 40 and 20 percentage points higher than the real figures. With regard to the socially undesirable behaviours, the opposite trend was seen; between a third and a half of those convicted of bankruptcy or drunken driving did not own up to the fact. A similar experiment was conducted in Italy: 55% of people officially registered as not having voted stated that they had voted. Moreover, the highest percentage of untrue replies was recorded among persons with a higher level of education – that is to say, among those more fully aware of the deviance of their behaviour.

Non-attitudes Another difficulty is constituted by non-attitudes. In social research, subjects are often asked about complex matters, such as how far the government should interfere in the economy, or whether taxes should be raised to pay for better social services, etc. Questions are often asked in the form of 'batteries': the subject is presented with a series of statements, and has to say whether he agrees or disagrees with each one. It is likely that some subjects have never thought seriously about some of the issues raised, and therefore do not have an opinion about them. In the interview situation, however, the respondent may feel *under pressure to answer* and – facilitated by the formulation of the 'closed question'[2] – *choose* one of the possible replies *at random*. At best, we have a situation in which opinions are formed on the spot (and are therefore highly unstable).

The long-known problem of non-attitudes was vigorously underscored in a celebrated 1970 essay by Philip Converse. On examining the results of a longitudinal survey conducted by re-interviewing the same subjects on different occasions, Converse noted some rather strange patterns (such as the low correlation between the replies given to the same question by the same individuals on different occasions). This prompted him to hypothesize the existence 'of two sharply discontinuous classes of respondents, the stable and the random'. The former are perfectly constant in their replies, while the latter are people 'with no real attitudes on the matter in question, but who for some reason felt obliged to try a response' (Converse, 1970: 175). As Converse points out, 'Whatever our intentions, the attitude questionnaire is approached as though it were an intelligence test, with 'don't know' and 'can't decide' confessions of mental incapacity' (1970: 177). Converse coined the term 'non-attitude' for this lack of opinion.

This problem has also been examined empirically by various researchers by asking a sample of subjects questions concerning nonexistent facts, in order to identify individuals who respond even though they have no opinion (in this case, all those who give any answer other than 'don't know'). For a more complete review of the numerous studies conducted (and of the problem of non-attitudes in general), the reader should refer to the specialized literature (e.g. Smith, 1984). Here, we will mention only two examples. Schuman and Presser (1981: 148 ff.) asked interviewees if they agreed or disagreed with certain government measures that did not actually exist (an 'Agricultural Trade Act' and a 'Monetary Control Bill'). In a series of similar experiments, Bishop et al. (1986) formulated their questions (again asking for opinions on non-existent laws) in various ways, and in some formulations explicitly included the option 'don't know' among the answers. In the various experiments, the standard question, which asked the subject plainly if he 'agreed' or 'disagreed' with the non-existent government measure, elicited a response from about one-third of interviewees (while only two-thirds admitted that they did not know, which in this case was the only right answer). These findings cast serious doubt on the reliability of the technique.

Intensity At this point, a further problem arises. Standardized questions elicit opinions but do not record the intensity or the staunchness of those opinions. A question that asks the respondent if he agrees or disagrees with a certain statement will elicit a number of positive and a number of negative responses, which will be undifferentiated; the researcher is therefore unable to distinguish, within each class of response, which opinions are deeply rooted and which are superficial, perhaps even formed on the spur of the moment. Thus, the sociologist is obliged to attach the same importance to fleeting whims that may change from one day to the next as to consolidated opinions that are entrenched in the respondent's personal history. Clearly, for instance, an anti-abortion opinion expressed in a detached manner and based on purely theoretical grounds differs markedly from the strong emotional involvement that prompts the individual to take part in anti-abortion demonstrations. And the behavioural consequences of the same opinion may be very different if that opinion embodies different degrees of emotional involvement.

4. QUESTION FORM AND SUBSTANCE

Having discussed the general problems of data collection by means of direct questioning, we will now focus on the tools used for this purpose. We will begin by looking at the general themes of the content of the questions and the distinction between open questions and closed questions.

A questionnaire may appear to be a series of banal, perhaps even obvious, questions, and drawing up a questionnaire may seem to be a fairly simple exercise. In reality, however, the formulation of a questionnaire is a difficult and complicated task requiring great effort and careful attention. Moreover, it is a task that is difficult to formalize, in that no precise rules exist; at best, we can make simple suggestions, which are based only partly on expressly conducted studies. In general, drawing up a good questionnaire requires: (a) an experienced researcher; (b) a knowledge of the population to which the questionnaire is to be administered, and (c) clarity of the research hypothesis. It may be added that the inexperienced researcher can get round the first point by carefully consulting questionnaires previously used in other studies on the same or similar themes. As Sudman and Bradburn (1982: 14) point out in one of the best-known manuals on the construction of questionnaires, copying questions from other questionnaires is not plagiarism. On the contrary, from the scientific viewpoint, it is recommended practice, in that it enables knowledge to be accumulated and comparisons to be made.

4.1 Sociographic data, attitudes and behaviours

First, we will look at the subject matter of the questions. Various subject classifications have been proposed. In spite of their differences, these classifications can ultimately be traced back to the tripartite division into basic sociographic properties, attitudes and behaviours.

Questions concerning basic sociographic properties These refer to the simple description of the basic social characteristics of the individual (hence the term 'sociographic'). By this, we mean the individual's permanent features, such as demographic features (gender, age, place of birth, etc.) and social connotations inherited from the family or acquired in youth (such as social background and education). In addition, the term also extends to those characteristics which – though not strictly permanent – nevertheless define the individual for a certain period of his life, such as occupation, marital status, geographical location and size of the municipality of residence, etc. Most of these questions are asked in all surveys (regardless of the object of the research) and there are standard formulations, which the researcher is advised to adopt.

Questions concerning attitudes   Here, the area under investigation has to do with opinions, motivation, orientation, feelings, evaluations, judgements and values. These properties of the individual are those that are most typically recorded through surveys; indeed, direct questioning of the individual seems to be the only way of gaining some insight into his thoughts. It is also the most difficult field to explore. Questions in this area can be answered more easily if the issue raised has given rise to some form of behaviour than if it is simply a matter of expressing an opinion. For example it is easier to ask whether someone has voted 'yes' or 'no' in a referendum on abortion, than to ask whether he is in favour of abortion or against.

Attitudes are often complex and multifaceted. For instance, the subject may be in favour of abortion in certain situations and against it in others; or he may not have a fixed opinion on the issue. Moreover, the subject himself may be unaware of the motivations underlying his action (someone might go to church regularly for reasons that are not altogether clear even to himself). Finally, as has been said, attitudes vary enormously from person to person in terms of intensity, and degrees of intensity are difficult to discover through a questionnaire. For all these reasons, and first of all on account of the intrinsic complexity and ambiguity involved, questions on attitudes are among the most difficult to formulate. Moreover, a response may be influenced by the way in which the question is expressed, by its position in the questionnaire, by the interviewer's approach, etc.

Questions concerning behaviours   In the previous case, we record what the interviewee says he thinks. In the present case, we record what he says he does or has done. We are therefore in the field of 'actions' which, for at least two reasons, constitutes much more solid ground. First of all, unlike attitudes, which depend upon psychological and mental states, behaviours are *unequivocal*. An action either takes place or does not, and questions about actions therefore have a precise answer.

Second, behaviours are empirically *observable*. An action can be observed by another person and may leave an objective trace (as opposed to the paramount subjectivity of attitudes); if a person goes on strike, this action is known to his work-mates; if he has voted, this fact is recorded in the electoral registers, etc. Actions are therefore empirically verifiable, though this does not mean that a respondent's answers will actually be verified. Nevertheless, the fact that a precise reply exists means that questions on behaviour are usually easier to answer; and the fact that replies can be verified objectively means that it is not so easy to lie (however, we shall not forget that problems exist for recalling past behaviour, as we will see later).

4.2 Open versus closed questions
In formulating a question, one of the first decisions to be taken by the researcher is whether it should be presented in the form of an *open question* or a *closed question* (strictly speaking, these should be called 'questions with open or closed answers', though the shorter form is commonly used). An open question is one in which the respondent is at liberty to formulate a reply as he wishes (the reply is transcribed *verbatim* by the interviewer). A closed question is one in which the interviewee is presented with a range of alternative answers to the question, and is asked to choose the most appropriate option

(the interviewer merely ticks the option selected).

By way of example, we will look at the two formulations of a question that is frequently asked in sociological questionnaires. Open question: 'What you think are the most serious problems facing the country today?' Closed question: 'I'll now read a list of social problems (the list reads: unemployment, inflation, crime, immigration, etc.). Which of these do you think are the most serious problems facing the country today?'

Clearly, the choice between the two formulations is directly linked to the problem of the standardization of data discussed earlier. But, in addition to deciding whether to standardize the question, we must also decide whether we wish – a priori – to standardize the answers.

Let us first look at the *open question*. Open questions are claimed to offer the advantage of freedom of expression. The basic difference between the two models lies in the spontaneity of the response on the one hand, as opposed to the constraint of the pre-coded response on the other. But is that an end to the matter? It should be borne in mind that the closed question, with its choice of answer from a pre-established set of options, already takes us to the final objective of data collection in quantitative research, that is to say the data-matrix (the classification of the answers according to a standardized scheme valid for all interviewees). By contrast, the open question takes us only halfway along the road to the data-matrix. Indeed, once the respondent's reply has been transcribed word for word, a so-called 'coding' phase will need to be undertaken, in order to classify the responses into a limited number of categories so that comparisons and subsequent quantitative analyses can be made. In other words, the answers have to be standardized in any case, so that the data-matrix can be constructed; if there is no pre-coding (before the answer, closed question), there will have to be post-coding (after the answer, open question).

But this post-coding involves a high degree of arbitrariness on the part of the coder. This may mean that the respondent's original answer is forced into a category, just as it was forced into a category a priori by the closed question. Indeed, open answers are frequently contradictory, incomprehensible, tautological, confused, generic and ambiguous.

Let us look again at the previous question regarding the 'serious problems facing the country'. How do we classify an answer that makes reference to 'the state'? Does the respondent have in mind the inefficiency of the public administration? Is she thinking of state centralism (she herself being in favour of devolution)? Or is it corruption among civil servants? Now let us look at another question: 'What features of a job do you consider to be important?' If the answer to this question is open, how do we classify, after the interview, an answer such as 'a job you like'? And what about generic answers such as 'good working conditions' (which may mean many different things: salary, chance of promotion, job security, hours, etc.)? Or answers that use a different frame of reference, and mention not a specific feature but a type of job, such as 'a civil servant'?

Things change if the interview envisions a guiding role on the part of the interviewer. Sudman and Bradburn (1982: 150) report the following example:

Int: What are the most important problems facing the nation today?
Resp: I don't know, there are so many.
Int: That's right, I'd just like to know what you think are the most important problems.
Resp: Well, there's certainly inflation, and then government spending.
Int: Government spending … how do you mean? Could you explain that a little? What do you have in mind when you say 'government spending'?
Resp: There's no end to it. We have to cut down federal spending somehow.
Int: Any others?
Resp: No, I think those are the most important ones.

In the hands of a capable interviewer, the open question always yields an unambiguous result that remains within the frame of reference laid down by the researcher. However, this way of working has a high cost and is not practicable on large numbers. A normal survey involves at least 1000 interviews and therefore dozens of interviewers. Moreover, if face-to-face interviews[3] are conducted on a nationwide sample, some interviewers will be allocated to distant areas, and thus be difficult to control. Indeed, as Cicourel (1964: 107) wonders, 'can we assume that interviewers … are all employing the same theoretical frame of reference and interpreting each event, respondent, etc. identically, that is, using the same meaning structures in different contexts with the same interpretive rules?'[4]

Therefore, for the essentially practical reasons of cost and feasibility, the open question has gradually been abandoned in large surveys. As we will see later, however, it is still applicable in studies involving small samples.

The *advantages* of the *closed question* may be seen as the other side of the coin with respect to what has just been said about the open question. These advantages are now listed.

- The closed question offers everyone the same frame of reference. Let us take, e.g. the question 'What do you think are the most important things that children should learn in order to be prepared for life?' This question was formulated in both the open and closed form in an experiment. In the closed form, the alternatives proposed were obedience, hard work, being responsible, helping others, etc. – that is, a series of virtues or values. Among the open responses, the most common was 'to get an education'; this obviously falls outside the researcher's frame of reference (which envisioned identifying the reference values of the respondents) (Schuman and Presser, 1981: 109). In other words, since the same question may be interpreted differently, the closed question clarifies the intended frame of reference through its pre-established options, and presents all respondents with the same frame of reference.
- The closed question is an aid to memory; the alternatives proposed act as a kind of checklist for the respondent.

- The closed question prompts thought and analysis; it forces the respondent to abandon vagueness and ambiguity. Moreover, it helps the respondent to discriminate among alternatives that might still be unclear in his mind. For example, in answer to the question of what makes a 'good' job, the respondent might be inclined to reply instinctively 'one that gives you satisfaction'; the closed options, however, would oblige him to think about salary, promotion, developing personal skills, etc.

In a corresponding fashion, we can also pick out three basic limitations of the closed question:

- The closed question omits all the alternative answers that the researcher has not thought of. By imposing the researcher's conceptual scheme on the situation studied, the theoretical horizon is prematurely closed; as we have already seen, this is a general limitation of quantitative research. As Cicourel notes, 'the questionnaire with fixed-choice response categories precludes the possibility of obtaining unanticipated definitions of the situation which reveal the subject's private thoughts and feelings' (1964: 105).
- The alternatives proposed by the closed question influence the answers. The fixed-choice categories may prompt a response from someone who has no opinion on the issue. The closed question therefore risks eliciting what we have called 'non-attitudes' or 'pseudo-opinions' – that is, random responses; this problem does not arise with the open question, since the respondent cannot hide his 'don't know' behind some pre-set option.
- The fixed options do not have the same meaning for all respondents. The pre-coding of responses, which is intended to facilitate comparison, may in reality be an illusion if single individuals attach different meanings to them. Indeed, the closed question requires a dual process of interpretation-comprehension on the part of the respondent, who has to understand not

only the question but also the array of response options. Thus, the risk of different interpretations among subjects is much greater than when the question is open. In this regard, it should be added that the closed category masks gross incomprehension of the question while, if the question is open, the interviewer can very often realize whether the respondent has actually understood what the question means.

From what has been said, it emerges that an absolutely essential condition of the closed question is that all the possible alternatives be presented in the array of options. The trick of adding the item 'other' at the bottom of the list is necessary, but not very effective. Indeed, the alternatives proposed will tend to attract the respondent's attention, and she will be likely to 'choose' from among these; unless she has a firm opinion on the issue, the respondent is unlikely to reject the options listed and to suggest her own. As a result, the closed-question category demands that a careful *exploratory study* be carried out beforehand – using the same questions in an open form, and on a (not too small) sample of subjects drawn from the same population to which the questionnaire is to be administered – in order to identify the full range of possible alternatives.

In some cases, the closed question is not practicable: when the possible response alternatives are not perfectly clear to the researcher; when they are too numerous or focus on issues that are too complex (for instance, why a child might have a conflict relationship with his parents); when the respondents have a very low level of education and are unfamiliar with the abstract language of the pre-coded responses; and when dealing with sensitive issues that can be investigated only through in-depth interviews (such as sexual behaviour, drug use, etc.).

The limitations of the closed question are therefore just as clear as those of the open question. Nevertheless, when *large numbers* are involved (and this essentially means research conducted on samples of several

hundred cases and upwards), there is no alternative to the closed question. In a small research group in which the research leader directly supervises the work of the interviewers, in which the interviewers are constantly in contact with one another and can interpret interview transcriptions on the basis of common frames of reference, and, above all, when the number of interviews is limited, a strategy based on open questions may be considered. This may take the form of what we have called the *'structured interview'*, which will be dealt with in the chapter on qualitative interviews (Chapter 10).

Such an approach cannot, however, be applied to large-scale surveys. When the study involves hundreds or thousands of subjects scattered over a wide area, and consequently a large number of interviewers, standardization of the data-collection tool is the only option. Without the standardization of questions and answers, of the interviewing technique, and of coding procedures, the result would be an enormous mass of patchy, incongruous information that cannot be interpreted or coded. For this reason, nearly all surveys on large samples are nowadays conducted by means of closed-category questionnaires.

5. FORMULATION OF THE QUESTIONS

An amusing anecdote shows the importance of how questions are worded (Sudman and Bradburn, 1982: 1):

> Two priests, a Dominican and a Jesuit, are discussing whether it is a sin to smoke and pray at the same time. After failing to reach a conclusion, each goes off to consult his respective superior. The next week they meet again. The Dominican says: 'Well, what did your superior say?' The Jesuit responds: 'He said it was all right.' 'That's funny,' the Dominican replies, 'my superior said it was a sin'. Jesuit: 'What did you ask him?' Reply: 'I asked him if it was all right to smoke while praying.' 'Oh,' says the Jesuit, 'I asked my superior if it was all right to pray while smoking.'

Saying that the way in which a question is formulated can influence the reply appears to be a banal statement. Nevertheless, this point cannot be overemphasized. Even slight changes in the wording of the question can lead to marked variations in the response. One of the first experiments on this phenomenon was carried out in the 1930s by Rugg (1941). What he did was to ask essentially the same question about freedom of speech in two different ways. In one case, subjects were asked: 'Do you think the US should allow public speeches against democracy?' In the other, the question was: 'Do you think the United States should forbid public speeches against democracy?' To the first question, 75% of respondents answered 'No', while to the second question, only 54% answered 'Yes' – a difference of some 21 percentage points. Although the meanings of the two verbs 'not allow' and 'forbid' are equivalent, the latter seems to imply much stricter prohibition, probably because it involves active opposition and not merely a withholding of support.

Another example is quoted by Schuman and Presser (1981: 284). The following question was asked: 'If a situation like Vietnam were to develop in another part of the world, do you think the US should or should not send troops?' The same question was then put to another sample of subjects, but this time with the words 'to stop a Communist takeover' inserted. In its first formulation, the question elicited an affirmative response from 18% of respondents; in the second formulation, almost twice as many (33%) said 'Yes'.

Innumerable examples of how the formulation of the question can influence the response are to be found in manuals dealing with questionnaire technique. While it is difficult to draw up precise rules on the subject, some suggestions can be made with regard to the language, syntax and content of the questions.

1. *Simplicity of language* Given that the questions are standardized, and therefore the same for everyone, language that is accessible to everyone should be used. For example, the following question appeared in a questionnaire used in France: 'Many experts maintain that preventive detention is of great public utility because it prevents potential criminals from committing further crimes or hiding evidence. Do you agree?' As it turned out, less than 50% of the respondents knew the exact meaning of the term 'preventive detention'. In general, it should be borne in mind that (a) the language of the questionnaire must be appropriate to the characteristics of the sample subjects – e.g. we would not use the same style of language for seasonal immigrant workers, the residents of an old peoples' home and university students; if different groups of people are to be interviewed with the same questionnaire, its language must be comprehensible to members of all the groups to be interviewed, especially the least sophisticated group; (b) the self-administered questionnaire has to use simpler language than a questionnaire administered by an interviewer, as no further explanations can be given; (c) even when an interviewer is present, many respondents will be too embarrassed to admit that they do not understand, and may respond at random rather than ask the interviewer to explain.

2. *Question length* As well as being formulated in simple language, questions should generally be concise. Questions that are too long not only take up more time but may also distract the respondent from the crux of the issue. Moreover, by the time the end of a long question is reached, the interviewee may have lost sight of the beginning and respond only on the basis of the final part. However, when complex issues are dealt with, a long question might actually be preferable, in that it (a) facilitates memory; (b) gives the respondent more time to think and, as the length of the answer is directly correlated with the length of the question; (c) prompts a more detailed answer. The longer question may therefore be

preferable when dealing with issues that are personal-sensitive, or require careful thought or the use of the memory. In such cases, the question may be introduced by underlining the problematic nature of the issue or by quoting examples such as 'As you know, there are different opinions on the question of … Some people think that … Others say that … Which position is closest to your opinion?', rather than simply asking 'Are you in favour or against …?'

3. *Number of response alternatives*   In closed questions, the response alternatives must not be too numerous. If they are read aloud by the interviewer, there should generally be no more than five; above this number, the respondent's memory of the first alternatives will begin to fade by the time the interviewer reads the last ones (Sudman and Bradburn, 1982: 172). When larger numbers of alternatives are presented, the respondent is usually shown a card which reports them in written form; but even in this case, they should not be too numerous.

4. *Slang*   Many subcultures are jealous of their slang. Attempts to use it on the part of the interviewer may cause irritation or seem ridiculous. In general, the interviewer can obtain cooperation more easily by underlining the scientific nature of his role than by pretending to be a member of the respondent's own subculture.

5. *Ambiguous or vague definitions*   Care must be taken to avoid using terms that are not clearly defined. e.g. the question 'Do you have a steady job?' implies a concept that does not have an unequivocal meaning. For instance, can a contract that must be renewed every year be called 'steady'? Similarly, in the question 'How many rooms are there in your house?', what is meant by room? Should the bathroom and kitchen be counted?

6. *Words with strong emotive connotations*   It is advisable to avoid emotive language. If we want to know whether a parent uses corporal punishment, we should not ask 'Do you hit your child?', as the word 'hit' has a strongly negative connotation. Thus, terms such as freedom, justice, equality, communism, boss, big business, etc. should also be avoided. Instead, paraphrases of such terms should be used, even if this means lengthening the question.

7. *Syntactically complex questions*   The syntax of the question should be linear and clear. For example, double negatives, as in the following question, are to be avoided: 'Do you agree or disagree with the statement: "It is not true that workers are as badly off as the trade unions say?"' Someone who disagrees with the negation believes that workers are badly off. But the question is complicated and very easy to misunderstand.

In general, the respondent should not be asked negative questions containing disapproval or condemnation of some object, person or behaviour. A respondent who approves of the behaviour will have to answer in the negative (in order to negate the negation), while one who disapproves of that behaviour will have to express agreement with the affirmation (which expresses condemnation). Thus, respondents often say that they 'disagree' when, in reality, they do not disagree with the statement but with the behaviour mentioned in the statement. Such problems do not arise if only affirmative statements are used.

8. *Questions with non-univocal answers*   Multiple questions and questions that are not sufficiently detailed should be avoided. By multiple questions, we mean those that are formulated in such a way as to include more than one question. For instance, if we ask 'Were your parents religious?', we exclude the possibility of answering that one parent was and the other was not. Likewise, faced with the question 'Do you believe the government's economic policy is fair and effective?', someone who believes that the policy is effective but unfair will not know how to answer. In such cases, the problem

is easily solved by splitting the question into two separate questions.

An example of an insufficiently detailed formulation is seen in the question 'Do you agree or disagree with abortion?', which does not allow the various positions within this issue to be distinguished (one might disagree with abortion in principle, but agree with it in the case of foetal malformation or when the mother's life is in danger). Similarly, asking a young person 'Do you work?', without specifying whether this includes summer jobs, temporary jobs, part-time work, baby-sitting, etc. is inappropriate.

9. *Non-discriminating questions* Questions should be constructed in such a way as to discriminate among sample subjects. A question which gets the same answer from 90% of respondents is normally a bad question, being of no practical use (except in particular cases in which we may want to isolate a specific minority). Consequently, when a range of response alternatives is presented, items that will obviously gain great consensus should be avoided. For instance, if the question is 'Which of the following groups of people do you trust most?' (neighbours, priests, workmates, teachers, etc.), the option 'members of your family' should not be included. Likewise, when asking 'Which of the following countries is the best place to live?', the respondent's own country should not be included (unless the aim is specifically to pick out lovers of foreign countries).

10. *Loaded questions.* Sometimes the researcher unwittingly constructs a question in which the adjectives used, the examples quoted or the collocation of words point the interviewee towards one of the possible response alternatives and away from the others. The following question was used in a survey on trade union militancy that was conducted many years ago in France: 'In our country 700 priests have declared that the Gospel is a message for the *poor* and *exploited*, and so they *live a poor life, work in factories* and *participate actively* in trade unions and political organizations in order to *help* workers to obtain greater *social rights*. Do you think these priests are right?' The text contains seven words and expressions (which we have written in italics) that clearly lend a positive connotation to the behaviour of the priests. As many respondents would be unfamiliar with the figure of the worker-priest, a description was required. In this description, however, the positive emphasis clearly pressurizes the respondent – unless he already has clear ideas on the issue – towards an affirmative answer.

Again with regard to the abortion question, markedly different results are obtained according to whether the question is placed within the perspective of responsible maternal choice or that of the unborn baby's right to life.

A form of tendentiousness may be seen in closed questions that fail to include some of the possible answers among the response options (the alternatives not explicitly presented will be under-represented in the responses, in comparison with their true value). Take the question 'How do you spend your free time, watching television or doing something else?'. Or again, the question 'Some people think that women should have an equal place with men in running offices and industries and in holding public positions. Others say that a woman's place is in the home and that a woman's main job is to bring up children and take care of the family. What do you think?'. Without the second part (Others say...), the question would be vitiated.

11. *Presumed behaviour* Behaviours must not be taken for granted. For instance, an interviewee must not be asked who he voted for in the last election, without first being asked if he voted. Preliminary questions which allow

respondents to be selected for further questioning are usually called 'filter questions', while questions that are asked only after the filter question has been answered in a certain way are known as 'conditional questions'. Without these filter questions, the interviewee might feel obliged to make a reply (at random or on the basis of social desirability) even when the question does not concern him.

12. *Time focus* In general, care should be taken over questions that refer to habitual behaviour or that require time averages to be calculated. For example, the questions 'How often do you usually read a newspaper?' and 'How many times a month do you go to the cinema?' run the risk of the interviewee's answering according to some perceived obligation, or to the image that she has, or wishes to give, of herself, rather than in accordance with her true behaviour (the issue of the socially desirable answer is dealt with later). It is therefore advisable to add a second question that has a specific time reference. Thus, in the two previous examples, the interviewee would be also asked if she read a newspaper yesterday (or today) and whether she has been to the cinema in the last two weeks. Focusing on a precise period of time is an aid to memory and makes it more difficult to superimpose ideal behaviour on actual behaviour.

The time focus also applies to situations that change over time. For example, it is advisable not to ask simply 'What was your father's occupation?', but 'What was your father's occupation when you were 14-years-old?'; a person's occupation may change over time, and the lack of a specific time reference may create difficulties for the interviewee.

13. *Concrete versus abstract* Similar observations can be made with regard to this point. An abstract question can easily give rise to a generic or stock reply (reflecting social norms rather than the respondent's true thoughts; see point 15). By contrast, a concrete question facilitates reflection and prompts the respondent to identify with the real issue; moreover, it helps to avoid misunderstandings. For example, in a study conducted in Italy on attitudes towards the death penalty, 42% of those interviewed answered 'No' to the general question 'Do you think the death penalty should be applied in cases of exceptionally serious crimes?' However, when examples of 'exceptionally serious crimes' were provided, this figure fell to 29%.

Another example of making an abstract attitude concrete is seen in the following question, which was used to gauge 'patriotism' in a sample of young people: 'Nobody wants war, but if a war broke out, do you think you would go and fight for your country?' Patriotic feeling is so abstract and difficult to define that only by evoking the image of a concrete situation, albeit a hypothetical one, can we make it the focus of a question.

Instead of asking an abstract question, it can sometimes be useful to tell a story and then ask the interviewee to take sides. In the following example, instead of asking an abstract question on the choice between ethical rigour and opportunistic relativism, the interviewer illustrates a concrete case:

Early one morning, Mr. Smith is cycling to work. Suddenly he pulls out of a side-street, right into the path of an oncoming car. The car swerves to avoid the cyclist and crashes into a lamp-post. Mr. Smith admits that the accident was his fault, says he will pay for the car to be repaired and promises to get in touch with the owner; as the car is an expensive one, the repairs are likely to be very costly. When he gets to work, Mr. Smith tells his workmates what has happened. His friends tell him he is a fool to offer to pay; there were no witnesses to the accident, and anyway, judging by the kind of car, the owner can probably afford to pay for the repairs himself without feeling the pinch. But Mr. Smith says he can't break his promise, particularly because he might have been killed if the car hadn't swerved. The interviewer then asks, 'Do you agree with Mr. Smith or with his friends?' (Marradi, 1996: 34)

Answers should also be concrete. For example, Groves (1989: 452) reports various studies on the different meanings attributed by respondents to the adverbs 'often', 'quite often', etc.; where possible, it is advisable to use a clearly defined time expression.

14. *Behaviours and attitudes*   As already mentioned, questionnaires frequently include questions about both behaviours and attitudes. It has also been said that attitudes are, by nature, much vaguer, more ambiguous and open to standard responses than behaviours are. It is therefore a good rule to focus the question on a behaviour rather than on an opinion, whenever the subject matter of the question permits. In the field of political involvement, for example, rather than asking the interviewee if he is interested in politics, it is preferable to ask whether he reads political news in the papers, or watches the news on television. Similarly, rather than asking whether it is right to give time and money to charity and to social solidarity initiatives, it is better to ask whether he personally gives money or time to such associations.

Another useful hint is to look for behaviours that can be verified empirically. Thus, in addition to asking the respondent if he keeps up to date with politics (an attitude) and if he reads the newspapers (a behaviour), questions can be asked that require specific knowledge: for instance, if he knows about a recent political event, or if he knows the name of the leader of a certain party or the mayor of his town.

To quote a final example on this point, we should not ask the generic question 'Do you read books?' Instead, we should ask how many books the respondent has read in the last six months and what the titles are.

15. *Social desirability bias*   This is one of the main difficulties in data collection through questioning. The problem has already been amply discussed from a general point of view; we will now see how it can be tackled from the technical standpoint, in the construction phase of the questionnaire.

First of all, the advice given earlier – to formulate questions as far as possible in a concrete manner – applies to this point, too. Indeed, abstract questions favour generic answers that reflect social norms, while the visualization of concrete cases forces the interviewee to take sides.

A specific suggestion regarding questions of this sort is to formulate the question in such a way as to make even the least desirable answer acceptable by providing a justification for it. Thus, instead of asking 'Do you read newspapers?', we might ask 'Do you normally find the time to read newspapers?' Similarly, we might say 'Political elections were held on 21st April this year. Many people did not vote because they were ill, or a long way from home, or they think voting is useless, or for some other reason. Did you vote?'

Another tactic is to depict a negative behaviour as normal or common (and therefore no longer deviant) – e.g. 'Nearly everyone has contemplated suicide at some time in their life. In some moment of depression, have you ever thought … etc?'.

Or again, the question may be formulated in a way that presents all possible answers as equally legitimate – e.g. 'Some people say that smoking marijuana is the first step on the road to hard drugs, while others say that it is completely harmless. What do you think?' This approach can be adopted in order to present various alternatives in a balanced way.

A further possibility involves pretending to take for granted that the interviewee indulges, or has indulged, in the socially disapproved behaviour, and leaving the respondent to deny it. This kind of artifice was use by Alfred Kinsey in his famous study of sexual behaviour in America; he did not ask single women if they had sexual relations, but how often they had them (Kinsey et al., 1953).

Some have suggested formulating the questions in the third person, thus shifting the focus to someone other than the respondent. While it is unrealistic to believe, for instance, that we can find out through a questionnaire whether a young person uses drugs, it may nevertheless be possible to discover something about the motivations underlying such behaviour by asking an indirect question, such as 'Many young people today use drugs; in your opinion, why do they do it?'

All the above tactics may help to reduce the effects of the social desirability bias, but they will never succeed in eliminating it entirely. If a question deals with an issue that is subject to some form of social expectation, it will inevitably engender a certain bias and, except for those rare cases in which the behaviour can be verified, the size of this bias will remain unknown.

16. *Embarrassing questions* A topic that is closely related to the previous one is that of so-called 'embarrassing questions'. There are sensitive issues, such as sexual behaviour, income, deviant behaviour (drug abuse, alcoholism), etc. that are extremely difficult to investigate by means of questionnaires. Such issues, however, can be explored fully only through non-structured interviews, in which highly skilled interviewers can succeed in gaining the trust of respondents. Kinsey, for example, who was the first to tackle the sensitive issue of sexual behaviour, gathered his empirical material exclusively through in-depth interviews which, for the most part, he himself conducted.

17. *No opinion and don't know* We have already discussed the difficulties that arise when the respondent has no opinion on the issue in question or, not having thought about the issue before, is prompted to make up an opinion on the spot. The problem can only be tackled by assuring the respondent that 'don't know' is as legitimate an answer as the rest, and including this option among the others. Instead of asking 'Do you think that quite a few of the people running the government are crooked, not very many are, or do you think hardly any of them are crooked?', the question could be formulated in exactly the same way, but adding at the end '... or do you not have an opinion on that?'. A slightly different method is to use a preliminary filter question, such as 'Some say that many of the people running the government are crooked; others say only a small minority are. Do you have an opinion about that?' Only if the respondent says that she does have an opinion will she then be asked 'Who do you agree with?'. Schuman and Presser (1981: 116 ff.) carried out experiments on this point, and found that the first version of this question elicited a 'don't know' response from 4.2% of respondents, while 20% answered 'don't know' to the second version.

It should be borne in mind that the interviewee who feels insecure, who has no opinion on the issue but is reluctant to say 'I don't know', may well choose a response at random or – more likely – search for some clue (in the wording of the question, in the interviewer's demeanour, tone of voice or facial expression) to the 'right' answer. The researcher will therefore have to be very careful to formulate the question in a neutral way and avoid any direct or indirect prompting.

18. *Attitude intensity* A problem related to the above is that of the intensity of

opinions. As we have already seen, respondents should not be regarded simply as being 'for' or 'against'; it is also important to understand the degree of intensity of their opinions, as this is what determines behaviour. For example, every opinion poll on gun control carried out in the US over the last 30 years or more has revealed that a large majority of the population is in favour, and yet, gun control legislation has not been passed. This is ascribed, among other reasons, to the fact that the minority opposing gun control is far more zealous than the majority in favour.

Schumann and Press (1981: 231 ff.) have proposed separating the question of the strength of attitudes into *intensity*, *centrality* and *committed action*. To the question 'Would you favor a law which would require a person to obtain a police permit before he could buy a gun, or do you think such a law would interfere too much with the right of citizens to own guns?', they added a question regarding intensity ('Compared with how you feel on other public issues, are your feelings about permits for guns extremely strong, very strong, fairly strong, not strong at all?'); a question on centrality ('How important is a candidate's position on permits for guns when you decide how to vote in a Congressional election? Is it one of the most important, very important, somewhat important, not too important?'); and a question on committed action ('Have you ever written a letter to a public official expressing your views on gun permits or given money to an organization concerned with this issue?'); The results of their research revealed that the minority who opposed gun control had much stronger feelings on the issue than the majority who were in favour.

As this example illustrates, the intensity of an attitude cannot be gauged simply by formulating the question more appropriately; further probing is required. This obviously has its costs and runs counter to the general economy of the questionnaire. Frequently, therefore, no attempt to assess intensity is made or, at best, the researcher inserts response categories such as 'Do you agree strongly, agree somewhat, neither agree nor disagree, disagree somewhat, disagree strongly?'

19. *Acquiescence and 'response set'* Acquiescence refers to the interviewee's tendency to choose answers that express agreement, giving affirmative answers (yea-saying) rather than negative ones. The phenomenon is more frequently encountered among the less educated and is generally attributed either to an attitude of deference towards the interviewer or to a tendency for these subjects to be less critical and more easily influenced. Schuman and Presser divided a sample of subjects into two groups; one group was asked 'Do you agree or disagree with the following statement: "Individuals are more to blame than social conditions for crime and lawlessness in this country"; the other group was asked the same question, but with the terms 'individuals' and 'social conditions' inverted ('Social conditions are more to blame than individuals for crime and lawlessness in this country'). In the first group, 59% of subjects agreed with the statement (individuals are more to blame), while in the second group, 57% agreed (social conditions are more to blame). These results were clearly contradictory. Subsequently, when the researchers formulated the question as 'Which in your opinion is more to blame for crime and lawlessness in this country: individuals or social conditions?', 54% of those interviewed said social conditions and 46% said individuals (Schumann and Presser, 1981: 204 ff.). It is not difficult to formulate the question – as in this example – in such a way as to take into account this possible source of bias; the important thing is that the person who

draws up the questionnaire be aware of the problem.

A similar form of response bias is that which goes under the name of *response set*. When faced with a battery of questions for which the same response alternatives are presented (e.g. agree strongly, somewhat, little, not at all), some respondents may, out of laziness (to get the interview over quickly) or lack of opinion, reply in the same way (e.g. 'agree somewhat') to every question, regardless of its content. This problem can be tackled by alternating the polarity of the answers so that the respondent will have to answer some questions affirmatively and others negatively in order to avoid contradicting himself (for instance, in a battery of questions on politics, two consecutive questions may be formulated in such a way that the traditionalist-conservative position corresponds to a positive answer in the first case and to a negative answer in the second).

Similar problems – again caused by acquiescence or laziness – may arise when the interviewee is faced with a list of alternatives and is called upon to make a choice (usually multiple, for example: 'Which of the following features do you think are most important in a good job: opportunities for promotion, salary, flexible hours … Choose the three you consider most important'). Research has revealed that, when the respondent can see the list of alternatives (on a card), she will tend to pick the first items listed; however, when she only hears the alternatives (read aloud by the interviewer), she will tend to pick the last items listed. This bias can be obviated by varying the order of the response alternatives from one interview to another.[5]

20. *Memory effects* Obviously, questions regarding past facts and behaviours encounter difficulties due to incomplete or imprecise memory. In compiling the questionnaire, strategies have been proposed in order to reinforce the validity of questions based on memory. One of these is to place a time limit on the memory. For instance, instead of asking how many times a person has been abroad, or if he has ever been the victim of a crime (theft, pick-pocketing, etc.), the interviewer will set the question within a limited period of time (in the last year, last six months, etc.).[6] Another tactic is to use prominent events as time markers. If, e.g. we want to know when the person bought a washing machine, we can ask whether it was before or after the birth of the last child, before or after the summer holidays, etc.

A further way of jogging the respondent's memory is to use a list of possible responses. In a question about how the interviewee went about looking for a job, for example, a list of different possible initiatives could be presented (advertisements in newspapers, employment exchange, applications to companies, competitive examinations, friends, relatives, acquaintances, etc.). The same structure could also be used in a question on television-watching, by drawing up a list of the programmes broadcast.

When the behaviour under investigation concerns not only the past, but also the present and future (in that the behaviour is still in progress at the time of recording), diaries or similar records can sometimes be used in order to avoid relying on memory. To record family budgets, national statistics institutions in all countries distribute diaries to selected families, in which various items of family expenditure are to be noted.[7]

Finally, it should be added that, when the respondent's attitude or behaviour has changed from the past to the present, he may well unconsciously attribute his current attitude or behaviour to the past as well.

21. *The order of the questions* In conclusion, how should we decide in what order the questions are to be asked? In considering

this point, we should bear in mind how the *interviewer-interviewee relationship* develops. This relationship is an asymmetrical one. On one side, we have the interviewer, who is familiar with the interview situation, who has already conducted dozens, perhaps hundreds, of interviews, who is aware of the objectives and able to foresee how the interview will unfold. On the other side, we have an individual who does not know why she is being questioned, why she has been singled out, or who the interviewer has been sent by; afraid of giving the wrong answers, she is fraught with doubt, anxiety and mistrust. The interviewer's first task is therefore to reassure the respondent and to show her that she has nothing to fear. The second is to help her learn the question-answer mechanism of the interview rapidly.

Thus, the objective of the first part of the interview is to put the respondent at ease and show her how the interview works. It is therefore generally advisable to begin with easy questions that are not too personal, based on facts rather than opinions. In short, questions that reassure and instruct. If potentially embarrassing questions are to be asked, it is recommended that these be placed in the middle of the questionnaire, when the interviewer has had time to gain the respondent's confidence. Some researchers recommend placing such questions at the end of the questionnaire, both to minimize the damage if the respondent should terminate the interview and, especially, to avoid the risk of spoiling the atmosphere of the interview right from the beginning.

The second criterion to be borne in mind is that of *interest and tiredness*. It is important to structure the questionnaire in such a way as to keep the respondent's attention alive. It has been found that the interviewee's attention and interest show an increasing trend up to about halfway through the interview and then

decline. Consequently, more demanding questions should be located in this middle phase of the interview, while questions that do not require much thought, such as those on sociographic characteristics, can be left to the end. This brings us to the issue of the length of the questionnaire. While it is difficult to establish general criteria, since length will depend heavily on the subject matter and the population studied, a face-to-face interview should last about 45 minutes on average, and a telephone interview about 20 minutes.

The third criterion concerns the *logical sequence* of the issues raised during the interview. As far as possible, the interview should flow like a natural conversation, without sudden leaps in subject (from one subject to a totally different one) or time (from the present to childhood and then back to the present, etc.). When moving on from one subject to another, it is advisable to introduce the new topic by means of expressions such as 'Let's move on to a subject that's different, but that ...', and the like. Questions should move from the general to the particular, following a 'funnel' sequence; broad, general questions should therefore be asked first, followed by progressively more specific ones – e.g. in investigating the role played by professional associations in orienting the votes of their members, the following sequence of questions could be asked: 'Do you work?'. (If yes): 'Are you an employee or self-employed?'. (If self-employed): 'Are you a member of any professional association?'. (If yes): 'Has your association given its members any indication on how to vote?'. (If yes): 'What kind of indication?'. (If it has suggested voting for a particular party or candidate): 'Did you follow this suggestion?'.

Regarding the sequence of the questions, the last point concerns the *contamination effect*; this is the phenomenon whereby the answer to a question may, in some cases, be influenced by the questions that precede it. Schuman and Presser (1981: 36 ff.) report the following example: when the question 'Do you think it should be possible for a pregnant woman to obtain a legal abortion if she is married and does not want any more children?' was asked on its own, 58% of respondents said 'Yes'. However, the figure fell to 42% when the same question was located within a series of questions on abortion, immediately following the question 'Do you think it should be possible for a pregnant woman to obtain a legal abortion if there is a strong chance of serious defect in the baby?'. In the second formulation, the prior mention of a situation in which abortion seems to be particularly justified makes the respondent more critical of a less justifiable motivation.

Having reached the end of this long list of the main controversial points regarding the construction of the questionnaire, the reader may be disconcerted by the thought of how sensitive this research tool is to the formulation of the questions, and come to the conclusion that this means of gathering information is completely unreliable and subject to manipulation by the researcher.

That answers are strongly influenced by the way in which the questions are formulated is certainly true. Nevertheless, it should be pointed out that this influence is particularly relevant in what is commonly called 'univariate analysis' – that is to say, in analysing the percentages of replies to single questions, taken separately. However, social researchers are not only interested in knowing how many citizens vote or how many are in favour of legalizing soft drugs; above all, they are concerned with studying the *relationships among* variables: in finding out, for example, whether such percentages vary according to gender, age, social class, level of education, political orientation, place of residence, etc., with a view to identifying what determines the social phenomenon under investigation, the factors that influence it, or are correlated with it.

In this perspective, even if the question is formulated in such a way as to yield a bias in favour of one of the response alternatives, or a percentage of 'don't knows' that is lower than it should be, the relationships between gender, age, social class, etc. and the variable studied will presumably not be altered too greatly, since any such bias should impact in more or less the same way on all respondents.[8] The researcher can therefore undertake comparisons and analyses of relationships among variables when all respondents have been asked the questions in the same form; however, when the questions have been formulated differently, even if only slightly, great caution will need to be exercised.

In conclusion, the advice given earlier – that whenever questionnaire data are presented, the exact formulation of the questions should *always* be reported – is more valid than ever. This is a basic scientific requisite (i.e. guaranteeing clarity and reproducibility) of this social research technique.

6. ITEM BATTERIES

It is frequently the case in questionnaires that questions formulated in the same way (same introductory question and response alternatives, but referring to different objects) are presented in single blocks. These compact formulations are called 'item batteries' and are used in order to:

- save questionnaire space and interview time;
- help the respondent to understand the response mechanism (which remains the same for all questions);
- improve response validity in that, when answering a single question, the respondent implicitly takes into account the answers he has given to the other items in the battery; and
- enable the researcher to construct synthetic indexes that summarize in a single score the various items in the battery.

TABLE 5.1 *Examples of item batteries*

Q. 1. Have you suffered from the following disorders in the last few days?

	No	Yes
– I take longer than usual to fall asleep at night	1 ☐	2 ☐
– I wake up often in the middle of the night	1 ☐	2 ☐
– I cannot concentrate easily when reading the papers	1 ☐	2 ☐
– I feel irritable or jittery	1 ☐	2 ☐
– Much of the time I am afraid but don't know the reason	1 ☐	2 ☐
– I am terrified and near panic	1 ☐	2 ☐
– I am having trouble with indigestion	1 ☐	2 ☐
– My heart sometimes beats faster than usual	1 ☐	2 ☐
– I have a lot of trouble with dizzy and faint feelings	1 ☐	2 ☐
– My hands shake so much that people can easily notice	1 ☐	2 ☐

Source: 'Carroll rating scale for depression' (Robinson et al., 1991: 211), quoted only with reference to insomnia, psychological anxiety, somatic anxiety.

Q. 2. Which members of your family know that you are homosexual?[a]

	Knows	Knows but pretends not to	Probably knows but we have never talked about it	Doesn't know	Is absent (deceased or other)
Mother	1 ☐	2 ☐	3 ☐	4 ☐	5 ☐
Father	1 ☐	2 ☐	3 ☐	4 ☐	5 ☐
Brother(s)	1 ☐	2 ☐	3 ☐	4 ☐	5 ☐
Sister(s)	1 ☐	2 ☐	3 ☐	4 ☐	5 ☐
Spouse	1 ☐	2 ☐	3 ☐	4 ☐	5 ☐
Child(ren)	1 ☐	2 ☐	3 ☐	4 ☐	5 ☐

[a]Research conducted on a sample of homosexuals

Q. 3. Do you consider yourself to be very satisfied, somewhat satisfied, somewhat dissatisfied, very dissatisfied with the following aspects of your job?

	Very satisfied	Somewhat satisfied	Somewhat dissatisfied	Very dissatisfied dissatisfied	Don't know
Independence	1 ☐	2 ☐	3 ☐	4 ☐	5 ☐
Responsibility	1 ☐	2 ☐	3 ☐	4 ☐	5 ☐
Level of competence	1 ☐	2 ☐	3 ☐	4 ☐	5 ☐
Pay	1 ☐	2 ☐	3 ☐	4 ☐	5 ☐
Career opportunities	1 ☐	2 ☐	3 ☐	4 ☐	5 ☐
Job security	1 ☐	2 ☐	3 ☐	4 ☐	5 ☐

Q. 4. I'm going to read you a list of things people often say. For each statement, please tell me if you agree strongly, agree somewhat, disagree somewhat, or disagree strongly.

	Agree strongly	Agree somewhat	Disagree somewhat	Disagree strongly	Don't know
When jobs are scarce, men should be given priority over women in getting a job	1 ☐	2 ☐	3 ☐	4 ☐	5 ☐
When jobs are scarce, people should be forced to retire early	1 ☐	2 ☐	3 ☐	4 ☐	5 ☐
When jobs are scarce, employers should give citizens of this country priority over immigrants	1 ☐	2 ☐	3 ☐	4 ☐	5 ☐
It's not right to give handicapped people jobs when people without physical handicaps can't find work	1 ☐	2 ☐	3 ☐	4 ☐	5 ☐

Some examples of batteries are reported in Table 5.1. In the first example, the interviewee is presented with a list of situations, objects, etc. and is asked to answer 'yes' or 'no' to each. Here, the items refer to psychological disorders (that the person may suffer from), but could equally concern personal possessions, actions performed, etc. The other three examples shown in Table 5.1 differ from the first in that several response alternatives are offered. In this type of question the interviewee is often asked to indicate the degree to which he/she agrees with a given statement, is satisfied with a given situation, supports a political position, etc., and obliged to express his/her answer by selecting among response categories similar to the following: 'very much', 'somewhat', 'a little', 'not at all'.

When the same question is applied to different objects, as in the case of batteries, it is important to distinguish questions formulated in *absolute terms* from those formulated in *relative terms*. In the above examples, the individual items in the battery are formulated in absolute terms, in the sense that each item in the battery is a self-contained unit, to which the interviewee can respond without reference to the other questions. For instance, when asked if it takes longer than usual to fall asleep at night, the respondent can reply 'yes' or 'no' whether or not this question is placed in a battery of similar questions.

By contrast, a question formulated in relative terms requires that a comparison be made with other possible response alternatives. Let us look at the question about 'problems facing the country' presented some pages back. This question could be presented in absolute terms, as follows: 'I'm going to read you a list of social problems. As I read each problem, tell me if you think it is very important, quite important, not very important or not important at all'. The interviewer then lists problems such as unemployment, inflation, crime, corruption, etc. Alternatively, the same question could be presented in relative terms: 'I'm going to read you a list ... etc. Tell me which three of these problems you think are the most important'. Similarly, a battery of items aimed at assessing

the popularity of well-known personalities may be presented in absolute terms by reading a list of names of politicians, e.g. and asking the respondent to score each one (for instance, on a scale from 1 to 10). Alternatively, the items may be presented in relative terms by asking the respondent to put the names of the politicians in order of preference, or to choose the one (or two or three, etc.) he prefers.

From the respondent's point of view, questions involving comparisons (that is, those formulated in relative terms) are often better, in that they enable the various positions to be distinguished more easily – e.g. most people are likely to be in favour of both tax cuts and improvements in social services. However, when faced with a choice, they will be forced to establish priorities, and therefore reveal their ideas more precisely. It should be added, however, that questions involving comparisons among a number of stimuli are more difficult to handle from the point of view of statistical analysis, and therefore tend to be used less frequently.

In social research, a procedure that makes frequent use of item batteries is *scaling*, which is applied especially in the area of so-called 'attitude measurement' (e.g. questions 3 and 4 in Table 5.1 are aimed at assessing the respondent's attitude towards his own job and discrimination at work). In the case of scaling, the most pressing reason for arranging the questions in batteries is the one quoted in the first paragraph of this section, the aim being to condense the answers into a single score in order to operationalize the particular attitude under investigation. The issue of scaling will be dealt with in detail in the next chapter.

Finally, it should be noted that the main advantage of item batteries, which lies in the ability to compress a range of multiple stimuli into a short time and a limited space, also embodies its greatest risk. The urgent tone of the battery and the repetitiveness of the response mechanism can easily produce two of the most common forms of response error: 'pseudo-opinions' (randomly given answers) and 'response sets' (giving always the same answer). The researcher and interviewer should therefore exercise caution in formulating and asking this kind of question.

7. TYPES OF QUESTIONNAIRE ADMINISTRATION

There are basically three ways of administering a questionnaire: the face-to-face interview, the telephone interview and the self-administered questionnaire.

For decades (at least from the beginning of the 1930s to the end of the 1970s), the most common method of questionnaire administration was the face-to-face interview. This typically involved calling at the interviewee's home, sitting down and asking questions. From the 1980s onwards, a number of factors (the widespread diffusion of the telephone, rising interview costs, public saturation with all kinds of interviews, increased mistrust of strangers owing to rising crime rates) prompted data-collection agencies to replace face-to-face interviews with telephone interviews as their standard procedure. Alongside these two methods, space has always been available for self-administered questionnaires; this category includes questionnaires sent by post, distributed directly to subjects (museum visitors, department store customers, etc.) and administered to groups (school classes, work departments, etc.), and web surveys.

The way the questionnaire is to be administered will, to some extent, affect how it is drawn up. While the points raised in the previous sections apply to all methods of administration, the fact remains that, in constructing the questionnaire, the researcher must bear in mind how it is to be administered, in that the solutions to the various problems that arise may vary according to the method of administration that will be adopted. Each mode of administration involves specific problems. These will be dealt with in the following pages.

7.1 Face-to-face interviews

In the face-to-face interview, the interviewer plays a central role. Indeed, the quality of the interview will depend to a great extent on the interviewer's performance – how he establishes and conducts the relationship with the interviewee.

The general question of the interaction between the observer and the phenomenon observed is discussed in Section 2.1 of this chapter, and we have seen that this is one of the principal dilemmas of the survey. There is no need, here, to resume discussion of the two alternative approaches: the *objectivist approach* (neutral detached interviewer) and the *constructivist approach* (interviewer-interview interaction). It should, however, be borne in mind that the technique presented here is that of the standardized questionnaire, which fits closely into the first of these two approaches. What we are talking about is a study typically involving at least 1000 interviews and several dozen interviewers; this means that the roles of researcher and interviewer do not coincide.

The problem is therefore one of minimizing the effect of the interviewers. This is done through training aimed at standardizing their behaviour and limiting their discretionary power. In a large-scale study, it is essential that interviewers *avoid any kind of behaviour that might influence the respondent*. They must therefore refrain from expressing approval or disapproval of what the subject says, and learn to respond with non-committal words or gestures whenever the interviewee looks for some reaction. At the same time, they must ensure that the respondent cooperates positively, does not suffer lapses of attention or interest, always understands what the questions mean and does not make gross mistakes in answering. It is a difficult balance to strike. From the point of view of the interpersonal relationship, interviewers need to adopt a friendly, but neutral, attitude – one that is basically permissive and implicitly able to get across the idea that there are no right or wrong answers, and that there exists a whole range of equally legitimate opinions and behaviours. Some of the characteristics required to achieve these objectives are discussed below.

Interviewer's features Textbooks on social research practice often dwell on the physical features of interviewers, from gender (they prefer women) to age (middle-aged), education (medium level, high-school diploma) and race (in multi-ethnic societies). They also suggest that the person should be willing to take on a job without great professional aspirations, which is discontinuous, part-time, modestly paid and largely done outside normal working hours. The resulting ideal identikit portrays a middle-aged, middle-class housewife with a high-school diploma. The textbooks often mention the interviewer's dress and appearance; as the first impression may be decisive in a situation of this kind, they recommend a neutral appearance that is neither showy nor eccentric.

There is no need to go to any great lengths on this subject, in that it can be tackled simply by applying a little common sense (not least because the interviewer's ideal features will depend to a great extent on those of the sample interviewed).

Interviewer's expectations It is important to remember that the interviewer's expectations may have a considerable influence on the respondent's answers. If the interviewer discovers that the respondent is a member of a particular political party, she will expect answers on political issues to follow the party line; if the respondent does not appear to be well-informed, she may tend to ask the questions hurriedly and to accept evasive answers or 'don't knows' too readily. Likewise, if the interviewer is convinced that a question is difficult, she will probably obtain a high number of 'don't knows', on account of both her lack of confidence in the respondent's ability to answer and her easier acceptance of evasive answers.

Such expectations are often transmitted unconsciously during the interview. They may be communicated by the interviewer's tone of voice and facial expressions (surprised looks, nodding of the head, etc.), or by the way questions or response alternatives are stressed. All these factors are likely to have an even greater influence on interviewees who feel insecure or uncertain, or who are tempted to try to please the interviewer.

Interviewer's Training All this underlines the importance of interviewer training. First of all, the interviewer must be made aware of the type of interaction that takes place between herself and the interviewee, and of the mechanisms of acquiescence and subliminal influence that are created. Second, since the interviewer has to be able to intervene if the respondent misunderstands or asks for clarification, etc., detailed instructions on what to do in such cases will need to be given, in order to minimize variations in interpretation and prevent discordant indications from being given to respondents. Questionnaires themselves often carry instructions for interviewers – e.g. 'What are the names of all other persons who are living here?' (Interviewer: list all persons staying here and all persons who usually live here who are absent. Be sure to include infants under one year of age). The researcher must also plan for briefings, i.e. meetings which precede fieldwork and in which interviewers are instructed about their tasks, as well as meetings during fieldwork in order to check on progress, identify and solve unforeseen problems, etc. The researcher will also have to engage supervisors for interviewers to call upon if they need help or advice.

Interviewer's motivation Finally, the interviewer's psychological disposition towards her task must also be considered. As has been said, the mechanisms of subliminal interaction and unconscious gestures, looks and tone of voice affect the interview. As a result, an attitude of passivity, tiredness and lack of motivation on the part of the interviewer cannot fail to impact negatively on the respondent. The interviewer must therefore be convinced of the importance of her work in general and of the research in particular. This means that researchers should be involved in the goals of the investigation, and it is important that briefings be used not only to sort out practical questions, but also to ensure that the research objectives are fully explained.

7.2 Telephone interviews

It has already been mentioned that, as a result of a range of concomitant factors, a boom in the use of telephone interviews has been seen in recent years. Indeed, in countries where a high percentage of the population has a telephone, this survey technique represents the most widespread mode of questionnaire administration. The advantages of telephone interviews are briefly outlined. This technique:

- speeds up data collection; with the right resources, a large (over 1000 cases) nationwide sample can be surveyed in as little as a few days; in some situations, this might be an essential requisite (e.g. in gauging the public's reaction to some news event);
- costs far less than face-to-face interviews: savings estimates range from 50% to 75% (Groves, 1989: 526–38; Klecka and Tuchfarber, 1978);
- enables subjects living in outlying districts to be reached at no additional cost; this means that the sample does not have to be concentrated in more easily accessible areas, as often happens with face-to-face interviews;
- greatly facilitates the tasks of interviewer training and supervision; as the interviews are centralized, the interviewers can form a close-knit group, located in a limited area and easily reachable for the purposes of training and supervision (moreover, supervisors can listen in to check how the interviews are being conducted);
- enables computer recording of data to be carried out directly. The telephone is generally used together with the computer (CATI: *Computer-assisted telephone interviewing*): the interview text is scrolled on the interviewer's monitor, the respondent's answers are immediately typed in and stored, the computer directs the interview (for example, in the 'funnel' sequence of questions, it automatically

moves on to the right question, without the interviewer having to follow 'arrows' on the questionnaire), and automatically signals any gross inconsistencies. In this way, the interview runs much more smoothly than a face-to-face interview, the risk of interviewer error is reduced, and elementary analyses of the data collected can be made at any stage of the proceedings (for instance, frequency checks to monitor the sample, communication of provisional data to those who have commissioned the study, etc.).

The disadvantages of the technique can be listed equally concisely:

- in the absence of personal contact, the interviewee feels less involved in the interview and is therefore more likely to give superficial, random or hurried answers; moreover, the interviewer will inevitably feel more detached (than in a face-to-face interview) and may make less effort to ensure the success of the interview;
- again because of the lack of personal contact, the interviewer-interviewee relationship tends to wear thin more quickly; as a result, telephone interviews have to be much shorter than face-to-face interviews (an average of 20 minutes versus 45 minutes);
- visual aids, such as written lists of complicated response alternatives, photographs or illustrations, cannot be used during the interview;
- as the interviewer cannot see the respondent or his home, she cannot record non-verbal data (such as the type of house, the interview environment, the social class of the family as deduced from furnishings, etc.; in face-to-face interviews, such features can be recorded);
- those who do not have a telephone – such as members of marginal sectors of society – cannot be reached; the growing use of answering machines, voice mail, and cellular phones causes a similar problem, in that they make it difficult to speak with their users;
- the elderly and the less educated are generally under-represented in telephone

interviews; while a skilful interviewer can usually persuade a reluctant elderly person to take part in a face-to-face interview, this is much more difficult in the case of a telephone interview, as there is usually a younger or better educated person at home who is likely to be called in to help ('I'll put my son/daughter on') (even though the interviewer's instructions specify otherwise);[9]

- the limited amount of time available means that questions have to be simpler, more concise and, in the final analysis, elementary; moreover, again because of the lack of personal contact, it is difficult to get interviewees to cooperate beyond the level of providing formal replies to formal questions.

Of the various limitations listed here, the most serious are probably the first (lack of contact) and the last (the pressure of time). The rapid pace of the interview allows little time for thought; as already mentioned, short succinct questions prompt short succinct answers, as the respondent perceives that he is required to answer briefly, immediately and without hesitation. There are no pauses in the conversation; silence becomes embarrassing since the respondent cannot use non-verbal signals to show that he is thinking about the answer.

In telephone interviews, the absence of personal contact makes the relationship more formal and less committed. The interviewee may therefore be prompted to answer in a 'bureaucratic' manner or at random; it is easier to confess that we have not understood to a person sitting in front of us than to a disembodied voice waiting for a reply (any reply) in order to go on to the next question. In short, the pressure (on the interviewee) to respond quickly and the anxiety (of the interviewer) to get through the questions in the allotted time strongly condition how the interview is played out. It is therefore with some justification that answers given on the telephone have been claimed to be more superficial than those obtained in direct interviews.

In conclusion, the telephone interview demands simplification of the issues investigated, brevity in questions and answers and a reduction in the number of response alternatives. The fact that it does not allow 'long' interviews to be conducted' or issues to be investigated in depth, means that this research tool is not well suited to deep analysis. On the other hand, its ability to reach large samples of the population, to yield immediate results, to bring together disparate issues (as in market research) into a single procedure, and, consequently, to lower costs makes it a highly appropriate technique for large-scale surveys.

7.3 Self-administered questionnaires

We will now look at questionnaires that subjects fill in on their own, without the participation of an interviewer. These are questionnaires handed out to students at school, to people attending public events, to the users of public services and so on. They also include questionnaires distributed to families and subsequently collected or, as is often the case, mailed to subjects or administered via web surveys.

The first advantage of the technique is obvious: an enormous saving on data-collection costs. For example, in the case of a questionnaire handed out at the entrance to some public event (a festival, exhibition, fair, etc.) and collected at the exit, a single field worker can gather information from hundreds of people in a single day; to obtain similar results through face-to-face interviews, dozens of interviewers would be kept busy for several days.

The main drawback to this technique is equally evident. In the techniques described earlier, the questionnaire is filled in by a trained worker (the interviewer), who has had time to learn the procedure and is unlikely to make gross mistakes. This is not so for the self-administered questionnaire; many interviewees will be filling in a questionnaire for the first time, some may never even have seen one before, and others may not know exactly what to do; the level of education of the subjects will probably vary widely; moreover, many may not bother to fill in the questionnaire, or to fill it in properly. As a result, self-administered questionnaires must be as brief, concise and simple as possible.

A further disadvantage lies in the self-selection of those who respond. To take the example of visitors at a public event, only a minority of subjects will actually hand the completed questionnaire back in. This would not matter if they represented a random sample of the entire population under investigation (all visitors). Unfortunately, they do not. Those who comply are likely to be more motivated, better educated, perhaps younger, etc. As a result, we do not know how far the data obtained can actually be extended to the whole population.

Two basic cases of self-administration can be distinguished: group administration and individual administration. An example of *group administration* may be seen when students in a class are given questionnaires by an operator, who then gives instructions, assists with compilation and collects the completed questionnaires at the end. In a case of this kind, the problems mentioned are considerably reduced. The fact that the operator is on hand to provide instructions and explanations makes gross error less likely; moreover, the operator will ensure that all questionnaires are completed and handed in, thus avoiding the phenomenon of self-selection. When group administration can be properly implemented, the self-administered questionnaire is generally a valid technique. However, outside of the school context, the situations in which it can actually be applied are somewhat rare.

With regard to *individual administration*, a distinction should be made between situations in which returning a completed questionnaire is optional and those in which it is mandatory. A case of *mandatory return* is that of the census, for example, in which an operator distributes questionnaires to families and calls back a week later to collect them. This obviates the two problems mentioned earlier; gross errors are avoided through a summary check carried out by the operator when the questionnaires are collected, and self-selection is avoided by the fact that the operator ensures that all completed questionnaires are collected.

This method does not offer very great savings in comparison with the face-to-face interview (it still requires the personal intervention of an operator, though this may be limited to a few minutes). Nevertheless, the procedure is commonly adopted by national statistical institutes not only in censuses but also for the collection of other data, especially when the information to be gathered is very detailed and is spread over a certain length of time. For example, in investigations on time budgets, as well as on family expenditure, daily schedules are distributed, on which subjects note how they spend their time and their money on each of the following days. Data gathered in this way are much more reliable than those that the subject reports from memory.

Finally, to return to the question of individual completion of optional return questionnaires, we will look in greater detail at the case of the *mail questionnaire*. This involves mailing questionnaires to a sample of subjects who represent the whole population under examination, together with a letter outlining the research and a stamped addressed envelope for return.

The advantages and disadvantages of this technique are briefly listed:

Advantages:

- very great savings on costs (the only immediate costs being those of printing and mailing);
- the questionnaire can be filled in at leisure, even at different times;
- greater guarantee of anonymity than in a face-to-face interview (the returned questionnaire does not contain any means of identification);

- no bias due to the presence of an interviewer;
- subjects living far away or in isolated areas can be reached.

Disadvantages:

- low percentage of returns (often well below 50%), partly because there is no interviewer present to urge compliance;
- sample bias due to self-selection; since those who respond tend to be different from those who do not (e.g. more educated, etc.), it is unlikely that we will have a random sample of the entire population;
- the level of education of the population studied has to be medium-high, in that subjects must have a certain familiarity with written communication;
- no control over completion of the questionnaire, which might be filled in by some other member of the family, or by a secretary;
- questionnaires must not be too complex; both questions and instructions must be simple (e.g. filter questions such as 'If you answer 'yes', go on to the next question; if 'no', go to question 25', etc. should be avoided);
- questionnaires have to be much shorter than in face-to-face interviews.

The main problem with this technique is the low percentage of returns. Babbie (1979: 335) calls a 50% return rate 'adequate', a 60% rate 'good' and a 70% rate or higher 'very good', but emphasizes that this is only a rule of thumb and that it is far more important to have an unbiased sample (though this is not easy to ascertain) than a large sample.[10] The rate of returns depends on various factors, four of which are as follows:

- the institution running the investigation, its prestige and how well it is known; for instance, a well-known public institution, such as a university, will tend to have greater success than some unknown research institute.

- the length and layout of the questionnaire; a questionnaire that is long, complicated and difficult will tend to put the interviewee off straightaway;
- the characteristics of the interviewees; a better outcome is achieved when the population studied is made up of subjects who share common features (members of an association, university graduates, members of a professional category, etc.);
- how questionnaires are followed up; reminders should be given at least once and preferably twice. The complete procedure should have four stages: (a) questionnaires and accompanying letters are sent out; (b) reminders are sent (a letter or postcard); (c) a further reminder is sent, together with another copy of the questionnaire (for those who may have lost the first one); (d) respondents are contacted by telephone.[11]

To conclude our discussion of telephone questionnaires and self-administered questionnaires, it should be said that in both cases *open questions are to be minimized*. The time limits imposed on telephone interviews oblige the respondent to answer quickly and briefly, leaving no room for the inevitable hesitations and explanations that accompany open questions. In the self-administered questionnaire, the absence of an interviewer removes one of the prerequisites of open questions, which make sense only if there is an interviewer on hand to guide, prompt and record. Without an interviewer, the open question lends itself to misunderstanding and, especially, to omitted or incomplete transcription of responses.

7.4 Computer-assisted interviews

We will now briefly mention interviews that utilize the computer in the data-collection phase. The case of *CATI* (*Computer-assisted telephone interviewing*) has already been mentioned. Another technique is that of *CAPI* (*Computer-assisted personal interviewing*); this is not very different from a normal face-to-face interview except for the fact that, instead of using a written questionnaire, the interviewer reads the questions from a portable personal computer and types in the answers directly. In this way, some of the steps between data recording and processing can be eliminated; the phases of data coding and input are no longer required (as they take place during the interview itself). At the end of the day's work, the interviewer – wherever she is – can transmit her interview files via modem to the research centre, where the data can be processed as they come in. In addition to this advantage, complex questionnaires (involving conditional questions, questions submitted to random subsets of the sample, randomly varied sequences of responses, checks on consistency among answers, etc.) can be handled more easily, as the computer can be programmed in advance to deal with these variants.

Another use of the computer in questionnaire administration is that of CASI (*Computer assisted self interviewing*), in which the respondent himself reads the questions on the monitor and types in the answers. In this case, the computer does not merely replace the paper copy of the questionnaire, but is a dynamic means of interaction between the respondent and the research centre. A terminal may be installed in the respondent's home and is linked by modem to the research centre, which sends out the questions and receives the answers. In terms of cost, the most obvious advantage of this technique is that the interviewer is eliminated (indeed, this is a self-administered questionnaire). There is, however, another important advantage: the possibility of conducting longitudinal surveys – that is, of repeating the survey over time on the same subjects. Successive interviews can be carried out in which the questionnaire is modified each time, thus allowing permanent monitoring of such phenomena as changes in public opinion or consumer spending patterns (for instance, how specific political events influence government popularity,

or how consumer spending is influenced by a particular advertising campaign). It is, then, a powerful tool (that is focused especially on short-term changes and has, to date, been used in the field of public opinion polls and marketing). It is not, however, free from problems, the main ones being the limits to self-administered questionnaires (we can never be sure which member of the family has actually answered the questionnaire) and the drawbacks to longitudinal surveys (the awareness of being under scrutiny may alter the subject's behaviour; see Section 9.2).

8.   ORGANIZING DATA COLLECTION

Having discussed question formulation and questionnaire administration at some length, we will now look briefly at the phases that precede the data collection itself: preliminary exploratory interviews, testing of the questionnaire, interviewer training (and supervision once fieldwork has begun), initial contact with interview subjects.

Exploratory study   It almost goes without saying that, in order to construct satisfactory questions, the researcher must first be fully conversant with the object of the research. This is especially true of standardized questionnaires; since these are made up of closed questions, the researcher must not only know exactly what to ask but also be aware of all the possible responses. According to Schuman and Presser, it is necessary that 'investigators begin with open questions on large samples of the target population and use these responses to construct closed alternatives that reflect the substance and wording of what people say spontaneously. This point is so obvious as to be embarrassing to state, yet it is probably violated in survey research more often than it is practiced.' (Schuman and Presser, 1981: 108).

This *preliminary exploratory phase* will be conducted through a multiplicity of techniques, which will gradually evolve from highly unstructured, typically qualitative initial tools to ever more structured techniques. This sequence includes unstructured interviews with key informants, interviews with some members of the population to be studied (focus groups, for example, see Chapter 10, Section 3.2), interviews with open responses (but standardized questions) conducted on the study population, and trials of questions or specific parts of the questionnaire carried out on acquaintances, friends and colleagues, in order to compare different formulations.

In all these cases, the interviews and trials will generally be carried out by members of the research team themselves, who will personally tackle the problem of understanding the various aspects and nuances of the phenomena under investigation.

Pre-testing On conclusion of the exploratory phase, the questionnaire is drawn up. When an almost definitive version has been produced, the *test phase* begins, by means of what is commonly called pre-testing. It should be borne in mind that one of the characteristics of the standardized questionnaire is its inflexibility. Once it has been printed and fieldwork has begun, it can no longer be modified. Any change made will be costly, in that data from interviews already conducted would be lost. It is therefore essential to spot any need for changes in advance. For this reason, a kind of 'dress rehearsal' embodying all the features of the real operation will be required.

With the exception of extremely costly research projects (for which pilot studies are to be recommended), a pre-test conducted on a few dozen cases will be sufficient.[12] This will be carried out on a sample of subjects who have the same characteristics as the members of the study population (taking care to cover a certain range in terms of gender, age, level of education, etc.), and the interviews will be conducted by the same interviewers and in the same conditions as the real interviews (in the interviewee's home, etc.).

One of the aims of the pre-test is to establish the duration of the interview; the pre-test version of the questionnaire is often longer than the final version and contains a certain over-abundance of questions, some of which will be dropped if the test interviews prove to be too long. It should be added that, if such modifications result in a much changed questionnaire, this new version will again have to be tested; as Sheatsley (1983: 228) points out, 'a common error is to write entirely new questions, change the wording of many others, or assume that one has cut 10 minutes of interviewing time by making certain deletions, and then to send the revised version into the field without trying it out.'

Interviewer training and supervision We have already mentioned the fact that if the study is to use interviewers (for face-to-face or telephone interviews), these will have to be trained beforehand and supervised throughout the data-collection procedure. The preparatory phase (*briefing*) consists of an initial meeting between the research team and the interviewers. The aim of this meeting is to outline the research (who it has been commissioned by and its scientific objectives), explain its design (sampling, selection of subjects, interview modality, etc.), and to illustrate the data-collection tool (the questionnaire) in detail.

Attempts will be made to identify all possible problems that might arise during fieldwork, in order to ensure that a common line of conduct is adhered to. This meeting will be followed by trial interviews (the pre-test), at the end of which another meeting will be held in order to discuss how the technique works.[13] Once the definitive version of the questionnaire has been produced, the data-collection phase will begin in earnest. During this phase, it is advisable to hold another meeting with the interviewers, to check how the work is proceeding and, again, to establish a common approach to any problems that may have arisen. During field-work, supervisors will be on duty both to advise and to check up on interviewers (by working together to solve any problems that arise, and by ensuring that interviews are being carried out properly).[14]

Initial contact The most delicate moment of the entire interview is probably the initial approach, when the subject has to decide whether or not to agree to being interviewed. The feelings of suspicion, mistrust and insecurity that may flit through the subject's mind need not be discussed here. However, since this is an on-the-spot decision, a decisive role will be played by the interviewer's approach, both in terms of appearance (dress, etc.) and in terms of the reasons she puts forward (not least the arguments used to sway the hesitant or unwilling subject).

In her introduction, the interviewer must make sure that she explains (a) who the research has been commissioned by; (b) what its objectives are, and (c) why the subject has been picked out; she must also (d) stress the importance of the subject's cooperation and (e) reassure him that his answers will remain anonymous. It is extremely useful to make this presentation by letter a few days in advance, if possible.

The most compelling argument used to overcome the subject's mistrust is that of anonymity. For example, it has been shown that answers regarding voting behaviour are easier to obtain when the questionnaire is unequivocally anonymous (simulated voting by placing a card into a 'ballot-box') than in face-to-face interviews.

Two further decisive elements are constituted by the institution commissioning the research and the figure of the interviewer. For example, if a study is commissioned by the city council and preceded by a letter of presentation and an appeal by the mayor for cooperation, the refusal rate will be lower than if the same research is presented by an unknown research institute. Studies carried out by the national statistics institute meet with far lower refusal rates than other surveys when data are gathered by the local councils themselves, which often conduct interviews through council employees who are known – especially in small towns – and trusted by the population.[15]

9. SECONDARY ANALYSES AND SURVEYS REPEATED OVER TIME

The survey procedure, as it has been implicitly presented so far, envisages a researcher conducting analyses (a) of data that he himself has collected (b) within the same time period (or at least within a limited period, such as a few weeks). However, this is not the only possibility. Today, research is frequently carried out on pre-existing databases or through surveys repeated over time. These two cases are analysed separately below.

9.1 Secondary analysis

When planning his research, the social scientist instinctively conceives of it in terms of a self-sufficient, self-contained process, in which he himself gathers the data to be analysed. He starts out (and rightly so) with the intention to tackle new and original issues, and the idea of utilizing data collected by others may appear demeaning. Nothing could be further from the truth. Indeed, there is no doubt that original research can be carried out on data collected by others. Sampson and Laub's study of deviance (*Crime in the Making*), which was presented in Chapter 2, is a case in point.

By *secondary analysis*, we mean *research carried out on previously collected survey data available in the form of the original data-matrix*; it therefore involves re-analyzing pre-existing files. It should be noted that the term 'secondary analysis' is applied only in cases in which the unit of analysis is the individual and data are available at the individual level. This is different from the case in which only aggregate data are available (e.g. at a territorial level, as in the case of official statistics, which will be dealt with in Chapter 7) or when we re-analyse tables or results from previous studies (as in meta-analysis, which will be discussed later in this section).

For decades, social research proceeded according to the traditional model, in which the researcher defines the issue, draws up the study design, collects the data and then analyses them. As time went on, however, this way of working proved to be inadequate. First of all, the development of the discipline placed ever greater demands on the researcher. For instance, those who first carried out empirical research on the relationship between social class and academic success could restrict their study to a single academic institution and still come up with something new. For those who came later, however, an original contribution could only be made by broadening the empirical base, in order to make comparisons among different institutions or social groups, between urban and rural areas, between the north and south of the country (and, subsequently, even among nations). Likewise, in earlier times, even a simple distribution of univariate frequency or simple bivariate tables could yield original findings; subsequently, however, the need arose for more sophisticated analyses that would simultaneously assess the effect of several variables (multivariate analysis), which involves the use of large samples. In short, the need for greater sophistication rapidly drove up the costs of data collection, placing it beyond the reach of most researchers.

Two developments ensued. First, it was realized that much of the research conducted in the past still offered ample scope for new and original in-depth treatment. Indeed, data analysis does not normally exploit the total data to their full potential. Moreover, ongoing theoretical developments in every discipline periodically raise new issues, and new data-processing techniques can also be used to analyse old issues. Researchers were therefore prompted to re-analyse old files.

Today, this task has been facilitated enormously by the development of information technology, which allows the researcher to download and use files from worldwide sources. It has also been facilitated by the establishment of *data archives*. These are institutions which collect files from previous studies, document the data-gathering techniques used, harmonize the criteria according to which the data are organized, and distribute the data (for a modest fee) to anyone who asks for them.

At the same time, the scientific community has streamlined the collection of new data by promoting agencies whose job is to pool the resources required for this costly operation, and subsequently to make the data available to all researchers. This has given rise to data-gathering for the specific purpose of secondary analysis. Though not focusing exclusively on a specific theme, this kind of data collection is sometimes linked to a particular area of interest (such as electoral behavior, the orientation of values, social mobility, etc.). On other occasions, 'multi-purpose' surveys are carried out, involving a wide range of social issues.

The advantages of these developments are clear: savings are made on data-gathering costs; the quality of the data is ensured when they are collected under the supervision of the scientific community, and even researchers on a low budget are enabled to make wide-ranging studies. In addition, when data collection is carried out by permanent institutions (such as those connected with foundations, universities, the scientific community, etc.), the same surveys can be repeated over long time-intervals, therefore enabling the 'time' variable to be included in social research (this will be dealt with in the following section).

The limitations of these developments should not, however, be overlooked. The lack of control over the phases of data collection may make it impossible for the researcher to judge the *quality of the data*. Moreover, data collected in the past may lack sufficient documentation regarding the data-collection techniques, the features of the sample, the procedures adopted by the interviewers, and non-response rates. In addition, any errors that may have been made in recording or processing data may no longer be detectable.

Nevertheless, with regard to secondary analysis, some serious limitations remain. While it is the researcher who establishes the issues to be examined and analyses the data, these data are collected by others. This may *limit the issues*, in that important questions may go unanswered as a result of insufficient data. Furthermore, this division of labour may produce *research motivated by available data* rather than on theoretical hypotheses: 'Some researchers obtain a data set, apply a currently popular statistical technique, and then look for a problem to investigate ... but the "data set in search of analysis" approach yields only trivial findings' (Kiecolt and Nathan, 1985: 14).

Meta-analysis Before concluding this section, we will briefly return to a point mentioned earlier: the distinction between secondary analysis and so-called *meta-analysis*. Meta-analysis is the name given to an approach that has gained ground in recent years in countries (particularly the US) in which the growth of social research has produced a huge body of empirical data requiring new forms of synthesis. This approach involves selecting, integrating and synthesizing studies that focus on the same object of analysis. Unlike secondary analysis, meta-analysis looks at the *results* of such studies, and not at the original data. It therefore involves 'integrating results' rather than 're-analysing subjects'. Glass, who introduced the term, writes:

> *Primary analysis* is the original analysis of data in a research study ... *Secondary analysis* in the re-analysis of data for the purpose of answering the original research questions with better statistical techniques, or answering new questions with old data ... *Meta analysis* refers to the analysis of analyses ... the statistical analysis of a large collection of analysis results from individual studies for the purpose of integrating the findings. (Glass, 1976: 3)

Meta-analysis uses statistical procedures to synthesize the results of the studies examined. This technique developed as the use of computerized cross-referencing increased; indeed, keyword searches enable studies conducted on a given issue to be picked out fairly easily. For instance, Glass and co-workers used this technique to investigate the influence of the size of school classes on learning. Analysis of the 80 or so studies that they found clearly revealed a close – almost linear – relationship between the level of learning and class size. They concluded that 'there is little doubt that, other things equal, more is learned in smaller class' (Glass et al., 1987: 42).

The same technique was used in a curious study conducted by Rotton and Kelly (1985). In order to test the popular belief that the phases of the moon influence human behaviour, they analysed 37 empirical studies on the relationship between the lunar cycle and various types of mentally or socially anomalous behaviour, such as admissions to psychiatric hospitals, suicide or self-inflicted injury, telephone calls to psychiatric help centres, homicide and other criminal acts, etc. Meta-analysis of the results of these studies revealed no statistically significant relationship between such behaviour and the phases of the moon.

9.2 Surveys repeated over time

In our introduction to the concept of the variable (Chapter 3, Section 5) and in our discussion of experimentation (Chapter 4, Section 5), the fact was mentioned that a variable may 'vary' both *among cases* (in the same time) and *over time* (in the same cases). For instance, if we wish to study the relationship between political conservatism and age, we can do so in two ways: we can either assess political conservatism on a sample of subjects of different ages to see how it varies with age; or we can study the same sample of subjects over time and, by repeating our measurement of their political opinions, see how these vary as the years pass. Studies of the first type are called *cross-sectional studies*, while those of the second type are *panel studies*.

So far, we have referred implicitly to cross-sectional surveys. However, the same techniques (especially that of the standardized questionnaire) may also be applied to longitudinal investigations. As mentioned earlier, a *panel study is one in which the study is repeated over time on the same subjects*. Naturally, this means tackling the arduous task of introducing the variable 'time' into social research. Although the study of *change* is fundamental in the social sciences, it is very difficult to carry out using the tools available today. The cross-sectional survey – in that it provides a kind of instant photograph taken at a specific moment – is a particularly inappropriate tool for the job. The panel survey offers a solution to the problem.

Panels surveys The panel[16] technique, which involves interviewing the same subjects at different time-points, was first proposed in the 1940s by Lazarsfeld (1948), who had applied it during his electoral studies. To examine the effects of election propaganda, he monitored a sample of Ohio voters for six months during the 1940 US presidential campaign.

There are some particular difficulties inherent in panel surveys. A major problem is the 'attrition' of the sample: this term refers to the constant decrease in the number of cases in each successive interview 'wave' due to various reasons (respondents may drop out, move away, die, etc.). Moreover, previous measurements may influence subsequent ones. As already mentioned, memory effects and learning effects may influence the subject's answers when the same questions are repeated. Finally, it should be remembered that the awareness of being under scrutiny may cause the subject to

change his behaviour (for instance, if he knows that he is going to be questioned about politics, he may keep himself better informed on the subject, etc.).

However, repeating measurements on the same subjects is not the only way to carry out a longitudinal study. An alternative is provided by the *retrospective survey*. This consists of a normal cross-sectional survey (carried out in a single session), with the difference that the respondents answer questions about their past. The shortcomings of this approach are obvious, since it relies on memory and on the faithful recounting of past behaviour.

Another solution involves *linking administrative and census files*, thus bringing together personal data from different sources (census, public records office, local health service centres, etc.). In this way, personal information (socio-economic variables, demographic events, health records, etc.) recorded by different sources at different times can be collated (e.g. variations at the individual level between two censuses). The limit to this approach stems from the scant nature of the information provided (which is substantially restricted to basic sociographic properties).

Repeated cross-sectional surveys One way of introducing the time factor into the investigation, without interviewing the same subjects twice, is to use *repeated cross-sectional surveys*. This involves recording the same information at different points in time on different samples of subjects. Obviously, such samples must be comparable (the sample designs must be absolutely identical) in order to ensure that any differences that may emerge among the various measurements are really due to changes in the population and not to variations in the composition of the sample. It should be pointed out that surveys of this kind can only record changes at an aggregate level (such as the overall religious values or patterns of consumption of a population) and not at an individual level. It is therefore very difficult to analyse the causes of any change; such causes are more easily identifiable when the change is recorded at the individual level (panels) and can consequently be seen in relation to other individual variables.

A classic example of cross-sectional surveys is seen in the various 'national election studies' that are conducted at election time in many countries. These involve representative samples of the electorate and utilize questionnaires that mainly ask the same questions. This enables variations in public opinion over time to be discerned.

The main drawback to all research designs that include the variable 'time' is their cost. An effective study of change cannot generally be based on only two measurements; the survey will normally have to be repeated over a long period of time (even decades). This means that investigations of this kind have to be carried out by permanent institutions, which can ensure the necessary long-term continuity that individual resear-chers or isolated research groups cannot provide.

10. DATA SETS AND ARCHIVES IN THE US AND THE UK

This section will discuss some of the many data sets in the US and UK which are part of a series, either in that they interview the same individuals over the course of time (panels), use the same instrument or survey to interview new sets of individuals over time (repeated cross-sections), or some combination of the two (rotating panels). Typically, these surveys cover economic and demographic behaviours, health status and behaviours, educational paths and progress, political participation, attitudes and opinions. The following data sets represent only a fraction of all such series, and an exploration of the holdings of data archives and official agencies will reveal many more.

10.1 Repeated cross-sections

Although more often considered to lie in the category of official statistics (discussed in Chapter 7), the decennial censuses in the US are also a rich source of individual level data. Unlike the traditional tables with aggregate statistics for different geographic areas, *the public use microdata samples (PUMS)* are drawn from the records of individual households and persons who were counted in the censuses between 1850 and 1990. Since 1960, the Census Bureau has produced those samples as part of their data dissemination efforts; samples prior to 1960 were created from census records on microfilm by a number of researchers. The actual method of sampling individuals and households differed by year, but provide representative samples ranging from the 5% samples available in 1980 and 1990 to the 1-in-760 sample for 1900.

As might be expected for a cross-sectional series spanning 150 years, the variables detailed in any census year vary, but the PUMS are consistently strongest in terms of characteristics such as age, gender, race, education, labor force participation and household composition. The usefulness of this census microdata as a repeated cross-section has been expanded greatly by the Minnesota Population Center, which has integrated and harmonized the coding of data across years, provided documentation on data-collection procedures, sampling procedure, variable definitions, changes in universes, and appropriate weighting, as well as construction of new variables, such as metropolitan status and imputed household relationships.

A second series of microdata produced by the US Census Bureau, the *Current Population Survey (CPS)*, is widely used for trend analysis. Strictly speaking, the CPS utilizes a rotating panel design, with households included in the sample for four consecutive monthly interviews and, following an eight-month fallow period, interviewed for an additional four months, but most commonly the data are treated as repeated cross-sections.[17] Although substantially smaller that the decennial census, the CPS includes 55,000 to 60,000 housing units, sufficient to provide the national and states estimates of labor force characteristics for which it was designed. In addition to questions about labor force participation, unemployment, hours and wages, supplemental questionnaires in selected months cover such topics as occupational mobility, school enrolment, fertility, birth expectations, marital history, childcare, health care coverage, voting, and use of public assistance. Although the CPS has been conducted since 1943, microdata are only available for 1964 and later. As with the microdata from the decennial census, researchers have made efforts to integrate and harmonize coding from multiple years; such integrated files are available for the March CPS supplements (which contain a broad array of demographic data, annual earnings, education, and public assistance), the October supplements (which focus on school enrolment), and the May supplements (which have information about usual weekly hours and union coverage).

Analogous to the CPS in the United States are the *Labor Force Surveys* (LFS) in the UK. The LFS was carried out from 1973 through 1983 as a biennial survey, between 1984 and 1991 as an annual survey, and since 1992 the data are released quarterly. The quarterly data reflect interviews with about 138,000 respondents, and provide information about age, gender, ethnicity, labor force participation, disabilities, household composition, and education. Many of the topics which are explored via supplements to the CPS in the US, however, are instead investigated in a *General Household Survey*. Since 1971, the GHS annually asks 9,000 households in Great Britain questions about family, housing, income, living arrangements, health, social class, smoking, drinking, contraception, either in a core questionnaire or in periodic supplements.

The US Census Bureau and Bureau of Labor Statistics (BLS) also conduct the *Consumer Expenditure Survey* (CES). The CES actually consists of two separate surveys – a quarterly Interview survey and the Diary survey – that provide information on the buying patterns of consumers, including detailed data on their expenditures and income, as well as race, gender, age and other standard characteristics. The interview portion of the CES employs a panel portion, with each consumer unit interviewed at three-month intervals over a 15-month period. In addition to its use by the BLS to revise the Consumer Price Index (CPI), the CES can be used by researchers to study the impact of policies on different socioeconomic groups, spending and saving patterns of varying household types, and trends in consumption. For more recent years (1980 through 1998), researchers at the National Bureau of Economic Research have compiled integrated family and individual files to aid in trend analysis.

In the UK, the *Family Expenditure Survey* (FES), like the CES in the US, is used to update the Retail Price Index, but also serves to investigate consumer purchase patterns and income, using both interview and detailed diary data. The FES has been conducted since 1957, and interviews about 10,000 households each year.

Researchers interested in US health and diet data may turn to the *National Health and Nutrition Examination Surveys*, conducted in three cycles between 1971 and 1994. Each cycle interviewed 25,000–34,000 persons, and the resultant data include both questionnaire-based responses and medical data obtained through direct examination. A panel portion to this data is available via reinterview of the first wave (1971–1975) of respondents in 1982–1984, in 1986 and in 1987. Another source of health data is the *National Health Interview Survey* (NHIS), an annual dataset starting in 1969. The NHIS reflects the health status, demographic characteristics, doctor visits, and hospitalizations of over 100,000 persons from each survey. Additional supplements in each year look at topics such as health insurance, accidents, prescriptions, smoking, alcohol consumption, knowledge and attitudes about AIDS, and mental health.

The *National Food Survey* (NFS) in the UK, collected since 1940 and available as microdata since 1974, provides a record of household food expenditures, consumption and diet for a sample of about 8000 households. The *Health Survey for England* (HSE), for which data are available from 1991 forward, provides measures of health status, disease and risk factors associated with health conditions, with varying supplemental questionnaires in each year which focus on such topics as the health of young people, heart disease, or ageing and social isolation.

The *American National Election Study* (ANES) series, starting in 1948, provides data on political participation, social and political attitudes and values, and opinions and perceptions of political figures, policies and groups. The samples for these studies range in size from 1000 to 2500 respondents, and also include sociographic variables like age, gender, race, religion, occupation and education. To aid in comparative analyses over time, a cumulative file containing core items from the biennial election surveys since 1952 has been created as well.

The *British Election Studies* began, under the title of *Political Change in Britain*, in 1963 and surveys have subsequently occurred after every general election since 1964. In addition to the election year surveys, there have been two off-year surveys and supplemental samples of Scottish, Welsh and minorities. The data are intended to make possible the analysis of long-term changes in political attitudes and behaviour, and cumulative files through 1994 have been constructed.

Monitoring the Future is a survey conducted in the US for a sample of approximately 16,000 high-school seniors each year since 1976. Each year's sample is divided into five or six subsamples, all of which respond to a core set of 115 questions on drug use and demographic characteristics, with each subsample responding to a different set of approximately 200 supplemental questions on other topics. Such supplemental topics include changing roles for women, attitudes toward religion and politics, marital plans and educational and occupational goals. A concatenated core file, containing responses in all years to the core questions, is also available.

The *General Social Survey* (GSS), perhaps one of the best-known social surveys, has been conducted since 1972 on an annual or biennial basis. The GSS fields an extensive core questionnaire, which includes questions on employment, occupation, education, the family, race relations, sex relations, religion and morals. In each year, the GSS also gathers data in a topical module, which explore issues such as work orientation, religion, gender, mental health, the role of government or social networks in more depth. Since 1985, topical modules on the GSS have gained a multi-national component through the International Social Science Program (ISSP), which fields the same survey in participating countries. The ISSP includes 34 member countries as of 2001.

The *British Social Attitudes* survey is an annual survey conducted since 1983, and is focused on social attitudes and changes in those attitudes over time. Topics covered include attitudes toward education, civil liberties, inequality, religion, politics, racism, health care, and morality. A standard core of demographic and personal information are obtained in each survey year.

In 1970, a series of surveys intended to measure public attitudes toward and support of the Common Market and EC institutions was launched, expanding in both topical scope and geographic inclusion over time. The 30-year-old *Eurobarometer* series grew to include coverage of the 15 member states of the European Union on an array of topics covering attitudes to nuclear power, religiosity, gender and work roles, racism, information technology, environmental problems and working conditions, as well a variety of other topics. Common core questions ask about age, gender, marital status, education, occupation, income, ethnicity, political leanings, subjective social class, religion and household composition.

Another international survey repeated at intervals, and which includes the US and UK (and over 50 other countries in the most recent waves), is the *World Values Survey (WVS) and European Values Survey*. Asking about such broad topic areas as the meaning and purpose of life, free will, satisfaction with life, current social issues and problems, trust in others, religion, work and leisure, the WVS was fielded in 10 Western European countries and replicated in 12 other countries in its first wave between 1981 and 1983. The survey was repeated and extended in 1990–1993, again in 1995–1997, and a fourth wave was fielded in 1999–2000.

10.2 Panel studies

The *National Longitudinal Surveys*, representing five cohorts of men, women and children in the US, were initiated in 1966 with data collection on a cohort of 5020 men aged 45–59. In the same year, a sample of men aged 14–24 was drawn, followed by a cohort of women aged 30–44 in 1967 and women aged 14–24 in 1968, all of similar size. These original cohorts were followed biennially, ending in 1981 for the group of young men, and in 1990 for the group of older men. The original cohorts of women have continued to be followed. In 1979, a new cohort of 12,686 young men and women who were 14–22-years-old were selected (the NLSY79), and were subsequently followed on an annual basis.

Data in these files reflect the start and end date for individual's work histories, with information about each job. Data is collected in a similar event history format for marital histories, fertility, spells on public assistance and unemployment receipt. Surveys of women have gathered data on the subjects of childcare, responsibility for household tasks, and attitudes towards women working, while surveys of the cohorts approaching retirement have also included focuses on pensions and retirement plans. The NLSY79 surveys are also enhanced with a battery of measures of education, aptitudes, skills and achievement scores, as well as detailed high-school transcripts.

The *National Child Development Study* (NCDS) follows the lives of children born in the US during a target week in 1958, with five follow-ups through 1991. Data collection has tracked childcare, education and training,

family relationships, demographic events, employment and income. The *British Cohort Study of 1970* (BCS70) follows children born during one week in April 1970, building on an initial survey of about 17,000 births to examine factors influencing neonatal mortality. Follow-ups have subsequently been conducted in 1975, 1980, 1986 and 1996, and examine physical, educational, familial and social development of this cohort. Data include both attitudinal and descriptive items. About 55% of the initial cohort remained in the sample at the most recent follow-up.

The *Panel Study of Income Dynamics* was fielded in 1968 among a sample of 4,800 households in the US, oversampled among low-income households, and followed through their lives as they move into new households. The sample was followed annually through 1997, and biennially since then. The survey was designed to investigate determinants of family income, and include questions on attitudes and personality, behaviors, income and work histories, assistance from family and friends, and demographic characteristics. For ease of use, extracts for individuals and families have been created, but a wealth of detailed supplemental files covering a broad range of topics are also available.

In Britain, *the British Household Panel Survey* (BHPS), also annually interviews more than 5000 households initially sampled in 1991. Individuals are followed to new households if they leave the original household. In 2000, Scottish and Welsh samples were increased to independent estimates of characteristics in those areas. The intent of the survey is to understand social and economic trends, and topical areas explored include housing, wealth, employment, income, household composition and demographic events driving changes in that composition, and social networks.

The *European Community Panel* (EHCP) is another similar survey that began in 1994. This survey is conducted by Eurostat (the statistical institute of the European Union) in many European nations. It is an annual face-to-face interview with about 6,000 families. It covers a broad range of topics including health, labour market conditions, household composition, education, level of well-being, and schooling.

A focus on income and wealth, and the impact of state and federal policies on the poverty status and well-being of individuals and families in the US, was the basis for the *Survey of Income and Program Participation* (SIPP), begun in 1984, and *the Survey of Program Dynamics* (SPD), fielded in 1997 as an extension of the 1993 and 1994 panels of the SIPP. The Census Bureau has conducted the SIPP almost yearly since 1984, including studies beginning in 1990, 1991, 1992, 1993, and 1996. Each of these studies consists of a multi-wave set of interviews with the same households three times each year for about two-and-a-half years. Each interview includes a repeated set of core items and a topical module with more detailed questions. The core questionnaire asks respondents about their participation in a wide range of public assistance programs, including Aid to Families with Dependent Children, Medi-Cal, Food Stamps, and Supplemental Security Income, as well as information about the composition of the household, demographic events, labor market activity and income. The SPD was initiated in response to dramatic changes in public assistance policies in 1996, and provides for the collection of 10 years of annual follow-up interviews for the entering SIPP panels of 1993 and 1994.

Longitudinal data focused on education and educational outcomes in the US include the *National Longitudinal Study of the Class of 1972* (NLSC72), the *National Education Longitudinal Study* (NELS), and *High School and Beyond* (HS&B). The NLSC72 spans the period from 1972 through 1986, and tracks the educational, vocational and personal progress of high-school seniors in 1972 with interviews 1973, 1974, 1976, 1979, and 1986. Events tracked include post-secondary education, family formation and dissolution, military experience, and employment. The HS&B tracks about 60,000 students who were high-school sophomores and seniors in 1980 through

1986 via three follow-up interviews. Data items cover work experience, unemployment history, education and other training, family formation, and income. The NELS tracks a cohort of 25,000 eighth-grade students in 1988 as they progress though secondary and post-secondary education. It includes information about the student's parents and their parental background, their learning environment, aspirations, and social relationships, and teachers and school administrators.

11. A FINAL NOTE: SOME EMERGING RISKS

That we have devoted considerable space to the issue of surveys should not surprise the reader. Indeed, the survey is, and has always been, the most widely used research technique in sociology, and probably in the entire field of social research. The procedures that it uses were worked out and tested through thousands of studies conducted in the United States and other Western countries in the 1950s and 1960s, and have been consolidated around a standard model that still remains valid.[18]

Nevertheless, recent years have witnessed the emergence of some rather worrying trends. Sets of ready-collected data on the most diverse social phenomena are now available for processing. Firms specializing in data collection offer high-speed, low-cost services that save the researcher the trouble of gathering data in the field. The growth of social research is demanding increasingly numerous samples that can only be managed by specialized agencies, with the result that small locally-based research is being squeezed out. These, and probably other, factors are all conspiring to create a situation in which research conducted through surveys, both nationally and internationally, is faced with an increasingly dramatic split between theoretical elaboration and data analysis on the one hand and data collection on the other.

The classical survey described in this chapter was organized in phases that were always controlled and directly run by the researcher (or research team). The researcher (or team) defined the hypotheses and, on the basis of these, constructed the first draught of the questionnaire. She handled much of the exploratory study personally, selected and trained the interviewers, kept in touch with them directly during data collection, organized and supervised the phases of codification and finally analysed the data. Although the role of the researcher was distinct from that of the interviewer, each step of the data collection process was directed and supervised by the researcher.

The two models most commonly adopted today both differ from the classical model. The one that differs more is the case in which the researcher merely analyses data collected by others, as happens in secondary analysis. The other case is that in which the researchers also draws up the questionnaire, but leaves the interviewing to a survey agency.

The 1970s manual of Michigan University's Institute for Social Research, though advocating a strongly behaviourist approach, recommended that interviewers be made aware of the objectives of every question and that the research director clarify every possible source of misunderstanding (ISR, 1976: 4). In other words, even in a model envisaging strict separation of roles, care was then taken to establish considerable contact between the researcher and the interviewer, and the researcher should inform the interviewer of the exact reasons behind each single question. Today, this no longer happens (or happens increasingly rarely). Obviously, such contact is missing when the researcher works on data that have already been collected and coded. Moreover, when data collection is carried out by a survey agency, the researcher has no direct contact with the interviewers, but only with the management of the agency. The interviewer's role is therefore reduced to that of a mere measuring tool, an adjunct to the questionnaire.

Professional interviewers are called upon to conduct interviews on anything from drug use among young people to the consumption of cosmetics or the popularity of a television personality. All such interviews will be carried out in the same professional and impersonal style. The sociologist conducting the study of drug use has no opportunity to convoke the interviewers, to explain the cognitive objectives of the research, or to discuss with them the reactions of those interviewed; in other words, the researcher cannot assemble a group and use the experience of its members to make contact, albeit indirectly, with the subjects of the research.

Thus, a distinction is created between the noble tasks in research (the formulation of theories, statistical analysis and interpretation of results) and humbler tasks (collecting information), which are farmed out to those we can call the hired hands of research. The researcher not only delegates these 'menial' tasks to others, but also forgoes control over them. As a result, less attention is devoted to data collection and the quality of the data is therefore jeopardized.

This decline is all the more disconcerting in that it is accompanied, in the current model of social research, by rigorous attention to data analysis. Thus, while more care is taken to work out models of multivariate analysis whose level of sophistication approaches that of econometrics, less concern is addressed to the question of what is really revealed by those so perfectly manipulated variables. It must therefore be forcefully underlined that the scant awareness of the accuracy of the data engenders a grave risk: that of sophisticated processing of insubstantial data leading to the production of worthless research (as denoted by the celebrated acronym *gigo*: 'garbage in, garbage out').

SUMMARY

1. A *survey* is a technique for gathering information by questioning individuals, who are the object of research and who belong to a representative sample, through a standardized questioning procedure, with the aim of studying the relationships among variables. A survey is made up of two

fundamental elements: question and answer. Both of these may be formulated in a standard way; alternatively, they may be freely expressed. When both are standardized, we have what we call a *questionnaire*, which is the main data-collection tool in surveys.

2. A researcher who wishes to explore social reality by posing questions to social actors faces two dilemmas. The first has to do with the tension between the view that social reality is objectively knowable (*objectivist* position) and the view that knowledge can only be generated by the interaction between the subject who studies and the subject that is studied (*constructivist* position). The second dilemma sets off those who feel that there exist, in the social world, empirical uniformities which can be classified (*uniformist* position) against those who believe that inter-individual differences cannot be eliminated (*individualistic* position). When the researcher decides to adopt a questionnaire and therefore the survey technique, he is solving both dilemmas by choosing the first alternative in both cases.

3. Another basic objection has to do with the reliability of the verbal behaviour. This question actually implies two distinct problems. The first concerns *social desirability*: if an attitude or behaviour has a strong positive or negative connotation in a certain culture, the respondent may be tempted to report a socially approved opinion or behaviour, rather than her actual thought or action. The second has to do with *non-attitudes* (or *pseudo-opinions*): in social research, subjects are often asked about complex matters, about which some subjects may have never thought seriously nor therefore formed an opinion.

4. Questions can be classified, according to their *content*, into three groups: questions concerning basic *sociographic properties*, *attitudes* and *behaviours*. In relation to their *form*, we may distinguish between *open* and *closed* questions. An open question is one in which the respondent is free to

formulate a reply as she wishes. A closed question is one in which a range of alternative answers is presented to the interviewee, who must choose her reply among them. When large numbers of interviewees are involved, the researcher must necessarily opt for closed questions.

5. The way in which a question is formulated can heavily influence the answer. Even slight changes in the wording of the question can lead to marked variations in the response. In order to avoid errors in question wording, there are many guidelines that can be followed regarding syntax, language, content, time focus, memory effects, question order, number of response alternatives, and how to avoid social desirability and non-attitude bias.

6. Item batteries are sets of questions formulated in the same way and submitted to interviewees in blocks. They allow the researcher to save questionnaire space and interview time, help the respondent to understand the response mechanism, improve response validity and construct synthetic indexes that summarize in a single score the various items in the battery.

7. There are basically three ways of administering a questionnaire: face-to-face interviews, telephone interviews and self-administered questionnaires. In the *face-to-face interview*, the interviewer plays a central role. The main problem is therefore the minimization of interviewer effects. *Telephone interviews* speed up data collection, cost far less than face-to-face interviews and greatly facilitate interviewer training and supervision. But the interviewee feels less involved in the interview; visual aids cannot be used; those who do not have a telephone cannot be included in the study; elderly and less educated individuals are more difficult to reach. *Self-administered questionnaires* are used in two different contexts: group administration and individual administration. Mail questionnaires are the most important tool in the case of individual administration.

8. Data collection is usually preceded by the following activities: preliminary exploratory interviews; questionnaire testing; interviewer training (and supervision once fieldwork has begun); initial contact with interview subjects.

9. *Secondary analysis* is carried out on previously collected survey data available in the form of the original data-matrix. It therefore involves re-analysing pre-existing files. Today secondary analysis is facilitated to a great degree by the development of information technology and the establishment of data archives.

We can introduce the time factor into empirical research by means of *panel studies* or *repeated cross-sectional surveys*. A panel study is one in which a survey is repeated over time on the same subjects, whereas repeated cross-sectional surveys record the same information at different points in time on different samples of subjects.

10. Many data sets in the US and UK are part of time series (panels or repeated cross-sections); typically, these surveys cover economic and demographic behaviour, health status and health-related behaviour, educational careers, political participation, and attitudes and opinions.

FURTHER READING

C. Marsh, *The Survey Method: The Contribution of Surveys to Sociological Explanation* (Allen & Unwin, 1982, pp. 180) is a friendly introduction to the history of surveys and provides an overview of the methodological debate on this technique.

For a discussion of standardization and a comparison between pre-defined questionnaires and flexible conversational interviewing, see H. Houtkoop-Steenstra, *Interaction and the Standardized Survey Interview: The Living Questionnaire* (Cambridge University Press, 2000, pp. 209).

On questionnaire design we suggest three books: J.M. Converse and S. Presser, *Survey Questions: Handcrafting the Standardized Questionnaire* (Sage, 1986, pp. 80), a short but comprehensive summary of relevant knowledge; F.J. Fowler Jr., *Improving Survey Questions* (Sage, 1995, pp. 191), which contains a lot of practical suggestions and hints; and S. Sudman, N.M. Bradburn and N. Schwarz, *Thinking About Answers: The Application of Cognitive Processes to Survey Methodology* (Jossey-Bass, 1996, pp. 304), a thorough discussion of the effects of questionnaire design on results.

For a brief review on telephone surveys, read R.M. Groves, *Theories and Methods of Telephone Surveys* (Annual Review of Sociology 1990); P.J. Lavrakas, *Telephone Survey Methods: Sampling, Selection and Supervision* (Sage, 1993, pp. 181) provides a more exhaustive and applied treatment. As regards mail surveys, one may choose between a short text, D.A. Dillman, 'The Design and Administration of Mail Surveys', *Annual Review of Sociology* 1991, and a more applied reading: T.W. Mangione, *Mail Surveys: Improving the Quality* (Sage, 1995, pp. 129).

See S. Menard, *Longitudinal Research* (Sage 1991, pp. 81), for a short treatment of longitudinal studies and panel surveys; for a collection of essays on all aspects of the design and analysis of panel surveys, see D. Kasprzyk, G. Duncan, G. Kalton and M.P. Singh (eds), *Panel Surveys* (Wiley, 1989, pp. 592). G. Firebaugh, *Analyzing Repeated Surveys* (Sage, 1997, pp. 71) is devoted to repeated cross-sectional surveys. Finally, a good text on secondary analysis is K.J. Kiecolt and L.E. Nathan, *Secondary Analysis of Survey Data* (Sage, 1985, pp. 87).

NOTES

1. Actual behaviours were checked either a priori (people whose names appeared in judicial records of convictions for bankruptcy or drunken driving were interviewed, without of course knowing that the researcher was aware of the fact) or a posteriori (after the interview, the electoral registers were checked to see if the people had actually voted, or libraries were contacted to see whether the respondents were actually members).

2. Closed question: the respondent chooses the answer from an array of options proposed by the interviewer (see Section 4.2).

3. Telephone interviews require fewer interviewers and, being centralized, the interviewers are easier to control. As we will see, this is one of the advantages of the technique. On the other hand, telephone interviews are subject to rigid time limits and do not therefore permit in-depth interviews or dialogues such as the one quoted earlier.

4. A solution that seems to combine the advantages of the open question with those of the closed question involves using what is called the 'field-coded question'. This consists of asking open questions which are coded on the spot by the interviewer into pre-coded categories (which are listed on the interviewer's copy of the questionnaire, but not seen by the respondent). However, in spite of its apparent advantages, those who have studied the problem in depth recommend that this solution be avoided. Indeed, 'interviewers do have the advantage of being able to ask respondents to elaborate further if there is doubt about the category an answer should fit into', but this is outweighed by the disadvantages: 'we do not know to what extent interviewers understand the categories in the intended way', and 'the pressure of the interview situation makes it likely that greater coder error will be introduced in a field-coding situation than in office coding' (Sudman and Bradburn, 1982: 153).

5. This tactic does not rule out the possibility of error on the part of the individual respondent, but it does at least avoid systematic error – that is, an error in the same direction on the part of all respondents.

6. It should be borne in mind that the memory is subject to a so-called 'telescoping effect', whereby events situated in the distant past are remembered as happening more recently.

7. A similar approach can be adopted with regard to 'time budgets'; subjects are given schedules on which they note the starting and finishing times of all their activities in a given period (generally a day or a week).

8. This supposition is not altogether justified, since the subjects who are 'the most easily affected by variations in question form should tend to be less educated, as well as less interested or involved in the particular issues asked about' (Schuman and Presser, 1981: 6).

9. The person who answers the telephone will not necessarily be interviewed; there are various ways of selecting a subject at random from the family unit (e.g. 'the person whose birthday is next', or similar).

10. Dillman reports that the response rates in the (American) studies analysed by him range from 60% to 75% (1978: 51).

11. Reminders may be sent to all subjects (a more costly procedure) or only to those who have not yet returned the questionnaire. In the latter case, each questionnaire will have to have an identification number, and will therefore no longer be anonymous (it can, however, be explained in the accompanying letter that the questionnaires will be processed anonymously).

12. Sheatsley (1983: 226) maintains that 'it usually takes no more than 15–25 cases to reveal the major difficulties and weaknesses in a pre-test questionnaire'.

13. On conclusion of these meetings, it is advisable to summarize all instructions in the form of a written list, to which the interviewer can refer during the course of the interviews.

14. Supervision can also serve to motivate interviewers (nothing is more demoralizing than the perception that no one will notice if the work is done well or badly). In general, random checks on interviewees are carried out, usually by telephone, in which some key questions are repeated in order to ensure that the answers are consistent with the information collected by the interviewer.

15. The problem of refusal will be discussed further in Chapter 8.

16. The term 'panel' was originally used in the US to indicate a group of citizens appointed for jury service in the lower courts; it subsequently came to mean a group of persons called upon to judge or discuss. The term was then applied to permanent groups of citizens asked to express their opinions through interviews repeated over time.

17. The sample for the CPS is a sample of housing units, rather then households or persons. No effort is made to follow movers, and attrition of persons in the housing unit is substantial over the course of the 16 months between the month

a housing unit is first interviewed and the month it leaves the sample.

18. Many of the survey manuals written in the US at the end of the 1960s and the beginning of the 1970s are still relevant today, and some are still on the market (after undergoing purely cosmetic changes).

6   Scaling

This chapter addresses one of the most difficult issues in social research: *measurement*. How can one translate complex social science concepts – such as emotional states, psychological traits, social interactions, and political attitudes – into empirical operations? After a preliminary theoretical overview and a brief history of measurement in social research, the chapter introduces some of the most simple and well-known scaling techniques; the final part describes a technique for assessing interpersonal relations among individuals in groups.

1. OPERATIONALIZING COMPLEX CONCEPTS

Scaling is the name given to a set of procedures drawn up by social research to 'measure' human beings and society. In the previous chapters, we discussed the complexity of the concepts used in the social sciences and the

fact that many concepts are not observable. Optimism, depression, racial prejudice, authoritarianism, religious devotion, intelligence, social integration, social conflict, etc. are typical concepts in the social sciences, and characterize the basic unit of these sciences: the human being. However, they do not translate easily into the language of empirical research.

This issue was dealt with in Chapter 3, in which we discussed concepts and indicators. As was said then, a general concept, such as religious devotion, can be operationalized by means of a specific concept known as an indicator, which is linked to it by a partial overlapping of meaning (thus, we can operationalize religious devotion by means of religious practice and political conservatism by means of the party voted for).

The technique of scaling serves to achieve this objective in a more systematic and formalized way. How scaling differs from the use of indicators is that it not only involves replacing a concept with one or more indicators that partially overlap it; rather, it replaces that concept with a coherent, organic set of indicators. Moreover, it sets up inter-individual criteria to ascertain whether the indicators and the concept really do overlap and whether the procedure is complete. We can therefore say that *a scale is a coherent set of items that are regarded as indicators of a more general concept*.

The *item* is therefore the single component (statement, question, behaviour, test response, attribute); the *scale* is the set of items. The underlying concept has different names according to the discipline; psychologists speak of 'latent trait', while sociologists often use the term 'latent variable'.

A test of mathematical ability is a scale; the existence of a general concept, 'mathematical ability', is hypothesized, and this is assessed by means of a range of specific tests (solving problems and equations, proving theorems, etc.), the results of which are combined into a single score. A further example can be seen in Table 5.1 of Chapter 5, which reports a series of psychophysical disorders taken from the 'Carroll rating scale for depression'. This too is a scale: the symptoms are the items of the scale and depression is the general concept; the final result of the scale is a score, which is based on the single responses and assigned to the individuals to whom the scale is adminis-tered. The researcher takes this score to be a measure of the level of depression.

In the field of sociology and social psychol-ogy, the most common application of scaling is seen in so-called *attitude measurement*, in which the unit of analysis is the individual, the general concept is an attitude and the specific concepts are opinions. By 'attitude' we mean – to use the definition given in a classic treatise on the issue – 'the sum-total of a man's inclinations and feelings, prejudice or bias, preconceived notions, ideas, fears, threats and convictions about any specific topic', while by 'opinion' we mean 'the verbal expression of attitude' (Thurstone and Chave, 1929: 6–7). Attitude is therefore a fundamental

belief that cannot be gauged directly, while opinion is one of the ways in which it is man-ifested; opinion is therefore an empirically assessable expression of attitude.

In our terminology, we could say that the attitude is the general concept and the opin-ions are its indicators. The process of assessing attitudes involves presenting the individuals under examination with a series of statements and asking them to express their opinions of them. By appropriately combining the responses, an individual score is obtained which estimates the position of each subject with regard to the attitude in question. Table 6.4 shows one of these scales, in which the attitude is 'sense of political efficacy', an aspect of political participation, which is assessed through the opinion expressed on single statements regarding politics, members of Parliament, etc. By attributing a score from 1 to 4 to each single response (1 to the minimum and 4 to the maximum sense of efficacy) and adding the scores, each individual interviewed is allocated an overall score of political efficacy ranging from a minimum of 9 (there are nine questions in the example) to a maximum of 36. The scale is constituted by the set of statements, the statements being the items of the scale.

Since scaling was first applied in the 1930s, sociologists and social psychologists have drawn up hundreds of scales, both to 'mea-sure' attitudes and, more generally, to gauge many latent dimensions of the human person-ality: emotional states (anxiety, depression, resentment), psychological traits (self-esteem, introversion), needs (self-fulfilment, power), social relations (social status, family integra-tion), and political orientation (left-right lean-ings, political alienation). Alongside these applications, we find the scales used in educa-tional science to assess skills and abilities (manual, mental) or learning (academic and professional assessment tests).[1]

However, while 'attitude measurement' is the most important field of application of scaling, it is not the only one. The technique can be used not only to assess the properties of individuals through their responses to a range of stimuli (the items of the scale), but also to attribute a score to the stimuli on the basis of individuals' responses. For instance, a social prestige score can be attributed to professions, or a rank-order list of the popularity of politicians can be established, on the basis of the judgements expressed by interview subjects. Moreover, scaling can also be used to gauge the properties of units other than individuals; e.g., to gauge the efficiency of institutions (governments, companies, public bodies, etc.), to assign a social cohesion score to a community, or to judge the power of a range of professional roles on the basis of authority-submission relationships at work, and so on.

Does scaling produce nominal, ordinal or interval variables? The underlying concept is generally taken to be a continuous property; the degree of racial prejudice or religious devotion varies gradually – or at least is thought to do so – from among individuals (indeed, social scientists often use the Latin word *continuum*). These continuous properties cannot be translated into interval variables only because we are unable to measure them – that is, to define a unit of measurement. Scaling is a way of dealing with this problem by means of procedures that yield interval variables. But has this objective been achieved? Indeed, can it be achieved?

Traditional scaling has given rise to variables that we have called 'quasi-interval' (see Chapter 3, Section 6), where 'quasi' serves to indicate that the objective of attributing complete numerical meaning to scale scores is unachievable. Recently, however, new theoretical developments and the availability of new data-processing resources have given rise to statistical models that are able to produce variables characterized by 'equal intervals' among its values, that is equivalent to having a unit of measurement. However, these applications are complex and infrequently used (we are referring to Rasch's scaling technique). It can therefore be said that the main body of social research techniques does not go beyond quasi-interval scales.

Early attempts to gauge attitudes through the use of scales date back to the middle of the 1920s and are seen in the work of Allport and Hartman, Bogardus, and Thurstone. It was Thurstone (1927; 1928; 1931) who first systematized the sector; the three different proposals (*Paired comparison, Rank order, Equal appearing intervals*) that he made were of considerable methodological interest (particularly the third), but have now been superseded, chiefly on account of their difficulty of application. By contrast, the simplicity of application of the proposal put forward by Likert in 1932 was met with considerable success (and still is today). Subsequently, an important contribution was made by Guttman (1944; 1950).

2. QUESTIONS WITH ORDERED ANSWERS: THE SEMANTIC AUTONOMY OF RESPONSE CATEGORIES

A scale is made up of several items, and in most cases these items are questions. To take up a notion introduced earlier (Chapter 5, Section 6), we can say that – in this most common case – *a scale is made up of a battery of questions*. Before going into the question of how the scales are constructed, we will look briefly at the issue of *question format*. In a closed-ended question, when the response alternatives presented to the interviewee are in (increasing or decreasing) order, these alternatives can be presented in three ways.

- The first of these involves presenting response alternatives which, even though they can be placed in order, are *semantically autonomous*; this means that each one has its own intrinsic complete meaning that does not need to be seen in relation to the meaning of the other alternatives presented in the scale in order to be understood. For instance, if we look at the questions and answers reported in Table 6.1, we will see that a subject who answers that he/she has a 'university degree' does not need to know what the other response alternatives are.

TABLE 6.1 *Questions with semantic authonomy of response categories*

1. Attendance of religious functions	2. School education
1. Never	1. Illiterate
2. Two-three times a year	2. Primary schooling
3. Once a month	3. Lower secondary
4. Two-three times a month	4. Upper secondary
5. Once or more a week	5. College or university

TABLE 6.2 *Questions with partial semantic authonomy of response categories*

In the present circumstances we cannot afford tax cuts	Would you say you are very interested in politics, somewhat interested, only a little, or not at all interested in politics?	Kind of town of residence
1. Agree strongly	1. Very interested	1. Urban
2. Agree somewhat	2. Somewhat interested	2. Mostly urban
3. Neither agree nor disagree	3. Only a little	3. Semi urban
4. Disagree somewhat	4. Not at all interested	4. Semi rural
5. Disagree strongly		5. Mostly rural
		6. Rural

- The second case is that in which the response alternatives show *partial semantic autonomy*. The most common example is that of responses listed in order: 'very much', 'somewhat', 'a little', 'not at all', or similar (see Table 6.2). In this case, the meaning of each category is only partially independent of the others. For instance, it is not entirely clear what is meant by 'somewhat' interested in politics, when the expression is taken on its own. However, in a series ranging from 'very much' to 'not at all', in which 'somewhat' comes after 'very much' and before 'a little', it is easier to attach a meaning to the word.

- Finally, we have the so-called *self-anchoring scales* (Cantril and Free, 1962), in which only the two extreme terms are given a meaning and the respondent is called upon to identify his position within a continuum – represented by boxes, numbers or a band – located between these two extremes. Table 6.3 shows three examples. The first of these concerns the left-right political spectrum; the second utilizes the so-called 'feelings thermometer'; and the

third refers to a very general question (satisfaction-unsatisfaction), in order to illustrate how the technique can be applied to any issue in which responses can be imagined within a continuum located between two opposite alternatives.

Regarding the type of variable produced by these three procedures, with reference to the distinction between *nominal, ordinal* and *interval* variables, the first of the three situations (semantic autonomy) yields ordinal variables; only the order of the categories is guaranteed, while the distances that separate them are totally unknown (because of the semantic autonomy of the categories, the respondent chooses them according to their content, regardless of their position in relation to the others).

Nor can it be said in the second case (partial semantic autonomy) that the different response categories are equidistant from one another; for one respondent, the term 'somewhat' might have a strong affirmative connotation and therefore be very close to 'very much' and more distant from 'a little', while for another respondent the opposite might be true. However, as the individual answers do not have an autonomous meaning, the respondent interprets them in relation to the other alternatives; this process is likely to trigger a mechanism of quantitative comparison, especially if the alternatives are fairly numerous.

This process of self-evaluation of the distance between one response category and the next is more likely to take place when the responses are self-anchoring. In attributing a meaning to the intermediate categories, the respondent automatically subdivides in her mind the semantic space between the two extremes, and establishes correspondences between the states of the property and the positions on the scale. Thus, if she is very satisfied or dissatisfied with a certain situation, or if she strongly agrees or disagrees with a certain statement, she will indicate her position as being towards one extreme or the other; if she feels her position to be equidistant between the two extremes, she will indicate the mid-point of the scale, etc. This mental subdivision of the continuum presumably involves breaking up the space into equal parts; the technique should therefore ensure that the categories are substantially equidistant from one another.

However, the fact that it is the respondent herself who implicitly establishes the unit of measurement of the scale means that the procedure is a subjective one. In other words, we do not have an external, inter-individual unit of measurement that is valid for all subjects studied, as well as for the researcher. For this reason, we do not have true interval variables, but rather what we have called *quasi-interval* variables.

There is general agreement among researchers that these variables can be treated as interval variables from the mathematical-statistical standpoint. Indeed, in social research practice, even variables of the first and second type are often treated as interval variables, generally by assigning numerical values in a simple sequence (1, 2, 3 ...) to the categories. This practice, however, has given rise to considerable controversy among social researchers.

We will conclude this section by mentioning some of the technical issues involved in question wording. Boxes 6.1 and 6.2 deal with problems concerning the presence of a neutral response option and the number of response categories.

BOX 6.1   THE NEUTRAL RESPONSE OPTION

When the variable has partial semantic autonomy, the question is raised as to whether the respondent should be given an explicitly neutral response option (e.g. 'agree strongly', 'agree somewhat', *'neither agree nor disagree'*, 'disagree somewhat', 'disagree strongly'), or whether he/she should be forced to take sides on the issue. There is no agreement among researchers on this point. On the one hand, offering a neutral position enables genuinely intermediate opinions to be recorded faithfully; on the other, it provides a loophole for those who prefer not to take sides or not to reveal what they really think.[2] Generally speaking, it appears preferable to offer a neutral option, unless the explicit intention is to force the subject to make a choice. Moreover, it is strongly advisable – as was pointed out in Chapter 5, Section 5 – always to provide the option 'don't know', in order to avoid what we have called 'pseudo-opinions'.[3]

BOX 6.2   THE NUMBER OF RESPONSE CATEGORIES

A further question is that of the number of response categories that should be offered. As a general rule, if the scale is made up of few questions (or even based on a single question), it is preferable to offer the respondent a wide range of possible answers (e.g. 5 or 7 alternatives). By contrast, if the scale contains numerous questions, the responses could – in the extreme case – all involve a binary choice (yes/no). Indeed, the objective of the scale is to identify the differences among subjects with regard to the property under examination. If a scale is made up of a single question and offers 10 possible response alternatives, the subjects can be distributed over 10 positions. If a scale is made up of 10 binary questions, we will still obtain (by summing the responses to the 10 questions) a final score over 10 positions. Moreover, it should be borne in mind that offering more alternatives makes the question more difficult to answer (it is easier to answer agree/disagree than to grade one's own level of agreement). Traditionally, specific solutions to this problem have been found within the various techniques (e.g. in the Likert scales, questions normally have 5 or 7 alternatives; in the Guttman scales, the responses are dichotomous).[4]

Regarding the self-anchoring scales, the examples reported in Table 6.3 show three *different response-sequence modalities*: empty boxes, a series of numbers (often from 1 to 7 or from 1 to 10, or, in the case of the feelings thermometer, from 1 to 100), and an unbroken line. There is no great difference between the first two formats. The unbroken-line formulation was introduced into the social sciences relatively recently, together with assessment modalities that have been successfully applied over the last 30 years in the field of physical sensations (luminosity, the intensity of sounds, tastes and smells, weight estimates, etc.; cf. Lodge, 1981). Typically, the interviewee is asked to draw a line proportional in length to his degree of approval of a given statement, liking for a certain person, confidence in a particular institution, etc. In the coding phase, the length of the line is measured and converted into a number. Advocates of this technique claim that the conventions regarding physical distances have a greater inter-subjectivity than those regarding semantic distances.

In this section, we have examined the structure of the single questions. Normally, however, a scale is made up of several questions or, to be more precise, several items. Nunnally (1978: 66–68) reports three reasons why *multi-item scales* are superior to *single-item scales*. First of all, the complexity of the concepts to be investigated makes it unlikely that they can be covered by a single indicator (cf. the discussion of the dimensions of complex concepts in Chapter 3, Section 7). Second, a single assessment lacks precision, in that it cannot uncover subtle distinctions among the various positions of the subjects with respect to the property considered. For example, in the very common case of dichotomous questions (such as agree/disagree), subjects are sorted into only two groups, and finer distinctions go unrecorded. Finally, single questions run a greater risk of random error; when the scale is based on several responses, any such error will have a lesser weight.

TABLE 6.3   *Self-anchoring scales*

Question 1. In politics one often talks about left and right. Where would you place yourself on this scale? And where will you place the different parties?

Left   Right   Don't know

| | | | | | | | | | | | |

Question 2. Now I want to ask you your opinion about some institutions, facts or parties whose names are written on these cards. This figure represents a thermometer marked in degrees from 0 to 100. Use this thermometer to express your degree of liking or disliking for the institutions written on the card. If you like it very much or your opinion is very positive, mark the card at 100 or perhaps at 90 to 95 degrees. If you dislike it very much or your opinion is very negative, mark the card at 0 or perhaps at 5 to 10. If your opinion is intermediate between the two extremes, mark the thermometer at 50 degrees or perhaps between 40 and 60.

Question 3. What is your level of satisfaction with the following aspects of your life? (Place a cross on the horizontal bar: if you are absolutely unsatisfied place your cross at the extreme left; if you are very satisfied place the cross on the extreme right; otherwise place the cross on the line in proportion to your degree of satisfaction or unsatisfaction)

	Unsatisfied	Satisfied	Don't know
Financial situation			☐
Relationship with your spouse			☐
Relationship with your children			☐
etc.			
etc.			

In conclusion, single-item scales are less valid, less accurate and less reliable. The following sections will therefore deal with the most common multi-item scaling techniques.

3.   THE LIKERT SCALE

This technique takes its name from the psychometrician Rensis Likert, who first proposed it at the beginning of the 1930s (Likert, 1932). The heading 'Likert scale' covers a wide variety of scales, which are also known as *summated rating scales*. This technique is still the most frequently used procedure in attitude assessment, and has been developed and enriched considerably since its introduction. In our illustration, we will also bring up some general considerations (wording of questions, scale validation, etc.) which are applicable to all techniques of scale construction.

The procedure on which the Likert scales are based is simple and intuitive. It is the first thing that would come to mind if anyone had to assign an overall score on the basis of the scores in single tests: add up the scores of the single tests. Thus, in a school test made up of 30 questions, we might give one point for each correct answer and then add up the points; a student who has made no mistakes will get 30. Likewise, in a football league, the total number of points of each team in the league is simply the sum of the points won in the individual matches.

The format of the single questions in the Likert scales is traditionally that of a series of statements, the respondent having to say if, and to what extent, he agrees with each one. In the initial version, Likert himself proposed seven alternatives (ranging from 'agree strongly' to 'disagree strongly'). The number was later reduced to five (or sometimes four by eliminating the middle category). In terms of the classification presented earlier, these are questions with answers that have partial semantic autonomy. There are four phases to the construction of the scale:

1. item conception and writing;
2. item administration;
3. item analysis, i.e. internal consistency evaluation and item selection; and
4. scale validation and unidimensionality checks.

In the *first phase*, the dimensions underlying the attitude to be studied are identified on the basis of the literature and theory, and statements are formulated to cover the various aspects of the general concept to be assessed. Adorno and co-workers, for example, picked out one of the components of authoritarianism as anti-intraception: 'a term that describes … an attitude if impatience with and opposition to the subjective and tender-minded … the anti-intraceptive individual … is afraid of genuine feelings because his emotions might get out of control' (Adorno et al., 1950: 235). On the basis of this consideration, they included in their scale F questions expressly aimed at gauging this particular personality trait.

The importance of this exquisitely theoretical phase must be stressed. The technique can be applied to any set of statements centred around a single theme, and statistical-mathematical operations can then be used, as we will see shortly, to select the statements that are pertinent to it and to discard those that are inconsistent. Nevertheless, the fact remains that the resulting scale will be more valid – that is, endowed with a greater ability to effectively gauge the underlying property for which it has been constructed – if the statements that it contains are formulated after the different aspects of the concepts to be assessed have been identified at the theoretical level. Such concepts are usually complex; they contain multiple dimensions which the scale must be able to cover (cf. the discussion of this problem – especially of the relationship between concepts and indicators – in Chapter 3, Section 7). To return to what is one

of the best-known examples of the application of this scale, *The Authoritarian Personality* (1980) by Adorno and co-workers, the authors examined previously empirical research, psychological studies and general literature on anti-semitism and fascism before identifying nine facets of the authoritarian personality, around which they then constructed the single questions-statements of the scale.

We can summarize this point (which applies not only to the Likert scales, but also to all the others) by stating that it is strongly advisable to adopt a *deductive* rather than an inductive approach.

In the *second phase*, the scale is administered to a sample of interviewees. The only noteworthy point here is the fact that this technique generally requires a good education on the part of the interviewees. Statements such as 'It would be preferable to raise taxes rather than reducing the social services provided by the state', or 'It is preferable to dispense with the use of nuclear power stations for the production of electrical energy, in that the economic advantages offered are outweighed by the dangers involved', may not be entirely comprehensible to a considerable portion of interviewees. Moreover, it is worth remembering what was said in Chapter 5, Section 6 with regard to item batteries: that they are particularly subject to errors caused by random responses (pseudo-opinions) or by mechanical repetition of the same answer throughout the battery (response-set: e.g. 'agree somewhat' in every case). This means that it is important to provide an explicit 'don't know' response option and to ensure that all the statements are not oriented in the same direction (so that the respondent will be forced to think, sometimes expressing agreement and sometimes disagreement, in order to avoid contradicting himself).

Table 6.4 reports a scale of 'political efficacy'. This concept was introduced in 1954 by the research group of Michigan University's Survey Research Center to indicate 'the feeling that individual political action does have, or can have, an impact on the political process' (Campbell et al., 1954: 187). This example is taken from a study in which the scale was made up of nine statements, five of which referred to national politics, and four to local politics (City Council).

Once interviewees have been asked the questions (or, to use a more general expression that can be extended to cases in which the scale is not administered through interviews, once the data have been collected), the next step is to evaluate whether the scale is really able to achieve the objective for which it has been constructed. As we know, the underlying supposition is that all the items that make up the scale are correlated with the same underlying latent concept; it is in this perspective that the items were chosen in the first phase. There is no guarantee, however, that the choice – which was made by the researcher on the basis of reflection about the concept to be gauged – was correct. After administration of the scale, it is therefore

necessary to establish an empirical criterion by which we can ascertain that all the items effectively share a common general concept. Indeed, some of the items in the scale may prove to be out of line with the others – that is to say, semantically linked to other concepts – and will therefore be eliminated. To use a more technical term: we must ensure *unidimensionality* of the scale.

This operation is carried out in the *third phase*. Two basic tools are used: the *item-scale correlation*, which serves to pick out scale items that are not consistent with the others, and the *alpha coefficient*, which serves to judge the scale's overall degree of internal consistency (see Boxes 6.3 and 6.4).

In eliminating unsatisfactory items from the scale, the researcher will take into account both the item-scale correlations and the alpha coefficient. The items with too low an item-scale correlation will be eliminated. This

---

BOX 6.3   ITEM-SCALE CORRELATION

To determine the item-scale correlation, each respondent's score over the whole scale is calculated and the coefficient of correlation between this overall score and the score on each single item is worked out.[5] The correlation coefficient measures the degree of relationship between two interval variables. If the two variables covary (i.e. as one varies so does the other), it takes on a high value (up to a maximum of 1 if the correlation is direct, and a maximum of –1 if the correlation is inverse);[6] if they are not correlated, the coefficient has a low value (0 indicating a total absence of correlation). In our case, the correlation coefficient tells us whether the score of each single item points in the same direction as the overall score, which takes all the other items into account.

If we are assessing authoritarianism, a person who gets a high overall score when the answers to all the questions are summed (and therefore proves to be 'authoritarian') should also have a fairly high score on any single item in the scale. Exceptions may of course be encountered at the individual level. However, if an item displays values that clash with the overall scores of a large number of respondents, we are forced to conclude that there is something wrong with that item. It may be ambiguous, badly worded, misunderstood by many respondents, or else it may be picking up something other than authoritarianism. In any case, the item is inconsistent with the rest of the scale and has to be eliminated.

BOX 6.4   INTERNAL CONSISTENCY OF THE SCALE: CRONBACH'S ALPHA

Several criteria for evaluating the *global internal consistency of the scale* have been drawn up. The best known of these indexes is *Cronbach's alpha*, which is based on the correlation matrix among all the items and on the number of items. Its formula is:

$$\alpha = \frac{n\bar{r}}{1+\bar{r}(n-1)}$$

where *n* is the number of items in the scale and $\bar{r}$ is their mean correlation.

Alpha is not a correlation coefficient, even though it looks like one; it normally has a positive[7] value between 0 and 1; the higher the values, the greater the internal consistency of the scale. Nunnally (1978: 245) suggests that the scale must have a 0.70 threshold in order to be acceptable. A lower value of alpha means that the items in the scale have little in common, or else that there are too few of them. If there are 10 items in the scale and the mean of all 45 correlations among them is 0.30, then $\alpha = 0.81$ (satisfactory). If there are five items and the mean correlation is the same, then $\alpha = 0.68$ (unsatisfactory). Alpha increases as the number of elements in the scale increases, and as their mean correlation increases.[8]

---

will raise the mean correlation $\bar{r}$ among the items, but it will also reduce the number of items *n*; these two manoeuvres will therefore have a contrasting influence on alpha. Thus, the items that have a lower item-scale correlation will be eliminated only as long as this operation produces an increase in alpha.

Table 6.4 reports alpha for the scale, the item-scale correlation coefficients and, for each item, the alpha value assumed by the scale if that item is eliminated. First of all, it will be seen that the scale displays a very high alpha value ($\alpha = 0.88$), and therefore seems immediately to be satisfactory. Analysis of the item-scale correlation reveals high values for all the items. The item showing the lowest correlation is no. 2 ($r = 0.47$); however, eliminating this item does not produce an increase in alpha (which remains = 0.88). Moreover, eliminating this item would mean removing the only cognitive statement ('Sometimes politics is so complicated…'); the researchers therefore decided not to eliminate it.

We now come to the *fourth phase*, in which the validity and unidimensionality of the scale are tested. With regard to *validity testing*, we will introduce a distinction between the classical application of scaling and a simplified application. In the traditional approach, the construction of the scale is an autonomous operation; for instance, a scale is drawn up to gauge self-esteem, anxiety, religious devotion, etc. with a view to creating an instrument that can also be applied to different populations from that for which the scale has been constructed. The process begins with a large number of items (as many as 50), which are administered to a fairly small sample of cases (generally 100–200); on the basis of this first trial, the inconsistent items are eliminated and the acceptability of the scale is established (by following the procedure described in the previous phase). The scale is then applied in different studies and, during the course of its application, further validity tests are undertaken (predictive validity, concomitant validity, validity for known groups,

TABLE 6.4 *Political efficacy scale. Question: I'm going to read you some opinions that people sometimes express. I want to know for each one of these opinions if you agree or disagree. Tell me exaclty if you strongly agree, somewhat agree, somewhat disagree or strongly disagree.*

	% Strongly agree + somewhat agree	Item-scale correlation[a]	Alpha if the item is excluded
1. People like me don't have any say about what the government does	62.9	0.58	0.87
2. Sometimes politics seem so complicated that a person like me can't really understand what's going on	79.6	0.47	0.88
3. I don't think public officials care much what people like me think	69.6	0.62	0.87
4. Usually those elected to Parliament soon lose touch with the people who elected them	82.5	0.60	0.87
5. The parties are only interested in the votes of the people, not in their opinions	67.7	0.64	0.87
6. People like me don't have any influence on local elected officials	50.1	0.70	0.86
7. Usually those elected to our city council soon lose touch with the people who elected them	47.4	0.71	0.86
8. People like me don't have any influence on the actions of the district representatives	46.8	0.67	0.87
9. Usually those elected as district representatives soon lose touch with the people who elected them	41.5	0.68	0.87
		Alfa = 0.88	

[a]Adjusted correlation = correlation between item and scale without that item

construct validity) to confirm that the scale is genuinely able to assess the property for which it has been constructed.[9]

This is the dominant approach in psychological research, in which the properties to be investigated are constituted by personality traits and multi-faceted psychological constructs located deep in the mind, and which therefore require very elaborate scales made up of dozens of items.[10] Among sociologists and political scientists, however, a simplified approach to scaling has been gaining ground. In this case, the scales are made up of about 10 items; several scales may co-exist within the same investigative tool (usually a questionnaire); the scale is only one aspect of the research (such as in a study on attitudes towards politics that utilizes a 'political efficacy' scale, a 'political participation' scale and a 'left-right self-placement' scale, in addition to many other questions on family socialization, education, occupation, religious devotion, etc.) In such cases, the scale is drawn up in a single operation, with no separation between 'construction' and 'application'; validity testing is scant and unsystematic, and the field of application is limited to the specific population under examination.

We will now look at the issue of *unidimensionality testing*. Although the 'item-analysis' procedure presented in the third phase is designed specifically to ascertain that all the items are indicators of the same property, it is not in fact sufficient to guarantee the unidimensionality of the scale. Indeed, the items might correspond to two distinct properties (such as authoritarianism and class ideology) that are correlated but very different. This would give rise to satisfactory values of the item-scale correlations and of the alpha coefficient, even if unidimensionality were lacking.

A very effective method of testing unidimensionality is *factorial analysis*. While this procedure is too complex to be dealt with in this volume, its use in testing the unidimensionality of scales can be understood without having to go into the details of the technique (see Box 6.5).

BOX 6.5   FACTORIAL ANALYSIS

The aim of factorial analysis is to reduce a set of correlated variables to a smaller number of hypothetical variables (factors or latent variables) that are independent of one another.[11]. The analysis starts out from a correlation matrix among the variables observed, and the goal is to explain these correlations through the existence of underlying factors. For example, the correlation between the marks obtained in algebra and in geometry by a given group of students (students who are good at algebra are good at geometry too, while those who are poor in one are poor in both) could be ascribed to the fact that both marks are influenced by an underlying factor – that is to say, a capacity for mathematical abstraction.

Table 6.5 reports the results of factorial analysis carried out on the items of the scale shown in Table 6.4. The 'factor loadings' reported in the table can be interpreted as coefficients of correlation between each item and the underlying factor. The analysis has revealed the existence of two factors: the first loaded by the first five questions and the second by the last four questions. Thus, the scale is not unidimensional, but bidimensional, since there are two underlying concepts. Interpretation of the two factors is fairly straightforward. The first is correlated with the questions on national politics, while the second is linked to political representatives at the local level.

TABLE 6.5   *Factor analysis on the political efficacy items*

Item n.	Factor loadings	
	Factor n. 1	Factor n. 2
1	**0.661**	0.295
2	**0.702**	0.104
3	**0.764**	0.245
4	**0.752**	0.224
5	**0.679**	0.360
6	0.346	**0.761**
7	0.300	**0.811**
8	0.210	**0.858**
9	0.204	**0.875**

Factorial analysis can be used to discover whether only one factor, or more than one factor, underlies the items in a scale that is presumed to be unidimensional. For example, a researcher may have constructed an anxiety scale that includes both psychological symptoms (fear, a feeling of being watched, etc.) and physical symptoms (sweating, rapid heartbeat, etc.). Through factorial analysis, she can discover whether the two sets of indicators really do have a single underlying concept (anxiety in this hypothesis), or whether instead they indicate two different concepts. In our example the factor analysis revealed the existence of two factors (see Box 6.5) and the researchers decided to split the questions into two 'political efficacy' scales: one referring to national politics and the other to local politics.

To sum up, the Likert scale is undoubtedly the most widely used technique for assessing continuous properties, and particularly attitudes, in the social sciences. Its popularity certainly stems from the simplicity of its theoretical basis and its ease of application (in principle, it does not even require the powerful data-processing resources of modern computing, which accounts for its great success in the 1950s–1970s).

Nevertheless, there are several drawbacks to the technique. The first of these concerns the scores assigned to the single items. Each item is an ordinal variable, generally of the 'partial semantic autonomy' kind, and usually involves five categories (from 'strongly agree' to 'strongly disagree', or similar), to which scores on a simple scale from 1 to 5 are assigned in a completely arbitrary manner; these scores are then treated as interval variables (e.g. in the item-scale correlation). Aware of this weakness, Likert himself initially proposed a more elaborate technique in which the response scores were assigned on the basis of the results of the assessment ('sigma method', Likert, 1932). He later abandoned this proposal as the simple scores based on the sequence of natural numbers proved to correlate closely with those calculated according to the more sophisticated criterion.

Another problem concerns the *lack of reproducibility* of the scale – that is to say, the fact that from the scale score it is not possible to work back to the answers to the single questions (the same score can be obtained by means of many different combinations of answers). It is therefore perfectly possible for two identical scores to be produced by very different answers.

Finally, it should be borne in mind that the final score on the scale does not constitute an interval variable; we are in no position to say, for example, that the distance between a score of 14 and one of 18 is the same as the distance between 8 and 12.

4. GUTTMAN'S SCALOGRAM

Guttman's proposal (1944; 1950) was an attempt to find a solution to the problem of the unidimensionality of the scale which, as we have seen, was one of the weaknesses of Likert's technique. Guttman's scale can be likened to a flight of steps, a series of items of increasing difficulty in which a subject who makes an affirmative response to any given question must have already made an affirmative response to all those that precede it in the scale of difficulty. It was this structure that gave rise to the name 'scalogram' or *cumulative scale* (as opposed to the term 'additive scale' attributed to the Likert technique, in which the items of the scale were all on the same level).

This cumulative nature of the scale items can be illustrated through the example of an old 'social distance scale' proposed in the 1920s by Bogardus (1925). This scale, which was designed to assess the respondents' degree of prejudice towards ethnic minorities, utilized a sequence of questions such as 'Would you be willing to accept a black person (a Korean, a Japanese, etc.) as a visitor to your country?' 'Would you be willing to have a black person living next door to you?' 'Would you be willing to make friends with a black person?' 'Would you be willing to marry a black person?'

TABLE 6.6 *Anwsers to the question: Would you like to have a black (Korean, Japanese, etc.) as visitor in your country, as neighbour, as personal friend, as spouse?*

As visitor	As neighbour	As friend	As spouse	Score
1	1	1	1	4
1	1	1	0	3
1	1	0	0	2
1	0	0	0	1
0	0	0	0	0

Obviously, someone who is willing to marry a black person will presumably have no objection to having a black friend or neighbour, while someone who would not accept personal friendship would presumably also refuse marriage. If the items in the scale are perfectly scaled, only certain response sequences are possible. If we score 1 for an affirmative answer and 0 for a negative answer, the only possible sequences should, in principle, be: 1111, 1110, 1100, 1000, and 0000 (Table 6.6). Thus, a sequence such as 1011 should not occur (as this would indicate a respondent who is willing to marry and make friends with a black person, but not have a black neighbour). As seen in Table 6.6, the possible responses give rise to a matrix divided into two triangles, one made up of all affirmative answers and the other made up of all negative answers.

By assigning a score of 1 to an affirmative answer and 0 to a negative answer, and summing the scores of each individual on all the items, we obtain each subject's overall score on the scale. It will be noted that we can work back from the subject's overall score to the responses given to each single scale item; for example, a subject who gets a score of 2 on the scale in Table 6.6 has given the response sequence 1100. We therefore know not only how many questions have been answered affirmatively but also which ones. This possibility of working back from the scale score to the responses to the single items is a typical feature of the Guttman scalogram and is known as *reproducibility* (since the answers to the single questions can be 'reproduced' from the score). Another noteworthy point is that

this technique only uses dichotomous items, such as questions with 'yes/no', 'agree/disagree' answers (unlike the Likert technique, in which the response is graded on a scale of intensity).

Of course, only an ideal scale gives rise solely to the response sequences shown in Table 6.6. Any real application will encounter responses that fall outside the sequences envisioned by the model; these will be regarded as 'errors'. The problem is to establish how many errors an acceptable scale can tolerate and what procedures can be adopted to minimize such errors.

As in the case of the Likert scale, the construction of the Guttman scale can be broken down into *three or four phases*: question wording, administration, item analysis with the establishment of an overall index of acceptance of the scale, plus a validation phase, if deemed necessary.

With regard to question wording (and item selection in general), the considerations made in our discussion of the Likert scale regarding the importance of conceptual reflection also apply here. Referring specifically to the Guttman scale, we can add two further observations. First – and to some degree this constitutes a simplification – the questions must be in binary form. Second, the questions must be designed with the final purpose in mind: a set of items of increasing intensity. Unlike the Likert scale, in which the questions may all be of approximately the same intensity, the Guttman scale has to cover the whole range of the underlying attitude continuum, in such a way as to produce a battery of items of increasing difficulty. For example, in

TABLE 6.7   *Error detection in a Guttman scale*

(a) original matrix
Items

Cases	n. 1	n. 2	n. 3	n. 4	n. 5	Score
A	1	1	1	1	1	5
B	0	0	0	0	1	1
C	0	0	1	0	1	2
D	0	1	0	1	1	3
E	0	1	1	0	1	3
F	0	0	0	0	0	0
G	1	0	1	0	0	2
H	0	1	1	1	1	4
No. of affirmative responses	2	4	5	3	6	

(b) ordered matrix
Items

Cases	n. 5	n. 3	n. 2	n. 4	n. 1	Score
A	1	1	1	1	1	5
H	1	1	1	1	0	4
E	1	1	1	0	0	3
D	1	0*	1	1*	0	3
C	1	1	0	0	0	2
G	0*	1	0	0	1*	2
B	1	0	0	0	0	1
F	0	0	0	0	0	0
No. of errors	1	1	0	1	1	
* error						

constructing a scale to gauge the progressive-conservative attitude in politics, the researcher will not only have to draw up a series of statements covering various fields (fiscal policy, employment policy, interpretation of historical events, etc.), but will also have to construct statements that cover the whole spectrum from extreme radical to extreme reactionary.

In the administration phase, the problems posed by the Guttman scale are fairly similar to those raised by the Likert scale, the main difference being the binary nature of the choices offered.

Where the Guttman scale really does differ is in the item analysis. The aim of this analysis is to evaluate the scalability of all the items, discard those that are least consistent with the model, establish a scalability index of

the scale and decide whether or not the scale is acceptable. This procedure first involves identifying what we have called the 'errors' in the scale – that is to say, those answers that do not fit into the sequences envisioned by the model. To this end, two different techniques have been proposed: the first is the one originally adopted by Guttman, while the second is the one subsequently proposed by Edwards (1957). Only this latter will be presented here, in that it is acknowledged to be superior to the former.

The procedure is carried out in the following way. Let us suppose that the initial data-matrix is that reported in Table 6.7a (for the sake of simplicity, we will imagine that the scale has been administered to only eight subjects). We will now rearrange the columns and lines of the matrix in such a way that the items are ordered from left to right according to the number of affirmative responses received, while the subjects are ordered from top to bottom according to the total score obtained. In this way, the 2-triangle structure of the matrix is seen (one triangle made up mainly of 1s and the other of 0s, Table 6.7b). From Table 6.7b, it immediately appears that two sequences are wrong: case D and case G. The errors are picked out by comparing the sequence observed with the theoretical correct sequence that should be obtained from that subject's overall score. Let us take case D: the sequence observed is 10110, with a final score of three. In order to keep the same final score, the correct sequence should be 11100; there are therefore two errors (there should be a 1 in the second position and a 0 in the fourth position).

Once the errors have been picked out (marked with an asterisk in Table 6.7b), it has to be decided whether they are sufficiently few to allow us to confirm the 'scalability' of the items. Guttman proposed an index, which he called the reproducibility coefficient, to measure the discrepancy between the scale observed and the perfect scale. Its formula is:

$$C_r = 1 - \frac{\text{n. errors}}{\text{n. total responses}} = 1 - \frac{\text{n. errors}}{\text{n. items} \times \text{n. cases}} = \frac{\text{n. correct responses}}{\text{n. total responses}}$$

In our example:

$$C_r = 1 - \frac{4}{5.8} = 0.90$$

As will easily be seen, this index can also be interpreted as the proportion of 'correct' responses (those which correspond to the theoretical sequences) over the total number of responses. Guttman suggested that the scale should have a value of $C_r \geq 0.90$ (errors in 10% or fewer of the responses) in order to be acceptable. If the scale displays a reproducibility coefficient lower than 0.90, the items with the largest number of errors are progressively eliminated and C_r is recalculated each time.

The reproducibility coefficient of the scale is the mean of the reproducibility coefficients of the single items (proportion of correct responses/total responses to each item). It can now be demonstrated that the reproducibility coefficient of each item cannot fall below its proportion of responses in the modal category.[12] For example, the modal response to item no. 1 in Table 6.7 is 'No' and its proportion is 0.75 (6 'No' responses out of 8); therefore, the reproducibility coefficient of item no.1 cannot fall below 0.75. Consequently, a Guttman scale made up only of very forceful statements that elicit, for example, 90% affirmative and 10% negative responses (or vice versa) will automatically obtain a C_r value of around 90%.

Once the non-scalable items have been eliminated and the scale judged acceptable, the scores are assigned to the subjects. If a subject presents a response sequence that is in line with the model, there is no problem; the scale score is the sum of the scores obtained on each single item. Even if the subject presents a sequence containing errors (e.g. 01010), the same criterion is applied (if the technique described here for determining the errors has been followed), and the subject's score remains equal to the sum of the positive responses given. At this point, the construction of the scale is deemed to have been completed.

Various ways of improving the yield of this technique have been suggested.[13] Here, we will focus on only three, all of which were proposed by Guttman himself. The first suggestion is to avoid items displaying acceptance or refusal rates that are too high (above 80%), in that they have little discrimination value and will raise the reproducibility coefficient of the scale artificially. Guttman also recommended using a sufficiently high number of items, and demonstrated that a scale of only four items can yield high C_r values even if the items are statistically independent of one another. In addition, Guttman warned that erroneous sequences should be carefully scrutinized, in that the frequent recurrence of a sequence not foreseen by the model may be indicative of another latent variable underlying the indicators.

BOX 6.6 MEASURES OF REPRODUCIBILITY

Edwards (1957) proposed a *minimal marginal reproducibility (MMR) index*, calculated by means of the following formula:

$$MMR = \frac{\sum \text{ proportion of responses in the modal category}}{N}$$

Where N is the number of items in the scale.
In our example from Table 6.7:

$$MMR = \frac{0.75 + 0.50 + 0.63 + 0.63 + 0.75}{5} = 0.65$$

This index shows the minimum value below which the reproducibility coefficient of the scale cannot fall, whatever the sequences of the responses might be. The Guttman coefficient of reproducibility C_r is then compared with the *MMR*. Only if the former, as well as being above 0.90, is also clearly higher than the latter, can it be stated that the good reproducibility of the scale is due to the true scalability of its items and not to the marginal distribution of the responses. In our example, this requisite is fulfilled.

In conclusion, we can say that the Guttman scalogram has played a fundamental role in the development of scaling. During the course of at least 30 years the debate that centred around this technique gave rise to numerous suggestions for its improvement (see McIver and Carmines, 1981). Nevertheless, some problems remain. First of all, the final score obtained on the latent variable remains – as for the Likert scales – substantially an ordinal variable; in this case too, we have no grounds for claiming that the distance between scores of 2 and 4 is the same as the distance between 5 and 7. Second, the Guttman technique is applicable in the case of attitudes (behaviours, events, etc.) that are clearly defined and scalable. However, when the attitude is complex, it may be difficult to scale in cumulative sequences; as the categories partially overlap,

numerous errors are likely to emerge at the end. Finally, the model proves to be rigidly deterministic, while social reality can only be interpreted correctly through probabilistic models that take into account the possibility of error and the gradual shift from one position to the next. This is the chief weakness of the Guttman model and the main reason why it has been superseded by the probabilistic scales (Rasch scales).

5. THE SEMANTIC DIFFERENTIAL

The semantic differential technique was developed in the 1950s by the American psychologist Charles Osgood and co-workers (Osgood, 1952; Osgood et al., 1957). The aim of these researchers was to create a highly standardized tool to gauge the meaning that concepts have for people: a tool capable of answering the question 'What does it (a concept such as mother, the country, war, etc.) mean to you?'.

The problem of what a term, social situation or object in general 'means' to a person is an extremely complex one, and one that is loaded with both philosophical and psychological significance. It is also of the utmost importance in the study of behaviour. As Nunnally asserts, 'Human behaviour is determined by the meaning of events rather than by intrinsic properties of events; a baby reacts approvingly to his mother's voice because that has acquired the meaning of nourishment, warmth, and protection' (1959: 383).

In the book in which they systematized their proposal, Osgood and colleagues wrote:

> Ordinarily, if we want to find out what something means to a person, we ask him to tell us ...: What does 'sophisticated' mean to you? Well ... I know what it means ... but it's hard to put into words. It's being clever and wise about people and things – knowing the ropes, so to speak. It's sort of smooth and polished, graceful but not awkward ... poised, 'savvy' you know ... (Osgood et al., 1957: 18).

As the authors point out, when the subjects studied are intelligent, educated people with excellent verbal skills, exploring meanings on the basis of the descriptions that they give may be a valid and sufficiently sensitive method; these people are able to express in words the distinctive and determining elements of what a particular concept means to them. However, with people who are endowed with lesser verbal skill, this system is likely to be found wanting; the spontaneous descriptions given may be too scant. Moreover, the numerous descriptions provided by these highly subjective procedures are very difficult to compare.

Osgood's semantic differential was designed to investigate the meanings of given concepts not through direct subjective descriptions provided by interviewees but through associations between those concepts and other concepts presented to all interviewees in a standardized manner. Thus, instead of asking: What does the word 'sophisticated' mean to you?, the interviewer asks a series of questions, such as: Is 'sophisticated' hard or soft? Pleasant or unpleasant? Fast or slow? And so on. To increase the sensitivity of the technique, the subject is also asked to grade the intensity of each impression on a 7-point scale. Therefore, as Osgood and co-workers assert, 'the semantic differential is essentially a combination of controlled association and scaling procedures' (1957: 20).

The format of the questions is illustrated in Figure 6.1. This example is taken from a study conducted in Italy on young people in which the interviewees were asked to evaluate four political parties (Sciolla and Ricolfi, 1989). As the figure shows, this technique utilizes a series of typical self-anchoring scales – as defined in Section 2 – in which only the extreme categories have autonomous meaning, while the (graded) meaning of the intermediate categories is established by the interviewee himself. Table 6.8 reports 50 pairs of opposite attributes used by Osgood and colleagues in their research. The authors applied these scales to persons (mother, foreigner, the self, politicians, etc.), concrete objects (knife, snow, engine, etc.), abstract objects (modern art, sin, leadership, etc.), events (debate, birth, etc.), and institutions (United Nations, hospital, family, etc.).

Osgood maintained that the pairs of bipolar attributes should bear no relation to the object under examination, and that the same pairs of adjectives should be used in every case. Even adjectives that apparently have nothing to do with the object under examination (e.g. the pairs masculine-feminine, young-old, black-white, etc. attributed to a motor car) may prove useful in revealing deep, and even subconscious, meanings that the object holds for the interviewee.[14]

Question: Let's talk about parties. Tell me how you would place each party on the following scales?

Socialist Party

	1	2	3	4	5	6	7	
Young	————————————————————————————	Old
Strong	————————————————————————————	Weak
Clean	————————————————————————————	Dirty
Fast	————————————————————————————	Slow
Close	————————————————————————————	Remote
Tolerant	————————————————————————————	Intolerant
Open	————————————————————————————	Closed
Indulgent	————————————————————————————	Strict
Winner	————————————————————————————	Loser
Left-wing	————————————————————————————	Right-wing
Cheerful	————————————————————————————	Sad
Efficient	————————————————————————————	Inefficient

Interviewer instruction:
• Show the card to the respondent and ask him to place for each of the scales a cross above the position which best corresponds to his image of the party.
• It's better if the respondent answers quickly without very much reflection.

FIGURE 6.1   *Example of semantic differential*

TABLE 6.8   *Semantic differential. Pairs of attributes used by Osgood et al. (1957)*

1.	Good-Bad	26.	Wet-Dry
2.	Large-Small	27.	Sacred-Profane
3.	Beautiful-Ugly	28.	Relaxed-Tense
4.	Yellow-Blue	29.	Brave-Cowardly
5.	Hard-Soft	30.	Long-Short
6.	Sweet-Sour	31.	Rich-Poor
7.	Strong-Weak	32.	Clear-Hazy
8.	Clean-Dirty	33.	Hot-Cold
9.	High-Low	34.	Thick-Thin
10.	Calm-Agitated	35.	Nice-Awful
11.	Tasty-Distasteful	36.	Bright-Dark
12.	Valuable-Worthless	37.	Bass-Treble
13.	Red-Green	38.	Angular-Rounded
14.	Young-Old	39.	Fragrant-Foul
15.	Kind-Cruel	40.	Honest-Dishonest
16.	Loud-Soft	41	Active-Passive
17.	Deep-Shallow	42.	Rough-Smooth
18.	Pleasant-Unpleasant	43.	Fresh-Stale
19.	Black-White	44.	Fast-Slow
20.	Bitter-Sweet	45.	Fair-Unfair
21.	Happy-Sad	46.	Rugged-Delicate
22.	Sharp-Dull	47.	Near-Far
23.	Empty-Full	48.	Pungent-Bland
24.	Ferocious-Peaceful	49.	Healthy-Sick
25.	Heavy-Light	50.	Wide-Narrow

The test is easy to administer and is generally well accepted by interviewees, even when the pairs of attributes appear to have little relevance to the object to which they are applied. On presentation of the battery of questions, interviewees are generally urged to respond instinctively, without thinking too much about each pair.

Regarding the number of bipolar attributes presented for the same object, the technique is very flexible. In the two examples that we have quoted here, the number ranges from the 12 presented in the research on political parties to the 50 initially proposed by Osgood. Similarly, the objects submitted for evaluation may be numerous (e.g. a series of 30 well-known personalities from the world of entertainment, politics, economics, etc.) or few (such as the four political parties mentioned earlier). The choice will depend on the aim of the study and on the importance of the role assigned to the technique within the general framework of the investigation. In its application to the political parties, the semantic differential formed part of a questionnaire that used other attitude assessment tools involving traditional Likert scale-like questions; for this reason, its application was limited in terms of both the objects submitted for evaluation and the pairs of attributes presented. By contrast, Osgood and colleagues report applications of the technique in the field of personality studies in which the assessment is entirely based on the semantic differential technique and the number of judgments required (the number of bipolar attributes multiplied by the number of objects for evaluation) may be as high as 400 (e.g. 40 bipolar pairs for each of 10 objects).

The responses obtained may be processed in various ways, which will be mentioned only briefly here. A summary description of the image of the object submitted for evaluation can be obtained by drawing a 'profile'. This is a graphic representation created by drawing a line in such a way as to join up the mean scores obtained by the object on each pair of attributes. For example, Figure 6.2 reports the profiles of the Green Party and the Christian Democrats in the application to Italian political parties. From these profiles, the image of the Christian Democrats emerges as 'old, right-wing, inefficient, dirty, closed, slow, and sad', while the Green Party is perceived as 'young, fast, cheerful, near, clean, open, tolerant, weak, and losing'. In the same study, the Italian Communist Party was deemed to be 'efficient, left-wing, strict and intolerant', while the Socialist Party was seen as being 'indulgent and fair' (Sciolla and Ricolfi, 1989: 109–10).

In this example, the profile is drawn up on the basis of the means of the judgments expressed by those interviewed, and its object is the concept (here the party). However, profiles of the interviewees themselves can be constructed on the basis of the individual subject's answers. This technique has been used in order to gauge self-esteem, by asking the interviewee to classify a battery of bipolar attributes according to the cognitive object 'Me, as I am' and 'Me, as I would like to be'. The gap between the two profiles enables the subject's degree of self-esteem to be gauged and, to quote one application of the technique, the progress made by a patient on psychotherapy can be evaluated by observing how this gap changes over time.

It is, however, in exploring the dimensions of meanings that the semantic differential is chiefly used. If an interviewee is asked to collocate a given cognitive object with 30 pairs of adjectives, each single decision will naturally be guided by the global vision ('the meaning') that the interviewee has of the object proposed. The supposition is that this vision is not unidimensional – that is to say, it is not oriented in a single direction but embodies various aspects which contribute to the overall meaning of that object. By means of factorial analysis, the fundamental dimensions underlying the judgements of a given sample of subjects can be determined.

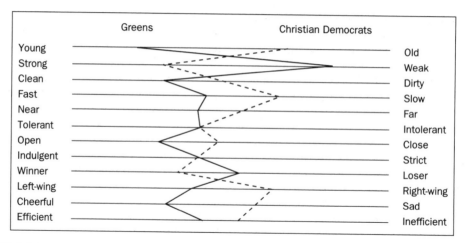

FIGURE 6.2   *Semantic differential. Examples of 'profiles'*
Adopted from Sciolla and Ricolfi, 1989

By using the same set of 50 bipolar adjectives (seen in Table 6.8) with a series of diverse cognitive objects and repeating the test on different samples of subjects, Osgood and colleagues were generally able to identify three fundamental dimensions underlying the various judgements: *evaluation* (linked to the pairs good-bad, positive-negative, beautiful-ugly, fair-unfair, valuable-worthless, etc.), *potency* (hard-soft, strong-weak, heavy-light, etc.) and *activity* (active-passive, fast-slow, hot-cold, etc.). These three factors are listed in order of importance; the first is the most relevant and seems to represent what, in the traditional scaling techniques, was generally called attitude (favourable or unfavourable) towards a certain cognitive object.

On the basis of this finding concerning the dimensions of the semantic space, the values recorded on the individual bipolar attributes can be summed[15] (according to the dimension that the attribute belongs to), thus yielding overall scores for each object on the three dimensions mentioned, not unlike what would happen with a Likert-type additive scale.[16] The score recorded on the dimension 'evaluation' is the one that is most directly comparable to the scores obtained with other scaling techniques. Indeed, Osgood and colleagues found a high correlation between the factor 'evaluation' in the semantic differential and the scores yielded by Thurstone's and Guttman's scales.

Osgood and colleagues claimed that the three dimensions they identified – evaluation, potency and activity – governed the semantic space of the vast majority of subjects, regardless of their culture (studies were carried out in various countries) and the concepts submitted for evaluation. Many researchers do not share this generalizing view, and several studies have found that the single judgements are underpinned by dimensions other than the three mentioned.

Although these facts clash with some of Osgood's theorization on the semantic space, they do not diminish interest in his technique as a means of delineating the *structure* of attitudes. The most original contribution of the semantic differential to attitude assessment probably lies in the fact that it revealed the multidimensionality of meanings; it brought, to a field of study that had operated within a unidimensional perspective, the resources of the multidimensional approach (this issue will be discussed further at the end of this chapter).

6. SOCIOMETRY

The objective of the technique presented in this section is quite different from that of the techniques described above. Indeed, it does not aim to assess latent variables, such as religious devotion or depression, nor attitudes towards particular cognitive objects, such as political parties or immigrants. Rather, sociometric techniques were worked out in order to assess *interpersonal relations* among individuals in groups. But then, as already said, this chapter does not only deal with attitude assessment: it also covers the main scaling techniques – that is to say, the procedures drawn up by the behavioural sciences, chiefly between the 1930s and 1960s, with the ambitious and somewhat naïve aim of 'measuring man and society'. Although they have failed to achieve this objective of 'measuring' – as we have pointed out several times – they have nevertheless provided highly valid means of studying human beings and their behaviour.

Sociometric testing was proposed in the 1940s by Jacob Moreno (1934), an eclectic scholar (physician, therapist, sociologist) of Romanian birth and American adoption.[17] Moreno's intention was to develop systematic standardized procedures to study the interpersonal relationships that are set up within small (or relatively small) groups. The ideal field of application of the technique is the school class. George Bastin (1961) introduced his book on this technique by giving an account of a very simple experiment. He picked out 12 first-year classes at a technical institute and, three months after the beginning of the school year, he selected four teachers per class from among the teachers who took the classes every day,

and asked them to describe the relationships that had formed among the pupils: friendships, sub-groups, leaders, isolated pupils, etc. On the whole, the teachers proved unable to unravel the network of relationships that had developed among their pupils. At the same time, Bastin administered a sociometric questionnaire to the classes. This proved to be perfectly capable of revealing the web of relationships among the students, and showed patterns that were completely unknown to the teachers.

In its simplest formulation, the sociometric test consists of a questionnaire made up of a small number of questions centred around the theme of liking/disliking the other members of the group. To carry on with the school example, the following four questions put to all the pupils in the class are enough to enable a complete sociometric test to be conducted:

– Which of your classmates would you like to have in class with you next year? Name as many as you want and put them in order of preference.
– Which of your classmates would you not like to have in class with you next year? Name as many as you want and put them in order, starting from the one you would least like to have.
– Guess which of your classmates have named you among those they would like to have in class with them next year.
– Guess which of your classmates have named you among those they would not like to have in class with them next year.

In this example, the questions were asked just before the end of the school year, and the pupils knew that new classes would be formed the following year; but they can also be applied to similar situations: the companions with whom you would like (or not like) to play, study, form a work group, go to the cinema; or that you would like (not like) to invite your house, to your birthday party, etc.

Handling the data is equally simple. A square matrix is constructed with the names of the group members listed along the top and down the left side; the favourable and unfavourable judgements are then registered in the boxes corresponding to each pair. The first step in processing the data involves analysing the individual sociometric status; this is done by analysing the number of approvals and disapprovals expressed and obtained by each subject. On the basis of the four questions, eight basic indexes can be worked out, which give rise to a graphic psychosocial portrait of the subject. Figure 6.3 reports these indexes and the graphic representation of two cases. These two subjects are both loners, in that they have received very few approvals (index *a* significantly low) and numerous disapprovals (index *b* significantly high); moreover, numerous companions feel disapproved of by these two (index *h* high). In this situation, subject S_1 is aware of his exclusion from the group (believing himself to have been rejected by a large number of companions: high index *f*) and has reacted by expressing a large number of rejections himself (high index *d*). By contrast, subject S_2 appears to be unaware of his own isolation (index *f* not significant) and does not engage in retaliatory behaviour (index *d* not significant).

In addition to analyses aimed at defining the relationship status of the individual subjects, operations are performed to uncover the *sociometric structure of the group*. Figure 6.4 shows a simple representation (*sociogram*) of the first two positive choices made by each member of a group of 12 students (Nunnally, 1959: 392). This reveals that the group is broken down into three sub-groups (all first choices and almost all second choices are made within the sub-groups), plus one isolated individual (no. 3). The group composed of subjects 5, 8, 11 and 12 presents a leader (no. 12, who is the first choice of all the others), while the structure of the other two groups presents greater parity (though there are clear differences among the subjects: e.g. in the group comprising subjects 1, 6, 7 and 9, subject 1 is more isolated from the others, in

that he only receives one second choice). Two of the three groups are connected through subjects 6 and 11, who function as intermediaries, while the third (nos 2, 4 and 10) is a closed group, in that all choices are made internally. The state of isolation and disorientation of subject 3 is made all the more evident by the fact that, in addition to not being chosen by any of the others, his own choices are directed towards subjects belonging to different groups.

Moreno and those scholars who followed him in developing the sociometric approach proposed numerous other ways of graphically representing both the structure of the group and the status of its members (for instance, by drawing concentric circles in which the most popular individuals are located at the centre and the least popular at the periphery). Furthermore, different sociograms can be constructed according to the questions considered (Figure 6.4 refers only to positive choices, but we could also consider rejections, imputed choices and rejections, reciprocal choices and rejections, etc.).

For a more detailed treatment of this subject, the reader should refer to the specialist literature. Here, we will restrict ourselves to observing that the technique proves useful in three ways. First, it is a tool for *individual diagnosis*, with a view to identifying relationships of dominance-dependence, isolation, affinity (liking and friendship) and conflict (disliking and enmity); second, it is a means of shedding light on the *relationship structure of the group*, communications networks, informal hierarchical organization, pathways of information, gossip, orders, etc; and, finally, it provides a method of studying *group psychology*, identifying tensions, the existence of social stratification, barriers of race, religion, language, gender, age, etc.

Sociometric testing is generally suited to the study of structured groups; it does not lend itself to the analysis of informal groups (such as the locals who frequent the same bar or children who happen to play together on a

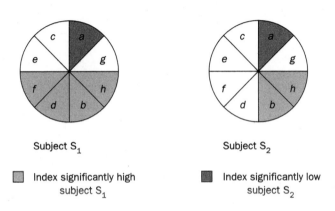

Positive indexes

Centrifugal indexes
(everything comes out from the subject)

Centrepetal indexes
(everything comes to the subject)

Negative indexes

a = n. of received choices
b = n. of received refusals
c = n. of expressed choices
d = n. expressed refusals

e = n. of choices that the subject thinks he received
f = n. of refusals that the subject thinks he received
g = n. of people who believe they were chosen by the subject
h = n. of people who believe they were refused by the subject

Subject S_1

Subject S_2

Index significantly high subject S_1

Index significantly low subject S_2

FIGURE 6.3   *Individual sociometric indexes (Bastin, 1961)*

beach), since it requires that the subject's range of choice be precisely circumscribed. As already mentioned, the technique is extremely useful in investigating relationship patterns within a school class. It has also been applied in the field of work (factory departments, company organization) and in the military context (e.g. to see whether the formal hierarchy corresponds to the actual hierarchy, or whether orders follow hierarchical channels of communication or alternative channels, etc.).

With reference to these latter applications, it should be pointed out that the technique was originally drawn up to investigate affective relationships within groups, and used criteria of choice based on friendship, liking and admiration (through questions such as 'Who would you like to play with?' or 'Who would you invite to dinner?'). Subsequently, it was extended to the study of functional relationships, and utilized choice criteria based on estimates of ability, competence and utility

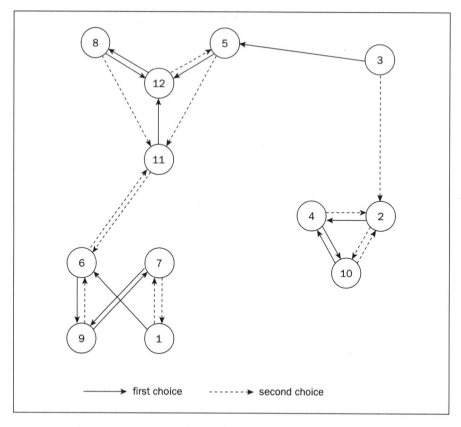

first choice   ------> second choice

FIGURE 6.4   *Sociogram of the two first choices in a group of 12 students (Nunnally, 1959)*

(through questions such as 'Who would you like to study with?' 'Who would you pick for your football team?' or 'Who would you want in your work group?'). Finally, it was applied (though to a lesser degree) to the study of communication processes (through 'interaction diagrams') within formal organizations.

Moreno's technique enjoyed great popularity in the 1950s and 1960s, and was applied in numerous fields. Subsequently, however, the interest of researchers waned, not least on account of the cracks that appeared in the theoretical edifice of 'sociometry', which Moreno had constructed for the purpose of social renewal rather than of scientific research. In more recent times, the systematic study of social

relationship networks has been revitalized by the *network analysis* approach. This has been given a boost by developments in the field of information technology and the new possibilities offered by personal computers for the management and analysis of data on relationships (Knoke and Kulinski, 1982; Wasserman and Faust, 1994).

7.   A FINAL NOTE: UNIDIMENSIONAL AND MULTIDIMENSIONAL SCALING

In the two previous sections we have to some extent digressed from the central theme of this chapter, which is scaling techniques designed to operationalize complex concepts. In the first four sections of the chapter we outlined the various paths taken by the social sciences in the attempt to 'measure' the human mind. However, only the so-called 'unidimensional' scales were discussed; that is to say, we looked at research situations in which a single fundamental dimension is presumed to underlie a set of observations.

The rationale behind that approach is the following. In attempting to assess a complex, latent concept (which cannot be directly operationalized), such as alienation or authoritarianism, the researcher has to choose – on the basis of purely theoretical considerations – manifest (or partly manifest) expressions of that concept; these expressions are constituted by opinions. Having submitted these opinions to the judgement of the interviewees, the researcher then ascertains that these variables correlate with one another in the responses given (as proof that they are determined by a single underlying latent property). The set of responses given by each subject is then used to operationalize the latent concept.

This sequence begins with the general concept under investigation, and indicators are identified to operationalize this. However, the problem of complex concepts underlying a set of observations can be tackled in another way. This involves beginning with the observations themselves and attempting to discover *how many and which* latent dimensions (concepts) underlie them. This is the technique of the so-called *multidimensional scales*.

Let us consider, for example, the research carried out in 1968 by Weisberg and Rusk (1970) on voters' opinions of the candidates in the American presidential election of that year. Respondents' preferences regarding the 12 candidates in the primary elections were recorded by means of the 'feelings thermometer'. The authors applied multidimensional scales to these data in order to identify the dimensions underlying the judgements expressed.

Such techniques of analysis start out from the correlations among the stimuli (or items, to use our terminology), which are regarded as a measure of *proximity*. If, for example, there is a high correlation between the scores obtained by Humphrey and Johnson (two of the candidates in this research), this means that these two candidates are close in the mental space of the respondents; a respondent who judges one positively will judge both positively. This conceptual space can be imagined as a physical space defined by dimensions (just as in geometry a plane is defined by two dimensions and space by three dimensions, and we may imagine spaces with *n* dimensions).

An interesting example is provided by Kruskal and Wish (1978: 7). Let us imagine that we are looking at a map and that we have been asked to draw up a table showing the distances in kilometres between the various cities on the map. This task can be performed quite easily by measuring the distances on the map in centimetres and then converting them into kilometres (by means of the scale of the map). Now let us suppose that we are faced with the opposite problem: we have a table showing the distances in kilometres and have to reconstruct the positions of the cities on the map. This task is much more difficult than the first, but there are geometrical procedures that enable us to tackle it.

The problem tackled by means of the multidimensional scaling technique resembles the process of constructing the map on the basis of the table of distances. Starting out from the distances between given objects (in our example, candidates), we attempt to reconstruct the conceptual space in which these objects are located (in the minds of the interviewees, if we are dealing with interview data). First of all, we have to find out whether there exists a space that is common to all respondents; then we have to work out how many dimensions this space has; finally, we should give a name to these dimensions (in the map example, the task was easier; we knew that there were two dimensions and that they were called latitude and longitude).

In the research mentioned earlier involving the American presidential candidates, two dimensions emerged (Figure 6.5 shows where

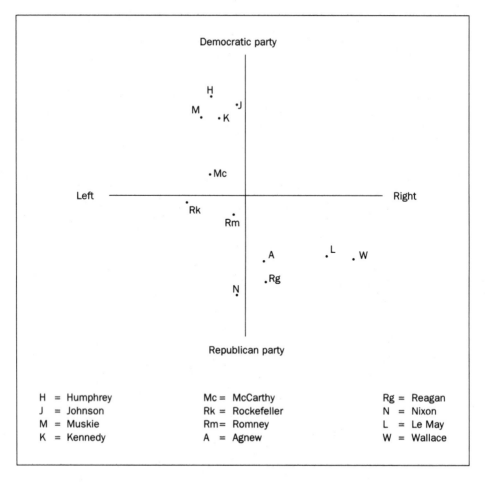

FIGURE 6.5   *Placement of the candidates in the 1968 American presidential elections in the space defined by the dimensions «party identification» and «ideology» (Weisberg and Rusk 1970)*

the 12 candidates were located in these dimensions). These dimensions were interpreted by the authors as the axis of party identity (Republican/Democratic) and the ideological axis (left/right). In other words, in expressing their preferences, the respondents followed, more or less unconsciously, two evaluation criteria: they judged each candidate on the basis of his party affiliation and progressive/conservative position. Humphrey, for example was judged to be fairly close to the centre on the ideological axis, while he was strongly identified with the Democratic Party. By contrast, Rockefeller was considered to occupy a central position between the Republicans and the Democrats (he was actually Republican but held liberal views), but with a strong left-leaning ideology.

The present manual does not deal with multidimensional scales in that the conceptual, mathematical and computational complexity of these techniques lies beyond its scope.

SUMMARY

1. *Scaling* denotes a set of procedures drawn up by social researchers to operationalize complex concepts. A *scale* is a coherent set of items that are regarded as indicators of a single, more general concept. An *item* is therefore a single component (statement, question, behavior, test response, attribute); a *scale* is the set of items. In sociology and social psychology, the most common application of scaling is represented by so-called *attitude measurement*. Scaling produces 'quasi-interval' variables in that they closely resemble interval variables.

2. In a closed question with ordered response alternatives, the latter may be *semantically autonomous*; or they can show *partial semantic autonomy*; or we have the so-called *self-anchoring scales*. In the first two cases, ordinal variables are generated; in the third case we obtain quasi-interval variables.

3. The term *Likert scale* covers a wide variety of scales, which are also known as *summated rating* or *additive* scales, since the scale score is assigned by summing the scores on the single items which make up the scale. There are four phases in the construction of a Likert scale: item conception and writing; item administration; item analysis (internal consistency evaluation and item selection); scale validation and unidimensionality checks.

4. The *Guttman's scalogram* is a *cumulative* scale (as opposed to the additive scale represented by the Likert scale). It is cumulative in the sense that it comprises a series of items of increasing difficulty; a subject who gives an affirmative response to any given question should also give affirmative responses to other items preceding it in the scale of difficulty. Item scalability is measured by the reproducibility coefficient.

5. Osgood's *semantic differential* was designed to investigate the meanings of given concepts, not through direct subjective descriptions provided by interviewees, but through associations between those concepts and other concepts presented to all interviewees in a standardized manner. Osgood identified three fundamental dimensions underlying judgements: evaluation, potency and activity.

6. The *sociometric* techniques proposed by Jacob Moreno seek to assess interpersonal relations among individuals in groups, by identifying the relationships which exist among them. In their most basic version, sociometric tests consist of a questionnaire made up of a small number of questions focusing on the topic of liking/disliking other members of the group.

FURTHER READING

A useful sourcebook on classic approaches to scaling (from Thurstone to unfolding scales) in the American empirical tradition is G.M. Maranell (ed.), *Scaling: A Sourcebook for Behavioral Scientists* (Aldine, 1974, pp. 436). An updated version which accommodates recent developments is offered by D. Krebs and P. Schmidt (eds), *New Directions in Attitude Measurement* (de Gruyter 1993, pp. 378).

For an introductory text on measurement and a practical guide to the construction of the simpler scales, see R.F. DeVellis, *Scale Development: Theory and Applications* (Sage, 1991, pp. 121).

A very useful guide to the construction and use of attitude scales is provided by two collections prepared by J.P. Robinson, P.R. Shaver and L.S. Wrightsman (eds): *Measures of Personality and Social Psychological Attitudes* (Academic Press, 1991, pp. 753), and *Measures of Political Attitudes* (Academic Press, 1998, pp. 801).

NOTES

1. There are inventories which report some of the most widely used attitude scales. The reader should see the two volumes by Robinson, Shaver and Wrightsman for Psychological attitudes (1991) and for Political attitudes (1999).

2. For a review of studies on the neutral position, see Schuman and Presser (1981, Chapter 6). For a more general overview of question formulation, see De Vellis (1991).

3. The question of how the answer 'don't know' should be treated in the data-analysis phase is a tricky one. The 'don't know' answer is frequently treated in the same way as an expression of neutrality, and is therefore given an intermediate score between the two extremes. In reality, this is a mistake: for example, when faced with a choice between higher taxes and fewer social services, the respondent who chooses an intermediate position, which may be interpreted as a balanced position between the two extremes, is not the same as the subject who answers 'don't know' either because he has not understood the question or because he has never thought about the issue.

4. With regard to the same point, it should be added that the increased use of telephone interviews, in which visual aids (such as cards showing the various response alternatives) cannot be used, has led to the formulation of questions involving *a series of binary choices*. In this way, the interviewee may be asked if he agrees or disagrees with a given statement; then, according to the answer given, he will be asked whether he agrees (or disagrees) 'strongly' or 'somewhat' and so on. This formulation appears to yield fairly similar results to those obtained by means of single questions for which all the response options are presented simultaneously (Groves, 1989: 467).

5. The most accurate procedure involves calculating the correlation between the score of each item and the score given by the sum (or by the mean) of all the *remaining* items ('adjusted' item-scale correlation).

6. Direct correlation: as one variable increases, the other also increases; inverse correlation: as one variable increases, the other decreases.

7. If the alpha value is negative, this means that some items are negatively correlated with one another, as a result of inconsistent polarity (e.g. the highest score indicates strong authoritarianism in one case, but weak authoritarianism in another). If all scores tend correctly in the same direction, alpha has only positive values.

8. This mathematical feature prompts many psychometricians to construct and administer scales containing too many items merely in order to increase the probability of obtaining a high alpha value. In such a case, however, it is also more likely that the interviewee will get tired and respond randomly.

9. We recall the definition of validity given in Chapter 3 Section 9: validity is the degree to which a given procedure for transforming a concept into a variable actually operationalizes the concept that it is intended to; for validity testing modalities, see the section mentioned.

10. Psychometricians generally work with single very long (to increase α) scales, and in laboratories; sociologists and political scientists insert (necessarily shorter) scales into questionnaires to be applied in the field.

11. The factors may also be correlated ('oblique rotation'), but here we are referring to the most elementary situation.

12. The modal category (or 'mode') of a nominal variable is that which displays the highest frequency. If the variable displays 40% 'Yes' responses and 60% 'No' responses, its mode is the category 'No' and its proportion is 0.60; if the responses are 90% and 10%, respectively, the proportion of the modal category is 0.90.

13. We may mention the fact that the Guttman technique can also be used with polytomous responses if these are first transformed into dichotomous responses by means of category aggregation (the point of subdivision can be chosen in such a way as to maximize the scalability of the scale – for example, by putting together the responses 'agree strongly' and 'agree somewhat' for certain items while, for other items, placing 'agree strongly' in opposition to all the other responses put together).

14. Osgood himself, however, often varied the list of attributes from one study to another; moreover, the technique has often been applied by using attributes specifically linked to the object

under investigation, in addition to the traditional pairs.

15. This sum is weighted, in that it uses the factorial scores of a factorial analysis.

16. With the difference that the responses in the Likert scale have partial semantic autonomy (e.g. very much, somewhat, a little, not at all), while in this case they are located on self-anchoring scales.

17. The figure of Moreno is rather singular; in addition to being a scholar, he was also a prophet and trend-setter, whose aim was to found a movement for the creation of a utopian society based on cooperation, solidarity and freedom. In general, the term 'sociometry' is used to indicate the whole range of Moreno's proposals, including psychodrama and sociodrama techniques, designed to give vent to creativity and spontaneity, chiefly for therapeutic purposes. Here, however, we will restrict our attention to 'sociometric testing', the technique proposed by Moreno for the investigation of relationships within groups.

7 Official Statistics

Modern societies produce a large quantity of data that derive from activities (such as the general population census) undertaken by governments in order to improve their knowledge about the societies they govern and normal administrative procedures of public bureaucracies (e.g. demographic statistics based on birth and death certificates, changes of residence, etc.). Such information represents a precious source of social knowledge and may constitute the empirical material for social research. This chapter describes such data, with special emphasis on official statistics in the US and in the UK.

1. A CLASSIC STUDY BASED ON OFFICIAL STATISTICS

In what can be regarded as the first sociological study, as well as one of the most brilliant examples of how to blend theoretical enquiry with empirical data, the French sociologist Emile Durkheim (1897) examined a phenomenon that was, in his day, highly controversial: suicide. His aim was to apply techniques of quantitative analysis to an issue that for centuries had only been the subject of philosophical speculation. The starting point of his analysis was a form of

empirical material that has not so far been mentioned in our text: official statistics.

Let us briefly describe Durkheim's approach to an aspect of this issue that he was to call 'egoistic suicide'. He began by wondering how the various religious faiths might influence suicide. By plotting the distribution of suicides on a map of Europe, he perceived that the phenomenon was much more frequent in Protestant countries than in Catholic ones. Faced with the possibility that this difference might be – as we would say today – 'spurious', that is to say, due not to religion but to other factors (for instance, cultural and economic) that differentiated between Catholic and Protestant countries, he decided that he would have to compare the effects of the two religions within the context of the same society. He therefore analysed suicide rates in the various provinces of the Kingdom of Bavaria; these provinces displayed marked differences in the numbers of Catholic and Protestant residents, while the variable 'society' was – as we would say today – 'kept under control' (or maintained constant), in that the provinces all belonged to the same state. Durkheim found that here, too, the suicide rate was directly proportional to the number of Protestants and inversely proportional to the number of Catholics.

Durkheim also found Switzerland to be an interesting case from this point of view. Since both French and German populations were to be found in the same country, he realized that the influence of religion could be observed separately on each of the two nationalities. He found that suicide rates were four or five times higher in the Protestant cantons than in the Catholic cantons, regardless of nationality. He therefore concluded that there was a genuine effect of religion on the suicide rate. Durkheim believed that this effect was due to the greater individualism of the Protestant faith, the only essential difference between Catholicism and Protestantism being that the latter allows the individual greater freedom of interpretation than the former; the Protestant is the chief author of his own faith, while the Catholic receives his faith 'ready-made' and is given no room for personal interpretation.

Having ascertained the influence of religion on the suicide rate in a given society through the analysis of these and other data, Durkheim turned his attention to other factors, particularly family and political factors. 'If one consults only the absolute figures,' – he wrote – 'unmarried persons seem to commit suicide less than married ones' to the extent that 'certain authors had once taught that marriage and family life multiply the chance of suicide' (Durkheim, 1897: 171). This interpretation was, however, erroneous, as it failed to take into account the absolute number of married and unmarried persons and the fact that the figure for the unmarried included children and youths, among whom suicide is very rare. However, when Durkheim restricted his analysis to persons over the age of 16 years, and also took into account the mean age of the married and the unmarried, he discovered that marriage reduced the risk of suicide by about half. He found that the 'protection coefficient' of marriage, which Durkheim established by working out the ratio between the suicide rates among the unmarried and the married, is constantly above the value of 1^1, meaning that the tendency to commit suicide is lower among married people. Next, Durkheim attempted to determine whether this protection factor exerted by marriage was due to conjugal life or to the presence of children. To this end, he compared suicide rates among married people – of the same gender, age and social condition – with and without children. He found that 'the immunity (towards suicide) of married persons in general is thus due ... to the influence not of coniugal society but of the family society' (1897: 189), and added that 'the family is the essential factor in the immunity of married persons, that is, the family as the whole group of parents and children' (1897: 198).

Finally, Durkheim tackled the question of the influence of what he called 'political society'. In this case too, his analysis yielded some very interesting results. On analysing variations in suicide rates in various countries and in various periods, Durkheim discovered that all forms of political unrest – from revolutions to war, and from riots to simple electoral crises – are accompanied by a drop in the suicide rate of the society involved. 'These facts' – he wrote – 'are therefore susceptible of only one interpretation; namely, that great social disturbances and great popular wars rouse collective sentiments ... and concentrating activity toward a single end ... cause(s) a stronger integration of society' (1897: 208).

Durkheim concluded this part of his research with the following considerations:

We have thus successively set up the three following propositions: (a) suicide varies inversely with the degree of integration of religious society; (b) suicide varies inversely with the degree of integration of domestic society; and (c) suicide varies inversely with the degree of integration of political society. The cause can only be found in a single quality possessed by all these social groups ... The only quality satisfying this condition is that they are all strongly integrated social groups. So we reach the general conclusion: suicide varies inversely with the degree of integration of the social groups of which the individual forms a part. (1897: 208–10)

2. MAIN FEATURES OF OFFICIAL STATISTICS

The above account illustrates the kind of analysis that Durkheim conducted, and especially the type of data that he used. As we have seen, he analysed the statistics available at that time, which were published by the government organizations of the day. This example clearly shows that official statistics constitute a very important empirical basis from which highly convincing results emerge.

for the quantitative analysis of collective phenomena.

Even today, we can distinguish two meanings of the word 'statistics': that of science which studies collective and mass phenomena through mathematical methods based on the probability theory; and that of sets of data intended to give an overview, even if only indicative, of given facts or phenomena. Thus, statistics may be 'science' (statistical science) or 'data' (statistical data).

In the present chapter, the term 'statistics' is used in this second sense. Thus, by

---

BOX 7.1   OFFICIAL STATISTICS IN SOCIAL RESEARCH

Empirical social research was born in Europe at the beginning of the twentieth century, on the basis of studies involving official statistics. Durkheim's *On Suicide* (1897) is but one of many such examples. It is worth mentioning, among others, André Siegfried's (*Tableau politique de la France de l'Ouest*, 1913) and Herbert Tingsten's (*Political Behaviour*, 1937) research in the field of political sociology. In spite of the limited number of variables available to these scholars, both conducted admirable historical-social studies by analysing territorial and temporal variations. The survey did not emerge as a research technique until the end of the 1930s with the development of social research in the US, which at that time did not keep official statistics. In the post-war period surveys became the dominant mode of social research, whereas official statistics assumed a secondary role.

The word 'statistics' comes from 'state', its original meaning being that of 'science that describes states'. The adjective 'statistic' was introduced by the Italian scholar Gerolamo Ghilini in 1589 with reference to this science. Subsequently, the noun 'statistics' arose to indicate that discipline which deals with the quantitative description of the main features of a nation. As the mathematical aspects of the discipline evolved, and especially with the introduction of probability theory, the term 'statistics' took on the more general meaning of *science of the collective*: a scientific method

demographic statistics we mean the tables which report the numbers of the population, births, deaths, marriages, migration, etc., subdivided by region and by year; similarly, judicial statistics are the figures concerning crimes, trials, prison inmates, and the activity of the judicial institutions in general; and likewise for the statistics on health, employment, education, etc. These data differ from other data normally used in social research – especially from those gathered through surveys – with regard to four aspects: production, unit of analysis, content, and breadth of what is recorded.

2.1 Production

In the title of this chapter ('Official Statistics'), the adjective 'official' (which could be replaced by 'public') indicates that these data sets are gathered almost entirely by public agencies. Census-taking dates back to ancient times, and traces have been found even in primitive civilizations. Broadly speaking, we can say that the need to 'count' the population, the number of families and goods, arose with the earliest forms of state organization and became consolidated as the great centralized empires of the ancient world emerged. Archaeological finds have pointed to the existence of such forms of statistical recording in the ancient civilization of the Sumerians (IV-II millennium B.C.), then in the Assyrian and Babylonian empires, in ancient Egypt, in imperial China, and in ancient Greece and Rome (the term 'census' comes from Latin).

In regard to the production of statistics by public agencies, a distinction should be made between data generated during the course of normal administrative procedures and data expressly gathered for cognitive purposes.

In any society that has some form of bureaucratic structure, a whole range of *administrative acts* will be registered; these leave traces which, if suitably collected and organized, will yield statistical data. We need only think, for example, of demographic statistics; in the event of births, deaths, marriage, divorce and transfer of residence, the citizen is obliged to fill in the appropriate forms. When such events are registered (for instance, the sum of all births on a given day in a given municipality) they give rise to statistical data. Further examples include: crime statistics resulting from the registration of reports made by citizens; statistics on foreign trade as revealed by customs documents; education statistics emerging from the registration of enrolments and withdrawals at educational institutions; health statistics (abortions, infectious diseases, causes of death, hospitalization) stemming from the records kept by doctors and healthcare institutions; welfare statistics based on the payment of pensions and benefits; statistics on family savings as revealed by bank deposits, and so on and so forth.

In this regard, it should however be pointed out that the use of administrative data for the purpose of compiling cognitive statistics is not applicable to all modern societies. European states have a long tradition of centralized bureaucracy and have used networks of administrative organizations (municipalities, counties, provinces, etc.) to compile records since the nineteenth century. Outside Europe, this is not the case, as in the US, for instance, on account of the lack of a centralized state structure and the presence of a marked tradition of diffidence towards any form of state intrusion into the life of the citizen.

With regard to cases in which statistical data are a by-product of administrative deeds, we can use the term *indirect recording*. In other cases, statistical data are produced through *direct recording*, in that the information is expressly gathered for the purpose of shedding light on a given social phenomenon. This is the case of the *census*, which is carried out by the state in order to map the features of the population. The modern census was established in 1801 in Britain and in France, and has been carried out every 10 years since then.

For many years, social statistics relied upon administrative and census data. More recently, however, these sources have been supplemented by other forms of direct recording. The use of data from administrative records offers the advantage that the cost of data collection is almost completely eliminated. At the same time, however, the problem arises that such data have been collected for other purposes and may therefore prove inadequate in revealing the social phenomenon under examination. Moreover, certain phenomena elude all administrative records; we need only think, for example, of new forms of family structure (*de facto* families, families with children from previous marriages, cohabitation among the elderly, etc.), of illegal immigration, of crimes that go unreported, etc. In recent years, therefore, national statistical institutes have implemented a range of *ad hoc surveys* in specific sectors, in order to study particular aspects of society. For instance, recent surveys of emergency rooms to investigate visits attributable to 'club' drugs were conducted by the Substance Abuse and Mental Health Services Administration in the US, while the Health and Safety Executive gathered self-reported information on work-related illnesses in the UK. While *ad hoc* surveys constitute a growth sector in all national statistical institutes, the use of administrative records for statistical purposes is likely to increase in the future as a result of the new possibilities offered by information technology; as the various sectors of the public administration become increasingly computerized, the scene is being set for ever closer links among the various administrative archives already in existence.

2.2 Units of analysis

A distinction that is 'traditionally' made between official statistics and the results of surveys concerns the unit of analysis; official statistics do not focus on the individual, but on *geographic areas*: electoral or census districts, municipalities, provinces, regions, counties, nations, etc. When Durkheim (1897) compared suicide rates in the provinces of Bavaria, his unit of analysis was the province. When he examined the trend in suicide rates over time in order to investigate possible variations during war years, his unit of analysis was the nation.

Although the basic information is collected on individuals (*recording unit*), the data are available for analysis only at the aggregate level (*unit of analysis*). Let us imagine a table in which the regions of a certain country are listed, each accompanied by three statistics in the form of percentages (or 'rates'): the divorce rate (as a percentage of all marriages), votes for the Socialist Party (as a percentage of all valid votes cast), and the number of cinema tickets sold (in relation to the total population). In this case, the unit of analysis – to which the data are assigned – is

a geographic area: here, a region. Only at this level can the data be analysed. For instance, we may be able to say that region A has a higher divorce rate than region B; that the mean number of cinema tickets sold in the region is 3.8 per person, or that there is a correlation at the regional level between the divorce rate and votes for the Socialist Party (that is to say, the regions with the highest percentages of Socialist Party votes also tend to have higher divorce rates). Clearly, all these statements are made with reference to regions, not individuals.

These are called *aggregate* data, as opposed to *individual* data. These terms underline the distinction between cases in which the unit of analysis is a group of individuals and those in which it is a single individual. In its literal meaning, the term 'aggregate' refers to a process of composition, or summing; and that is exactly what happens. Aggregate data are the result of a *counting* operation performed on the individuals of a group; this gives a total, which is in turn normalized on the basis of the total population of the group, in order to compensate for size differences among the groups, and hence to be able to compare the groups.

In the case of official statistics, the group (which could generally be constituted by any set of individuals, such as firms, army divisions, educational institutes, etc.) is a *geographic area*. Thus, by counting the numbers of divorces, votes for a given political party, or cinema tickets sold, and relating these to a reference value (which may vary from case to case; in our example, the total numbers of marriages, valid votes, and population, respectively), we obtain a *statistical ratio*, which constitutes the aggregate variable and enables comparisons to be made.

In most cases, information is collected on individuals (persons who get divorced, individuals who vote, etc.), but is only available at the aggregate level. Why so? First of all, the information may be produced at the individual level, but registered only at the aggregate level for reasons of privacy. This is what happens in elections, when the vote cast by an individual is registered (and thus knowable) only as part of the total number of votes for a given party in a given area.

Sometimes the information is initially gathered at the individual level for administrative purposes regarding the mere occurrence of a given social phenomenon, with no further specification of the characteristics of the individual. This is the case, for instance, with demographic statistics regarding births, deaths, and marriages on a given day in a given municipality, in which no further information on the individuals is recorded except for a few basic features such as gender, age and marital status (as in the case of suicide, in which the data are provided by the record of the cause of death). As a result, such data are kept and made public only in aggregate form, and breakdowns are limited to a few variables (e.g. the number of deaths by gender and age in a given year in a given municipality).

On other occasions, the information may be collected and *recorded* in some detail at the individual level, but published (and therefore made available for research) only as aggregate data for organizational reasons. Let us take the case of the census. The information is collected by an interviewer who questions individuals (or families). In principle, therefore, the information collected is not unlike that yielded by surveys. Before the advent of the computer age, however, it was inconceivable that census forms could be analysed at an individual level (and thus handled in the same way as survey questionnaires). Indeed, it was impossible to imagine storing and analysing millions of individual records, except in the form of summarized tables per municipality (or other geographic area).

Finally, the information may come from administrative data recorded from the outset at an aggregate level (e.g. sales of tickets in various cinemas).

All the above concerns the traditional approach to official statistics. Today, however, some things are changing; as a result of modern information technology, data from official statistical sources are being made increasingly available not only in aggregate and table form, but also in the form of individual records.

Nevertheless, even today, the vast majority of official statistics are expressed as aggregate data at the level of some geographic area. Moreover, even when the data are made available to the researcher in the form of individual-based files, this does not mean that they cannot be used at geographic area level; it should also be added that such form facilitates immediate consultation, while the analysis of individual data requires a higher level of technical competence.

2.3 Contents

The information provided by administrative records is not yielded by observation or questioning, but by the registration of events or facts (a birth, a purchase, a change of residence, hospital admissions, school enrolments, etc.). We are therefore dealing with what, in Chapter 5, Section 4.1, has been called 'sociographic data'. This means that opinions, attitudes and motivations are excluded.

This feature of information drawn from statistical sources is preserved even when such information is not derived from administrative records, but from *ad hoc* surveys conducted for cognitive purposes. The census is usually limited to collecting factual data; and even the special investigations conducted by the various national statistical institutes on samples of the population which cover specific social issues do not generally tackle attitudinal issues.

This self-limitation stems, first of all, from the original characteristics of official statistics, which, since they are derived from administrative records, regard only actions, behaviours and facts. Moreover, since the material collected is to be handled by the state (or other public bodies), greater care must be taken to safeguard the privacy of the citizen than might be taken by a private body. A final consideration is the volume of data handled. Even in the case of surveys, official statistics – as we shall see – are collected on large samples by large numbers of collectors; efforts are therefore directed to ensuring that the distributions of the variables are representative of the population, rather than at attempting to investigate motivations or attitudes.

2.4 The breadth of data gathering

A final characteristic of 'traditional' statistical data is that they are gathered on the entire population. In this case, a choice has to be made between *exhaustive* (total) collection and *sampling* (or partial collection). Traditional statistical data from administrative sources are exhaustive, in that they are derived from records of the whole population: all births, deaths, hospital admissions, judicial proceedings, etc. in a given municipality in a given year (indeed, modern techniques of sampling are fairly recent, arising in the 1930s and 1940s, while the collection of statistics dates back to the beginning of the nineteenth century).

The census itself has traditionally been carried out on the entire population, and this is still the case. The census operations carried out in 1990–1991 in nine of the 12 countries which at that time made up the European Union were conducted on the entire population. In two countries, Denmark and the Netherlands, the traditional operations were replaced by a computer linkage of administrative files; only in Germany[2] was the census conducted by means of sampling (1% of the population).

The advantages and disadvantages of sampling, as opposed to total collection, are obvious. Sampling: (a) *reduces the cost* of data collection; (b) *reduces the time* required to collect and process the data (which is considerable in the case of total collection, since delays in a few units can hold up the whole process); (c) *reduces the organizational load*, in that it is not necessary to recruit, train and manage huge numbers of data gatherers; and (d) *enables in-depth analysis to be made*, as the smaller number of data gatherers means that they can be adequately trained to conduct more complex surveys, while the lesser organizational complexity enables resources to be concentrated on quality control.

On the other hand, it is clear that only total data collection enables analyses to be carried out on the smallest geographic units. While sampling is sufficient to reveal the features of the whole population of the country, or of large geographic areas such as regions, total data collection will be required in order to reveal the characteristics of the population of small municipalities. For this reason, the census, precisely because it yields an inventory of the human and material resources of the nation, is conducted on the whole population. It aims to provide a picture of the *stock information* of the nation every 10 years, while the so-called *flow information* will be provided by administrative records and periodic surveys. However, the most recent *ad hoc* investigations carried out by the various national statistical institutes into particular and hitherto little explored aspects of society have generally been conducted through sampling. The samples studied are in general quite large (usually comprising tens of thousands of cases). By contrast, a survey conducted by a private organization on a sample of the national population normally deals with between 1000 and 3000 cases.

The reason for this difference lies in the particular objective of official data gathering. Rather than attempting to study a social question, to verify a theory empirically, or to identify the possible causes of a given phenomenon, the primary goal of official statistics is, and always has been, essentially a descriptive one. Moreover, the strongly geographic character of this objective requires that reliable estimates of the phenomena studied should also be obtained at the sub-national level.

3. US AND UK OFFICIAL STATISTICS

Although the term 'official statistics' may convey the sense of a unified and monolithic system of data, the production, review, maintenance and distribution of statistics gathered through official venues can be variable and widely dispersed. The nature of the data collection, the degree of centralization or dispersion of data gathering and compilation, the agencies involved in the production of statistics, the geographic coverage and detail, and the manner of distribution all vary from one set of statistics to another. Some statistics may be gathered from administrative records for local governmental units and distributed by those same units. Other statistics may be gathered locally, but are compiled and released at a higher and more inclusive regional or administrative level. Other statistics derive from surveys resulting from coordinated national efforts at data collection, and are systematically collated, reviewed, and distributed from a central agency.

3.1 Official agencies

Agencies play many different roles within the organization of a national statistical system as a whole. In the US, the Office of Management and Budget (OMB) is responsible for the coordination of the federal statistical system, but responsibility for the collection, review, analysis and distribution of official statistics is diluted among separate agencies and different levels of government. At the federal level, for example, 15 statistical agencies are devoted solely to the creation and analysis of statistics in selected areas, and at least 90 other agencies maintain statistical programs which provide the planning of surveys or studies, data collection, data analysis, or dissemination of their own statistics or statistics collected by others.

For example, the SOI Division of the Internal Revenue Service provides summary annual income, financial, and tax data for states, counties, and zip codes based on tax returns. Since returns of tax filers may be linked across years, this division also provides estimates of state-to-state and county-to-county migration. The National Center for Education Statistics not only gathers administrative data (indirectly via surveys of state education departments from their own administrative records), but also sponsors large surveys and compiles comparative

statistics for regions (e.g. other countries) in which it had no hand in the collection of the data. The Bureau of Labor Statistics (BLS) collects, analyses, and disseminates administrative and survey data, and maintains links to the individual state agencies who compile and prepare their own labor market data in conjunction with the BLS.

The US Census Bureau is, perhaps, the largest single producer of federal statistics. In addition to the better known decennial censuses of population and housing, the Bureau also conducts censuses of agriculture (in years ending in a 4 or 9), an economic census of retail, wholesale, and service trades, a census of manufacturers, a census of transportation and a census of governments (all in years ending in 2 or 7). It also tabulates on foreign trade, and conducts repeated cross-sectional and longitudinal surveys like the Survey of Income and Program Participation, Current Population Surveys, and American Community Surveys.

In the UK, the Office of National Statistics (ONS) was formed through the merger of the Central Statistical Office (CSO) and the Office of Population Censuses and Surveys (OCPS) in 1996. The ONS is responsible for collecting economic and social statistics, assembling a database of key statistics from a variety of sources, conducting the census and social surveys, developing statistical standards and classifications, analysing statistical information and disseminating the results. The ONS, together with the more than 40 statistics branches within all government departments and agencies, form the Government Statistical Service (GSS). The director of the ONS is also the head of the GSS, and the registrar general for England and Wales.

While the ONS plays a larger role in the UK statistical system than does the OMB in the US, a number of other agencies and departments play key roles. For example, the Department for Work and Pension produces statistics on income support, pensions, housing benefits and unemployment benefits. The Department for Education and Skills carries out an annual census of schools in England, maintains the National Information System for Vocational Qualifications and provides statistical publications of their own and other departments' data. The Department for Transport, Local Government and the Regions collects, analyses and publishes a range of information on housing, local government, environment and countryside issues, construction, transport and traffic.

In short, in both the US and UK the collection and production of official statistics is distributed across a number of distinct departmental entities, whose actions are coordinated to some extent by a central agency. Because of advances in technology, however, the distribution of official statistics is becoming increasingly unified (in many senses). The linkage of data distribution from separate agencies and sources, even when those agencies continue to separately maintain and distribute their holdings, can be drawn together via links from a single site on the internet.

3.2 Distribution through official venues

Official statistical data is becoming increasingly ubiquitous. Its production has spread substantially, moving from simple centralized enumerations to programs of systematic coverage by a broad range of governmental units. Both the increase in the numbers of statistics available and the range of sources from which they can be obtained can lead to a haphazard embarrassment of riches. Both the US and UK, while maintaining a level of dispersion in statistical activities, have made an effort to integrate the distribution of statistics. In terms of published materials, an array of statistics may be found in a handful of reference books.

In the UK, key print publications include *The Annual Abstract of Statistics*, which contains statistics on the country's economy, industry, society and demography. It is compiled from roughly 100 sources and has more than 10,000 series contained in 330 tables. The *Official Yearbook of the United Kingdom* is a series which began in the 1940s which, although less numerically oriented than the Annual Abstract, contains 600 pages of simple tables,

maps, and text about the people and institutions of the UK. The *Monthly Digest of Statistics*, as its name suggests, contains updates to economic and social series of statistics in 130 tables. *Regional Trends* provides not only statistics for UK regions, but also for sub-regions within the UK and the regions within the European Union, and covers topical areas on population, households, education and training, the labour market, housing, health, lifestyles, crime and justice, transport, the environment, regional accounts, and industry and agriculture. A compendium of the *Regional Trends* publication since its inception in 1965 is available on a CD-ROM. Since 1970, *Social Trends* has provided a reference source aimed at a non-technical audience with key statistics, text, and charts organized around topics similar to those in the *Regional Trends*.

In the US, key print publications include the *Statistical Abstract of the US*, the *County and City Data Book*, the *State and Metropolitan Data Book*, and the *Historical Statistics of the United States*. The *Statistical Abstract* has been published since 1878, and contains 1500 tables detailing characteristics of the population, geography, political structure, economy and budget, transportation, environment and natural resources, trade, and international statistics, usually in the form of time series. Tables are usually for the nation as a whole, although many series are provided for states or Metropolitan Areas (see the following section on geography). The *State and Metropolitan Data Book* has been published at four to five-year intervals since 1979, and provides similarly detailed time series for smaller geographies. These geographies include not only state and metropolitan areas, but also central cities and suburbs for a number of items. *The County and City Data Book* focuses on even smaller geographies and has, since 1947, provided summary statistics on the characteristics of the population and economy of these areas. The *Historical Statistics*, covering from colonial times through to 1970, provide national statistics, and the sources for those statistics, over a longer span of time.

Increasingly – and fortunately for social scientists interested in using official statistics – statistics are becoming more broadly available in electronic form. Many of the original print publications identified above, for example, are now provided on CD-ROM or posted as documents directly downloadable from the internet. Similarly, the statistical series from which these publications draw are frequently available as spreadsheets or data files. In many cases interactive applications have been designed to assist users in selecting the geographic areas and topical series available,[3] and the ability to do some analyses, like cross tabulations of counts or mean values, may be available. Equally importantly, centralized government sites which attempt to draw together the entire range of official statistics are a major objective of national governments in both the US and UK.

In the US, the *FedStats* site, http://www.fedstats.gov/, is the 'gateway to statistics from over 100 US Federal agencies'. It does not, and is not intended to, actually house the statistical series from those agencies. Instead, it operates like a table of contents or index to statistical resources maintained on the individual sites of those agencies. It is possible to browse categories of topics (from Acute Conditions through Weekly Earnings), search statistical agencies for statistics identified with a key word or phrase, or obtain statistical profiles incorporating pre-defined sets of characteristics for the nation, states, counties, or judicial districts. Links are also maintained with each of the statistical agencies and the key statistics maintained at those agencies which are available online.

The National Statistics site for the UK, http://www.statistics.gov.uk/, provides a central point of access to official statistics as well as maintaining those statistics on site. Statistics organized around 13 topical themes (including agriculture, fishing and forestry, commerce, energy and industry, crime and justice, economy, education and training, health and care, labor market, population and migration, social and welfare, and transport, travel and tourism). Access to the statistics are

provided via the consolidated database called StatBase. Thematic items and series pertaining to each theme can be found by series or subject, and interactive queries based on items with which the series can be cross-classified (such as geographic area, year, or age groups) permit more detail and flexibility. Limitations on the number of items which can be extracted at one time make this more of an exploratory tool, however. Detailed tables are available for a larger range of data and series are also possible through other tools, however, as is metadata for the series and statistics in each series.

3.3 Metadata

Metadata (information about the data) is particularly important in the environment in which official statistics have increasingly become available. In traditional circumstances in which a statistic was embedded in explanatory text, or within a table with footnotes and contextural headings and associations, much of the information which allows the researcher to understand the statistic was immediately evident. Even in situations where a statistic was shorn of metadata, as with a plain text file, usually the process through which data was imported into a statistical analysis program was sufficiently laborious that close attention to a codebook which provided metadata was necessary.

As researchers and research organizations anxious to share statistical series placed statistics on the internet, and as governmental and private organizations began to disseminate statistics in the absence of well-defined standards, statistics often became disassociated with the information which made them interpretable. A series showing unemployment rates among women, for example, may vary in terms of a denominator. In some years, it may include all women over 14, in others it may be limited to the 'experienced' labor force who have held jobs, while in others it may include all women between the ages of 16 and 64 who are either looking for work or are at work. Without information about the universe for which it is defined, information on how the data was gathered, how it may have been processed, or what kind of statistic (e.g. a count, a percent, a median) it represents, seemingly straightforward statistics can be misleading. While standards are still evolving, elements including source, title, coverage, producer, format, date, subject, data type and description are usually suggested. The Dublin Core and the data type definitions of the Data Documentation Initiative (DDI) seek to provide standards for necessary metadata and appropriate tags for attaching such information to electronic data accessed on the internet. Researchers should be aware that, even when such information is not present, its absence should create some doubt about the statistics being used.

3.4 Geography

The geography for which official data may be provided is complex and may be inconsistent between systems of statistics. For example, census data in the US is provided at the national level, in the 4 census divisions into which the US is split, the 9 census regions into which divisions are split, and each of the 50 states, which are further subdivided into 3141 counties. Counties are subsequently broken into civil divisions and places, which are then split into census tracts, which are further broken out into block groups and subsequently blocks. For local level analyses, census tracts, containing on average 4000 persons, are the most commonly used geographic unit.

Large economically integrated urban counties may also be classified as Metropolitan Statistical Areas (MSAs), which may be aggregated up into Consolidated Metropolitan Statistical Areas (CMSAs), or split into central cities and suburbs. Each of these previous geographic levels tend to, with some exceptions, nest within a higher level of geography. Independent of this basic hierarchy are political, administrative, or use-based boundaries, such as congressional districts, American Indian Reservations, school districts, zip code tabulation areas, traffic analysis zones, labor market areas, or urban and rural areas.

Correspondences between different units of geography for recent US censuses can be determined using a *geographic correspondence engine*, created and maintained by the Consortium for Earth Science Information Network (CIESIN). Using the lowest level of geography defined by the census – the census block – the proportions of different geographies which overlap can be associated with the identifiers about those areas. For example, based on these correspondences, the relationship between Voting Tabulation Districts and census tracts can be defined, even though one such area may not nest completely within another, by noting the proportional allocation of one area within others. Although, unfortunately, these correspondences cannot be established for geographic units prior to 1990, documentation on changes in geography between censuses, and centroids marking the longitude and latitude of many census geographies are available in earlier periods. For county and state boundaries, digitization of historic paper maps also provides documentation of geographic changes since 1790.

In Great Britain, the most finely grained units of census geography are enumeration districts (EDs) in England and Wales and output areas (OAs) in Scotland. These 150,000 geographic units are contained within wards and postcode sectors, which are themselves contained within local authority districts (metropolitan, non-metropolitan, London boroughs, and unitary authorities), and then into counties (where applicable), and subsequently Governmental Office Regions (GORs) and countries.

Other UK geographies commonly used for statistical reporting include Standard Statistical Regions (which GORs replaced), Environmental Agency areas, National Health Service Regional Office areas, Police Force areas, Department of Trade and Industry Regions, and Tourist Board regions. Reporting of areas based on postal code aggregates are also frequently employed.

The *Gazetteer of the Old and New Geographies of the United Kingdom* provides a reference source showing correspondences between statistical regions, local authorities and health authorities, as well linking the local authorities with the UK NUTS. The NUTS (Nomenclature of Territorial Statistics) is a hierarchical classification of areas that spans the European Union's economic territory. In additional, a Neighborhood Statistics Database which is geographically referenced at a low level and aggregated into higher level geographies will permit the linkage and publication of economic and social data collected by the government at a consistent small-area geography. Maps identifying these higher level boundaries can be found on the UK National Statistics web site.

3.5 Standards and classifications

Official statistics should ideally provide a consistent measure of the highest available quality for the item being recorded. The existence of appropriate metadata and geographic referencing serve as the basis for insuring that the universe being counted and the territory for which it is counted are consistent and explicit (or at least knowing when it is not). The consistency of the categories being used for tabulation, and the documentation of changes in the categories, are another hallmark of official statistics.

Although, as we have already noted, official statistics tend to reflect facts rather than opinions, the categories of interest and the way they are defined are socially governed. Statistics on suicide may seem clear – Is a person dead? Did they die by their own hand? Was the death intentional? – but the attribution of suicide and its subsequent recording by officials may indicate the evaluation by coroners, doctors, family members, and police of ambiguous information. For more amorphous categories – occupation, unemployment, class – the social aspects to factual counts are even more clear. Official agencies set standards for the classification of these social facts, ideally at national levels, but such standards may change. Standard Occupational Classifications, Standard Industrial Classifications, the North American Industry Classification System, or the International Harmonized System Commodity Classification all represent efforts to impose a consistent definition of a category or class. The existence of such schemes limits the amount of interpretation and variability that individuals recording data introduce, but interpretation – both officially imposed and individual – still remain.

Impacts of changes in classifications are particularly apparent when comparing data over the long temporal spans that some official statistics cover. Modern understandings of occupation and industry have evolved a great deal over the periods covered by censuses in the US and UK. Some inconsistency is inevitable, but documentation of changes in standards of the sort national statistical agencies now routinely prepare will aid in adjusting for and understanding those inconsistencies.

In many cases, national agencies are unable to impose a standard, either because an internal consensus does not exist or because collectors and producers of the data are unwilling to agree. This can be particularly true of administrative data gathered at local levels, and aggregated or distributed at higher levels. The greater the degree of decentralization, the more potential exists for local idiosyncrasies in the collection of data, variation in the categories for which they are tabulated, or selectivity in the aggregate totals which are forwarded to regional or national offices. For example, early statistics on school attendance in the US were often based on different bases of measurement: in some states, attendance might be based on the number of students in school on a selected day, while in other states it reflected the number of students who attended school at any time during the year.[4]

3.6 Non-governmental distribution

The dissemination of data directly by the producers (or indirectly through official media or internet sites) is a primary channel for statistics. The users of these sites and sources are varied, and access may be pitched toward news agencies, teachers, other governmental agencies, businesses or individuals in search of quick fact to bolster an argument. Another avenue for official statistics lies in academic data archives, which provide resources which are more likely to be structured toward and supportive of social science research.

The two most prominent data archives in the US and UK are the Inter-university Consortium for Political and Social Research (ICPSR) at the University of Michigan and the Economic and Social Research Council (ESRC) data archive at the University of Essex. Online, these archives can be found at http://www.icpsr. umich.edu and at http://www.data-archive. ac.uk/. ICPSR, founded in 1962, is probably the largest single data archive in the world. In addition to its role in housing and maintaining its extensive data holdings, ICPSR provides training in quantitative methods, instructional materials for teaching, and archives of combined data and information necessary to permit other researchers to replicate a corresponding published article, book, or dissertation. It also offers online analysis of selected data sets, many of which are data gathered by governmental agencies for the purpose of creating official statistics. ICPSR is a non-profit membership-based archive, with over 400 member colleges and universities from around the world.

The ESRC archive, founded in 1967, houses the largest collection of accessible computer-readable data in the social sciences and humanities in the United Kingdom. It distributes data to users in the UK and, by arrangement with other archives and approved individual researchers, internationally. In addition to British cross-sectional studies from academic, government and commercial sources, the archive holds time-series data, major longitudinal studies, and panel surveys. Online analysis capabilities are provided for some data sets using NESSTAR, created by a consortium including the UK, Danish, and Norwegian archives in combination with five other partners. NESSTAR is based on DDI (Data Documentation Initiate) data and metadata, and at ESRC supports analysis of British Election data.

With the expansion of the internet and subsequent integration of electronic resources, physical locality becomes less important, although it may still influence specialization

of holdings, possible fees for access, or level of assistance for users. As a result, a large number of archives also provide useful access to official statistics. Some archives of interest include the University of Edinburgh Data Library (http://datalib.ed.ac.uk/), Manchester Information and Associated Services (MIMAS) census tools accessed at http://www.census.ac. uk/cdu/, the Urban Information Center (UIC) at the University of Missouri (http:// www.oseda.missouri.edu/uic/), the Geospacial and Statistical Data center at the University of Virginia (http://fisher.lib.virginia.edu/), and the Resource Centre for Access to Data on Europe (http://www-rcade.dur.ac.uk/) which provides statistical data from Eurostat, the United Nations Industries Development Organization (UNIDO), UNESCO and the International Labor Organization (ILO). Many more such archives could be listed, but a reasonable search strategy is to begin at these academic data archives and investigate the current links which they provide to other archives. Those links are most likely to reflect archivists' up-to-date evaluations of the most useful and accessible holdings for the purposes of research.

3.7 Aggregate data and microdata

As we have already seen, one of the defining characteristics of official statistics are that they are aggregates: tabulations of counts, ratios, medians, means, or some other summary provided for a particular geographic area. The advent of surveys for the provision of official statistics, in combination with the release of microdata samples from national censuses, makes the use of the individual level data on which these summaries are based an attractive possibility.

Two factors which may make the use of summary totals more useful than the underlying microdata lie in the level of geographic detail available. Aggregate statistics, particularly from censuses, are often available for extremely small geographies. In the US, data for census tracts, block groups and blocks can provide detail on neighbourhoods and localities not identifiable using the Public Use

Microdata Samples (PUMS). In the UK, the Small Area and Local Base Statistics (SAS/LBS) provide the same fine geographic grain, which can't be equalled using the Samples of Anonymised Records (SARs). Related to this geographic detail are researchers' interests in characteristics of entire geographies. Some measures like indices of segregation, while they reflect and influence social processes at the individual level, can only be defined at higher levels. Frequently, researchers' use of aggregate statistics lies precisely in linking contextual characteristics of an area – such as high poverty areas, high crime areas, racially segregated areas – with individual level data for which they have (usually confidential) precise geographic information in order to investigate the influences of surroundings on individuals' behaviors.

However, if these limitations are not of concern, the flexibility offered by microdata is available to social scientists. In Chapter 5, Section 10 we identified many of the data sets underlying the official statistics in the UK and US. Data users interested in both individual level official data and international comparisons may also be interested in the International Public Use Microdata Samples. Like the PUMS discussed in Chapter 5, the International IPUMS will provide census microdata which has been coded and harmonized to match categories to the extent possible. The international microdata are intended to be provided for 21 countries on six continents, with multiple censuses included for each county, allowing comparisons both across time and across national geographies.

4.   A FINAL NOTE: THE STUDY OF SOCIAL STRUCTURES

Official statistical sources provide a wealth of opportunity for social research. They yield huge amounts of data on every area and every stage of social life: education, work, family, health, dealings with institutions, etc. For the social scientist, official statistics are indispensable in at least four sectors of research.

The first of these sectors concerns the *structure of society*: demographic features, migration, distribution of employment and voter orientation, class structure, social mobility, mobility of labour, structure of the economy and of families (children, cohabitation, the elderly), deviance (crime and judicial procedures), social deprivation, welfare and so on.

The second sector covered by official statistics is the *geographic breakdown* of the country. This reveals territorial differences (among various regions, between metropolitan and rural areas, etc.) with regard to crime rates, unemployment figures, economic structure, political and religious orientation and so on. Such differences can only be analyzed on the basis of data which refer to the entire area (or are derived from representative samples at a sub-national level), and only official statistics can fulfil this requirement.

Another field in which official statistics are essential is that of *comparative studies among nations*. Fairly recent times have seen the introduction of surveys using standardized sampling techniques (the same questionnaire, type of interview and sample structure) which, through the coordination of national research groups, enable comparisons to be made among nations. However, such techniques have been used only sporadically and in restricted sectors. Moreover, increasing co-ordination among central statistical institutes in various countries (e.g. Eurostat in the European Union) is leading to ever greater integration, and therefore comparability, of the official statistics of various nations.

Further, official data are indispensable to *time studies*. Indeed, only through official statistics can we study the long-term evolution (sometimes over decades or even centuries) of such phenomena as demographic patterns, trends in voting, employment in the various economic sectors, migration, etc. Furthermore, in addition to the analysis of such long-term trends (time-series analyses), the study of earlier societies relies heavily on official sources; in order to reconstruct the social structures and relationships of former times, statistics regarding elections, judicial proceedings, employment, incomes, commerce, taxation, etc. are of fundamental importance.

Naturally, the use of official statistics has its limits. First of all, *the data may not meet the researcher's needs,* as they have been compiled with other objectives in mind (and sometimes – as we have seen – for administrative rather than cognitive purposes). If, for instance, we take as indicators of religiosity in Spain the abortion rate or the number of copies of the official national Catholic magazine sold per 1000 residents, we will be using, for the concept that we wish to operationalize, very partial indicators in that – to return to a notion introduced in Chapter 3 – their 'indicating part' is limited. It would be far more appropriate to our objective to look at church attendance; however, this information will not be found in any statistical sources. In research based on official statistics, the selection of indicators therefore constitutes a serious problem, and the researcher will have to take the utmost care to ensure that they fit the phenomena to be examined.

A further difficulty lies in the fact that official statistics are *limited to factual variables* – that is to say, to objective and behavioural data. The whole subjective sphere of opinions, attitudes and motivations is therefore excluded. Thus, while official statistics enable us to conduct in-depth studies of the trends in electoral abstentions in a given country, its geographical distribution, its territorial correlation with economic and social indicators, its distribution according to gender, age, profession, educational qualification, etc., they can tell us nothing about why people do not turn out to vote. Only a tailor-made survey can shed light on this aspect of the phenomenon.

Finally, there remains the fact that official statistics – when they are known only at an aggregate level – *are not suited to the analysis of individual behaviours.* Even if we find a correlation at aggregate level (*ecological correlation*) between the percentage of manual workers and the percentage of votes for left-wing parties, we cannot draw the conclusion that manual workers vote for the left. This is the well-known problem of the *ecological fallacy,* which places strict limits on the conclusions that can be drawn from official statistics. Indeed, it is worth repeating that such data are extremely useful for the study of social structures, but are totally inadequate when the analysis focuses on individual behaviours.

SUMMARY

1.   The first important sociological study based on official statistics was Emile Durkheim's *On Suicide,* carried out at the end of the nineteenth century. By analyzing suicide rates in various European nations, Durkheim was able to empirically corroborate a complex theory of social integration that continues to be valid and stimulating.

2.   Official statistics differ from other data normally used in social research – especially from those gathered through surveys – with regard to four aspects: production, units of analysis, content and breadth.

  2.1.   *Production* Official statistics data are gathered by public agencies and are generated by two differnt types of procedure: indirect recording, when data are produced during the course of normal administrative procedures (e.g. demographic statistics based on birth and death certificates, marriages, divorces, changes of residence, etc.); and direct recording when data are collected by public agencies with the express intention of improving knowledge about the societies they govern (e.g. the general population census).

  2.2.   *Units of analysis* Unlike most data collected in social research, the unit of analysis in official statistics usually corresponds to geographical areas (provinces, counties, regions, municipalities, etc.), not individuals. This is why they are called *aggregate* data, as opposed to individual data.

2.3. *Content* Information provided by administrative records is obtained by recording events or facts; this means that opinions, attitudes and motivations are usually excluded.

2.4. *Breadth* Traditional statistical data are gathered on the entire population (consider once again the general population census and demographic statistics) rather than on samples (as is usual in other areas of social research).

3. The nature of the data collection, the degree of centralization or dispersion of data gathering and compilation, the agencies involved in the production of statistics, the manner of distribution, geographic coverage and detail, classification standards, publishing and distribution of findings may all vary greatly from country to country. This chapter described some of the main features of official statistics available in the US and the UK.

FURTHER READING

In the suggested readings for Chapter 3, Carley (1981) was mentioned on the topic of social indicators. A more recent book adopts a more pragmatic approach and speaks of 'statistical indicators': R.V. Horn, *Statistical Indicators for the Economic & Social Sciences* (Cambridge University Press, 1993, pp. 227).

To better grasp the usefulness of official statistics for studying social change and cross-national comparison, one may resort to the books published by the Comparative Charting of Social Change (CCSC) international

programme: T. Caplow, H.M. Bahr, J. Modell and B.A. Chadwick, *Recent Social Trends in the United States 1960–1990* (McGill-Queen's University Press, 1991, pp. 591) deals with the US. Other similar titles (*Recent Social Trends in …*) have been published on Germany, France, Québec, Greece, Spain, Italy, the Soviet Union, and Canada.

For the use of statistics concerning the UK, see A.H. Halsey and J. Webb (eds), *Twentieth-Century British Social Trends* (Macmillan, 2000, pp. 760): this is the most recent volume of a series that periodically attempts to 'photograph' social change in the UK since the early 20th century. For an analogous description of social change in the US, see T. Caplow, L. Hicks and B.J. Wattenberg, *The First Measured Century: An Illustrated Guide to Trends in America, 1900–2000* (AEI Press, 2001, pp. 307).

NOTES

1. A protection coefficient of 1 means that the rate of suicide in the two categories is equal; a coefficient of 2 means that the rate of suicide is twice as high among the unmarried as among the married.

2. It should, however, be pointed out that the German census originally scheduled for 1983 was conducted only a few years before, in 1987.

3. An example of such an application is the *Historical Census Data Browser* which can be found at http://fisher.lib.virginia.edu/census/. Based on the *Historical Demographic, Economic and Social Data: The United States, 1790–1970* archived at ICPSR, this application allows users to pick selected characteristics from censuses starting in 1790, and report those at the state or county level.

4. A more detailed description of how the division of educational statistics between agencies and levels of government have shaped and constrained modern education statistics appears in Weiss and Gruber (1987).

8 Sampling

In most cases social research cannot be carried out on a social reality in its entirety; the researcher usually has to settle for a sub-set of this reality. Thus sampling procedures are often the first empirical operations in which the researcher must engage. This chapter deals with sampling and contains a brief history of its introduction into social research, an overview of its mathematical bases, and a discussion of main sampling designs. The final section of the chapter addresses the special problems that sampling poses in social research.

1. POPULATION AND SAMPLE

Sampling – that is to say, observing a part in order to glean information about the whole – is an almost instinctive human act. We need only think of a cook tasting food to see whether salt should be added, an examiner questioning a student on part of the examination syllabus, or a journalist questioning a taxi driver to find out what 'the people' think of some topical issue. Although commonplace, however, the process of sampling was scientifically systematized only in very recent times, with the introduction of the notions of chance and randomization. Here, some clarification is required. In everyday speech, when we say that someone or something is chosen 'at random' from a set of people or objects, we usually have in mind an action that is much closer to a 'haphazard' choice rather than to the adoption of a rigorous procedure based on the notion of *chance* in a probabilistic sense. If we interview a person we come across by chance in the street, we do not carry out random sampling. Indeed, we have to distinguish between a *haphazard sample* and a *probability sample*. A random choice is by no means a choice without rules; on the contrary, the procedure of random sampling has to follow very precise criteria and chance – that is to say, true probabilistic chance has its laws. Indeed, contrary to what common sense would seem to suggest, if there is one phenomenon that is perfectly known to science (to the point that its manifestations can be represented in the form of mathematical expressions), it is *chance* (for instance, the probability of getting a pair of 'sixes' in 10 throws of a pair of dice can be calculated exactly).

Sampling is the procedure through which we pick out, from a set of units that make up the object of study (the *population*), a limited number of cases (*sample*) chosen according to

- *cost* of data collection;
- *time* required for the collection and processing of data;
- *organization*, in that there is no need to recruit, train and supervise huge numbers of interviewers, as is the case for a census of population; and

---

BOX 8.1   HISTORY OF SAMPLING

The idea of replacing data collection for the whole population with partial collection was first put forward in 1895 by the Norwegian statistician Anders Kiaer, but was not met with enthusiasm. Kiaer's method did not involve random selection, but rather was based on the use of information yielded by censuses, according to a procedure that would later be called *judgement sampling*. Several years later, in 1926, Kiaer's initial suggestion was formulated in more rigorous terms by the statistician A.L. Bowley, who introduced the concept of *simple random sampling*. However, another decade passed before the theoretical systematization of the entire field was achieved. This was the result of work done by the Polish statistician Jerzy Neyman, who drew a distinction between *judgement sampling* and *probability sampling* and established the theoretical framework of the latter, which relies on chance to select the units for inclusion in the sample.

---

criteria that enable the results obtained by studying the sample to be extrapolated to the whole population. The mathematical formulations of sampling have been studied in depth, giving rise to a specific branch of statistics known as *sampling theory*. In the present treatise, however, we will not go into the details of these aspects; indeed, the social scientist is not required to master the details of sampling theory, but rather to be familiar with its essential features and its underlying inspiration.

It is easy to see why sampling is used in social research. It offers several advantages in terms of:

- *depth* and *accuracy*, in that the lesser organizational complexity enables resources to be concentrated on quality control.

With regard to the application of probability sampling, a fundamental contribution to the spread of this procedure was made by opinion poll agencies. Probability sampling was definitively accepted as a result of a particular episode, which is quoted in all the methodology manuals on account of its ability to illustrate the advantages of the procedure. In an attempt to predict the outcome of the 1936 US presidential election, the popular American magazine *Literary Digest* sent out a facsimile of a paper ballot to over 10 million people, whose names were taken from telephone directories and registers of car owners. Two million responses were returned, which constituted an immense sample. Only 41% of the respondents said they would have voted for Franklin D. Roosevelt, thus foreshadowing a resounding victory for his opponent Alf Landon. This prediction was subsequently turned on its head when Roosevelt was elected with about 61% of the vote. The true outcome of the election was, however, correctly predicted by the opinion poll agencies Gallup, Roper and Crossley, which had worked on far smaller samples taken randomly from the entire population.

Where had the *Literary Digest* gone wrong? First of all – referring back to the discussion of various types of error in Chapter 3, Section 8 – a *coverage error* was made: the lists used to assemble the study population were incomplete. Having no Public Records Office to draw upon (the institution does not exist in the US), the organizers of the survey turned to telephone directories and lists of car owners. However, the citizens identified in this way were not representative of the entire population, but rather of the wealthier classes (especially since this was the period of the Great Depression) who tended to vote Republican.

A further distortion of the sample in comparison with the population stemmed from *non-response error*: a form of self-selection. Indeed, those who responded to the questionnaire were not the same as those who did not (the former probably being better educated, habitual readers of the magazine and so on, all of which correlates with voter orientation).

The opinion poll agencies succeeded in predicting the election result far more accurately because their sample, though smaller, was more *representative* of the population. This success, which made a great impact on the media and public opinion, established the pre-eminence of small probability samples over the large samples inspired by the logic of the census.

2. SAMPLING ERROR

By *population*, we mean an *aggregate N (population size)* of units (also called *statistical units* or *units of analysis*) which constitute the object of our study. The term 'population' suggests a set of human beings; in statistics, however, it has a much more general meaning and is applied to any set of objects (people, houses, businesses, geographical areas, manufactured goods, living organisms, inanimate objects, events, etc.). We might think, for example, of the municipalities in a given county, the crimes committed in a given year, the goods manufactured daily by a machine, etc.[1]

The variables (properties) X, Y, Z, etc. of these units are what we intend to study. The aim is to estimate a few characteristic values of these variables, called *parameters*, which are able to describe the overall distribution of the variables or the relationships among the variables themselves. For example, if the unit is the individual and the variable X is income, and we wish to know the mean income, the population parameter that we wish to know is a *mean*. If the variable Y is voter preference and we wish to discover the proportion of the electorate that voted for party A, the population parameter that we wish to know is a *proportion*. If we intend to study the relationship between the variables X and Z, the parameter that we wish to know is a *correlation* coefficient.

In order to find out the mean income of the population (or a proportion, or a correlation …), we would need to know the incomes X_i of all the units that make up the population. Since we do not have this information, and often cannot obtain it, we will measure income on a sub-set of the population.

The *sample* is the set of n (sample size) sampling units (which we call *cases*) selected from among the N units that make up the population, and which represent that population (hence the expression 'representative sample') for the purposes of our study. The population is the object to be investigated; the sample is our investigative tool. The procedure that we follow in order to select the *n* sampling units from the total of the *N* units of the population is called *sampling*.[2]

The advantages of operating on a reduced set, *n*, rather than on the whole population, *N*, have already been mentioned. There are, however, drawbacks. Whereas a study on an entire population yields the *exact value* of the investigated parameter, sampling yields only an *estimate*, i.e., an approximate value. For instance, if we use total measurement in order to discover the mean monthly income of a population, we will be able to state that 'the mean income of this population is £761'. If, however, our measurement is carried out on a sample of the population, our final statement will be something like: 'There is a 95% probability that the mean income of the population is £756 ± £15'.

This latter statement contains two elements of uncertainty, or rather one element of probability and one of approximation. First of all, the statement is not certain, but probable; the researcher is not 100% sure that the mean income falls between £741 and £771, since there is a 5% probability that the real value lies outside this range. Second, the researcher is unable to calculate the mean income of the population precisely, but can only establish a range within which to place this mean (between a minimum and a maximum). In more technical terms, this estimate involves a certain *level of confidence* and involves the determination of a *confidence interval* within which the population parameter probably occurs.

In other words, the estimate made on the sample will be subject to an error, which we call *sampling error*. If we use *V* to indicate the (unknown) value of the population parameter (a mean, a proportion, a correlation coefficient, etc.), *v* to indicate the value yielded by the sample (i.e. its estimate), and *e* as the sampling error, we have:[3]

V	=	*v*	±	*e*
population parameter (unknown)		sample estimate		sampling error

It is not difficult to calculate the estimate *v*, which is directly provided by the sample data; *the real problem lies in calculating the sampling error*. This is a major difficulty. Indeed, in order to establish the magnitude of this error, we would clearly need to know something about the population. But nothing may actually be known. Nevertheless, if the sample has been chosen according to a rigorously random procedure – that is to say, it is a *probability sample* – the magnitude of the sampling error can be calculated using statistical theory. If we look at the simplest case (cf. Section 4), in which 'simple random sampling' is used and the parameter to be studied is a mean, the sampling error is given by the equation:

$$e = z\sigma\,(\bar{X}) = z\,\frac{s}{\sqrt{n}}\,\sqrt{1-f}$$

where:

$\sigma\,(\bar{X})$ = standard error of the sample mean;

z = level of confidence of the estimate (in the case of 95% = 1.96);

s = sampling standard deviation of the variable analysed;

n = sample size;

$1 - f$ = finite population correction factor, where f = sampling fraction = n/N, where N = population size.

It should be noted that the size of the error increases:

- as the confidence level placed on the estimate is raised; if a 95%[4] confidence level is judged to be sufficient, then $z = 1.96$; if a level of 99% is required, then $z = 2.58$, and so on;
- as the variability of the variable studied increases; if we wish to estimate the mean income of the residents of a city neighbourhood, all other conditions being equal, the sampling error will be higher in a mixed neighbourhood than in a socially homogeneous one; and
- as the sample size diminishes (as is fairly obvious).

Finally, we have the *finite population correction factor* $\sqrt{1-f}$, where f = the sampling fraction, which is the ratio between the sample size and the population size (n/N). It should be noted that, if the population is infinite, or in any case much greater than n (as when the sample is less than 5% of the population), the correction factor becomes so close to 1 that it can be disregarded. In that case, the population size N does not even figure in the error formula. We can therefore say that the population size affects the sampling error only secondarily, when the sample is not too small in relation to the population. Indeed, *it is the sample size, rather than the sampling fraction, that determines the magnitude of the error*. This important issue will be dealt with later.

All the above applies when the population parameter to be estimated is a mean. In the case of categorical variables, the most common synthetic measure is the *proportion* (proportion of votes for party A, proportion of those agreeing with a certain statement, proportion of Catholics, proportion of ethnic minorities, etc.). In this case, the sampling error formula changes slightly, becoming:

$$e = z \sqrt{\frac{pq}{n-1}} \sqrt{1-f}$$

where z, n and f have the same meaning as in the previous formula, while: p = proportion of the sample accounted for by the category in question, and $q = 1 - p$

This formula corresponds to the previous formula for the mean if we consider that for categorical variables we have the standard deviation $\sigma = \sqrt{PQ}$.[5] Since P and Q, which refer to the population, are unknown, they have been replaced in the formula by the corresponding values p and q yielded by the sample data.

3.   SAMPLE SIZE

'How big should my sample be?' This is probably the first question asked by a researcher who is about to conduct a study based on sampling. Indeed, the size of the sample has to be established in advance – even if approximately – since this constitutes one of the basic criteria for defining the scope of the study and hence for estimating its cost.

3.1 One variable

On the basis of the sampling error formulae discussed earlier, it is easy to establish the size of the sample; it is sufficient to replace e with the error that we are prepared to accept and then solve the equation for n. For the moment, let us suppose that the population is so large in relation to the sample that the finite population correction factor can be ignored; to estimate a mean or a proportion, we can then solve the equation for n:

$$n = \left(\frac{zs}{e}\right)^2 \qquad n \cong n - 1 = \frac{z^2 pq}{e^2}$$

Sample size is therefore directly proportional to the desired confidence level of the estimate (z) and to the variability of the phenomenon being investigated, and it is inversely proportional to the error that the researcher is prepared to accept (or, in other words, directly proportional to the accuracy desired). It should be noted that z and e are fixed by the researcher (who establishes the reliability and accuracy required from the estimates), while s, p (and q) are as yet unknown, in that the researcher wishes to know, *before* beginning the sampling, how many cases will need to be included in the sample. Approximate estimates of s and p can be obtained from previous studies, from the opinion of experts or from a pilot study, whose cases may constitute the first part of the sample.

It is important to draw the reader's attention to the role of population size N in the sample size formula. It is a commonly held belief that the size of the sample should be proportional to that of the population. Thus, for example, in selecting two samples of the populations of two municipalities of 10,000 and 100,000 residents, respectively, the

**BOX 8.2   THE FINITE POPULATION CORREC-
TION FOR THE SAMPLE SIZE FORMULAE**

The formulae presented in the text for the sample size n do not take into account the finite population correction factor $\sqrt{1-f}$, which is introduced when the sample constitutes more than 5% of the population ($f = n/N > 0.05$). Taking this factor into account, we have:

$$n = \left(\frac{zs}{e}\right)^2 (1-f) \qquad\qquad n = \frac{z^2 pq}{e^2} (1-f)$$

If we replace f with its value n/N, and solve the equation for n, we obtain rather complex formulae. To simplify their handling, these formulae are usually split into two successive steps; as a first approximation, the previous formulae are applied, which provide a rough estimate n_0 of the sample size (where $n_0 = n/(1-f)$):

$$n_0 = \left(\frac{zs}{e}\right)^2 \qquad\qquad n_0 = \frac{z^2 pq}{e^2}$$

If the value of n_0 calculated in this way proves to be smaller than 5% of N, it can be regarded as definitive. If, however, it proves to be higher, the correction factor will be introduced and the correct value of n can be obtained as follows:

$$n = \frac{n_0}{1 + \dfrac{n_0}{N}}$$

unwitting researcher who relies on common sense may well be led to construct a sample 10 times larger in the latter case than in the former. This is a mistake. From what has already been said, it clearly emerges that population size does not even figure in the first approximation in the formula used to calculate the sample size n.

Only in the second approximation – with the introduction of the finite population correction factor (see Box 8.2) – does it come into play – that is to say, only when the size of the sample is not negligible in relation to the size of the population (i.e. greater than 5% of N).

In determining sample size, therefore, if the confidence level and sampling error remain the same, only the variability s (or $\sqrt{pq}$) of the variable studied comes into play in the first instance. In the case of the two municipalities mentioned earlier, it is quite possible that a sample of 1000 cases will be sufficient to yield an estimate that is *equally accurate* for both municipalities in spite of their different population sizes.

3.2 Several variables

So far, we have determined sample size with reference to the parameters of a single

TABLE 8.1 *Size n of a simple random sample required for a given precision of the estimate (maximum error, in absolute percentage points) and a given size N of the whole population (for a 95% confidence level).*

Precision of the estimate					
5%		**2%**		**1%**	
N	n	N	n	N	n
100	80	100	96	100	99
300	170	300	270	300	296
500	220	500	415	500	475
1000	285	1000	715	1000	910
5000	370	5000	1660	5000	3330
> 8000	400 (n_0)	10000	2000	10000	5000
		> 50000	2500 (n_0)	20000	6350
				> 200000	10000 (n_0)

variable. In general, however, the researcher wants to evaluate the parameters of several variables. If so, the method described above can be applied to each of the most important variables separately; the highest value of n found among these can then be taken as the sample size. If the researcher only has to evaluate proportions, as is usually the case in social research, the matter is simplified. Indeed, as the variability is measured by $\sqrt{pq}$, it is easy to see that this index assumes its highest value when $p = q = 0.50$. The sample size required is therefore calculated for the least favourable case – that is to say, when $p = q = 0.50$; this sample will be all the more sufficient for the variables that display proportions other than 0.50.

Thus we can construct a table (Table 8.1) which – at a confidence level of 95% – reports sample size for three different degrees of 'absolute' error (5, 2 and 1 percentage points) and for various values of the population size N. For example, if the population is of 10,000 units and the maximum error ('accuracy of the estimate') is of 2 percentage points, the sample size required is 2000 cases; if an accuracy of 5 percentage points is deemed sufficient, the sample size is 400 cases. It should be pointed out that, while an error of 5 percentage points is fairly high, a 2-point error is very low (since it means that, if we have an estimate of 40%, the true population value has a 95% probability of lying between 38 and 42%).

It is clear from the table that 2500 cases are sufficient in order to obtain estimates that are accurate to within 2 percentage points (and only 400 cases for estimates with an accuracy of ± 5 percentage points) *whatever the size of the population* (even if it were the population of the entire nation or the whole world!) This may surprise the reader. Indeed, it is tempting to think that a good estimate on such a huge population would necessitate a sample of hundreds of thousands of cases. However, it must be borne in mind that what has been said is applicable only if we have a rigorous *simple random sample*. In the case of the world population, for example, this would mean having a list of all the inhabitants of the earth, picking out 2500 names and travelling around the world until every person has been interviewed (leaving aside the possibility that some may be untraceable or may refuse to answer). Obviously, this cannot be done.

3.3 Multivariate analysis

This consideration regarding the feasibility of sampling in the social sciences prompts us to raise another question specifically related to social research. The statistical approach illustrated above is underpinned by a 'univariate' logic – that is to say, it considers the variables one by one, and not the relationships among them. Let us consider the following example:

Suppose we have selected a sample of 420 subjects by means of simple random sampling from the 50,000 residents of a neighbourhood, and that we have discovered by means of a questionnaire that 25.7% of our subjects are practising Catholics. Application of the formula seen earlier yields the following equation (the correction factor $\sqrt{1-f}$ being disregarded in that it is close to 1, as the sample is very small in relation to the population):

$$e = z \sqrt{\frac{pq}{n-1}} = 1.96 \sqrt{\frac{0.257 \cdot 0.743}{419}} = 0.042$$

This gives an error of 4.2 percentage points; we can therefore say that, with a probability of 95%, the percentage of practising Catholics is 25.7% ± 4.2%. However, the social researcher will probably not be content with this simple summary of religious practice; she may, for example, wish to see whether religious practice varies with the level of education. To do so, she will construct a table in which religious practice is reported separately for educated and uneducated persons. Let us now suppose that 265 of the subjects possess a diploma of higher education and that 22.6% of these are practising Catholics. What is the sampling error for this estimate? On applying the same formulae as before, we now find that the estimates are 22.6% ± 5.0, thus revealing that the percentage of practising Catholics among the educated falls between 17.6% and 27.6%. The error has increased considerably in comparison with the previous estimate. This is explained simply by the fact that, by splitting the subjects into two categories, we have divided our sample into two sub-samples of reduced size; as we know, the sampling error increases as the sample size diminishes.

Once having ascertained the existence of a relationship between education and religious practice, the researcher may decide to subdivide the sample further into three age-groups, in order to ensure that the relationship between education and religious practice is not a spurious one due to the effect of age. This further fragmentation of the sample leads to a further increase in the sampling error.

In social research, the size of the sample cannot therefore be established by the researcher only on the basis of the distributions of the single variables (univariate analysis); rather, it must be established with reference to the type of analysis to be undertaken, starting from the consideration of the breakdowns that the sample will undergo in order to be analysed (multivariate analysis).

For example, in a study on how people vote, the researcher may wish to analyse the social characteristics of those who vote for small parties that win only about 5% of the total number of valid votes. It should be borne in mind that out of 1000 valid replies (to the researcher's questions) a figure of around 5% will correspond to about 50 cases; this number might be sufficient to estimate the number of votes cast in favour of a party of this size, but it is far too small to enable any analysis of the characteristics of these voters to be made. We cannot, for instance, relate votes for that party to the gender, educational level, etc. of its supporters, in that this would involve breaking down our very small sample even further. As a general rule, the more the phenomenon under investigation is a minority phenomenon, the greater the overall sample size will need to be.

Similarly, if we carry out an investigation into social mobility in which the occupation of the interviewee is seen in relation to that of his or her father, and we split the analysis according to gender and age-group, we will have to break down the sample considerably. A table of mobility that considered seven classes of occupation for both child and father would break down the sample into 49 cells; if the cases were then subdivided into male and female and into two age-groups, we would have a breakdown into 196 cells. This means that 2000 cases would be too few for an analysis of this kind, since with a mean of only 10 cases per cell, many cells corresponding to the less common occupations would contain very few cases, or none at all. It is not surprising, therefore, that studies of social mobility are generally conducted on much larger samples.

4. PROBABILITY SAMPLING DESIGNS

A sample is said to be a *probability sample*[6] when:

- each unit has non-zero probability of selection;
- probability of selection for all units is known; and
- the selection is completely random.

The *Literary Digest* sample mentioned in Section 1 was not probabilistic since, on the one hand, people who did not have a car or a telephone had a zero probability of being included in the sample while; on the other hand, those who possessed both a car and a telephone had a (unknown) more than proportionate probability of being included. In this section, we will illustrate the essential features of the main probability sampling designs.

Simple random sampling Among probability samples, the most elementary case is that of simple random sampling. From a formal standpoint, a simple random sample is obtained when all the units in the reference population have the *same probability* of being included in the sample. In order to implement this sampling design, the researcher will, first of all, need a complete list of the members of the population; a number will then be assigned to each of the N units in the list, and the n numbers corresponding to the subjects for inclusion in the sample will be picked out at random[7]. Simple random sampling is the basis of random-digit-dialing (RDD) sampling used in many telephone surveys, especially in the US. RDD methods were developed so that telephone samples could include households whose telephone numbers are not included in telephone directories.[8]

Except for telephone interviewing, simple random sampling is rarely used in social research, both because selection relies entirely on chance and does not incorporate information that is already known about the population, and because in large-scale studies it involves a data-collection scheme that is costly and difficult to organize. Moreover, a complete list of the members of the population is often unavailable.

Systematic sampling – A procedure that is statistically equivalent to simple random sampling – from the point of view of the result (in the sense that it produces a simple random sample) – is that of *systematic sampling*. The only difference lies in the technique of picking out the subjects. The sampling units are no longer selected by lottery (or random number tables), but by scrolling the list of subjects and systematically selecting one unit at every given interval. If the size N of the reference population is known and the size n of the sample has been established, one unit every $k = N/n$ units of the population is selected, beginning with a number chosen at random between 1 and k (k is called the *sampling interval*). For instance, if a sample of $n = 500$ units is to be picked out from among a population of $N = 8235$ units, one unit every 16 ($k = 8235/500 = 16.7$) will be picked out, beginning with a number chosen at random between 1 and 16. If this number is 12, the subjects selected will be the 12th, the 28th, the 44th and so on.

Systematic sampling is equivalent to random sampling except in those (fairly rare) situations in which the sampling interval coincides with some periodic feature of the reference population. For example, the employees in a company may be listed according to their department and, within each department, according to their length of service. In such a case, if the sampling interval were to coincide with the size of the departments, our sample might well include only employees who have worked for the company for the same length of time.

The utility of systematic sampling does not lie so much in its simplification of the selection procedure as in its ability to produce random samples even when no list of the population is available and the population size (i.e. N) is unknown. In social research, systematic sampling is often used precisely because in many cases no list of the reference population is available. For example, in the case of exit polls – in which voters leaving the polling station are asked to report the vote they have just cast – one voter of every k is generally interviewed. Similarly, in market research, one customer of every k who leave the shop or supermarket is interviewed.[9]

Stratified sampling   As already mentioned with regard to sampling error, the accuracy of sampling estimates depends – among other things – on sample size and on the degree of variability in the distribution of the phenomenon studied within the reference population. Accuracy declines as sample size diminishes and as the distribution variability of the phenomenon increases. This means that if the variability of the phenomenon under investigation is very high, then the sample analysed will need to be larger, in order to maintain a certain level of accuracy in the estimate. Alternatively, if the phenomenon displays areas of greater homogeneity, it is possible to increase sample *efficiency* (greater accuracy for the same sample size) by adopting *stratified sampling*.

This sampling design is organized in three phases. First of all, the reference population is subdivided into sub-populations (called *strata*) that are as homogeneous as possible in terms of the phenomenon to be studied; this is done by using as a stratification criterion a variable that is correlated with the phenomenon. Second, a sample is selected from each stratum by means of a random procedure. Finally, the samples drawn from each stratum are pooled in order to produce an overall sample. For instance, if the phenomenon under investigation is income, the members of the reference population can be subdivided into strata based on the variable 'occupation', which

strongly correlates with income. If, for example, there are four strata (manual workers, clerical workers, middle-class self-employed and professionals) a sample will be selected from each of these strata (considered separately from the others). These four partial samples will then be pooled into a single sample. In this way, a heterogeneous population (which would have required a very large sample) is subdivided into relatively homogeneous strata that can be studied by using relatively small samples. The sum of these smaller samples is less than the size of the sample that would have had to be drawn from the entire reference population.

Within each single stratum, subjects are selected by means of a simple random sampling procedure. The sample is said to be proportionate (or self-weighting) if its composition is the same as that of the strata in the population. For example, if the four occupational categories mentioned above constitute 40%, 40%, 15% and 5% of the population, respectively, and we construct an overall sample of 1000 cases made up of 400 manual workers, 400 clerical workers, 150 self-employed and 50 professionals, we obtain a proportionate stratified sample.

By contrast, if we decide to over-represent some strata and to under-represent others, we obtain a *non-proportionate stratified* sample. For instance, we may decide to over-represent strata containing few subjects, so as to be able to conduct in-depth investigations on these, too. Alternatively, we may opt for a sample in which all strata are of the same size. In all such cases, if the overall sample does not reflect the composition of the population, a *weighting* operation (cf. Section 7) will be carried out in order to re-establish – within the sample – the correct composition of the population.

Among the various types of non-proportionate stratified sampling, the one that is theoretically most efficient is *optimum allocation stratified sampling*. In this procedure, the size of the sample drawn from each stratum is proportional to the variability of the phenomenon under examination within each stratum.

Multistage sampling This technique does not offer greater efficiency than simple random sampling, but it does simplify the selection procedure and reduce the cost of data-collection. Multistage sampling is the only viable option in some situations, such as when a complete list of the reference population is unavailable, or when – on account of the extreme dispersion of the population – the members of the sample produced by simple random sampling or stratified sampling would be spread over too vast an area (e.g. the whole country) and thus difficult to reach.

In multistage sampling, the population is subdivided into hierarchical levels, which are selected successively through a process of 'narrowing down'. For example, in order to draw up a national sample of elementary school teachers, we would first subdivide this population into *primary units*, constituted by the education districts to which the teachers belong, and then into *secondary units*, constituted by the teachers themselves. Sampling is carried out in two stages – that is to say, through two successive selection procedures. In the first stage, a sample of primary units (e.g. 50 education districts) is drawn up; for this purpose, a complete list of the primary units will be required. In the second stage, a sample of secondary units (teachers) will be selected from each of the primary units previously selected. This will necessitate having (or creating) a complete list of the teachers, but *only* for the primary units selected in the first stage. Naturally, the sampling stages may be more than two.

Multistage sampling offers two main advantages: (a) there is no need to have a list of the entire reference population, but only lists of the sub-populations of the higher-order units selected; and (b) data collection involves only the units selected, thereby reducing costs considerably. There are, however, disadvantages. Multistage sampling

leads to a loss of efficiency, in that cases belonging to a single higher-order unit tend partly to resemble one another. Moreover, the statistical theory involved in this sampling design is somewhat complex.

Cluster sampling This procedure is used when the population can be subdivided into groups. This is the case of families, school classes, works departments, hospital wards and so on. Such groupings are called clusters, hence the name *cluster sampling*. In this procedure, it is not the units (the individuals) that are selected, but the clusters; all the units belonging to the clusters selected are then included in the sample. In this way, advantage is taken of the spatial proximity among individuals belonging to the same cluster. For example, in a study of football supporters, a set of fans travelling on a train to watch their team play an away match may be taken as the reference population; two compartments of each carriage may be selected by means of systematic sampling, and all the individuals in those compartments interviewed. The procedure is extremely useful when – as in this example – no list of the units is available, but clusters can be selected by means of a random procedure.

A widely used technique is to combine multistage sampling with cluster sampling. An example is provided by the studies on the workforce conducted in many European countries by the national statistics institutes. In this case, a sample of municipalities is first drawn; then, within each municipality, a sample of families is selected, and all the members of these families are interviewed.

Area sampling A variant of multistage sampling is area sampling. This approach is adopted when no list of the reference population exists. For instance, a sample of the population resident in an area would usually be selected (in Europe) from the local Public Records Office. However, if no such office exists (that is to say, there is no list of the reference units) the procedure cannot be followed. In this case, area sampling will be used.

By way of example, we may mention the sample used by the Survey Research Center of the University of Michigan, which is structured as follows. The nation (US) is divided into *primary areas* (counties, groups of counties or metropolitan areas). The Center has chosen 74 of these. Each of the primary areas is subdivided into locations (e.g. one large city, a group of 4–5 medium-sized cities, a fairly large rural area and so on). In turn, each location is subdivided into *chunks*, areas generally identified by natural boundaries (medium-small towns, large city neighbourhoods, rural areas delimited by roads or rivers and so on). Each chunk is then divided into *segments* (city blocks or rural areas bounded by roads), each containing 4–16 housing units; these units are then selected for interview purposes. At all hierarchical levels, selection is carried out by means of a probability sampling. If a random selection has to be made within the individual family units (for instance, if the interview is to be conducted on citizens over 18 years of age and three members of the family unit qualify), random selection is again used (e.g. by listing the subjects in decreasing order of age and choosing one with the help of a pre-assigned random number table).

Area sampling is useful not only when lists of the population at the level are lacking, but also when they are incomplete. For instance, this technique offers a greater probability of encompassing such persons as illegal immigrants, temporary residents and so on.

5. NON-PROBABILITY SAMPLING DESIGNS

When a probability sample is not feasible, or when it is known in advance that it cannot be implemented in the data-collection phase, a *non-probability sample design* will be adopted from the outset. The most common types are presented in this section.

Quota sampling   This is probably the most widely used sample design, especially in market research and in opinion polls. To implement the procedure, the population must first be subdivided into a certain number of strata defined by a few variables of which the distribution is known (e.g. gender, age-group and level of education). Next, the proportional 'weight' of each stratum is calculated – that is to say, the portion of the overall population that belongs to each group (the sum of these weights must obviously equal 1). Finally, the quotas – that is to say, the number of interviews to be conducted in each stratum – are established by multiplying these weights by the sample size n.

Up to this point, quota sampling is no different from stratified sampling. Where it does differ, however, is in the fact that, within the limits placed on the overall size of each quota (e.g. 20 educated young males have to be interviewed), *the interviewer is free to choose the interview subjects at his discretion*. Thus, quota sampling is stratified sampling with the choice of the units left to the interviewer, whereby the size of the quota restricts this freedom of choice and ensures that the overall sample reproduces the population distribution in regard to the variables on which the quotas are based.

The limitations of quota sampling are plain to see. The interviewer's freedom of choice means that, within the pre-established constraints, she may well adopt utilitarian selection criteria by favouring the most easily accessible cases (acquaintances, subjects living in the same area or belonging to the same social group and so on), avoiding situations that may involve any degree of difficulty and not persisting when subjects are reluctant to be interviewed.

The most celebrated failure of quota sampling occurred, once again, in the field of election forecasts. In 1948, the three most respected American survey institutes predicted on the basis of quota sampling that Thomas Dewey would defeat Harry Truman in the presidential race. In reality, Truman won 50% of the vote and Dewey 45%. In that case, the error lay in the subjective choices of the interviewers; while satisfying the conditions on which the quotas were based (place of residence, age, race, socioeconomic status), the interviewers unconsciously favoured Republican supporters. This experience prompted the survey institutes to modify their strategy and to place greater constraints on the interviewers' freedom of choice; interviewers were given an area to work in and were instructed to call at pre-established homes and to move on only if the subject refused to be interviewed or did not possess the characteristics required.

Unfortunately, however, even when the interviewer works within these constraints, selection is still distorted in favour of those subjects who are more accessible; when the interviewer does not find a person at home, he will simply knock at the next door. This means that those who are more difficult to reach or reluctant to be interviewed will be under-represented (and both these social groups have characteristics that may be correlated with the variables studied).

Quota sampling has long been a subject of controversy. Naturally, statisticians do not recommend it, owing to its lack of scientific rigour. Moreover, in a probability sample, the most evident distortions can be detected by comparing the distribution of some of the variables (e.g. age, gender or educational level) known in the population with the corresponding distribution observed in the sample. In quota sampling, however, any distortion will be masked by the quotas themselves. On the other hand, quota sampling has enjoyed considerable popularity among market researchers and surveyors of public opinion, who maintain that it yields satisfactory results at low cost. Their conviction is that it is not worth investing large sums in probability sampling while other important sources of error remain.

Snowball sampling This sample design is particularly useful in the study of those social groups whose members tend to hide their identity for moral, legal, ideological or political reasons. These include illegal immigrants, members of religious sects, activists in outlawed political groups, homosexuals, tax evaders, moonlighters, the homeless, drug users, criminals and so on. The procedure is also used to study 'rare elements': small groups scattered over a large area but which keep in touch with one another in some way (members of minority religions, particular groups and associations, etc.).

Snowball sampling involves identifying subjects for inclusion in the sample by referrals from other subjects. The process begins with a small number of subjects who have the desired requisites, through whom further individuals with the same characteristics are identified. As the process goes on, the number of subjects should increase exponentially, hence the snowball analogy.

This design has the disadvantage of selecting individuals who are socially most active and most visible (albeit within the restricted framework of the group). Moreover, there is a risk that this chain of selection may be channelled along pathways that are too specific. In order to avoid such risks, it is generally necessary – as in the case of quota sampling – to impose constraints based on what is already known of the phenomenon being studied.

Judgement sampling In this procedure, the sampling units are not chosen in a random manner, but on the basis of some of their characteristics. This kind of sampling is used, for instance, on very small samples in order to avoid chance fluctuations that might excessively distance the sample from the characteristics of the population. For example, in selecting city neighbourhoods, it may be decided that the sample should contain an equal number of inner-city and suburban areas, or of working-class and middle-class neighbourhoods. In a study conducted in Italy, judgement sampling was used to select 100 municipalities from among a total of 8,000. This involved classifying all municipalities into 20 strata on the basis of both size (five categories) and geographical location (four categories). Within each stratum, the number of municipalities to be included in the sample was proportional to the demographic 'weight' of the corresponding population. These were, nevertheless, chosen on the basis of rational criteria; for instance, it was ensured that all 20 Regions were represented by at least one provincial capital, that the smaller municipalities were no further than 15 km from the provincial capital, that there was a university city in every Region, etc. The entire selection procedure was therefore based on rational considerations, and at no stage was random selection utilized.

A variant of this procedure is seen in *balanced sampling*. This involves selecting the units in such a way that, with regard to certain variables, the mean of the sample is close to the mean of the population (for instance, the sample of municipalities could be constructed under the constraint that, in each sample stratum, the mean number of votes for the left and for the right in political elections must not differ by more than 3 percentage points from the mean of the corresponding stratum in the population).

Judgement sampling does not of course offer the guarantees provided by probability sampling, nor the simplicity of implementation seen in quota sampling. Nevertheless, as has been said, it finds a convenient application in the case of very small samples (especially when the units of analysis are not individuals, but institutions, municipalities, etc.).

6. PROBLEMS OF SAMPLING IN SOCIAL RESEARCH

In the social sciences, the most common (though not exclusive) application of the technique of sampling is constituted by the *survey*, in which a sample of subjects to be interviewed is drawn from a population of individuals. In such cases, constructing a sample is an unavoidable necessity. In spite of this, however, one of the fields in which sampling theory is most difficult to apply is precisely that of the survey, in which the reference population (in the statistical sense) is made up of individual human beings and the data-gathering tool is a questionnaire or interview. This is due to the fact that, as was mentioned in Chapter 3, Section 8, so-called 'selection error' involves not only sampling error but also two other components: coverage error and non-response error.

6.1 Coverage error

Coverage error stems from the problem of obtaining a *list of the population*. As already mentioned, in order to construct a probability sample, all units of the population have to have a known probability of being selected. But what if the units themselves are not known? How, for instance, can a random sample of the immigrants in a region be selected if a list of all the immigrants in that region does not exist? Nor can we, in such a case, utilize systematic sampling, since our subjects are not physically located in a single place where individuals can be picked out at given intervals.[10]

Generally speaking, we can say that in Europe serious problems are not encountered when the investigation concerns entire populations (even of whole countries). Municipal Public Records Offices (which register all residents) and electoral rolls (for citizens over the age of 18 years) can provide a complete list of the population, from which the sample can be drawn by means of a random procedure.

The problem does arise, however, when the investigation focuses on particular sectors of the population. Except for cases in which the subjects studied belong to an institution or a formally constituted association, or have in some way come into contact with the public administration, population lists are not generally available. This is so when studies are conducted on segments of the population such as workers, the unemployed, immigrants, etc. Moreover, in such cases, the subjects are not located in any one place where they can all be screened by the researcher for the purpose of systematic sampling.

This is the situation when the unit of analysis is the individual. When the unit is a group, the scenario is slightly brighter, since sets of individuals (schools, universities, companies, hospitals, businesses) are normally officially registered. Outside these official entities, however, things are more complicated (sports clubs, theatre companies, computer courses, etc.).

Without a population list (or equivalent means of enabling the researcher theoretically to reach the entire population) *probability sampling designs cannot be implemented*. Indeed, in such cases, we cannot assign a known probability of selection to *all* the units of the population.

Of course, it is not enough that such lists exist; problems of up-dating, duplication and omission must be taken into account. The problem of omission, or *incompleteness of the list*, is the most serious. As the *Literary Digest* survey so aptly demonstrated, the use of telephone directories and registers of car owners as a surrogate for electoral rolls excluded a considerable number of people who possessed neither a car nor a telephone. The problem is not one of omission in itself; if the subjects present in the list were a random sample of the total population, there would be no difficulty. What is a problem, however, is that those listed tend to be different from those who are left out.[11]

In such situations, the social researcher has three options:

- redefine the population, for instance by stating explicitly that the research has not been conducted on shopkeepers but on the members of shopkeepers' associations, explaining the reasons behind this decision and dealing with its consequences in the data-interpretation phase;
- neglect excluded subjects. If the omission does not involve a large portion of the total (e.g. 10–15%) and there are good reasons to believe that those excluded

from the list are not very different – in terms of the issues investigated – from those included, the error may fall within the range tolerated in the social sciences, which, as we know, have several possible sources of error;[12]

- resort to a dual-frame sample. For instance, if 25% of the population does not have a telephone, a sample of subjects interviewed by telephone might be supplemented by ensuring that 25% of the final sample is made up of individuals without a telephone (who, of course, would probably have to be sampled in a different way).

6.2 Non-response error

Having a list of the population and selecting a sample by means of a rigorous random selection procedure is not enough to produce a genuine probability sample. Indeed, once the sample has been drawn up on paper, the problem of data collection remains. When the population is made up of human beings, setbacks may be encountered, and a sample that starts out as a probability sample may well no longer be so at the end of the data-collection phase. This is *non-response error*, which may have two distinct causes:

- failure to contact the subjects selected;
- refusal of some subjects to be interviewed.

Failure to contact the subjects selected is principally a question of cost, though this does not make the problem any less serious or easy to solve. It may be due to two factors, one of which is simply (a) *the difficulty of reaching the subjects* while staying within the data-collection budget. For example, in a study involving the entire national population – presuming that a complete list of the population is available – it is difficult to imagine constructing a sample based on simple random selection and then setting off to conducts face-to-face interviews with subjects scattered throughout the country. The second factor is (b) *the inability to trace the subjects*. Again, this is mainly due to economic constraints whereby a subject who is not found at home after two or three visits by the interviewer[13] is replaced by a subject from a reserve list.

Although the difficulties of making contact with the sample subjects seriously hinder the proper implementation of the probability selection, they can be overcome. For instance, alternative sampling designs (such as multistage sampling) may be used, or resources may be allocated to tracing the subjects (e.g. by not placing a limit on the number of times the interviewer calls at the subject's home).

Refusal to be interviewed This problem is a much more serious one, in that there are good grounds for claiming that subjects who refuse to respond are different from those who agree to respond. It is often the elderly, the poorly educated, women, people who live alone, or those who are very busy who refuse to respond. Then again, the decision to respond may be influenced by other personal characteristics of the subject; e.g. in a study of teachers, refusal is more likely to come from those who are less motivated and less involved in their profession. In other cases, refusal may be prompted by ideological factors or by some form of apprehension connected with the specific context of the interview; in a study of factory workers commissioned by management, for instance, those who are politically most active may refuse to respond. Similar examples could be quoted with regard to a refusal to answer specific questions; if, for instance, subjects are asked whether they are members of a political party, reticence is more likely to be shown by party members than by non-members, by members of an opposition party than by those of a governing party, and by manual workers than by professionals.

What percentage of non-responses is normally encountered in surveys? In the US, the non-response rate for a national sample of the entire adult population is about 25% for face-to-face interviews (Schuman and Presser, 1982: 16–17). Telephone interviews deserve a particular mention. Studies have revealed higher non-response rates for telephone interviews than for equivalent face-to-face interviews. In the US, the difference seems to range from 5 to 10 percentage points. In the UK, identical surveys carried out partly face-to-face and partly on the telephone displayed even greater differences (Collins et al., 1988: 217).

Clearly, for one reason or another, a considerable number of subjects included in the sample are not interviewed. In practice, this problem can be overcome by replacing these subjects with reserve subjects chosen at random from the population. This does not, however, obviate the risk of distorting the sample. If, for example, those who are not interviewed are the more marginal citizens (the elderly, the unedu- cated, those living on the outskirts of the city, etc.), and we replace them with other subjects randomly selected from the population, we are in fact replacing a segment of the population that has particular characteristics with a group of 'average' citizens. We therefore end up with a sample in which the marginal citizens are under-represented.

Few resources are available to offset non-response error. The first, and most obvious, step that the researcher can take is to try to reduce the number of untraceable subjects by repeatedly returning to the homes of absentees; naturally, the cost of such persistence would have to be budgeted for in advance. Second, *weighting* techniques can be applied after data collection has been concluded. This procedure involves attributing to those persons who have not been interviewed the mean responses given by the social group to which they belong. The following section deals with this issue.

7. WEIGHTING

'Weighting' is a method of artificially modifying the composition of the sample (by means of mathematical operations during the data-processing stage) in order to bring it more closely in line with that of the population. It involves attributing to the cases sampled a 'weight', which varies according to their characteristics. Weighting procedures can be extremely complex, and here we will present only their basic forms. These can essentially be reduced to three, according to whether they are based on:

- the probability of inclusion in the sample;
- what is known about the population; or
- what is known about the non-respondents.

As will be seen, a clear distinction must be made between the first case and the other two.

The probability of inclusion in the sample Often, the samples used in social research do not correspond to the ideal situation in which all units have an equal probability of being selected (self-weighting sample), as is suggested by the image of drawing lots. We have already mentioned cases of stratified sampling in which the number of sampling units included in the strata is deliberately non-proportional to their presence in the population (over-representation of some strata and under-representation of others). Let us suppose, for example, that women entrepreneurs make up 2.5% of the population, but we include them at a rate of 5% in order to obtain a sufficient number of cases to allow estimates to be made on this specific category. Subsequently, during the data-processing phase, the true weight of this category within the population will have to be restored before estimates can be made on the entire population; therefore, a coefficient will have to be applied to every case of women entrepreneurs sampled in order to halve their weight within the sample. In this case, the weighting operation is required by the structure of the sample design itself, and the terms of this operation are known at the outset.

There are, however, situations in which the selection procedure produces different probabilities of inclusion in the sample. Let us suppose that we wish to obtain a sample of families, and that only a list of individual citizens is available. In this case, we could pick out a sample of individuals and include in our sample the families to which they belong. In this way, however, large families would have a greater probability of being selected than small families. Consequently, in the data-processing phase, the data will have to be weighted (by attributing to each family a weight that is inversely proportional to its probability of inclusion, i.e. to the number of its members).

In all these cases, the probability of inclusion is not equal for all the units. However, it is known; and knowing the probability enables us to calculate the weights to be applied in the weighting procedure. We are still, therefore, within the bounds of probability sampling. The situation is very different, however, when the sample is not a probability sample (the probability of inclusion is not known), or is fraught with serious errors of coverage or non-response (which in reality make it a non-probability sample, even if the initial design was drawn up as a probability sample). In such cases, weighting involves adjustment operations designed to limit the errors and distortions; these operations are based on what is known of the population or the non-respondents.

What is known about the population The most common case in which weighting is carried out on the basis of what is known of the population is that of so-called *post-stratification*. As the term suggests, this involves stratification of the sample after data collection has been concluded. If the distribution of some variables in the population is known from external sources, such as census data for example, this distribution is compared with the distribution obtained from the sample; the sample data are then corrected so as to match the data distribution for these variables in the population. This operation is carried out by multiplying each case in the sample by a weighting coefficient (*weight*) equal to the ratio *'true' proportion/observed proportion* of the category (or stratum if we consider more than one variable at the same time) to which it belongs.

For instance, if male subjects make up 58% (observed proportion) of the sample instead of 49% (true proportion known from census data), each male will be multiplied by the weight 49/58 = 0.84,[14] and each female by the weight 51/42 = 1.21. It is as if – while maintaining the size of the sample – we reduced the number of males by counting each male not as one unit, but as 0.84 units, while increasing the number of females by counting each of them as 1.21 units. In this way, as has been said, the total number of subjects remains the same, while the proportion of males and females in the sample is rearranged. The new proportion will figure in all subsequent data-processing operations (frequencies, means, correlations, etc.).

Weighting according to what is known of the population can be carried out on the basis of any variable whose distribution in the population is known. In a pre-election opinion poll, for instance, in order to attenuate the risk of sample distortions, respondents may be asked how they voted in the previous elections. The sample can then be weighted on the basis of the fact that in the population the variable 'result of the previous election' is known.

What is known about the non-respondents The third situation to be considered arises when weighting is carried out on the basis of what is known of the non-respondents. This procedure is used to compensate for non-response error, though – unlike the previous procedure – it can do nothing to remedy coverage errors. In exit polls, for example, the interviewer can classify subjects who refuse to respond according to two variables (gender and age-group). The interviews recorded are then weighted by assigning them a weight that takes the refusals into account. Thus, if 9% of the total number of individuals intercepted by the interviewer are elderly women, but only a portion of these – equal to 5% of the total number – agree to be interviewed, those who are interviewed will be given a weight of 9/5 = 1.8. In this case, the weighting coefficient (weight) corresponds to the reciprocal of the response rate for each category.[15]

Why weight? If we accepted the results yielded by the sample in their unmodified form (and, by inference, extended them to the entire population), it would be as if we attributed to the non-respondents the mean behaviour of the responders. This would often be a mistake (it is well-known that non-respondents are more commonly found among elderly people, women, the poorly educated, etc.). It is therefore preferable to assign to non-respondents the mean behaviour of persons belonging to the same social group rather than the mean behaviour of the entire population (if, for instance, there are 35 young women among the responders instead of 46, we multiply these by a weight of 1.31, thus transforming them from 35 to 46 and thereby attributing the mean responses of the young women interviewed to the 11 young women who have not been interviewed).

The weighting procedure – as described earlier with regard to the correction of coverage and non-response errors – is sometimes criticized as constituting undue manipulation of the data. Nevertheless, it should be borne in mind that, while weighting involves an arbitrary element, the lack of weighting leads to almost certain error. If the sample is patently distorted with regard to base variables correlated with the phenomena investigated, it is clearly a mistake to extend the results to the whole population. In such cases, weighting certainly helps to reduce the distortion present in the data.

The real problem, however, is that weighting – as already observed for quota sampling – masks the distortions in the sample by means of an accounting artifice. The researcher must therefore explicitly state that a weighting procedure has been used.

Alternatively, the distortions should be allowed to appear clearly, so that both the analyst and the reader can be made aware of the inadequacy of the data and the need for caution in their interpretation.

8. A FINAL NOTE: SAMPLE ACCURACY

Two factors contribute to the scientific validity of a sample: its precision and its accuracy. A sample's *precision* is the inverse of the standard error of the estimates, i.e. what we defined 'sampling error' in Section 2. Its *accuracy* is the inverse of the total selection error (see Figure 3.5), which includes the previous sampling error, as well as non-coverage and non-response errors (the last two together are also called 'non-sampling error' or 'bias') (cf. Kish, 1965: 25).

As we have already mentioned, the *precision* of a sample depends largely upon its size: if the sample is too small, the standard error of the estimates will be too high and the confidence intervals very wide. For instance, a sample of 10 cases – even if chosen in a perfectly random manner – will yield estimates that are so imprecise as to be practically useless for most purposes.

Yet, in order to have a 'good' (i.e. *accurate*) sample, more than precision is needed. Even a very large sample can be a 'bad' sample if it contains non-sampling errors (bias), such as non-coverage or non-response errors. But, as we have argued above, in the social sciences it is practically impossible to avoid completely non-coverage or non-response errors. Nevertheless, the researcher can *minimize* them by ensuring that the sampling procedure is as close as possible to the probability sampling model.

The two goals of sampling error reduction (related to sample size) and non-sampling error reduction may sometimes clash. If resources are invested with a view to reducing non-sampling error (e.g. by stubbornly pursuing sampled subjects even when they are very difficult to track down), sacrifices will have to be made in terms of the number of subjects included in the sample. Clearly, we have to strike a balance between these two objectives. Indeed, it would not make much sense to invest a lot of energy to guarantee the absolute absence of non-response and non-coverage errors in a sample of only 50 cases; on the other hand, it would be equally senseless to devote large resources to collecting, coding and analysing 20,000 questionnaires from a patently biased sample.

As a general rule, we can say that, of these two requisites – large sample size and lack of bias – lack of bias is more important. For instance, if a study is carried out on teachers in a certain district, it is preferable to interview 300 teachers randomly selected from a complete list provided by the education authority, rather than to interview 1,000 teachers contacted through friends and acquaintances, or by means of self-administered questionnaires left in school staff-rooms. Likewise, in a study on doctors, it is better to interview 300 randomly selected subjects and pursue them doggedly until they all respond, rather than to obtain 1,000 responses to questionnaires mailed to 10,000 individuals (9,000 of whom do not respond). The improper choice of subjects, due both to the method of selection and to the phenomenon of self-selection (only the most highly motivated respond), will bias the sample; and when the researcher loses control over the sample, the impact on the results may be devastating.

At this point, some reflection on the purpose of the research is in order. Indeed, the structure of a sample depends heavily on the research objective. At one end of the scale, there are studies designed to estimate the means (or proportions) of a few variables as accurately as possible. In election forecasts, for instance, an error of only a few percentage points might result in the wrong conclusion (by predicting victory for the eventual loser). At the other end of the scale, there are studies designed to analyse the relationships among variables. Again with regard to elections, the researcher may be investigating the influence of gender, age, social class and religion on how people vote. In this case, the accuracy of the overall estimate (the percentage of the electorate voting for party A) is secondary. What does matter is having a large number of cases, so that the sample can be broken down to reveal, for example, how young non-religious working-class males vote.

To take up a well-known distinction, we can contrast *descriptive studies* with *explanatory studies*. If the objective is a descriptive one (to describe the distribution of single variables as accurately as possible), the sample must be as free of bias as possible. If, on the other hand, the objective is explanatory, then this requirement is less binding. In a study on the relationship between age and voting, the fact that young people in the sample may be over-represented in comparison with the elderly does not mean that the relationship will be distorted; indeed, if the elderly tend to vote for conservative parties, this tendency will remain even if we have sampled fewer senior citizens than we should have.[16] Nevertheless, it should be said that, while exclusively descriptive research is frequently carried out (such as polls aimed at forecasting the outcome of elections), it is difficult to imagine a study that totally disregards the marginal frequencies of the variables.

SUMMARY

1. Sampling offers several advantages to social research in terms of *cost* of data collection; *time* required for the collection and processing of data; *organization*, in that there is no need to recruit, train and supervise large numbers of interviewers, as is the case for a census of population; *depth* and *accuracy*, in that the lesser organizational complexity allows resources to be concentrated on quality control.

2. Whereas a study on an entire population yields the *exact value* of the investigated parameter, sampling yields only an *estimate*, for example an approximate value. This estimate involves a certain *level of confidence* and involves the determination of a *confidence interval* within which the population parameter probably occurs. In other words, the estimate based on a sample is subject to error, which we call *sampling error*. If the sample has been chosen according to a rigorously random procedure – that is to say, it is a *probability sample* – the magnitude of the sampling error can be calculated using statistical theory.

3. Sample size is directly proportional to the desired confidence level of the estimate and the variability of the phenomenon being investigated, and it is inversely proportional to the error that the researcher is prepared to accept (or, in other words, directly proportional to the accuracy desired). Sampling error depends only to a small degree on population size N: a sample of 1,000 produces estimates which are affected by similar errors whether they are drawn from a population of 20,000 or 100,000 subjects. Sampling error is, however, strongly influenced by sample size n: a sample of 1,000 cases entails much greater errors than a sample of 2,000 cases.

4. A sample is said to be a *probability sample* when each unit has non-zero probability of selection; probability of selection for all units is known; and the unit selection is completely random. The main kinds of probability sample designs are simple random sampling, systematic sampling, stratified sampling, multistage sampling, cluster sampling and area sampling.

5. The main types of non-probability sample designs are quota sampling, snowball sampling and judgement sampling.

6. In social surveys the application of sampling theory is quite difficult, because of the existence of so-called 'selection error', which involves not only sampling error

but also two other components: coverage error and non-response error. *Coverage error* stems from the fact than often in social research we have no access to a comprehensive list of the members of the population. *Non-response error* may have two distinct causes: failure to contact selected subjects selected, and some subjects' refusal to be interviewed.

7. *Weighting* is a technique for artificially modifying the composition of a sample (by means of mathematical operations during the data-processing stage) in order to make it resemble the population to a greater extent. The most common weighting procedures are based on the probability of inclusion in the sample, what is known about the population, and what is known about the non-respondents.

FURTHER READING

A non-technical introductory book on sampling is G.T. Henry, *Practical Sampling* (Sage, 1990, pp. 139); another short and readable summary of basic sampling theory (slightly more statistically-oriented then the previous one) is G. Kalton, *Introduction to Survey Sampling* (Sage, 1983, pp. 96).

A comprehensive work on sampling, with many examples and illustrations, which has been the basic reference text for generations of survey samplers, is the classic L. Kish, *Survey Sampling* (Wiley, 1965, pp. 643); the standard statistical text on sampling is W.G. Cochran, *Sampling Techniques* (Wiley, 1977, pp. 448).

NOTES

1. The use of the term 'population' stems from what was one of the first fields of the application of statistics: demography. Many statisticians use the terms 'population' and 'universe' interchangeably, while others apply the former to a set of *real* (finite) cases, and the latter to hypothetical (infinite) sets. We prefer to adopt this

distinction and, as we will always be referring to real sets of units, will use only the term 'population'.

2. A clear distinction needs to be made among *sample design* (the predetermined theoretical procedure), *sampling* (the implementation of the design) and *sample* (the product of sampling). For example, a sample design may be random (it is decided that the sampling units included in the sample will be chosen by drawing lots), but the resulting sample may not be so, owing to incomplete implementation of the plan. In the case of surveys, for instance, if a sizeable proportion of the subjects selected for interview cannot or will not be interviewed, the resulting sample cannot really be regarded as random.

3. By convention, capital letters are used to indicate values in the population, and small letters to indicate corresponding values in the sample.

4. A 95% probability that the confidence interval $\bar{X} \pm e$ will contain the unknown mean of the population.

5. This is a dichotomous variable, which assumes only the values 0 and 1 (even if the variable is polytomous, it can always be reduced to dichotomous terms by opposing each category to the aggregate of all the others).

6. The adjectives 'probabilistic' and 'random' have the same meaning in this context; the terms probability sample and random sample can therefore be used interchangeably.

7. Numbered balls can be picked out of a metaphorical hat (as in a lottery); tables of random numbers can be used, or a sequence of random numbers can be generated by means of computer.

8. In the US, RDD samples basically append random numbers to known telephone prefixes. For example, a telephone number in the US could be generated as 415-321-XXXX, where XXXX is a randomly generated 4-digit number. The first part of the number corresponds to a specific geographic area, depending on the population to be included in the survey. Since the last part of the telephone number is generated at random, all households in that area are included in the sampling frame.

9. This k is different from the k in the previous paragraph in that it cannot be calculated in advance as a ratio N/n.

10. Strictly speaking, it is not necessary to have an actual list of the population in order to

assign to all subjects a known probability of being selected. In multistage (two-stage) sampling, it is sufficient to have a list of the primary units and of the secondary units belonging to the primary units selected (and likewise if there are more than two stages); in area sampling, a list of the areas at the various levels is sufficient. Systematic sampling can be conducted even in the absence of a prior list, as long as the whole population is localized in one place and the researcher has access to all the subjects during the course of selection (e.g. by interviewing one person in every 10 who leave a polling station or a museum). In all these situations each member of the population might get interviewed and therefore has a known probability of being included in the sample.

11. By analogy, this reasoning can be extended to probability samples that are not based on a list in the strict sense, e.g. systematic, cluster and area samples. If systematic sampling is used to interview football fans travelling by train to an away match, the sample will be biased, as it neglects those fans who travel by car (who will surely be different – older and wealthier – from those on the train).

12. For instance, in a country where today 85% of families have a telephone, and only 5% of telephone numbers are not listed in public directories, it is fairly standard practice to regard the list of telephone subscribers as an acceptable list of the population of families and therefore to conduct telephone surveys on samples of that population.

13. The example refers to face-to-face interviews conducted at the subject's home, but the same problem arises for other interview modalities.

14. This calculation stems from a simple proportion: if individuals of weight 1 add up to 58, how much would they have to weigh in order to add up to 49? ($X : 49 = 1 : 58$). As is clear from the example, if weighting is undertaken, all the strata in which the population is subdivided will be weighted.

15. Another situation in which weighting on the basis of non-responses is strongly recommended is that of telephone surveys, which normally present high non-response rates, especially within particular sectors of the population (poorly educated, elderly people). In such cases of refusal, it is advisable to try to find out the subject's age (and, if possible, the gender, which can often be deduced from the voice); in this way, the responses can be weighted as in the example reported in the text.

16. In other words, marginal frequencies vary more than correlations.

Part Three

Qualitative Techniques

The next three chapters deal with a new sector of social research techniques. In reality, this topic is not completely new to our reader, as it harks back to the issue of qualitative research, which was introduced in Chapter 2. Nevertheless, the present section is clearly distinct from the previous chapters, particularly in view of the fact that qualitative research not only involves completely different techniques from those used in quantitative research, but also requires a radically different cast of mind and basic philosophy. This is inevitably the case; between these two approaches there is a paradigm shift, from the positivist to the interpretative.

From the conceptual and terminological points of view, clear distinctions cannot be made among the techniques of qualitative analysis. For example, the terms *ethnographic research, field studies, community studies, participant observation, naturalistic research* are all used – albeit improperly – as synonyms. Likewise, the terms *in-depth interviews, unstructured interviews, clinical interviews, oral history, biographical approach,* etc. are used to indicate data-gathering techniques that sometimes differ only subtly.

Nor are the techniques of qualitative analysis distinct in terms of their application; they are often applied simultaneously, and the researcher may interweave several of them during the course of the same study.

Finally, it is difficult to map out the pathway of qualitative research into separate stages; the same two basic moments of collection and analysis of data, which are so clearly distinct and sequential in quantitative research, do not follow the same inflexible order, but intersect and overlap.

This state of affairs prompted Bryman and Burgess (1994: 2) to claim that, in qualitative research, we should speak not so much of 'techniques' or 'stages' as of a 'process' of research. They maintain '… that qualitative research cannot be reduced to particular techniques nor to set stages, but rather that a dynamic process is involved which links together problems, theories and methods'. Consequently, 'the research process is not a clear-cut sequence of procedures following a neat pattern, but a messy interaction between the conceptual and empirical world, deduction and induction occurring at the same time' (Bechhofer, 1974: 73, quoted in Bryman and Burgess, 1994).

This situation has been further underscored by other recent developments in qualitative research, which – in its exploration of novel approaches and new outlooks on research – has enriched the old toolbox of classical techniques, containing participant observation of ethnographic origin and non-structured interviews, with 'a collection of a variety of empirical materials – case study; personal experience, introspection; life story; … artifacts; cultural texts and productions; observational, historical, interactional, and visual texts – that describe routine and problematic moments and meanings in individuals' lives' (Denzin and Lincoln, 2000: 3).

That the process of qualitative research lacks the linearity normally seen in quantitative research is beyond doubt. Nevertheless, this does not mean that techniques or groups of techniques cannot be distinguished within it. Nor does the fact that these techniques are often used in conjunction prevent us from examining them separately. This is what will be done in the three chapters of this section.

The data-gathering techniques used in qualitative research may be grouped into three broad categories which are based on *direct observation*, *in-depth interviews* and the *use of documents*. These can be roughly linked to three primary actions that people implement to investigate the surrounding social situation: *observing*, *asking* and *reading*.

Through observation, researchers analyse a given social phenomenon first of all by immersing themselves in it, so as to experience it from the inside and to be able to give a direct description of it. By means of interviews, they plumb the experiences, feelings and opinions of the subjects studied, in order to register their behaviour and motivations. Finally, the use of documents involves analysing a given social situation from the standpoint of the material – generally, but not solely, in written form – that the society has produced, and produces, both through individuals (autobiographical accounts, letters, etc.) and through institutions (news bulletins, the press, legal reports, etc.).

While the techniques of qualitative research can be grouped in this manner, it is much more difficult to isolate the stages through which it proceeds. For this reason, we have not devoted a preliminary chapter to presenting this research process and its stages. Rather, we will deal directly with the single techniques.

9   Participant Observation

This chapter is devoted to the most classic qualitative research technique. 'Participant observation' combines observation as a tool for collecting social data and the full immersion of the researcher in the social reality studied. The chapter outlines the historical evolution of participant observation, with special regard for its origins in ethnography, the stages of a study based on this technique and the practical and theoretical issues it raises. The text also discusses the various fields in which participant observation may be applied and how they have changed over time: once a technique for studying 'different' societies, participant observation is now one of the main tools for analysing everyday actions in modern society.

1.   OBSERVATION AND PARTICIPANT OBSERVATION

It is not without significance that this chapter is entitled 'participant observation' and not, simply, 'observation'. By 'observation' we mean the principal technique for gathering data on non-verbal behaviour; by 'participant observation' we mean, rather than simple observation, the researcher's direct involvement with the object studied. A chapter on 'observation' might include techniques like the laboratory-based observation of interactions between individuals (such as Bales' experiments (1951) which consisted of putting subjects in a room, getting them to talk about a certain subject, observing their behaviour from the outside during the course of the discussion, and codifying it into a series of elementary actions); or like the observation techniques used in natural settings (for instance, studying the dynamics of a school class in which the interaction between the teacher and students is videotaped and subsequently analysed in minute detail). In such cases, however, a fundamental element of the technique that we are presenting here is lacking, namely the involvement of the researcher in the social situation studied and his interaction with the subjects involved. In other words, the above-mentioned techniques could still fall within the positivist approach.

Participant observation, on the other hand, is fully located within the *interpretative paradigm*.

Why, then, do we use the terms 'observation' and 'participant'? *Observation* implies watching and listening. But at the same time this technique entails personal and intense contact between the subject who studies and the subject who is studied, a prolonged interaction that may even last years. Indeed, it is the researcher's involvement (*participation*) in the situation under investigation that constitutes the distinctive element. The researcher not only *observes* the life of the subjects being studied, but also *participates* in it. And it is this second aspect which differentiates this research technique from all others in social research. In structured interviews, in statistical data analysis, in experiments, in the analysis of documents, even in in-depth interviews, the researcher does *not* become part of the social phenomenon studied. Nor does this occur under pure and simple observation. In participant observation the researcher 'steps into the field' and immerses herself in the social context that she wants to study, lives *like* and *with* the people who are the object of the study, shares in their daily lives, asks them questions, discovers their hopes and pains, their worldviews and motivations, in order to develop that 'vision from within' that is the prerequisite of *comprehension*.

This approach therefore has two underlying principles: (a) that a full social awareness can be achieved only through understanding the subjects' point of view, through a process of identification with their lives; and (b) that this identification is attainable only through complete participation in their daily lives, by interacting continuously and directly with the subjects being studied.

Thus, we can define participant observation as a research strategy in which the researcher enters:

- directly,
- for a relatively long period of time into a given social group,
- in its natural setting,
- establishing a relationship of personal interaction with its members,
- in order to describe their actions and understand their motivations, through a process of identification.

The reader will have grasped the five elements of this definition: (a) observation must be conducted first-hand by the researcher, without being delegated to others (as in survey interviews); (b) the period spent with the group studied must be relatively long (from a few months up to a few years); (c) this participation occurs in the group's natural habitat and not in artificial surroundings created in order to facilitate research tasks; (d) the research is not limited to observing a situation from the outside, but implies interacting with the people who are being studied; and (e) the final aim is to describe and 'understand', in a Weberian sense – that is, to 'see the world through the eyes of the subjects studied'.

In this perspective the researcher must not be afraid of contaminating the data through a process of subjective and personal interpretation, in that the subjectivity of the interaction, and therefore of the interpretation, is one of the very features of the technique. *Involvement* and *identification* are not to be avoided, but actively pursued (whereas *objectivity* and *distance*, which were basic elements of the neopositivist approaches, are no longer considered values).

In this process of involvement, the researcher must maintain a balance between two extremes, which Davis (1973) called 'the Martian' and 'the convert'. Both start off by assuming that 'the human's social world is a wholly constructed one' (1973: 337), but they end up drawing opposing conclusions. The 'Martian' attempts to get involved as little as possible in the social situation that is being studied. He listens sceptically to what the members of society say about themselves and their world, regarding their stories as misleading in that they are bound to one particular vision and culture. He regards the task of the social researcher as that of stripping away all cultural and cognitive assumptions (including his own) in order to grasp the real essence of social processes. The 'convert', on the other hand, does not fear that the culture of the society studied constitutes 'cognitive entrapment'. On the contrary, he thinks that only total immersion in it can provide the necessary means of understanding. However, by 'total immersion' he means 'a passionate identification with the life scheme of others' (1973: 338), and goes through an existential experience similar to that of the religious convert, who sees in his conversion a radical transformation of his own identity.

The solution to the *involvement/separation* dilemma probably lies in striking a balance between the two perspectives: if an excessive distance hinders understanding, complete identification can also be an obstacle in that, as we shall see, the social researcher has to be able to bring to the research situation questions that derive from his own culture and experience.

Participant observation was developed by anthropologists at the beginning of the twentieth century in order to study primitive societies. With the disappearance of primitive societies, anthropology shifted its interest to the study of modern societies, and concentrated on specific social and cultural areas (urban anthropology, anthropology of medicine, etc.); at the same time, its research model was adopted by other disciplines, such as sociology. In the sociological field, the activities of the Chicago School in the 1920s and 1930s deserve particular mention. Under the guidance of Robert Ezra Park, the Department of Sociology of the University of Chicago conducted a series of studies on American urban society – focusing particularly on deviance and social marginalization – that still today constitute a fundamental reference point in the history and development of sociological research. Park's explicit intent was to apply to the study of urban culture the same approach that anthropologists such as Francis Boas and Robert Lowie had used to study Native Americans. These experiences enriched and developed Malinowski's initial

---

BOX 9.1 PARTICIPANT OBSERVATION IN ETHNOGRAPHY

Participant observation was developed in anthropological research at the beginning of the twentieth century. It was the great English anthropologist (of Polish origin) Bronislaw Malinowski who codified the principles of this approach in the *Introduction* to *Argonauts of the Western Pacific* – defined as the book of Genesis of modern anthropology. The traditional model of eighteenth-century anthropology (which viewed native peoples as 'primitive savages' who had to be educated according to the tenets of Western civilization, and which conducted research by compiling reports from the government offices of colonies or missions) was radically overhauled by the introduction of the objective 'to grasp the native's point of view, his relation to life, to realize *his* vision of *his* world' (Malinowski, 1922). He conducted his research in the Trobriand Islands, 120 miles north-east of New Guinea, far from the commercial shipping lanes of the time. His model consisted of spending long periods (even more than one year) in a primitive society, sharing in its members' lives, and severing all contact with the Western world for the entire length of the observation period.

model, but left the underlying characteristics substantially unaltered: residence *in loco* of the scholar, sharing life with the subjects of study, observation of social interaction in the natural environment, and the use of key personalities as informers.

Within the context of anthropological-ethnographical research (or *field study*), participant observation is not the only technique that the researcher can use. The participating observer must observe, listen and ask and, in asking, she takes up the tools of the interviewer. At the same time, she must document facts that happen and have happened, explore any existing documentary material on the community being studied, and any that the community itself produces (historical accounts, autobiographies, letters, statements, reports, newspaper articles, etc.). In this, her research uses the instruments of documentary analysis. Later chapters will deal with interviewing techniques and documentary analysis, which are also used in other areas of social research besides ethnography. The fact remains, however, that the principal instrument of this type of research is participant observation.

In the following pages, we will describe the basic features of participant observation. However, as previously mentioned in introducing qualitative techniques this technique is not structured in a linear manner, with stages arranged in a pre-ordained sequence. Participant observation is a technique that is difficult to codify and difficult to teach, in that it is more of an experience than a set of coordinated procedures, which unfolds essentially according to the complex, ever-changing interaction that is set up among the issue under investigation, the researcher and the subjects of the study.

2. FIELDS OF APPLICATION AND RECENT DEVELOPMENTS IN PARTICIPANT OBSERVATION

Participant observation can be applied to the study of all human activities and all groupings of human beings, above all – as has been said – if one wants to discover the worldview of others 'from the inside'. There are, however, sectors in which this technique is especially useful because of the nature of the subjects studied. According to Jorgensen participant observation is especially appropriate for scholarly problems when:

- 'little is known about the phenomenon (a newly formed group or movement, ... improvised human conduct);
- there are important differences between the views of insiders as opposed to outsiders (ethnic groups, labour unions, subcultures such as occultists, poker players ... and even occupations like physicians, newscasters ...);
- the phenomenon is somehow obscured from the view of outsiders (private, intimate interactions and groups, such as physical and mental illness, teenage sexuality, family life, or religious ritual);
- the phenomenon is hidden from public view (crime and deviance, secretive groups and organizations, such as drug users and dealers, cultic and sectarian religions)' (Jorgensen, 1989: 12).

Participant observation emerges as a natural investigative tool when the researcher intends to study a situation in which he has taken (or takes) part himself, thus giving rise to what has been called *autobiographical sociology*. Examples taken from the extremely vast literature include the research on gamblers by Scott (1968), a long-time frequenter of illicit gambling schools; on jazz musicians by Becker (1963), a musician; on the socialization of children to the dancing profession by Hall (1976), who was a student at a dance school for 16 years; on Mexican women who illegally cross the US-Mexico border every week to work for American families by Mary Romero (1992), who was a servant for a family in El Paso at the age of 15, along with her mother and sisters; on American prisons by Irwin (1970; 1980), who started a five-year prison term at the age of 21; and by Jacqueline

Wiseman (1979), a long-time on the world that revolves around the used-clothes commerce, used-clothing store owner.

Autobiographical sociology also includes studies which take advantage of any life-transforming experience as an occasion for research. Whyte (1984: 31) for example, recalls the case of a student, Jose Moreno, who was sent from Cornell University to the Dominican Republic to study village life. As soon as he arrived, he found himself in the middle of a rebellion. He sympathized with the rebels, joined them, and later published a book based on material collected during this experience (Moreno, 1970).

Autobiography that turns into research is not the ideal type of participant observation, and is open to many criticisms. Ethnographic research is a *meeting of cultures*; the studying culture looks at the culture under study through the naïve eyes of the foreigner who knows little or nothing about it and immerses himself in a new world without knowing its language, customs, norms and values. From such observation, a fertile dynamic emerges that enables the observer to discover aspects and meanings which are hidden from those who have always belonged to the studied culture.

As already mentioned, participant observation – in the wake of ethnographic experience – is above all used to study cultures. In sociological research it has been applied basically to two objectives: to study in depth small autonomous societies located in specific territories and possessing a culturally closed universe that contains all aspects of life (e.g. a farming community, a small provincial town, a mining village, etc.); and to study subcultures that arise within specific sectors of a complex society. These may represent aspects of the dominant culture (youth culture, the rich, lawyers, the workers of a large industrial complex, the military, a political party, soccer fans, etc.) or be in partial conflict with it (a religious sect, a revolutionary party, gamblers, ethnic minorities, etc.) or even in open conflict (terrorist groups, prison inmates, radical political movements, deviant groups in general). Studies of the first type are called

community studies, while those of the second type are called *subculture studies*.

Community studies are more strongly influenced by the ethnographic model. These studies, which are usually conducted on small (or relatively small) social communities located in specific areas, oblige the researcher to live for a certain period of time in the community studied. A classic in this field is the study conducted by the Lynds, a couple who in 1924 moved to a small provincial American town (Muncie, Indiana, where they lived for three years) in order to study:

> … the interwoven trends that are the life of a small American city … with the approach of the cultural anthropologist. There are, after all, despite infinite variations in detail, not so many major things that people do. Whether in an Arunta village in Central Australia or in our own seemingly intricate institutional life … human behavior appears to consist in variations upon a few major lines of activity …. This study, accordingly, proceeds on the assumption that all the things people do in this American city may be viewed as falling under one or another of the following six main-trunk activities: getting a living; making a home; training the young; using leisure … ; engaging in religious practice; engaging in community activities. (Lynd and Lynd, 1929: 3,4)

It is evident that the whole existential universe of society is studied through an approach – as emphasized by the authors – that is very similar to that used by the anthropologist who studies primitive tribes.

Another example of community study is the one conducted in Italy in the 1950s by the American scholar Edward Banfield. He lived for nine months, with his wife and two children, in a town of 3000 inhabitants, mostly poor peasants and labourers, in Southern Italy, in order to study 'cultural, psychological, and moral conditions of political and other organizations' (Banfield, 1958: 9). Using the same method as the Lynds, the author concentrated on one particular aspect of social life – political and social participation – and identified a strongly individualistic culture, centred around the family, that conditioned the entire political and economic life of the small town to the point that 'the extreme poverty and backwardness could be explained largely ... by the inability of the villagers to act together for their common good' (1958: 9–10).

With regard to *subculture studies*, it may be noted that cultures that were different from the dominant one were among the first to attract the attention of sociologists. The research of the Chicago School in the 1920s and 1930s mostly involved social marginalization resulting from immigration and urbanization: vagabonds, gangs, prostitutes, black ghettos, slums, immigrant communities, etc.

One of the best known studies – often considered a prototype of this kind of research – is *Street Corner Society* (1943), which was carried out by William Foote Whyte in 1936–1937 in a slum on the outskirts of Boston. Having decided to study small-time organized crime for his doctoral dissertation, Whyte, then a 23-year-old Harvard student, moved into the most run-down neighbourhood in the city and led the life of any other inhabitant. In a crucial encounter he met Doc, the leader of one of the local youth gangs, who introduced him to all the local groups, in particular, to the youth gangs. The path of his research is vividly described in the appendix to the second edition (published in 1950) of the book, which rapidly became a sort of methodological guide for participant observation.

Another example is seen in Sánchez-Jankowski's research on gangs, which was described in Chapter 2. As mentioned in that chapter, the research is based on participant observation of a large number of cases (some 37 gangs located in three cities, observed over the course of 10 years), which is somewhat exceptional for a technique that usually involves studying only one social situation.

Among the classics, one can also cite *The Hobo* by Nels Anderson, which inaugurated the 1923 *Sociological Series* of the Department of Sociology of the University of Chicago, devoted to the city's urban problems. This research focused on the marginal proletariat that had developed around the construction of the great American railroad network. The 'hobos' were homeless migrant workers, who worked mainly in construction for limited periods of time (generally until that specific job was finished) and then moved on to look for work elsewhere. These individuals belonged to a world that had a well-defined cultural connotation, in which mobility, travel and a sense of transience were more a matter of lifestyle choice than of constraint. Anderson's research was partly the result of his own background (his father had been a hobo and the author himself had been through the experience in the early years of his working life). It was also a classic case of participant observation. When the author decided to do his doctoral dissertation on the life of the hobos, he moved to the Chicago neighbourhood where the greatest number of homeless people could be found.

From those early studies of deviant cultures or of groups living on the fringe of society, participant observation gradually came to be used to study the culture of sectors of 'official' society. Several studies on the lives and social conditions of specific categories of workers, for example, were conducted by researchers who took jobs among these workers in order to describe their lifestyles, worldviews and living conditions.

A classic study of this kind was conducted in the 1940s by Donald Roy (1952), a young American scholar who studied the life of factory workers and specifically wanted to explore the phenomenon of self-limitation of productivity; that is to say, he wanted to understand why workers deliberately limited the productivity of the machines on which they worked, even when bonuses were paid for every piece manufactured beyond a set minimum output. In order to investigate this phenomenon and, more generally, to enter into the worker culture, the researcher – then a graduate student from the University of Chicago – worked for 10 months (between 1944 and 1945) in a small workshop that produced components for railway carriages. He revealed his intentions to no-one – neither his boss when he was hired, nor his colleagues afterwards. His analysis was illuminating, as it refuted both the radical Marxist view, which regarded worker self-limitation (the tendency to produce less than possible) as an expression of class consciousness and the effect of the inevitable conflict between capital and labour, and the functionalist interpretation, which attributed limitations on productivity to poor communication between workers and management and inadequate attention to the human aspects of the work. Instead, in self-limitation behaviour, he identified a certain rationality on the part of the workers, who acted in accordance with their own interests; they thought that higher productivity would immediately induce management to raise the minimum standard of production, or else that the financial incentives were too low to justify the extra effort.

A similar study was conducted exactly 30 years later by another American scholar, Michael Burawoy (1979). He took a job in the same factory where Roy had worked, mainly in order to investigate the changes that had taken place in factory work since the first study. Like Roy, Burawoy used participant observation. Curiously, however, he conducted overt observation, revealing the aims of the study both to the owners and to his workmates. He was able to do so because tension between management and workers in the factory had eased over the previous 30 years, and because the management now showed greater awareness of social research tools.

As the focus of participant observation shifted from fringe cultures to 'normal society', research was conducted on the values, networks of social relationships and interpersonal dynamics that develop inside institutions and social organizations. This so-called *organizational ethnography* consists of analysing organizations as cultures. Such studies examine the culture of an organization (the implicit knowledge shared by members of the same institution, the reference models used to interpret reality, the unwritten rules that guide an individual's action) and the way in which this culture is expressed in action and social interaction (formal and informal groups, the structure of decision-making processes, interpersonal relationships, symbols and rituals).

With regard to productive organizations, we may quote the studies conducted by Gouldner, which were published in 1954 in the volumes *Patterns of Industrial Bureaucracy* and *The Wildcat Strike*. These two studies were the result of participant observation that lasted three years, from 1948 to 1951, in an American mining company of about 200 employees, some of whom worked underground while others were involved in above-ground mineral-processing operations. Data collection was carried out by a group of researchers made up mostly of university students from a nearby campus; they had free access to the factory and the mine, and their presence soon became familiar to the workers and miners. The empirical material of the study came from a variety of sources: observation, the analysis of company documents, non-directive interviews conducted by the students – after careful training and under constant supervision (this organizational model differs, in part, from the classic participant observation model in that an actual research team was engaged in the study and some of the data were collected through interviews).

In the first book, Gouldner's analysis focuses on company organization, beginning from the Weberian ideal type of bureaucracy, within which he tries to identify sub-types. Since his research was conducted during a transition phase in management (from an old, paternalistic and permissive manager to a younger one with a more efficient, hands-on approach), Gouldner focuses on the problem of succession in a bureaucracy. In the second volume, he takes advantage of a lucky coincidence; during the study period, a wildcat strike was called, which enabled him to observe an infrequent social phenomenon first-hand. This became an observation platform from which he was able to develop a general theory on group tensions.

Health institutions have also been studied through participant observation. For example,

Atkinson (1995) investigated the culture of physicians and the ways in which disease is construed and defined within the framework of extreme specialization and compartmentalization of modern medicine. In order to do this, he frequented the haematology-oncology department of a Boston hospital and for 10 weeks closely followed the work of three doctors, attending all their meetings and taping their conversations. In this way he was able to observe a whole range of formal and informal interaction, from routine daily encounters to case consultations, and from relations with the younger interns to meetings with more experienced, senior colleagues. All this was done with the objective of studying how interaction occurs among doctors, how they describe their clinical cases to their colleagues, how they try to persuade one another of their diagnoses, how the training of new generations is carried out; in short, how medical culture is produced and reproduced in a highly specialized and technologically advanced sector.

Participant observation has also been used to study political institutions. The research conducted by Dahl, Polsby and Wolfinger in New Haven, Connecticut, on democracy and power in an American city is a classic study. The aim of this research was to explore the question of 'who governs' in all its various ramifications: the real centres of power, decision-making dynamics, pressure groups, negotiation mechanisms between opposing interests, relationships between representatives and those represented, etc. (Dahl, 1961; Polsby, 1963; Wolfinger, 1973). The study is very complex and uses multiple techniques of data collection and analysis, including participant observation. Wolfinger obtained permission from the city's mayor to stay in his office for a period of time, observing the day's events, people contacted, filters used to select contacts, the dynamics of interaction, the role of assistants and councillors, etc., thus reconstructing in detail a series of decision-making processes.

One of the most original applications of participant observation to the study of specific cultural contexts within a larger society concerns studies on 'the culture of children'. Research conducted in the United States and in Italy by the American scholar William Corsaro (Corsaro and Rizzo, 1990) was based on access to an infant community (he worked mostly in nursery schools, with 3 to 5–year-old children). The fieldwork consisted partly of pure observation (videotaping behaviour and dialogue) and partly of interaction with the children. The researcher accomplished this by introducing himself into the class, observing the children, interacting with them, and taking part in their games, attempting to acquire the status of group member in order to grasp the children's views and interpretations, just like the researcher who attempts to participate in the life of an adult community. In this case, too, as in classic participant observation, great importance was placed on the subjects' interpretations and explanations, as gleaned from apparently casual conversations with the observer (who asked the children about the meanings of their behaviour while he played with them), and on the analysis of conversations among the children.

These examples involving the study of subcultures that are part of the multifaceted culture of a complex society must not obscure what was stated at the beginning of this section, that participant observation is extremely useful for studying 'particular cultures', autonomous cultural universes which often diverge markedly from the dominant culture. It remains the ideal technique for studying deviance, social marginalization, ethnic minorities, religious cults, closed organizations and 'alternative' groups of any kind.

3. OVERT AND COVERT OBSERVATION: ACCESS AND INFORMANTS

With regard to participant observation, an important distinction must be made between overt and covert observation. Indeed, the researcher may reveal or disguise his true objectives. He may openly declare at the outset that he is a researcher, that he wishes to be part of a given social group not because he agrees with its goals, but only to study it; or he may infiltrate the group by pretending to join it and to be a member just like any other.

The main advantage of covert observation stems from the fact that human beings, if they know that they are being observed, are not likely to behave naturally. This is what Labov called the *paradox of the observer*: we want to observe how people act when they are not being observed. Thus, covert observation should allow us to view their genuine behaviour. The argument is certainly valid. Moreover, it has already been stressed that the 'reactivity' of humans is one of the main factors that differentiate research in the social sciences from research in the natural sciences.

There are, nonetheless, convincing arguments against covert observation. Assuming a false identity to play a role that could be likened to that of a 'spy' is, in itself, reprehensible, and can be justified only if there are compelling ethical reasons for it. It is doubtful that the objective of social research has such a high moral value as to justify deceit and taking advantage of other people's good faith. Moreover, the awareness of his own deceit could create anxiety and unnatural behaviour in the researcher. Even the unscrupulous may find it difficult to cultivate bogus interpersonal relationships. In covert observation, there is a constant risk of being discovered, and the consequences of discovery may be unpredictable (from the abrupt interruption of the relationship to even more dire consequences when deviant groups or groups engaged in illegal activities are involved). In certain cases, concealing the researcher's role can even be an obstacle to the final objective of observation: understanding. Sometimes, explicit interviews and persistent questioning are simply impossible if the researcher does not reveal his role and objectives. By contrast, the overt participant observer can take advantage of his declared 'incompetence' in order to ask naïve questions, and elicit explanations of banal matters, thus

accumulating information concerning the natives' accounts and viewpoints.

Many experienced researchers have raised another important point. While the reason for engaging in covert observation (that is to say, someone being observed behaves differently) is valid during the early stages of observation, it is also true that, in the case of overt observation, the behaviour of the subjects observed will gradually return to normal as the researcher's presence becomes more familiar.

Sometimes the question of revealing the role of the observer does not arise. When the observed environment is public and open, it is not necessary (at times it would be impossible or ridiculous) to reveal the observation; we need only think, for example, of studies on crowd behaviour at football matches, on the courtship rituals of young people in a dance hall, or on the dynamics of speeches at political rallies or trade union meetings. Nor does the question arise (or arises to a lesser degree) when the researcher studies situations to which she already naturally belongs (for example, a teacher who studies classroom dynamics, or an assistant in a drug rehabilitation facility who studies the problem of drug dependency).

In other cases the question is not so much one of plain deceit as of omission: simply not declaring one's role. For example, a researcher might get a job in a factory in order to study the living conditions of workers; or a journalist with an Arab-like appearance might join a group of illegal immigrants from North Africa to study immigration routes and illegal workers in Italy; or again, a researcher might move to a small town or village in order to conduct a community study of life there. In these cases the researcher often combines normal work activities with the objectives of the study, and does not need to make his true intentions known, unless he wants to go beyond normal relationships (work, neighbours, etc.), e.g. through in-depth interviews with privileged observers to whom he will reveal his aims. In these cases, in which the role of the observer is revealed only to some members of the observed community, the term 'semi-overt role' has been proposed (Whyte, 1984; 30).

In general, when the investigated population is a private group that lies beyond the observer's experience and is accessible only to someone with certain requisites, it is strongly advisable for the researcher to specify his reasons for participation. Whyte states that 'in a community study, maintaining a covert role is generally out of question. People will not put up with interviews and observations for which no purpose is explained' (1984: 31). In other situations, general guidelines cannot be given, and the decision to reveal or conceal one's role will be taken on a case-by-case basis.

Once the case to be studied has been chosen and the mode of observation (overt or covert) established, the first problem that the researcher has to deal with is 'access'. Gaining access to the study environment is probably one of the most difficult tasks in participant observation. Patton (1990: 250) states that researchers' accounts bring to mind Kafka's *The Castle*, in which the protagonist, identified only by the letter K, wanders around outside the castle, desperately seeking to become part of the world inside; all efforts to contact the invisible authority that regulates access only cause frustration and anxiety; he begins to doubt himself, falls into despair and is racked with guilt for his own ineptitude.

Kafka's character never manages to enter the castle. The participant observer usually gains entry to the field of study, but it is never simple. The most common way of solving this problem is through a *cultural mediator*. This tactic is based on appealing to the prestige and credibility of one of the members of the group to legitimize the observer and get him accepted by the group. The cultural mediator is a person who is trusted by the population and who, because of his cultural characteristics, is also able to understand the motivations and the necessities of the ethnographer.

In his analysis of 10 different experiences of access, Whyte (1984: 37) distinguishes between informal and formal groups. The classic example of the informal group is found in Whyte's above-mentioned research, *Street Corner Society* (1943). In the appendix, he recounts his initial attempts to make real contact with the inhabitants of 'Cornerville' (the fictitious name of the neighbourhood studied). At first, he worked with a private agency that concerned itself with housing matters, in order to have an excuse to knock on people's doors, have a look inside their homes and ask them about their living conditions. However, the psychological burden of this intrusion and unnatural character of the situation soon forced him to interrupt this experiment. Subsequently, he attempted to approach some young women in one of the bars frequented by the neighbourhood youth, hoping to persuade them to tell him about their lives by offering them a drink. The attempt failed abysmally. Many other frustrating experiences followed until, in the end, a social worker in the neighbourhood suggested that he contact Doc, an intelligent youth who had worked for a time with the public housing social service. Whyte claims that 'in a sense, my study began on the evening of February 4, 1937, when the social worker called me in to meet Doc'. Doc understood Whyte's intentions and offered to introduce him to the various neighbourhood groups as a friend. Doc's prestige was so great that these introductions were sufficient to open doors to all the local groups and obtain cooperation from all of the local inhabitants, especially the young people who were the main object of Whyte's study.

This is an example of entry into an informal group. When the social group studied is an institution, the situation is different. Sometimes, formal rules of access exist; in other cases, permission has to be obtained from 'gate-keepers' – that is, the people who control access. One classic example is that of the researcher who took a job in a company in order to study the world of work. Whyte (1984) cites the case of Robert Cole, an American researcher who, during the 1970s, wanted to study Japanese work culture by applying a Weberian model of bureaucratic rationality. In order to get hired, he followed both the formal route (in this case, by answering newspaper advertisements) and the informal route (revealing his research objectives to personnel managers and asking to be admitted among the workers for a certain period of time). Both approaches turned out to be difficult: the first because, in the Japanese business world, a job application from a westerner was extremely unusual (unless the work was highly specialized); the second because research of this kind was completely unknown in Japan, which meant that his request was either misunderstood or viewed with suspicion. Finally, he found a job in a small factory. Even here, however, the intervention of informal mediators was essential for his subsequent observation work. Indeed, Cole was brought into contact with the people of greatest interest for his research by two workmates, one who did the most menial jobs, and therefore mixed directly with the unskilled workers, and a union representative, both of whom had been informed of his research goals (Cole, 1979).

Cole was 28 years old at that time, more or less the same age as the colleagues he met in the factory, which he found helpful. Some years later, however, when he conducted a similar study in a car factory in which most of his workmates were only about 20 years old, Cole found the age gap something of a hindrance to his research. This observation opens a brief digression on the effect that some of the observer's most visible features, such as age, gender and race, can have on relationships with those being observed. There are situations in which participant observation demands that the observer be similar to those observed. For example, it is difficult to imagine how Whyte could have conducted his research among Cornerville's youth gangs if he had been a young woman or an elderly professor.

Naturally, once access has been gained to the study environment, the researcher's work is only beginning. The trust of those being observed must be earned, day after day, through patient application. This makes demands upon the researcher's personality and psychological characteristics, his sensitivity, his ability to handle relationships, not only

with others but also with himself: frustration, emotional involvement, etc. (Lofland and Lofland, 1995: Chapter 4). In some cases, the opposite problem may arise; excessive identification of the observer with the group being studied can impair the critical assessment of observed facts. In his appendix to *Street Corner Society* (1943), Whyte points out that at one stage his excessive integration with the youths engendered a risk that he might evolve from being a 'non-participating observer' to a 'non-observing participant'.

Having earned the trust of the cultural intermediaries and gained access to the study group, the observer will still need to construct privileged relationships with some of the subjects studied. Insiders whom the observer uses to acquire information and interpretation from within the culture studied are usually called *informants* (or *key informants*). The researcher establishes an intense personal relationship, and sometimes true friendship, with these individuals. They may be people who occupy positions that are strategic for the knowledge of the environment (such as the manager of a grocery store who knows the neighbourhood well). Or they may be ordinary people whom we can simply call 'main contacts'.

We can make a distinction between 'institutional informants' and 'non-institutional informants'. The former are people who have a formal role in an organization (e.g. in a study on prisons, the governor, social workers, the chaplain, etc.). Given their role, their interpretation of social circumstances may be influenced by their loyalty to the institution. Non-institutional informants are more important; they belong directly to the culture under examination (in the above example, the prison inmates) and, as such, can provide their interpretation of facts and their motivation for action, crucial elements for the observer's 'comprehension'. It must be added that the person most willing to cooperate may not always be the best informed. Moreover, if the choice falls on an unpopular person or one who is not respected in the community, this could have a negative impact on the observer's integration into the group. The researcher should therefore consolidate a relationship with an informant only after being in the group for some time, and scrutinize the informant thoroughly before beginning any collaboration.

4. WHAT TO OBSERVE

Participant observation has to be selective; it cannot create an all-embracing picture. On the contrary, some objects will be brought into focus while others remain in the background; and some will be entirely excluded from the observer's frame.

In the first instance, it is theory which establishes what is to be observed. Regarding the role of theory in qualitative research in general and in participant observation in particular, some distinctions should be made. In Chapter 3, which deals with the connection between theory and research in the case of quantitative research, a standard model is proposed (Figure 3.1) which assigns to theory a dominant role in guiding research. However, as has already been pointed out, while quantitative research based on neopositivism generally subscribes to a deductive approach, and therefore assigns a guiding role to theory, research based on the interpretative paradigm gives much greater autonomy to empirical observation. There are, nevertheless, marked differences within both paradigms. With regard to qualitative research in particular, we have already mentioned (in the Introduction to 'Part Two') the extreme case of *grounded theory*, which stresses the importance of 'discovering' theory during the course of research and goes so far as to recommend that the researcher should ignore the sociological literature on the issue to be investigated, in order to prevent preconceived notions from conditioning the enterprise of discovery.

In such a situation, however, the researcher may be overwhelmed by the chaotic multitude of stimuli which assail him; having no guidelines, he will be unable to order these stimuli or to choose among the myriad ways of interpreting them.

The present treatise will therefore stay on a more moderate track and will substantially follow Blumer's notion of 'sensitizing concepts', as mentioned in Chapter 2, Section 3.1. According to this approach, participant observation (like any qualitative research) is not conducted in a vacuum, nor does it start out from a kind of *tabula rasa*; rather, it is guided, especially at the beginning, by a particular 'sensitivity' towards certain concepts rather than others. For instance, the researcher investigating juvenile delinquency will pay particular attention to the problems of childhood socialization, relationships with parents, early experiences of social institutions such as school, peer group relationships, etc., while research into conflicts in the workplace will involve an awareness of matters related to the ideology of the working environment, hierarchical structure, work expectations and frustrations, relationship networks among colleagues, forms of communication between different hierarchical levels, etc.

At the same time, it must of course be borne in mind that 'field studies differ from other methods of research in that the researcher performs the tasks of selecting topics, decides what questions to ask, and forges interest *in the course of the research itself*. This is in sharp contrast to many 'theory-driven' and 'hypothesis-testing' methods of research in which the topics of observation and analysis ... are all carefully and clearly specified before one begins to gather data' (Lofland and Lofland, 1995: 5).

Theory, then, provides some indication of what to observe. Let us now look at the possible subjects of observation. These may be classified into the following areas: (a) physical setting; (b) social setting; (c) formal interactions; (d) informal interactions; and (e) interpretations of the social actors. It should be pointed out immediately that this classification of 'what to observe' is only one of many possible classifications. Nevertheless, participant observation will always involve a preliminary descriptive phase, in which the external visible features of the study environment are outlined, followed by a phase of genuine interaction with the protagonists.

Physical setting It is usually fairly important for the researcher to scrutinize the structural layout of the areas in which the behaviour to be studied takes place (and later to give a detailed account of this in the research report). This is done not only to communicate the observational experiences more clearly to the reader, but also because physical characteristics almost always reflect social characteristics (as well as conditioning social behaviour). Indeed, as Patton reports, 'During site visits to early childhood education programs, we found a close association between the attractiveness of the facility (child-made decorations, and colorful posters on the walls, well-organized materials, orderly teacher area) and other program attributes (parent involvement, staff morale, clarity of the program's theory of action)' (1990: 220).

Needless to say, the researcher should not attempt to emulate the novelist; he should provide descriptions rather than evaluations or impressions. Thus, rather than referring to a neighbourhood as 'depressing' or 'socially deprived', he should describe the state of the roads, the shops, typical housing, means of transport and public facilities (churches, schools, post offices, etc.). If the study is conducted within a firm, information should be provided on the location of offices, the position of common areas (canteen, etc.), the internal division of office space among the various grades of staff, etc.

Social setting The human element will be described in the same way as the physical environment. In the above example of the neighbourhood, this will involve describing the people seen in the streets at the various times of day and night, how they dress, and the purpose of their movements (shopping, going to work, loitering, etc.); data will also be gleaned regarding family income, expenditure and so on. In the case of the firm, a scheme of the staff and departments will be provided, and the characteristics, roles and tasks of the staff will be described. If a community is divided into groups and subgroups, the researcher will document the size of these groups, the individuals they comprise, the frequency of their interactions and their channels of communication (in a works canteen, for instance, how groups are formed at the table: whether on the basis of ascribed characteristics – the women sit together, young and old sit at separate tables, etc. – or whether groups form on a departmental basis, whether hierarchical grades mix or remain separate, whether there is a stable structure or whether groupings change each day, etc.). In this case too, at least in the initial presentation of the setting, the researcher should confine himself to description (if possible, detailed and analytical) rather than introducing elements of interpretation.

In attempting to understand a given community, history plays an important role, especially when the study focuses on social change. Whyte provides some interesting illustrations of this point. For instance, in a study of the changes that had taken place in a Peruvian village over the previous five years, he notes: 'important changes did take place even in that short period, yet we came to recognize that understanding the dynamics of current social processes required us to extend the time line back many decades or even centuries' (Whyte, 1984: 161).

Formal interactions By formal interactions we mean those which take place among individuals within institutions and organizations in which roles are pre-established and relationships are played out within a framework of predetermined constraints. In this regard, the researcher might examine how communication takes place among the various hierarchical levels of a firm. Or she might study the dynamics of a public meeting. With reference to the two points mentioned above, she will begin by describing the physical and social settings (the size of the hall, the number and visible characteristics of those present – gender, age, race, social class, as revealed for example by their clothing, etc. – the layout of the speakers and the audience, etc.). She will then move on to the actions and interactions: who opens the meeting, what he says, the order of speeches, audience reaction, etc. Or again, if a trial in a courtroom is being observed, the researcher will note the ceremonial aspects of the occasion (the courtroom, the judge's robes, the seating arrangements, the opening rituals, the swearing-in, the questioning of witnesses, etc.), the various ways in which the judge's questions are formulated, how the accused and the witnesses reply, how the public prosecutor and the defence lawyer play their roles, how the public participate or react to the sentence, etc.

In a study of the decision-making processes of a formal organization, decisions could be classified according to type (from the most important to the routine); we could note who takes which type of decision (an individual or a committee) and whether the process involves consultation (formal or informal, with whom and how, etc.); how the decision is communicated once it has been taken; what happens if the decision turns out to be wrong and so on.

Informal interactions   In most cases, informal interactions constitute the core of participant observation. By their very nature, such interactions are difficult to study. Moreover, since their observation involves scrutinizing a multitude of different situations, it is impossible to provide rules or even general guidelines. Nevertheless, we will attempt to highlight certain aspects.

First of all, the observer can begin with physical interactions. As Spradley points out, every social situation is defined by three elements: the place, the actors and the actions. In observing the actions, 'at first, the ethnographer may see only a stream of behavior, hundreds of acts that all seem indistinct. With repeated observations individual acts begin to fall into recognizable patterns of activity like hunting, sprinting, ordering drinks, selecting a seat on the bus, and bagging groceries at the supermarket check-out counter' (Spradley, 1980: 41).

Participant observation often starts with ordinary, everyday behaviour, which is the most difficult to analyse in that it is made up of a whole range of mechanical actions of which the individual is hardly aware. The person waiting in a bus queue scarcely notices what is happening around him (others in the queue, how they are dressed, what they are doing, the traffic passing, a child on a bicycle, a beggar, etc.); nor is he very aware of his own behaviour, precisely because it is ordinary, repetitive and mechanical. The participant observer, however, has to become aware of all these scraps of everyday life; if he wishes to analyse them, he must learn to observe and isolate them. He must also be able to pick up the interactions among the people he observes: how they get on the bus, whether they jostle or step aside, how they take their seats, the schoolchildren making a noise, the reactions of the other passengers, the strangers who bump into each other, the two ladies gossiping, their tone of voice, gestures and facial expressions, etc.

It is important to learn to focus on those interactions that are of interest. At first, the researcher's field of observation will be very broad, but gradually he will become more selective. Let us imagine a researcher intent on studying the customer-assistant relationship in shops. After observation in various types of shop, he realizes that he has to restrict his attention to one particular category: bookshops. He then realizes that most interactions take place on the way out, at the cash desk, and so stations himself near the exit and observes. He may decide to restrict his field of observation even further, for instance by focusing on the conflicts that arise between the customer and the assistant over payment or when a customer is caught trying to slip out without paying for a book. In this case, he will observe the incident in minute detail: how it evolves, the characteristics of those involved (gender, age, profession, etc.), the reactions of the various individuals (customer, sales assistant, bystanders, etc.) and any subsequent developments (apologies, payment of compensation, police involvement, etc.). In the end, it may well turn out that our researcher's initial generic intention to study customer-assistant relationships has become a study of attempted theft in bookshops. However, the researcher does not always have such freedom to define the subject of his study while the investigation is in progress. Sometimes his choices will be limited by external constraints (for instance, the study may have been commissioned). The fact remains, however, that the observation will gradually focus more closely on specific objects and social processes.

Social actors' interpretations   We know that in the interpretative paradigm the individual studied is not merely a passive object of research, but becomes an active protagonist; his interpretation of reality is therefore a constituent part (and not simply an accessory) of scientific knowledge. In this perspective, his verbal communication with the observer becomes a preferential channel of communication. As Hammersley and Atkinson point out:

'All human behavior has an expressive dimension. Ecological arrangements, clothes, gesture and manner all convey messages about people. They may be taken to indicate gender, social status, occupational role, group membership, attitudes, etc. However, the expressive power of language provides the most important resource for accounts ... In everyday life people continually provide linguistic accounts to one other: retailing news about "what happened" on particular occasions, discussing each other's motives, moral character, and abilities, etc.' (Hammersley and Atkinson, 1983: 107).

All this takes place among the subjects themselves, but it may also take place between the researcher and the subjects studied. The researcher 'participates', observes and asks questions; and this *questioning*, both through informal conversation and formal interviews,

is used as an investigative tool alongside observation. Participant observation implies both looking and asking, and informal conversation aimed at eliciting information and understanding the subject's views and motives is just as much a part of the researcher's arsenal as the formal interview.

Clearly, the interview situation differs from that of the informal conversation and is, in a sense, 'artificial' in that the role of the researcher is all too evident. Indeed, the fact that he is obviously an outsider may make the observation itself less natural. Nevertheless, as Hammersley and Atkinson state, 'The distinctiveness of the interview setting must not be exaggerated, and it can be viewed as a resource rather than as a problem ... to the extent that the aim in ethnography goes beyond the provision of a description ... There may be positive advantages to be gained from subjecting people to verbal stimuli different from those prevalent in the setting in which they normally operate' (1983: 119).

The interview can also be used autonomously as a tool for data collection in social research. This issue will be dealt with separately in the next chapter. The reader should, however, be aware of the fact that it is widely used in the field of participant observation.

5.   RECORDING OBSERVATIONS

In every type of scientific research, whether in the natural sciences or the social sciences, the process of recording observations is of fundamental importance. In the case of participant observation, this basically involves writing up notes day by day. The result is a sort of ship's log in which everything that the researcher has observed during the course of the day will be meticulously recorded, along with his personal reflections. This record is an integral part of participant observation. Indeed, as the Loflands point out, 'Aside from getting along in the setting, the fundamental concrete task of the observer is the taking of field notes. If you are not doing so, you might as well not be in the setting'. They also specify that *the logging record is, in a very real sense, the data ... the data are not the researcher's memories ... the data consist of whatever is logged* (Lofland and Lofland, 1995: 67, 89). Hammersley and Atkinson (1983: 150) suggest that, if the observation is too exacting and leaves little time for writing up notes, the researcher should alternate periods of observation and writing, so as not to risk neglecting the latter.

Needless to say, relying on the memory to store data is completely unacceptable, as this will almost certainly lead to error. There are obvious limits to the amount of information that the human brain can memorize and, more importantly, our memory is highly (and unconsciously) selective, which means that memorized material is very likely to be distorted. For instance, the researcher's memory may retain material that is in line with a certain interpretation and remove material that would contradict this interpretation. If, however, the material is recorded immediately after it has been collected, the risk of such distortion is greatly diminished.

The researcher's daily notes arise out of the interaction between the observer and the situation observed; they will therefore consist of two basic components: the *description* of facts, events, places and persons; and the researcher's *interpretation* of these events together with his reactions, impressions and reflections. The dual nature of this process – objective representation and subjective comprehension – needs to be emphasized. Clearly, it is not easy to keep these two components separate; even the most 'objective' description will necessarily be influenced by the observer's cultural slant (cf. Geertz, 1973). Ethnographic recording constitutes the first formalization of the meeting between two cultures: that which studies and that which is studied. The researcher must be aware of this fact, and this awareness must orient the way in which notes are written up and the material observed is organized.

The act of recording observations will be examined further by splitting it into its three constituent parts: 'when' to record, 'what' to record, and 'how' to record it.

When   As soon as possible. As time passes, the vividness of the event will tend to fade and new events will tend to obscure older ones. Ideally, notes should be taken as the events occur, but this is not normally possible. It is obviously impossible when the observation is covert, but even when overt observation is undertaken it will be difficult to take notes without disturbing the environment studied. It is advisable for the observer to carry a notebook at all times and to take brief notes (for instance, slipping away for a few moments on some pretext), which will be written up at a more appropriate time; alternatively, she could carry a portable tape-recorder, perhaps equipped with a small hidden microphone, to record her impressions during the course of observation. In any case, all ethnography manuals suggest – or rather prescribe – keeping a daily log of events, in which the observer arranges the material gathered during the day, notes his own observations, and takes stock of the situation.

What   We have already mentioned that the researcher's notes should include (a) a description of events and (b) his own interpretation of them. To these we can add a third component: (c) the interpretations of the subjects studied. The description of events must be detailed and contain all relevant particulars. Clearly, not everything can be described, and the observer will have to be selective. However, especially at the beginning, descriptions should be extensive and cover as much as possible of the situation observed. Subsequently, the focus of the analysis will probably become more restricted, but this process of narrowing down will only take place as the research proceeds. Moreover, the focus of attention may shift during the course of the investigation; it is therefore advisable to keep the field of observation as broad as possible in the early stages.

The researcher's interpretation will generally be made up of two parts: theoretical reflections and emotional reactions. The former are directly linked to the primary objective of the observation and constitute an early attempt to glean material and ideas – which would largely be lost if they were not recorded immediately – to be incorporated into the final report. The latter component, however, which involves the researcher's own feelings, must not be overlooked. Participant observation requires an involvement on the part of the researcher which goes beyond the purely intellectual commitment; indeed, emotional participation is one of the means through which understanding can be achieved. Expressing and recording one's own feelings, therefore, constitute not only a form of analysis that is useful in maintaining self-control during the course of the field-work, but also provide documentation that can be used *a posteriori* to reconstruct the relationship that grows up between the observer and those observed. Moreover, through critical reassessment of the data collected, such reconstruction may also enable us to pick out possible distortions generated by the researcher's emotions.

The third aspect of this documentation involves the subjects' own interpretations, as they emerge from comments overheard, from informal conversations with the observer and from more formalized interviews. This aspect is far from secondary. As Hammersley and Atkinson point out, 'the accounts produced by the people under study must be treated in exactly the same way as those of the researcher' (Hammersley and Atkinson, 1983: 126).

How These three components of the notes – descriptions, observer's interpretations and subjects' interpretations – must be kept clearly distinct. The detailed account of an event must be kept separate from the researcher's comment. Moreover, within the researcher's comment, theoretical reflections must be clearly separated from emotional reactions. Finally, the interpretations expressed by the subjects involved must be clearly attributed to the individuals who make them, and not merely lumped together into one confused mass. In registering notes, therefore, the first principle is *separateness*.

The second principle is *accuracy*. This is especially important when the notes concern the subjects' own comments: the expressions they use, including slang, must be quoted exactly. Indeed, the lively speech of a protagonist is likely to be very different from a bland summary written by the observer. In this regard, taping formal interviews can be very useful. The tape-recorder should, however, be used with caution, as it will tend to exacerbate the artificial nature of the formal interview. It is therefore advisable to tape interviews only when there is firm trust between the interviewer and the interviewee, and only when the role of the researcher has already been fully accepted by the community being studied.

Again with regard to 'how', we should mention the technology that is now available to the researcher engaged in observation. The traditional means of audio-visual recording (photography and voice recording) have been supplemented by the video camera, which has opened up new horizons in observation. Moreover, the widespread use of personal computers and the creation of software specifically designed for the management of ethnographic observations now enable the researcher to organize data more efficiently, to read summarized accounts of events, to connect heterogeneous materials that have points in common, etc.

6. ANALYSIS OF EMPIRICAL MATERIAL

The analysis of the empirical material collected and the writing up of the final report are probably the most difficult tasks of research conducted through participant observation. It is through the analysis of empirical documentation that we take the delicate step from the language of the 'natives' to the conceptual categories of sociological theory.

While it is true that the aim of participant observation is to comprehend the point of view of the 'natives', such research also has the objective of bringing out aspects that the natives themselves are unaware of. According to Van Maanen, the observer has to view the social situation from two angles. One is the view from within, or *insider perspective*, which 'compels a researcher to actually enter the world of the studied and attempt to come forth with a close reading of that world in terms of the interpretive standards found there (as embedded in the actions, language, symbolic forms, and emotions of the studied)' (Van Maanen et al., 1982: 17). The other is the *outsider perspective*, which tries to highlight those aspects of the social world studied that are unknown to the protagonists themselves.

Analysing and interpreting empirical material is clearly arduous whatever technique of data gathering is used. However, as already mentioned, the lack of standardized procedures in qualitative research means that the success of this phase of the study will depend heavily on the ability of the individual researcher. Moreover, in the case of participant observation, the work will be complicated even further by the enormous amount of material collected, which is often heterogeneous and fragmentary, and which the researcher may find very difficult to cope with.

Methodology manuals generally provide practical rules on how to organize empirical material, and advise the student to draw up classifications, diagrams, schemes etc., in order to summarize the material and draw general conclusions. Advice of this kind has commonly been given since the 1980s, when the growing popularity of qualitative research ran up against the lack of standardized procedures, thus leaving many an inexperienced researcher at a total loss.

However, I remain to be convinced that such efforts have been in any way useful. Often, what is provided is merely a 'cook book' offering almost laughably banal suggestions; others are frankly irritating, in that they can make no better recommendation than to ape quantitative research procedures of statistical origin. Participant observation is characterized by a relationship of empathy between the researcher and the social reality observed. In this relationship, the individuality of the subjects involved is crucial, and it is the particular interaction that takes place which constitutes the main source of sociological 'comprehension'. Consequently, we can offer only a few general guidelines on how to analyze data and draw theoretical implications.

First of all, we can say that analysis of the data gathered through participant observation is a *continuous* process, and is partly carried out during the course of the observation itself.[1] This interweaving of observation and analysis is, in fact, indispensable, in that amassing large amounts of data without pausing to reflect is likely to produce disorderly heaps of material that will be difficult to cope with. By contrast, analysing data as they are collected, and formulating preliminary theoretical considerations, can help the researcher to see more clearly, to identify preferential channels of observation, and to begin the process of focusing on the main issues. Data analysis therefore has *retroactive* and *cyclical* features; as theoretical reflection proceeds, it goes back to observations already analysed and re-examines them in the light of new acquisitions or re-utilizes empirical material in new interpretations located at a higher level of abstraction, thus linking different levels of analysis.

A common problem that the researcher involved in participant observation will inevitably have to face is what Lofland called the 'agony of omitting'. The pathway of analysis taken in participant observation is rather like a funnel, in that the focus of the analysis narrows progressively. This inevitably involves increasingly drastic selection, and much of the material collected will have to be discarded. As Lofland points out, it is often the researcher's favourite material, the insights he regards as most felicitous, that has to be set aside. On this point, however, the researcher must make no concessions; it is more important to maintain a firm line of argument and a compelling style in his treatise than to indulge in digressions that may well provide a wealth of insights, but may also cause the reader to lose the thread of the analysis.

Description In practical terms, the first phase tackled by the researcher – in each of the topics dealt with – is the description. In the field of social research, description is often regarded as the poor relation of explanation, and particularly causal explanation (which, according to the positivist approach, is the only path to true scientific knowledge). In participant observation, however, description takes on the status of a full 'scientific product'; it is fundamental to sociological comprehension and not merely a background scenery used to highlight more noble structures are to be built.

In participant observation, the description is not simply a sensory account of what the observers sees and hears; it must be what the anthropologist Clifford Geertz quaintly called a 'thick' description. In other words, what the researcher sees and hears (which would constitute a 'thin' description) must be enriched with meanings and interpretations, and be recorded within a cultural and historical context and within a network of social relationships. Geertz writes, 'Consider two boys rapidly contracting the eyelids of their right eyes. In one, this is an involuntary twitch; in the other a conspiratorial signal to a friend. The two movements are, as movements, identical ... ; yet the difference, however unphotographable, between a twitch and a wink is vast' (Geertz, 1973: 6). A *thick description*, then, is one which is enriched with meaning; but that meaning is often equivocal in that 'the ethnographer is in fact faced with ... a multiplicity of complex conceptual structures, many of them superimposed upon or knotted into one another (1973: 10). Thus the anthropologist's description is itself an account of a complex plot that is open to different interpretations: it is 'thick'.

Furthermore, the description produced by the participant observer is a genuine 'construction', resulting from the assembly of different materials: 'narratives' (yielded by in-depth interviews, life stories, live recordings), newspaper reports, texts of speeches, documentary material of every kind, etc., in addition to the visual accounts of the social environments, events and persons observed. Even in this respect, it is never a pure description; every choice of material to be included is based on an implicit interpretation, and even the simplest visual description involves a specific cultural slant.

Classification The phase that follows description is classification. In observing the social world, the physical appearance of environments and groups, individual and collective behaviour, single acts and complex actions, the researcher will pick out both temporal recurrences and similarities among various objects that will enable him to draw up classifications. In Chapter 2, Section 3.4, we mentioned the process of classification in qualitative research: how types are picked out and typologies constructed; some examples were also given. We will now return briefly to this question.

Perhaps the simplest form of classification is that of establishing the time sequence. In their research on prisons in Italy, Ricci and Salierno (1971) broke down the process of prison entry into a sequence of elementary steps that remained almost the same in all cases examined: arrest, transportation to police headquarters, fingerprinting, notification of the arrest warrant, transportation to the prison, ritual entry through the reception area, 'matriculation' (the bureaucratic procedure of assigning an inmate number), body search, the issue of blankets and mess tin, and solitary confinement. The authors interpret these sequential acts as successive steps in the process of de-personalizing the inmate, who is stripped of all personal possessions in order to be transformed from an individual with a name into an anonymous recluse identified by a number.

Identifying time sequences involves breaking up a continuous flow of events into blocks separated in time. Another method of classification – the method most closely linked to the common meaning and etymology of the term ('divide into classes') – involves arranging a mass of different objects into classes according to their similarity/dissimilarity. A wide range of social objects can be classified in this way: persons, behaviours, institutions, events, etc.

An example of the classification of behaviour is provided by the research conducted by Walum (1974) into the 'changing door ceremony'[2] that takes place whenever two strangers try to walk through the same door at the same time. Walum studied this ceremony in a particularly meaningful circumstance: when the two strangers are of different gender; this situation involves values such as masculinity and femininity, initiative and passivity, conformism and non-conformism, and even, in certain periods and environments, political ideology. Walum observed how this ritual was enacted in the doorways of the American college where he taught, and classified the subjects observed into five types according to their behaviour: the 'confused' (who do not know what to do and end up bumping into each other), the 'testers' (who are aware of what the ritual implies in terms of interaction between the sexes and use this to challenge one another),[3] the 'humanitarians' (who open the door for the other person in order to be helpful or just courteous, regardless of the other person's gender), the 'defenders' (who know that the etiquette of door-opening has changed but refuse to accept the change), and the 'rebels' (who deliberately break the current rules).

Dimensions of typologies The process of classification often produces a 'typology', e.g. a set of types, ideal models of the different situations observed (in the examples just mentioned, we have seen five 'types' of 'door ceremony'). The various types are generally identified by the observer on the basis of personal assessment of similarity/dissimilarity, through a synthetic and intuitive mental process. Proceeding in his analytical and conceptual reflection, the researcher will now attempt to reveal the conceptual structure of classification by identifying the characteristics that distinguish the various types from one another.

An example can be seen in the research into work organization conducted by Rothschild-Whitt (1979). He observed six labour co-operatives operating in southern California and compared their organization and working methods with the traditional structure of work organization in western society. He identified eight dimensions in which the two models differ: authority (vested either in individuals at the head of the organization or in the collective), rules (either formalized and defined in detail or minimal and established case by case), social control (entrusted either to designated controllers or to the collective), social relations (either impersonal or personal), hiring (based either on pre-established rules or on personal connections), incentive structures (either monetary or moral), social stratification (either hierarchical or egalitarian), and division of labour (either with separation between manual and intellectual work, or with different combinations of tasks assigned to the same persons).

This process of identifying the dimensions of a typology enables us to reveal the conceptual structure of the classification and to arrive at the theoretical abstractions, or *ideal types*, that were mentioned in the first two chapters of this book.

Cultural themes Perhaps the most general way of dealing with the material collected through participant observation is to identify what Spradley calls the 'cultural themes' running through the society studied. He points out that the research of the participant observer must always move on two levels: 'One examines small details of a culture and at the same time seeks to chart the broader features of the cultural landscape … statements that convey a sense of the whole' (Spradley, 1980: 140). Spradley takes up the concept of the cultural theme from the anthropologist Morris Opler, who used it to describe the culture of the Apaches. In Opler's study, one of the cultural themes was that 'the men are physically, mentally and morally superior to the women', and this tacit premise was one of the bases of their view of the world and underlay much of their behaviour in the social and family sphere.

Returning to a familiar example, one of the cultural themes discerned in the world of the gangs studied by Sánchez-Jankovski (1991) was what he defined as the 'Darwinian view' of social relationships. According to this view, life is a continuing struggle for survival; each day sees competition for the scarce resources available, every companion is looked upon as an enemy, and only the strongest and those who act according to the principle of *mors tua vita mea* survive.

Identifying cultural themes is one of the ultimate goals of anthropology-based studies and, once picked out, the theme often sheds light on the entire research. This was the case of the previously mentioned research conducted by Edward Banfield in the 1950s in a village in Southern Italy. Banfield identified a cultural trait of *amoral familism* which pervaded every ramification of the life of the local people, and which consisted of their total inability 'to act together for their common good or, indeed, for any end transcending the immediate, material, interest of the nuclear family' (Banfield, 1958: 10). This is a cultural theme that runs through the whole of Banfield's analysis, and is used by the author to interpret a wide range of observations: there are no voluntary charitable organizations in the village; even the Church leads a wretched life (few attend Sunday Mass, almost only women, scant offerings in the collection plate); political parties are almost entirely absent; there are no voluntary associations (except for a recreational club that is no more than a venue for card-players); initiatives taken by the professional classes in the interests of the community come to nothing (though they have an interest in good road communications, shopkeepers have never taken any steps – not even a letter from any individual to the provincial authorities – to urge improvements in the lamentable road system). The examples are innumerable.

Naturally, the researcher is not always able to find a cultural theme strong enough to interpret such a wide range of observations. Nevertheless, the fact remains that the analysis of empirical material has to move from the specific to the general, by proposing general explanations that stem from the specific situations observed.

Style of writing   We will conclude this section with a note on the style of writing used in the concluding report of a study conducted through participant observation. Two adjectives are generally used to describe this way of writing: *reflexive* and *narrative*.

Participant research is 'reflexive' in the sense that the researcher is a part of the world he studies. Therefore, just as the entire path of the participant observer's research is neither impersonal nor neutral, the style of writing is also closely linked to the personality and culture of the researcher. This differs markedly from the style of the survey (the prototype of quantitative research). In the survey, results are presented in an impersonal, formal style, and the third person of the verb is generally used. In participant observation, the style is more informal and impressionistic, and the first person is used. Moreover, the ethnographic report is not written as a final and separate phase of the research, after data collection and analysis (as is the case in quantitative research). Indeed, some of the writing is done, as we have already seen, during the course of the observation itself, through the writing up of notes, etc. The final product, therefore, is partly an assembly of these texts. Thus, the researcher's feelings and personal reactions become a living part of the written account.

The concluding report of a study conducted through participant observation is often accompanied by an autobiographical appendix in which the researcher gives an account of his personal experience: what prompted the research, how the specific case was selected, access to the group, acceptance, cultural mediators, informers, problems encountered, development of theoretical reflections, changes in perspective, etc; it will also include his emotional reactions, the mistakes made and the difficulties that arose. As well as providing information, this account will have methodological utility. Since this kind of research bears the marks of the researcher's subjective decisions, this reconstruction can help the reader to assess the validity of the work, to interpret the meaning of its conclusions, to estimate the possible effects of distortions caused by the action (indeed the very presence) of the observer, to understand how far a result enables generalizations to be made, or is conditioned by outside constraints that make it a unique case.

The style must be 'narrative' – that is to say, close to the literary style of an account or a newspaper story, and therefore far removed both from the conceptual abstraction of a theoretical elaboration and from the arithmetical abstraction of quantitative research. The narrative style is a concrete and direct way of writing; it includes detailed descriptions and integral accounts of events, presents characters just like those in a story, and reports samples of the protagonists' direct speech. As Spradley explains, 'In our field-notes we identify an infant with a specific name, held by a specific mother, nursing at that mother's breast, at a specific time and in a specific place' (1980: 162). The participant observer does not want to attach a general identity to the subject observed, by discarding his local and personal connotations; on the contrary, it is this specific and unrepeatable nature of the concrete situation which enables the researcher to achieve comprehension and to communicate that comprehension to the reader.

The writer should describe the social situation in a 'natural' way, almost as if 'telling a story' (Van Maanen, 1988). His objective is to get across to the reader as much of his observational experience as he can; by producing an account that is rich in colour and feeling, he will enable the reader to conjure up a detailed image of the culture observed. Hammersley and Atkinson, for instance, point to the literary affinities between Malinowski's work and the novels of Conrad, and between the writings of reformers and scholars of English urban life at the end of the nineteenth century, such as Booth and Rowntree, and the novels of Dickens. Of course, as Hammersley and Atkinson add, 'what is normally thought of as 'story-telling' is only a part of the ethnographer's task. He or she is, to one degree or another, also engaged in the explication of theory, the development of causal models, and the construction of typologies' (1983: 210). Indeed, while much of the corpus of the ethnographic account is made up of 'thick description', we should not lose sight of the fact that the ultimate goal of social research – and therefore also of participant observation – is to work out some form of generalization. The level of analysis, at least in the concluding stage of the report, must therefore rise above the particular, in order to identify typologies and cultural themes, and to formulate theories.

7. OBSERVATION IN MICROSOCIOLOGY

7.1 From the study of 'others' to the study of 'ourselves'

Before leaving the issue of participant observation, we will look at some developments of the observational method that are not always grouped under the more general heading of ethnography-based participant observation, but which nevertheless spring from the same origin and share several of the features of its empirical procedures.

As has been amply pointed out, the technique of participant observation grew up within anthropology as a tool for studying and describing a culture that was 'different' (from that of the observer). In its early applications within the field of sociology, participant observation maintained its original features as a technique for studying 'other' cultures. From the study of primitive tribes, it was extended to the study of 'urban tribes', but continued to focus on those who were 'different'. These were segments of society that lay outside the mainstream and whose subculture was distinct from the dominant culture, whether they were social groups (youth gangs, religious sects, ethnic minorities, deviant groups, etc.) or territorial communities (slums, urban neighbourhoods, provincial towns, etc.).

However, as the focus of study gradually shifted from distant tribes to those closer to home, it soon became apparent that the method could be used not only to study 'others', but also to study ourselves. Moreover, it was realized that any field of human activity that had its own cultural specificity could be analysed through the ethnographic approach and participant observation. Indeed, just as youth gangs or football fans have their own subculture, so also can subcultures be identified within hospitals, business organizations, political parties or professional associations.

At the same time, it gradually became clear that not only the organized aspects of our social life have their own culture; even the most mundane routine activities, mechanical everyday behaviour, carry a hidden culture and are loaded with implicit meanings that even the performers themselves are unaware of. Within a branch of sociology, a challenge gradually emerged: that of 'giving serious sociological attention to seemingly mundane events and activities ... By the very act of making trivia a topic of study and recognizing its prevalence and importance in everyday life, (these) sociologists ... change the very thing they seek to study. That is, trivia is no longer trivial; it now becomes important' (Schwartz and Jacobs, 1979: 183).

We will not attempt to make a detailed analysis of the currents leading up to what is sometimes called *microsociology*, in that it deals with 'relatively small slices of space, time, and numbers of persons: with the individual and the interaction, with behavior and consciousness' (Collins, 1988: 3). We will merely mention the fact that the early writings of George Herbert Mead and Herbert Blumer in the 1930s helped to open up this interest in the minute details of social life. Blumer applied Mead's teachings to social research, thus giving rise to the school of

symbolic interactionism. The core of his approach lies in the importance he attached to the process of interpretation. He claimed that human behaviour was determined by the various *meanings* that things and persons conveyed (a woman may be a mother or a shop assistant; a chair may be something to sit on or an object to admire; a school means different things to teachers, pupils, parents, clerical staff and those without children). These meanings stem from the way in which people act towards those things or persons; each meaning is not individual, but social, and is learnt by the individual through the process of social *interaction* with his fellows; what we call 'culture' is nothing other than a set of shared meanings. Finally, these meanings are absorbed by the individual through a process of *interpretation* of the social phenomena that surround him, a process which depends on the individual's cultural premises.

This approach is perfectly in line with the methodological premises of participant observation, which arise out of the need to grasp the meanings that individuals attribute to their actions, and to see the world through their eyes. At the same time, focusing the analysis on verbal and non-verbal communication, on the definition of situations, and on the mechanisms of interpretation, involves meticulous reconstruction of social interactions, which prompts the researcher to shift his attention towards small events rather than broad social processes.

This shift towards the analysis of everyday life was given a powerful boost in the 1960s and 1970s by the work of Erving Goffman. He dealt mainly with social interaction and its rituals, and strove to identify models, by analysing what happens in offices, kitchens, formal dinners, conversations, etc. He also studied behaviour in public places (what people do in a launderette, how they pass each other in the street, the way they dress and adorn themselves, etc.). In what is probably his most famous book (Goffman, 1959), he used the theatre as a metaphor for life, seeing life as a series of plays complete with actors and audiences; formal dramas are played out on the stage, while informal interactions take place behind the scenes. As an example, he points to workers who act in a certain way in front of the boss and then stop acting as soon as he goes away. Just like those workers, judges, doctors, students and the rest of us all have our moments in the spotlight and behind the scenes. According to Goffman, all social life is guided by rituals, from casual conversation to etiquette, to the most intimate personal relationships. Violation of these ceremonial roles is interpreted by society as a sign of mental illness.

7.2 Ethnomethodology

This concentration on the minute interactions of daily life reached its peak with *ethno-methodology*, a term[4] coined by Garfinkel in the 1940s and derived from the Greek words *éthnos* (people), *méthodos* (method) and *lógos* (speech). The term refers to the 'analysis of the ordinary methods that ordinary people use to perform their ordinary actions' (Coulon, 1995: 2). Just as ethnobotany and ethnomedicine study the ways in which various cultures classify plants or practise medicine, ethnomethodology is the study of the methods and practices used by ordinary people to decipher the world, to give it a meaning, and to perform any action; it is the study of 'practical reasoning', 'the science of everyday life'.

According to this approach, everyday activities are regulated by well-defined norms governing the interaction among people. These are implicit norms, of which the subject – the individual human being – is unaware, even as he conforms to them. In order to bring such norms to light, these scholars proposed that these tacit conventions be broken. Thus, so-called ethnomethodological experiments were worked out. These involved such ploys as moving excessively close to a person during conversation, drinking out of other people's glasses at the table, talking to oneself in the street, taking off one's shoes in a formal business meeting, etc. According to these researchers, the embarrassment, or even patent annoyance, aroused by such behaviour pro- vides explicit confirmation that the behaviour

in question has violated an implicit norm governing social interaction.

The approaches that we have briefly out- lined here – symbolic interactionism, Goffman's contribution and ethnomethodo- logy – display common features as well as marked differences. In particular, they all take everyday actions as their *object* and set their *objective* as that of interpreting these actions on the basis of a process that could be called 'making a problem of the obvious'.

This line of investigation yielded new mate- rial for study and opened up new research horizons in sociology, and in particular in research conducted through observational techniques. However, returning to our start- ing point – that is to say, our reflection on par- ticipant observation – it should be pointed out that often these studies do not make full use of this technique; as we will see from the following examples, observation is often carried out without participation.

Among the studies most directly inspired by Goffman's theories, we can quote the work of Adam Kendon (1990) on how people behave in close-range encounters. Starting from the consideration that the eyes are an eloquent means of communication, he investi- gated the role that they play in conversations between two persons. Conducted towards the middle of the 1960s, Kenton's research involved the audio-visual recording of half- hour conversations between couples of people facing each other. These recordings were used to track eye movements during the conversation and to correlate them with the content of the conversation.

Another study by Kenton looked at how people greet each other. Observation was car- ried out at private garden parties, where greetings between hosts and guests, and among the guests themselves, were video- taped. Kenton writes: 'in the manner in which the greeting ritual is performed, the greeters signal to each other their respective social status, their degree of familiarity, their degree of liking for one other, and also, very often, what roles they will play in the encounter that is about to begin' (1990: 154).

Quarrelling has also been the subject of study. This kind of interaction takes place in all social contexts (at home and at work), between persons of all ages (whether children or adults), and at all levels of intimacy (lovers or strangers). Although the situations in which quarrels arise may vary considerably, it is not difficult to pick out common structures. Indeed, the different phases of the conflict – opening, reasoning, denials, accusations, threats, challenges, apologies, negotiations, closing – tend to follow the same basic order.

Allen Grimshaw (1990) compiled a collection of studies on quarrelling, which included research by Corsaro and Rizzo (1990) into quarrels between children aged from 3 to 5 years. Conducted through field observation and conversations recorded in an American and an Italian infant school, this study revealed similarities and differences between the two infant cultures. Grimshaw's collection also reports a study on family quarrels, in which the conversations of 64 American families of different social classes and races were recorded at the dinner table (Vuchinich, 1990). The study identified five ways in which conflicts are brought to an end: one of the parties gives in; a third person in a position of authority (usually a parent) intervenes; a compromise is reached; the quarrel is interrupted (e.g. by some external factor); one of the parties withdraws (e.g. by refusing to argue further and leaving the table, etc.). Clearly, the aim of the research is to pick out recurring models, the analysis being conducted through the classic method of identifying patterns that can be generalized.

Further examples can be seen in studies on collective behaviour. Heritage and Greatbatch (1986) studied how applause is elicited by analyzing recordings of 476 political speeches delivered at party congresses in Britain in 1981. By analyzing the parts of the speeches followed by applause, these authors were able to identify the rhetorical devices (the structure of the argument, sequences of affirmative and negative statements, tone of voice, pauses, etc.) used by the speakers to elicit applause. They discovered that, three-quarters of the time, applause followed seven clearly distinguishable rhetorical devices, regardless of the content of the statements and the political party involved.

On a very similar theme, Clayman (1993) examined how audiences show disapproval (booing) by analysing political speeches in the US and Britain. This author looked at the various phases of the phenomenon: precursors to the open expression of disapproval (murmuring, sporadic whistles, etc.); the beginnings and build-up of dissent (starting with a small group and spreading through the audience, the reactions of faithful supporters, etc.), and the speaker's reactions (explicit defence, silence, changes in tone of voice, attempts to carry on regardless, etc.).

The ethnomethodological approach to revealing the rules and the hidden structure of everyday behaviour can also be seen in studies on how people move in the streets. When people walk along a busy city street, the manoeuvres they use to avoid bumping into others seem to be part of a set of natural behaviours. Indeed, they are governed by precise rules, which are learnt at an early age (the anthropologist Lyn Lofland points out that one of the classic ways in which the cinema portrays the 'country boy' is through his inability to negotiate city crowds without bumping into people). Various studies have focused on this issue, including one by the British researchers Collet and Marsh (1974), who set up a television camera in a building overlooking Oxford Circus in London to record the movements of pedestrians crossing the street below. Their observation consisted of picking out two people walking towards each other and filming all their movements, from the approach on a collision course to the moment when they pass and subsequently walk on. By analyzing the various manoeuvres involved, these researchers were able to codify the moment when the two pedestrians pass, and to classify body movements (of the shoulders, arms, head) and dynamic features (lines of approach, time taken, passing on the right or left, etc.). Among other things, they discovered that men and women behave differently (men usually face the other person as they pass, while women tend to turn their backs; women make greater use of their arms as a protective barrier, etc.). They also examined bodily communication – that is to say, a whole range of mainly subliminal messages (the unconscious signalling of one's intentions, movements in response to these signals, the role of glances, etc.) that trigger the kind of coordinated mass movement (the 'dance of the pedestrians', as the authors call it) that is manifested by a crowd crossing the street.

Another classic theme in studies of this kind is queuing. Mann regarded people waiting in a queue as 'an embryonic social system ... the queue culture provides direction on such matters as place-keeping privileges, sanctions against pushing in, and rights of temporary absence from the waiting line' (1969: 340). He observed very long queues in various cultures: sports fans in Melbourne queuing up for football final tickets (in 1965, 25,000 people queued for 12,500 tickets, some for over a week); the weekly queue for tickets outside New York's Metropolitan Opera House; queues outside house rental agencies in Tokyo; at bus stops in London; at transport booking agencies in Mexico; outside food shops in Russia and Cuba, and wash-houses in Nigeria.

Mann analysed queuing from various points of view: the self-organization of the people when the queue lasts for some days; the sanctions imposed on those who violate the rules; the 'commerce' that springs up around the queue (people who are paid to queue up on behalf of others; children charging people a few cents to count the number of those in front of them, etc.); the reasons why people stay in the queue even when there is no hope (as in the case of the interminable line of children outside a Melbourne cinema waiting for the Batman T-shirts that would be handed out to the first 25), and so on. Moreover, the author discerned a link between the way of queuing and the degree of egalitarianism and social order in the national culture, and concluded that in England the 'democratic queue' was actually a 'way of life' (Mann, 1973: 56).

A particular area in which research inspired by ethnomethodology flourished – almost to the point of becoming a field in itself – is the analysis of conversation. This starts from the premise that conversation is one of the most common forms of interaction between individuals, and that, like all forms of interaction, it does not take place haphazardly; rather, it follows a set of unspoken rules and standard patterns, of which the interlocutors themselves are unaware, and which are an integral part of the culture to which they belong. The analysis of conversation aims to uncover this underlying structure by breaking down the conversation into elementary units and identifying typical sequences of the various stages.

In order to do this, a transcription technique has been worked out. In addition to transcribing the text of the conversation, this technique utilizes special symbols to represent such forms of communication as emphasis, tone of voice, pauses, interruptions, unfinished words, overlapping of sentences, sighs, murmurs, etc. By breaking down conversations in this way and analysing the various stages, such studies have shed light on some recurrent structures: rules governing whose turn it is to speak, ways of opening and closing conversations, ways of correcting oneself and one's interlocutor, how sympathy, involvement or disinterest are shown, implicit and rhetorical questions, and the differences among the various types of conversation (informal between friends, formal at a business meeting, asymmetrical between judge and accused, doctor and patient, etc.).

It will not have escaped the reader that this 'microsociological' research is far removed from classic research based on participant observation. The difference is seen not only in the content (here deliberately limited to small everyday actions), but also in the procedures used; the analysis of ordinary behaviour and interactions is often based on *pure observation*, on the reconstruction of a social mechanism made up of elementary actions, rather than on *participant* observation aimed at grasping the individual's subjective perception. Nor will the reader have overlooked the thread that links this approach, which attempts to discover the hidden meaning of tiny common practices (like crossing the road), to the study of the meanings, values and cultural themes that underlie more complex behaviours (like voting or taking part in a religious service). This link justifies placing this issue in the present chapter.

8. A FINAL NOTE: LIMITS AND RESOURCES

Needless to say, the technique of participant observation is not free from problems. Three of these are: (a) subjectivity; (b) non-generalizability; and (c) non-standardization.

Subjectivity (of the researcher) It has been said that in participant observation the observer is the *instrument* of research, in that all observations are filtered through his eyes, senses, sensitivity and ability to identify with the subjects studied. In addition to such strictly personal conditioning, we should also mention cultural conditioning. In the words of Spradley, ethnographic research is a 'a culture studying a culture' (1980: 13); and, as such, its results will depend not only on the culture studied, but also on the culture that is studying. As the anthropologist Clifford Geertz maintains, 'what we call our data are really our own constructions of other people's constructions of what they and their compatriots are up to' (Geertz, 1973: 9). In other words, when the ethnographer describes another culture, he also describes himself; the questions he asks, his selection of facts, and the interpretations he gives depend on his point of observation and on the windows that he opens in his mind. If an Indian and a Norwegian observer were to be faced with the same object of study (for instance, a motorway being built through a jungle or in a Berber village), they would undoubtedly give extremely different descriptions of it.

Non-generalizability (of the cases studied) The subjectivity of the researcher is not the only obstacle to making generalizations from data collected through participant observation; another problem is the subjectivity of the cases studied. Participant observation usually involves one case or a few cases; such research is intense but small-scale. This has given rise to accusations that such studies focus on situations that represent only themselves: 'Because their results describe unique phenomena, not classes of phenomena, their conclusions cannot be applied to any group other than the one investigated' (Borman et al., 1986: 48).

Non-standardization (of the procedures used) As was pointed out at the beginning of this chapter, it is difficult to describe, much less teach, the technique of participant observation, on account of the lack of universally applicable standardized procedures and the specific nature of each pathway of research. For the same reasons, such studies are not reproducible. Indeed, if the researcher changes, so also will the subjects and the settings observed, the modes of observation, the sequence of recordings, the data-gathering procedures, and therefore the very characteristics of the empirical material used. And without reproducibility, we lack one of the basic requisites of scientific research (as it is traditionally understood).

Thus, in participant observation, the subjectivity of the observational process, the uniqueness of the case studied and the irreproducibility of the pathway followed constitute a *limit*. At the same time, however, they constitute a *resource*. Indeed, this technique does not suffer from an 'objectivity complex'. On the contrary, it affirms the value of its own subjectivity, maintaining that comprehension can be achieved only through personal involvement, and that true knowledge emerges only from direct experience. It should also be added that even those who do not share this view, or who subscribe to a different epistemological vision, cannot deny that studies inspired by the ethnographic method have made a valuable contribution to social research.

Finally, it is worth mentioning a somewhat peripheral aspect of participant observation: the *difficulty of implementation*. Participant observation requires a large investment in terms of time and psychological resources. It takes time to understand the pattern of other ways of thinking, to grasp the values, norms and codes of communication of another culture. And not everybody has the time. As John Madge points out, 'It has never been easy to induce people to become participant observers. They must be dedicated to research, free from domestic ties or other responsibilities' (1962: 217). It is therefore no coincidence that among the finest pieces of sociological research conducted through participant observation we find a good number of studies derived from doctoral theses; that is to say, studies that stem from fieldwork carried out when the authors were young and had plenty of time (and enthusiasm).

In terms of psychological resources, the investment is equally onerous. Fieldwork necessitates involvement with the social situation studied and its protagonists. This may place on the researcher an emotional strain that is difficult to bear. Therefore, in addition to being psychologically resilient, the researcher has to be able to keep his feelings under control and to handle difficult interpersonal relationships.

Furthermore, during the course of participant observation, the researcher may have to cope with his own isolation. As already mentioned, the researcher is the instrument of the research, in that everything is channelled through his personal ability to see and understand; he must therefore bear the entire burden alone. Since there are no pre-set routes or statistical procedures to guide and support him, and no standardized models to shore up his weaknesses, he may fall prey to feelings of loneliness, disorientation and confusion.

SUMMARY

1. Participant observation is a research strategy in which the researcher enters directly and for a relatively long period of time into a given social group in its natural setting, and establishes a relationship of personal interaction with its members in order to observe their actions and understand their motivations, through a process of self-identification. In participant observation *involvement* and *identification* are not to be avoided; indeed, they are actively pursued (whereas *objectivity* and *distance*, which were basic features of the neopositivist approach, are no longer considered desirable).

2. Participant observation is usually employed for studying two kinds of groups: small, autonomous societies located in specific territories and possessing a culturally closed universe (*community studies*); and sub cultures that arise within specific sectors of a complex society, which may represent aspects of the dominant culture or be in conflict with it (*subculture studies*).

3. In participant observation the researcher may openly declare at the outset her true objectives, that she wishes to be part of a given social group not because she agrees with its goals, but only to study it (*overt participation*); or she may infiltrate the group by pretending to join it and being a member just like any other (*covert participation*). To gain access to the field of study, the researcher often resorts to the services of a *cultural mediator*. A cultural mediator is a person who is trusted by the target population and, because of his cultural characteristics, is also able to understand the motivations and the necessities of the ethnographer. *Informants* (or *key informants*) are 'insiders' whom the observer uses to acquire information and interpretations from within the target culture.

4. In order to understand 'what to observe', potential subjects of observation can be classified into the following areas: physical settings, social settings, formal interaction, informal interaction and interpretations of social actors.

5. In participant observation the process of recording observations is of fundamental importance. When should observations be recorded? As soon as possible. What should be recorded? Descriptions of events, the researcher's interpretations, the interpretations of the subjects studied. How should this information be recorded? By applying criteria of *separateness* (between descriptions, observer's and subjects' interpretations) and *accuracy* (in reporting subjects' comments, viewpoints, etc.).

6. When he analyses the empirical material, the researcher must engage in the following activities: description, classification, identification of the dimensions of typologies (this process reveals the conceptual structure of the classification and helps formulate theoretical abstractions, or *ideal types*). The most general way of dealing with the material collected through participant observation is to identify *cultural themes* that run through the society studied.

7. Participant observation developed within anthropology is a tool for studying 'other' cultures. From the study of primitive tribes, it was extended to the study of 'urban tribes', but continued to focus on those who were considered 'different'. Later it was realized that any field of human activity that had its own cultural specificity could be analysed by means of the ethnographic approach and participant observation. *Microsociology* is the study of small everyday actions; and *ethnomethodology* is the study of the methods and practices used by ordinary people to decipher the world, give it meaning and perform actions. Everyday activities are regulated by well-defined (implicit) norms governing interaction among people. *Ethnomethodology* attempts to unveil and study such norms.

FURTHER READING

P. Spradley, *Participant observation* (Holt, Rinehart & Winston, 1980, pp. 195),

J. Lofland and L.H. Lofland, *Analyzing Social Settings* (Wadsworth 1995 2nd ed., pp. 186) and M. Hammersley and P. Atkinson, *Ethnography: Principles in Practice* (Routledge, 2nd ed. 1995, pp. 312) are three classic texts that introduce readers to ethnographical approaches to social research in a manner that combines theoretical concerns and practical suggestions.

N. Denzin, *Interpretive Ethnography: Ethnographic Practices for the Twenty-first Century* (Sage, 1997, pp. 326) offers a discussion of recent trends and a post-modern perspective.

An interesting treatment of ethnographic social research, developed from a 'positivist' standpoint, is J. Goldthorpe, *Sociological Ethnography Today: Problems and Possibilities*, in Goldthorpe (2000).

Finally, D.W. Maynard and S.E. Clayman, 'The Diversity of Ethnomethodology', *Annual Review of Sociology 1991*, is an introduction to ethnomethodology. For a more exhaustive treatment see J. Heritage, *Garfinkel and Ethnomethodology* (Polity Press, 1984, pp. 336).

NOTES

1. This is the basic idea underlying *grounded theory*: observation and theoretical elaboration go hand in hand in a continuous interaction that has no 'before' or 'after'.

2. The concept of social ceremony was formulated by Goffman (1967).

3. A typical exchange might be: 'Female: Well, aren't you going to open the door for me?. Male: I didn't know that girls still like for boys to do that. Female: I'm not in Women's Lib.' (Walum, 1974: 512).

4. The term should not be interpreted as 'ethno-methodology' (the methodology of ethnology), but as 'ethnomethodo-logy', the study of 'ethnomethods', i.e. the methods of interpretation and action used by various peoples in everyday life.

10   The Qualitative Interview

Qualitative interviews, no differently from surveys, attempt to collect data by asking people questions pursuing, however, the typical goal of qualitative research of exploring the interviewee's individuality and seeing the world through his eyes. This chapter illustrates the differences between qualitative and quantitative interviews; it then describes the various types of qualitative interview, how to conduct such interviews and the stages through which they are carried out. The chapter finally offers suggestions concerning how to analyse the material collected with this technique.

1. COLLECTING DATA BY ASKING QUESTIONS

The qualitative interview can be seen as the verbal counterpart to participant observation, the former involving questioning and the latter involving observing. In participant observation, the researcher strives to identify with the subjects studied and thereby to see the world through their eyes. With qualitative interviews the researcher strives for the same

goal. It should be pointed out, however, that the qualitative interview cannot offer that same depth of penetration. Nevertheless, its basic objective remains that of *grasping the subject's perspective*: understanding his mental categories, his interpretations, his perceptions and feelings, and the motives underlying his actions.

The qualitative interview can be defined as a conversation that has the following characteristics:

- it is elicited by the interviewer;
- interviewees are selected on the basis of a data-gathering plan;
- a considerable number of subjects are interviewed;
- it has a cognitive objective;
- it is guided by the interviewer;
- it is based on a flexible, non-standardized pattern of questioning.

We will now examine the various features of this definition. First of all, the interview is elicited by the interviewer; in this respect, it differs from chance conversation. This is not to say that casual conversations cannot provide valuable information for the social researcher; on the contrary, the participant observer makes ample use of such conversations in order to reach a fuller understanding of the social reality in which she is immersed. However, the qualitative interview is something different; it is a conversation that is explicitly requested by the interviewer (the meeting generally taking place by appointment).

Second, subjects are selected for interview on the basis of a systematic data-gathering plan, meaning that they are chosen according to their characteristics (e.g. their belonging to certain social categories or having been through some particular experience). Moreover, these subjects must be fairly numerous (as a general indication, at least some tens[1]) in order to yield information that can be generalized to a larger population (though the intention is not to construct a truly statistical sample).

In conducting qualitative interviews, the researcher pursues a cognitive objective. Our definition therefore excludes the psychiatrist-patient interview (which has a therapeutic objective) and the job interview (for purposes of selection).

Finally, the qualitative interview is not an ordinary conversation, a normal dialogue between two evenly-matched individuals; rather, it is a guided conversation in which the interviewer establishes the topic and ensures that the interview is conducted according to the cognitive aims set. The interviewer may impart guidance at various degrees, but will substantially allow the interviewee to structure his answer, or even the entire conversation, as she thinks fit (unlike the case of the survey and the questionnaire).

2. QUANTITATIVE AND QUALITATIVE INTERVIEWING

The last point mentioned lies at the core of the distinction between the quantitative and qualitative approaches to *questioning* human

beings in order to obtain knowledge of society. Indeed, information can be gathered through questioning by means of two instruments: the standardized questionnaire (with rigidly structured questions and answers) and the 'free' interview (which does not have a preconceived rigid scheme).[2] These two techniques are only apparently similar; in their substance they are very different, in that they are backed by two philosophies of research – two paradigms – that differ markedly.

In our discussion of surveys in Chapter 5, we mentioned the fundamental differences between these two approaches to social research. We will now return to these in greater detail, this time starting out from the characteristics of the qualitative interview.

2.1 Absence of standardization
As has already been said, this is the basic difference between the questionnaire and the interview, and it is from this difference that all the others arise. While the questionnaire attempts to place the subject within the researcher's pre-established schemes (the answers to a closed question), the interview is aimed at revealing the mental categories of the subject, without reference to preconceived ideas. As Michael Patton puts it, 'The purpose of qualitative interviewing is to understand how the subjects studied see the world, to learn *their* terminology and judgements, and to capture the complexities of *their* individual perceptions and experiences. ... The fundamental principle of qualitative interviewing is to provide a framework within which respondents can express *their own* understandings in their own terms' (Patton, 1990: 290; original italics).

The quantitative approach, whose instrument is the questionnaire, forces the respondent to limit his answers. If he wishes to qualify his ideas, for example, to explain why – on the basis of his personal experience – he thinks that hospitals should be run privately rather than publicly, he is not allowed to do so. His personal reflections on the issue are not considered to be relevant and are not recorded by the interviewer, who simply wishes to know whether he is 'strongly, somewhat, not much or not at all' in favour of privatizing the health service. If the respondent wants to expound at length on some topic that he feels strongly about and on which he has worked out firm convictions, or if he prefers to skate over an issue that does not interest him or on which he doesn't have an opinion, he is prevented from doing so, as the structure of the questionnaire is inflexible; the interviewer has to ask all respondents the same questions, without skipping any or introducing new topics. Likewise, the interviewee cannot steer the conversation round to topics that are better suited to his personality and experience.

In all these cases, the interviewer's voice prevails over that of the interviewee. In the qualitative interview, by contrast, notwithstanding the interviewer's task of establishing the topics of conversation, *the dominant voice is that of the respondent*. In the extreme case (and in some respects the ideal case), the interviewer will speak very little; he will merely prompt and encourage the respondent, who will be totally free to express his thoughts, motivations and points of view as he wishes.

If the goal is to *grasp the subject's perspective*, then it necessarily follows that the interview relationship must be an individual one; the data-gathering tool must therefore be flexible enough to be adapted to the personalities of the different respondents. The interviewee must be given complete freedom of expression, so that he can bring out his own point of view using his own mental categories and his own language. In short, interviewing tools cannot be standardized to any great extent.

2.2 Comprehension versus documentation (context of discovery versus context of justification)

Questioning can be regarded both as a means of collecting information and as a means of understanding social reality. The quantitative approach uses questioning in order to collect information on people, their behaviour and social features. If the information we need could be recorded in some other way, for example, by photographing the person, we could replace the questions with photographs. By contrast, the qualitative approach does *not* use the interview – in the first instance – to gather information on people, but to understand them from the inside.

The difference between these two approaches – which can be seen as the difference between quantity and quality, between breadth and depth – also has implications for the number of subjects to be interviewed. Let us suppose, for example, that we wish to study the phenomenon of street crime – bag-snatching, theft, minor assault, vandalism – in a city neighbourhood, and that our aim is to assess its quantitative incidence: the most common types of crime and the social strata affected. Since many minor offences (such as the theft of a bicycle, attempted bag-snatching or shoplifting) are not reported to the police, they can only be recorded by questioning people. In this case, questioning is used to gather data. A sample of citizens will be asked whether, in the last few months, they have been the victims of any of the crimes listed, and so on. Alternatively, with regard to the same issue, we might decide to use questioning not to quantify this kind of crime but to investigate its consequences on the citizens' sense of security, faith in public institutions, degree of apprehension, fear and anxiety, and changes in habits. In other words, the aim is not to collect data, but to grasp the citizens' own perceptions of this social phenomenon.

In the first of these two cases, an extensive collection of data will be undertaken (a sample of at least some hundreds of subjects will be interviewed), as the aim is to obtain a representative picture of the social situation and then to analyse the data by means of statistical instruments. In the second case, recording will be carried out in greater depth; a single subject with whom the interviewer has been able to establish a relationship of fruitful empathy may be worth more, in terms of understanding and interpreting a certain social phenomenon, than dozens of questionnaires.

The distinction between the objective of data collection and that of understanding social reality brings us to Reichenbach's distinction between the *context of discovery* (the moment when a new idea is conceived) and the *context of justification* (the moment of empirical testing) (1951). When standardized questioning is carried out, the dominant context is that of justification; if the respondent is asked why she agrees or disagrees with the death penalty, and is required to choose a reason from a list of response alternatives, then the researcher presumably believes that he knows enough about the phenomenon to have been able to draw up a complete list of all possible responses, and therefore intends only to 'record the data', in order to quantify the weights of the different alternatives and to correlate the answers with other variables.

If, on the other hand, the researcher does not know the reasons why people agree or disagree with the death penalty, and wishes to 'discover' these reasons through questioning, she will use a non-standardized form of interview; in this case, her primary objective will be to *understand* the phenomenon studied. However, *this latter objective does not exclude the former*; as we will see later, there are research situations in which the qualitative interview is *also* used to gather data on the social reality studied. Nevertheless, the *principal objective* remains that of understanding, and the quantitative data gathered will constitute a by-product, eviscerated and impoverished in order to make them amenable to comparison and weakened by the modest size of the sample.

2.3 Absence of a representative sample

Another difference between the questionnaire and the interview arises out of the two points mentioned above: that of the sample. A fundamental requirement of questionnaire-based research (i.e. surveys) is that it must be carried out on a 'representative' sample – that is, a sample constructed in such a way as to reproduce the characteristics of the population on a small scale.

The qualitative interview does not aspire to this objective. Even when interview subjects are picked out systematically (and we will see some examples later), this procedure stems more from the need to cover the range of social situations than from the desire to reproduce the features of the population on a small scale. Not that this is an undesirable objective; rather, it would prove to be merely fanciful and, in any case, given the small size of the sample, unattainable. Studies based on qualitative interviews often involve samples of about 100 cases, far too few to be representative.

If the sample does not have to be representative, then there is no need to adopt a strategy of random selection of subjects for inclusion. The selection procedure is generally carried out as follows. A few (normally from two to four) variables relevant to the issue under investigation are identified and a table is drawn up containing cells generated by the intersection of the columns and rows corresponding to the values of the (nominal) variables. For each cell generated in this way, the same number of subjects will be interviewed. For example, if the variables selected are gender, age (youth, adults, senior citizens) and education (lower, higher), their combination will generate 12 cells, for each of which we will interview the same number of people (e.g. 10 young, uneducated males, and so on, up to 10 older, well-educated females, for an overall total of 120 cases). The subjects will be chosen according to the criterion of quota sampling; this means that, within the constraints imposed by the quota, the interviewer will be free to choose which subjects to interview.

For example, in Alberoni's study of militants in the Communist and Christian Democrat parties in Italy in the 1960s (Alberoni et al., 1967) 108 activists were interviewed according to a sampling design based on the variables 'party' (dichotomic: Italian Communist Party and Christian Democrats) and 'city of residence' (considering six different cities). The intersections between these two variables generated 12 cells (2×6); nine subjects were allocated to each cell, for a total of 108 interviews (54 per party, 18 per city).

Once it had been established that nine militants from each of the two parties had to be interviewed in each city, the interviewer was given the freedom to pick out these subjects.

Similarly, in a study conducted in the US in the 1980s (Riessman, 1990) on the personal and social reorganization of life following divorce, 52 men and 52 women were interviewed; in each group of subjects, 1/3 had been separated for less than one year, 1/3 for between one and two years, and 1/3 for between two and three years.

It should be noted that the sample generated by this procedure does not reproduce the characteristics of the population. However – as first mentioned in Chapter 2, Section 3.2 – the qualitative researcher does not follow a criterion of statistical representativeness, but rather one of substantive representativeness, in that the aim is to cover all the social situations that are relevant to the research, rather than attempting to reproduce the characteristics of the population in full.

Very often, however, no sampling design is drawn up in advance in qualitative research. While the researcher nevertheless follows a criterion in selecting the subjects to be interviewed, this may be a criterion of relevance which is built up during the course of the research itself. The researcher will choose subjects not on the basis of their distribution in the population but on account of the interest that they seem to hold, an interest which may, moreover, change during the course of the research. Sometimes a predefined systematic plan of sampling may be rendered impossible by the very nature of the issue under investigation, on account of the rarity of the phenomenon or the difficulty of identifying *a priori* which subjects are of interest to the research.

In her study of how women react to the experience of divorce, Terry Arendell (1986) initially tried to follow a classic sampling procedure, by collecting the names of 200 divorced women from the registers of two American courts and sending out letters to these women. However, since this strategy yielded only 20 suitable cases, she was forced to adopt a less systematic procedure; only by placing advertisements in strategic locations (local newspapers, nurseries, churches, companies employing female staff, etc.) was she able to reach her goal of 60 interviews.

Sometimes – especially if a 'clandestine' population is being studied – the technique of 'snowball' sampling is adopted. In his research on crime, Barbagli (1995) determined to interview criminals (particularly thieves and fences), subjects who, for obvious reasons, are difficult to identify (unless they are prison inmates, who in any case constitute a particular selection of the reference population; moreover, the condition of imprisonment will make it difficult to obtain a sincere interview). The author nevertheless managed to interview 65 criminals, who had been picked out by means of snowball sampling starting from the personal acquaintances of the interviewers, who had had previous contact with the criminal underworld.

2.4 Case-centred approach versus variable-centred approach

From these points, it follows that the researcher's interest focuses on the understanding of social facts on the basis of an overall interpretation of the phenomena and, especially, of the subjects studied. Since this issue has already been amply discussed in Chapter 2, Section 3.3, it will be recalled only briefly here. In analysing the data yielded by qualitative interviews, individuals are not broken down into variables and then studied in this form. Frequencies and correlations are not produced; rather, *stories are reconstructed*. As we have already pointed out, the objective is not to pick out the relationships among variables, but to understand individual manifestations. The intention is to reconstruct models, typologies and sequences of the basis of cases analysed in their entirety. The starting point (both of data analysis and of theoretical reflection) is the individual, not the variable.

3. TYPES OF INTERVIEW

Interviews differ in terms of their degree of standardization – that is to say, the varying degree of freedom/constraint placed on the two participants, the interviewer and the respondent. The distinction has already been made between standardized instruments (questionnaire) and non-standardized instruments (interview) in data collection through questioning. However, this distinction needs to be examined in greater depth, particularly with regard to the interview. A characteristic of the interview is that it is an open instrument; it is flexible, adaptable to the various empirical contexts and can be shaped during the course of interaction. However, it has varying degrees of flexibility. Three basic types of interview can be distinguished: *structured*, *semi-structured* and *unstructured*. These are examined below.

3.1 Structured, semi-structured and unstructured interviews

Structured interviews   These are interviews in which all respondents are asked the same questions *with the same wording and in the same sequence*. The 'stimulus' is therefore the same for all respondents. Interviewees are, however, completely free to answer as they wish. To return to a distinction introduced in Chapter 5, the interview is, in effect, a *questionnaire with open questions*. Although answers are freely expressed, and even if the interviewer is careful to 'let the interviewee speak', the mere fact that the same questions are asked in the same order introduces a considerable degree of rigidity into the interview.

Throughout this volume, a clear distinction has always been made between quantitative and qualitative methods, in that they are derived from two different paradigms and are therefore somewhat incompatible. Nevertheless, it should be pointed out that the structured interview constitutes the most genuine – and probably the only – example of a technique which seeks to mediate between the two approaches. The fact that questions are

pre-established places serious limitations on the objective of flexibility and adaptability to the specific situation analysed, which is one of the presuppositions of the qualitative approach. On the other hand, the respondent's freedom to answer as he wishes is in line with the tenets of this paradigm. Similarly, the fact that open answers can be (and usually are) coded in a data-matrix – as we will see shortly – is a typical feature of quantitative techniques. At the same time, however, they are analysed as integral texts, without being reduced to general categories which is a typical mode of qualitative analysis.

The structured interview is therefore a somewhat hybrid technique, in that it offers the standardization of information required by the 'context of justification', while remaining receptive to those unknown and unforeseen elements that belong to the 'context of discovery'. This attempt to meet the needs of both objectives simultaneously means, of course, that neither is met fully. Indeed, the structured interview offers a lesser degree of standardization than the questionnaire, and at the same time is unable to probe as deeply as the unstructured interview. However, this very ambivalence is an advantage when the researcher does not want to discard the objective of standardization of results – that is to say, of 'gathering data' in order to describe a given social phenomenon quantitatively – but, at the same time, does not know enough about that phenomenon to be able to utilize a classic questionnaire with closed questions.

A researcher might choose to make use of structured interviews for three reasons. One of these is the extreme *individuality of the situations* investigated. When each situation differs from the others, the researcher will be prevented from drawing up an exhaustive range of response alternatives before conducting the interview. An example is provided by a research project carried out in the UK in the 1960s and 1970s (Newson and Newson, 1978). This study focused on ways of bringing up children and involved a sample of 700 mothers living in the Nottingham area, who were interviewed on three successive occasions:

when the child was one, four and seven years old. Table 10.1 reports a brief extract, taken from the third wave of interviews, on the theme of discipline and punishment. In one question, designed to pick out the main areas of friction between mother and child, mothers were asked 'What about disagreements? What sort of things make you get on each other's nerves now, you and your child?' Clearly, such a question cannot be 'closed' in advance, as all the possible points of conflict cannot be foreseen.

On other occasions, the researcher may opt for the structured interview not because she knows little about the issue under investigation, but because *it involves so many aspects* that an exhaustive list would have to contain an infinite number of response categories. Questions such as 'What were your mother's greatest faults?' or, to return to the Newsons research, 'How you feel about smacking children of his age?', are liable to generate such a variety and complexity of answers that it would be totally unrealistic to try to draw up an exhaustive list of response alternatives.

Finally, the researcher's choice of the structured interview may be dictated by the *respondents' level of education*. We might think, for example of a study involving elderly peasant women in which the researcher wants to reconstruct their lives around the time of their marriage (meeting their future husband, engagement, dowry, wedding reception, honeymoon, cohabitation with the family of origin, etc.); or of a study involving primary schoolchildren and their relationship with school (an extract from the latter can be seen in Table 10.1).

In all the above situations, it is not difficult to conduct an interview that resembles a natural conversation, with questions being followed by free answers; by contrast, it would be difficult to implement an unnatural format in which the answers are to be chosen from a list of predetermined alternatives. It should be borne in mind that, while the question may be easy for the interviewee to understand (e.g. the question 'Could you tell me why you go to school?' in Table 10.1), understanding the

response alternatives is much more difficult, in that this requires a good capacity for abstraction; moreover, the predetermined alternatives may be worded according to mental categories that are remote from those of the respondent.

Semi-structured interviews   When conducting a semi-structured interview, the interviewer makes reference to an 'outline' of the topics to be covered during the course of the conversation. The order in which the various topics are dealt with and the wording of the questions are left to the interviewer's discretion. Within each topic, the interviewer is free to conduct the conversation as he thinks fit, to ask the questions he deems appropriate in the words he considers best, to give explanations and ask for clarification if the answer is not clear, to prompt the respondent to elucidate further if necessary, and to establish his own style of conversation.

The interviewer's outline may contain varying degrees of specification and detail. It may simply be a checklist of the topics to be dealt with, or a list of questions (usually of a general nature) having the goal of supplying the interviewer with guidelines. Table 10.2 shows a few extracts taken from two outlines of structured interviews. The first was used in the study *The Party Activist* mentioned earlier (Alberoni et al., 1967). This part of the interview deals with 'the activist's political commitment'. As can be seen, the outline consists solely of the headings of the topics to be covered during the course of the interview. The second outline is taken from the study *Getting a Job*, which explored the strategies used by the respondents in order to find a job, with a view to gauging the importance of personal contacts, and in particular 'weak' and less structured contacts (Granovetter, 1995).

This way of conducting the interview gives both the interviewer and the respondent ample freedom, while at the same time ensuring that all the relevant themes are dealt with and all the necessary information collected. The interviewer's guidelines draw the

TABLE 10.1   *Examples of structured interviews and subsequent coding*

a)   *Extract from interviews with 700 mothers on their relationships with their 7-year-old children* (Newson and Newson, 1978)

156.   What about disagreements? What sort of things make you get on each other's nerves now, you and N?
157.   Do you find that N takes a long time over doing as you ask him?
158.   What do you do if he is being very slow over this sort of thing?
159.   What happens if he simply refuses to do something you want him to do?
160.   How do you feel about smacking children of his age?
161.   Do you think parents should try to do without smacking altogether, or do you think smacking is a good way of training children?
162.   In general, do you think smacking has good results with children of this age?
163.   Any bad results?
164.   What effect does smacking have on you? Do you feel relieved or upset in any way (or is it part of the routine)?

Coding of questions 160–163

1.   Generally approves of smacking
2.   Thinks it unfortunate but necessary
3.   Generally disapproves of smacking

Coding of question 164

1.   Unemotional – just routine
2.   Feels relieved
3.   Feels guilty or upset

b) *Extract from interviews with children* (Capecchi and Livolsi, 1973)

2.1   Do you like going to school?
2.2.1   What do you like best about school?
2.2.2   What do you like least about school?
2.3   What is the best thing and what is the worst thing about your teacher?
2.4   Why do children go to school? (investigate whether for educational-cultural reasons, to learn a trade, out of duty)
2.5   Is there anything you'd like to do at school that you can't do now?
2.6   Are you made to do things at school that you'd rather not do?

Coding (attitude toward school)

1.   Rejection of school (specify reasons)
2.   Little or no participation
3.   Passive acceptance of school
4.   Keen acceptance of school (specify reasons for liking to go to school)

boundaries within which the interviewer is able to decide not only the order and the wording of the questions but also which themes to investigate in greater depth. While the interviewer will not generally tackle issues that are not laid down in the guidelines, he is nevertheless free to develop any themes arising during the course of the interview which he deems important for a fuller understanding of the respondent, even if these have not been raised in other interviews. This flexibility, albeit within a predetermined scheme, is not provided by the structured interview.

Unstructured interviews   In the structured interview, the questions are predetermined both in content and in form. In the

---

TABLE 10.2   *Extracts from outlines of semi-structured interviews*

a) Extract from interviews with party activists (Alberoni et al., 1967)

Concerning 'the activist's political
commitment'

1. Joining the party:
– image of the party
– how the activist was introduced to the party
– type of initial involvement (gradual or sudden)
– subsequent phases of commitment

2. Indoctrination:
– sources of training (courses, conventions,
   basic texts, official documents,
   university faculty, etc.)
– duty to undergo doctrinal training
– choice of current (for Christian Democrats)

3. Proselytism:
– field of activity
– occasions
– ways and means
– duty and meaning of commitment to proselytism

4. Times, places and ways of exercising
   political commitment:
– during the day
– during the week
– during the year
– at election time

5. Characteristics of a good activist

6. Integration in the party:
– practical meaning and rewards of political
   commitment
– sharing of the party's objectives and
   procedures
– interpersonal relationships within the party

Note. The extract reported here represents about 1/5 of the complete outline; the other parts concern the activist's family background, personal experience, habitual behaviour, conception of the party and conception of society.

b) Extract from interviews about job finding and career patterns (Granovetter, 1995)

. . .

2. Was there a point in your previous job when you *decided* to look for a new one, or did something just 'come along'?

3. How did you find the job you hold now?

Ascertain also:
  – if R searched, did some search methods fail to turn up offers?
  – where offers made and rejected in roughly the same period as the accepted one? How
    did they arise?

. . .

5. When you took your job, do you know whether you replaced anyone in particular? (If not, probe to determine exactly how the new job was created).

. . .

7. The job you held before your present one – do you remember how you found that? (trace complete work history backwards like this, to the first full-time job. If too many jobs, find out about first full-time job and one or two longest duration; estimate total number.

. . .

---

semi-structured interview, the content, but not the form, of the questions is predetermined. In the third case, that of the unstructured interview, neither the content nor the form of the questions is predetermined, and may vary from one respondent to another.

The characteristic feature of the unstructured interview lies in the individual nature of both the issues discussed and the dynamics of the interview. The interviewer's only task is to raise the topics that are to be dealt with during the conversation. Thus, the interviewer might elicit conversation on consumer spending, how to bring up children, involvement in politics, the practice of religion, or whatever theme has been chosen for investigation. The respondent will be allowed to develop the chosen theme as he wishes and to maintain the initiative in the conversation, while the interviewer will restrict himself to encouraging the respondent to elucidate further whenever he touches upon a topic that seems interesting. Naturally, the interviewer will also have to exercise a degree of control by leading the respondent back to the point if he begins to digress towards subjects that have nothing to do with the issue under examination. For instance, in an interview concerning work, the respondent might go on to discuss at length such aspects as work practices, relationships on the job, remuneration or career prospects, according to where his own interest takes him; but the conversation will still be about work and not, for example, about dating women. Should the respondent go off at a tangent, the interviewer will bring him back to the main theme.

Though the basic theme of the conversation has been chosen beforehand, unforeseen sub-themes may nevertheless arise during the interview. If these are seen to be relevant and important, they will be developed further. Thus, different interviews might emphasize different topics. Moreover, some respondents have more to say than others; some are more outgoing, while others are more reserved. In addition, the empathetic relationship that is built up during the course of the interview varies from case to case; some interviewees will get on the same wavelength as the interviewer, develop a relationship of trust with him and reveal their innermost feelings and personal reflections, while in other cases this mechanism is not

triggered. It therefore follows that the interviews will have an extremely individual character and will differ widely in terms of both the topics discussed and the length of the interview itself.

An example of the use of unstructured interviews can be seen in the research conducted by Judith Wallerstein and Joan Kelly (1980) on the adaptation processes implemented by ex-spouses and their children following divorce. The interviews were something akin to those conducted in clinical assessment and dealt with a wide range of basic issues (financial and working conditions during marriage, the causes of the break-up, how the decision to divorce was taken, how the family was prepared for the divorce, relationships between parents and children during the marriage and after the divorce, and the present financial and working situation). However, the way in which these issues were handled depended on the natural evolution of the interview rather than on any constraints imposed by the interviewer. Thus, some interviewees talked in greater detail about financial problems or the relationships with their families of origin, while others dwelt on the question of their children's upbringing or of professional self-fulfilment.

Finally, it should be noted that, in order to allow the respondent to express himself as freely as possible, the timing of such interviews will be determined by the respondent himself; the interview may last several hours, be conducted in successive sessions, or even take on the features of an autobiographical account.

How to choose? The choice among these three types of interview will depend on the *research objectives* and the *characteristics of the phenomenon studied*. In the first example reported (that of the mother-child relationship), the researchers could have chosen the unstructured interview rather than the structured interview, thereby allowing the mothers to talk freely about the various aspects of their relationships with their children. In this study, however, the researchers also wanted to quantify the social phenomena and to correlate the variables – e.g. they wanted to analyse any differences that might emerge among mothers of different social classes and to ascertain whether the mothers behaved differently according to whether the child was male or female. For this reason, the structured interview was chosen. Indeed, this technique enables a larger number of cases to be studied (in this example, some 700 mothers) and comparisons to be made, as the interviews have a common base. In this study, the choice was determined by the research objectives.

A case in which the choice of interview was dictated by the nature of the issue investigated is that of the research by Terry Arendell on divorced women. The researcher began her work of data collection through a sort of structured interview in which, as she herself states, 'the instrument listed all the basic questions I wanted to ask in the formal interview; however, I quickly found that strict adherence to its structure tended to interfere with the interviewee's train of thought'. Therefore, having revised the concept of the interview as a 'social process (with) not wholly predictable dimensions', she decided to adopt an unstructured approach, though ensuring that 'each of the particular areas covered by the instrument were discussed at some point in each interview' (Arendell, 1986: 164).

If the research design envisions interviewing a large number of subjects, numerous interviewers will be required, which means that a structured approach will have to be adopted. As we will see later, the interviewer plays a crucial role in the qualitative interview, in that his relationship with the respondent will strongly influence how the conversation unfolds. If the interviewers are numerous, it will be necessary to limit the subjectivity of this relationship by obliging them to adhere to a pre-established scheme that is common to all; this may even mean conducting structured interviews in which the format of all the questions is predetermined.

Finally, it should be added that the distinction between semi-structured and unstructured interviews is somewhat blurred, the real difference being between these two and the structured interview. When the interviewer is provided with a schematic outline of the interview, it may be difficult to say whether the relationship is semi-structured or unstructured. If, on the other hand, a series of predetermined questions is used, then what we have is clearly a structured interview, in which the respondent is closely guided by the interviewer.

3.2 Special cases

Non-directive and clinical interviews In the three types of interview described so far, interaction is in some way guided (or at least controlled) by the interviewer, who establishes the topics and the bounds of the conversation, if nothing else. In the non-directive interview, however, not even the topic of conversation is pre-established; the interviewer simply follows the interviewee, who is free to lead the conversation wherever he wishes, and the very fact that the interviewee raises one topic rather than another is taken as a diagnostic element. The interviewer therefore does not know where the conversation will lead; to return to a previous example, the interviewee may begin by talking about work and end up by talking about dating women. This type of interview originated in dynamic psychology and psychotherapy, in which its purpose is to help the patient bring to light deep-seated, and even subconscious, feelings.

The *clinical interview* is different in that it is closely guided by the interviewer (psychologist, doctor, social worker). Its aim is to examine the personal history of the individual, by means of an in-depth interview not unlike the unstructured interview illustrated earlier, in order to reconstruct the pathway that has led to a certain outcome, for example, deviant behaviour such as drug use, delinquency, etc.

In both these types of interview, the objective is therapeutic rather than cognitive. They are used not so much to gather information on a given social phenomenon as to delve into the patient's personality. For this reason, non-directive and clinical interviews are of no great concern to the sociologist, who wishes to understand social phenomena rather than to penetrate deeply into the structure of the interviewee's personality. As McCracken puts it, the sociological interview 'departs from the "depth" interview practiced by the psychological inquirer in so far as it is concerned with cultural categories and shared meanings rather than individual affective states' (McCracken, 1988: 7).

Interviews with key informants In the various types of interview presented so far, the persons interviewed are themselves the object of the study. If we wish to study political militants, we interview militants; if we wish to study delinquents, we interview delinquents. We may, however, decide to interview individuals who are not a part of the phenomenon under investigation, but who have special expertise or knowledge of that phenomenon. On account of their privileged observational position, these subjects are called 'key informants'.

For example, in his research on criminals, Barbagli (1995) interviewed not only 65 convicted criminals but also 28 other subjects, including lawyers, magistrates, police officers, bank managers, etc. These were interviewed because their professional experience brought them into close contact with crime and criminals. Likewise, in their study of a therapeutic prison in UK, devoted to providing therapeutic treatment of offenders with mental disorders, the authors interviewed, besides 640 inmates (the principal unit of analysis of their study), various prison staff members such as social workers, warders, doctors and psychologists, etc., whose professional roles endowed them with a profound knowledge of the object of the research (Genders and Player, 1995).

Sometimes, the key informant is a member of the population under investigation, but occupies a particular position within that population. This would be the case, for instance, of an opinion leader or a community leader, who is interviewed because she reflects the opinions of the group to which she belongs. Alternatively, the key informant may have a thorough knowledge of the object of

the study on account of his own personal experiences; in the study on prisons, particular attention was devoted to interviewing long-term inmates who had amassed a rich and varied knowledge of the prison system throughout their years spent in various penitentiaries.

Key informants are often sought out during the preliminary phase of research, when the boundaries of the object of study are yet to be established. They are often used in this exploratory function in quantitative research, too; for instance, before drawing up a questionnaire for use in a survey, the researcher may wish to analyse the phenomenon under investigation by first interviewing those who know it well.

One case in which key informants play a particularly important documentary role is when the research is of the ethnographic type. As we saw in the previous chapter, this kind of research is based chiefly on participant observation, though it is integrated by interviews with so-called 'informants' – characters who are typical of the social environment observed, group leaders and so on, who are literally 'privileged observers'. The term 'ethnographic interview' has been coined for this type of interview, though the model is clearly – to use our terminology – that of the unstructured interview. In such cases, the interviewee is allowed to talk at length, though the interviewer needs to be skilful in prompting the witness to explain himself clearly, to provide further detail, and to elucidate on matters that may seem obvious to him but not to the interviewer, in order to make him reveal all he knows.

Clearly, interviews with key informants are absolutely heterogeneous; each one is unique and has its own development and its own focus. This stems from the fact that the subjects interviewed are very diverse, and each has a different story to tell; we need only look back to the list of subjects interviewed in the above-mentioned research on crime (from lawyers to bank managers) or on prisons (social workers, prison chaplains, probation officers, etc.).

Focus groups So far, we have only discussed interviews with individuals. If, for example, we are interviewing a political party activist, and we wish to find out how he divides his time each day among family, work and the party, the fact that his wife is present at the interview may constitute an element of disturbance and distortion. In certain cases, however, interaction – particularly among members of a group – may produce deeper discussion, thereby aiding the researcher's understanding. For example, in order to understand soccer violence, it may be useful to bring together a group of 10 hard-core fans and discuss the causes of violence with them. Such discussion may uncover motivations that would not emerge in individual interviews. Moreover, group discussion may be better able to reveal the intensity of feelings, thus facilitating comparisons among different positions. For instance, motivations linked to competition among the various groups of supporters of the same team might prove to be much stronger than those linked to hostility towards opposing teams; this aspect would probably not emerge from interviews with individuals (which would reveal whether one motivation is more widespread than another, but would indicate little of their respective intensities). By contrast, the heated exchanges that would be likely to arise among the participants in a collective discussion might well expose the emotive charge present in conflicts among groups operating on the same territory.

Very often, as pointed out by Herbert Blumer, one of the theoreticians of qualitative research, 'a small number of such individuals, brought together as a discussion and resource group, is more valuable many times over than any representative sample. Such a group, discussing collectively their sphere of life and probing into it as they meet one another's disagreements, will do more to lift the veils covering the sphere of life than any other device that I know of' (Blumer, 1969: 41).

Group interviews were first proposed in a systematic fashion in the social research carried out by Merton et al. (1956), who coined the term *focused interview* (hence *focus group*). They write, 'First of all, the persons interviewed are known to have been involved in a *particular situation*: they have seen a film, heard a radio program ... taken part in a social situation (e.g. a political rally, a ritual or a riot)' (1956: 3). On the basis of their common experience (which may even be devised by the researcher, as, for example, in the case of a film shown to a number of subjects), the individuals are interviewed in a group by an interviewer who has previously studied the situation under examination and whose task is to lead the discussion in such a way as to reveal the subjects' different interpretations, emotional reactions and critical judgements; the debate is therefore focused on a precise event.

Group interviews date back a long way in the social sciences; apparently they were used by Malinowski (1922) in his anthropological research. This technique was also used by Merton et al. (1956) to study the impact of political propaganda, and now finds broad application in market research, in which 'focus groups' are used to assess consumer reactions to new products, advertising campaigns, etc. A focus group is generally made up of about 10 people, a number which is large enough to encompass various viewpoints and yet small enough to allow all the participants to interact. The discussion is led by a professional interviewer, who has thoroughly analysed the topic in advance. In guiding the debate, the interviewer will do his utmost to bring out all aspects of the question and to regulate the interaction of the participants (by preventing the more assertive members of the group from monopolizing the discussion and by encouraging the more reserved individuals to take part, while at the same time taking care not to stifle the free expression of the participants). In general, the researcher will try to form a group of fairly homogeneous subjects (in the example of soccer violence, groups of football hooligans; in a discussion of how citizens have perceived the President's address to the nation, separate groups of blue-collar workers, white-collar workers, housewives, students and so on will be formed). A further requisite is that all participants must be familiar with the question under discussion.

Finally, the cost-effectiveness of the group interview should not be underestimated, in that 10 people can be interviewed in approximately the same time as it would take to interview one person. Naturally, the product is different; individual data cannot be gathered in group interviews. To return to a dichotomy introduced at the beginning of this chapter, the group interview is a valuable tool for understanding the phenomenon under investigation rather than for documenting it.

4. CONDUCTING INTERVIEWS

Conducting a good qualitative interview is a difficult art. The problem is not merely one of getting the subject to agree to be interviewed and to answer questions sincerely. The most difficult part is 'getting the interviewee to talk' – that is, eliciting a fluid account in which the interviewer restricts himself to listening and occasionally to asking for clarification or to steering the conversation cautiously back to its central issues. It is a matter of gaining access – if not to the inner mind – then at least to the sphere of the interviewee's feelings and to his most genuine thoughts. It should be pointed out that in the psychotherapy interview this deep access is generally easier to achieve, in that it is the patient himself who wishes it; in the case of the interview conducted for cognitive purposes, however, even gaining the subject's confidence may prove very difficult. In order to obtain the interviewee's full cooperation, the interviewer has to be able to establish a relationship of trust, not as a professional but as a person. This is no easy thing to do, given the very limited time available; indeed, the interview is often conducted in a single session and sometimes without any preliminary preparation (unlike the psychotherapy relationship, which is built up over a long period and through numerous meetings).

The qualitative interview does not simply involve recording information; it is a process of social interaction between two individuals. Consequently, it is difficult to lay down general rules on how it should be conducted, in that the way it develops is strongly influenced by subjective components. We will therefore restrict ourselves to making a few suggestions.

Preliminary explanations The problem of making contact with the subjects and persuading them to agree to being interviewed was raised in Chapter 5, Section 7. As was pointed out, the main difficulty is that of overcoming the individual's initial diffidence and insecurity in the face of a new and unknown situation. In the case of the qualitative interview, this problem is not so acutely felt, as the interview is generally prepared for in advance. The interviewer is not just a stranger knocking at the door; An approach has already been made (by means of a letter of presentation, a telephone call asking for an appointment, and sometimes an introduction by an acquaintance, etc.). This is made possible by the fact that fewer contacts are required for qualitative interviews than for surveys (and therefore greater attention may be given to each individual case); moreover, as these are in-depth interviews, any doubt or cause for reticence has to be dispelled in advance, otherwise the objective of the interview will certainly not be attained.

The problem to be tackled during the initial contact is therefore not so much one of overcoming the interviewee's diffidence as of *explaining what we want from him*. This will mean describing the objective of the research, explaining why he has been chosen and why he is going to be asked certain, perhaps personal, questions and, if necessary, justifying the fact that the conversation will be recorded, etc.

Primary and secondary questions According to the distinction made by Kahn and Cannel (1967: 205), 'by *primary question* we mean any question which introduces a new topic or asks for new content. *Secondary questions*, by contrast, are intended to elicit more fully the information already asked for by a primary question.' Using a classification drawn up by Spradley (1979: 59) with reference to what he called the ethnographic interview, but which can be applied to any qualitative interview, we can distinguish three types of primary question. First, there are *descriptive questions*, such as 'Can you tell me about your job?' or 'What is your working day like?' Then there are *structural questions* aimed at discovering how the interviewee structures his knowledge and perceives social reality, e.g. 'Could you tell me what sort of people work in your place? or 'How can someone get ahead in your company?' And, finally, we have what Spradley calls *contrast questions*, which are based on comparisons, e.g. 'What's the difference between a "carpenter" and a "joiner"?' or 'In what ways is your present job better than your previous one?'

Probing An interview does not involve simply asking a given question and recording the answer. An essential ingredient of the interviewer's skill is the ability to uncover and to highlight the subject's true positions, even those that are most deeply hidden. To this end, the interviewer will make use of so-called 'probe questions'. These are not so much genuine questions as neutral prompts designed to encourage the interviewee to lower his defensive barriers, to elucidate further and to provide more detail. Such intervention is intended to spur the subject's initiative, to get him to talk, though without influencing what he says; therefore, rather than answering questions, the subject will follow the course of his own reasoning, choosing which issues to discuss further and how to expound upon them. This kind of probing may take various forms:

- *Repeating the question* Sometimes it is enough for the interviewer to repeat the question in different words, or to stress some words rather than others.
- *Repeating or summarizing the answers given* This involves picking up and repeating the subject's answers, either in the same words or in a summary form, in order to prompt him to clarify or develop what he has said. e.g. 'Well, you told me that … (followed by repetition of the words used). But what exactly do you mean by …?' Or: 'So, if I get your meaning,… (followed by a synthesis of what the interviewee has just said). Now then, are there any other reasons…? Is there anything else…? Would you like to say anything else about that?'
- *Encouraging and expressing interest* The interviewer can express interest in what the subject is saying either through verbal expressions and interjections, such as 'uh-huh', or through non-verbal signals, such as nodding. The timely use of expressions like 'Yes?' 'That's interesting'. 'Do go on'. 'I see'. 'Really?' shows that the interviewer is interested and prompts the subject to continue.
- *Pausing* If there are pauses in the conversation, the interviewer need not be too hasty to break the silence. Sometimes silence can encourage the interviewee to make confidential revelations; on other occasions, the vague feeling of embarrassment caused by the silence may goad the interviewee into continuing his account.
- *Asking for elucidation* Sometimes the interviewee will have to be asked explicitly to clarify or to say more about a point. In such cases, the interviewer may use expressions such as 'Tell me more about …'. 'I'd like to know more about what you think of …'. 'I'm not sure I really understand what you mean …'. 'And why did you feel that way about it?'

Language In our discussion of questionnaires, we saw that the problem of language was one of clarity; standardization of the instrument means that questions have to be worded in such a way that they are comprehensible to everyone. In the qualitative interview, this problem does not arise, as the language of the questions can be adapted to suit the characteristics of the interviewee. However, it should be borne in mind that language is the fundamental means of establishing a climate of empathy, and therefore of communication, between the interviewer and the interviewee. As Kahn and Cannel point out:

> Language plays an additional role in the interview by supplying cues to both interviewer and respondent as to the kind of person that the other is. Some of the first indications which the respondent gets as to whether the interviewer is a person very much like himself or very different will come from the language the interviewer employs in introducing himself and his subject … If interviewer and respondent 'speak the same language', they are more likely to have had similar backgrounds and experience and are therefore more likely to be capable of understanding each other (Kahn and Cannel, 1967: 111).

Of course, it is not always necessary (nor always possible) for the interviewer and the respondent to speak the same language. Often, the language and appearance of the interviewer are those of a scholar, and she will be accepted as such as long as she shows genuine interest and the respondent perceives her to be a person capable of understanding (we need only think of ethnographic research in which the researcher is a foreigner who does not know the respondent's world but wishes to understand it). Nevertheless, there may be situations in which the respondent has an acute sense of difference and mistrust towards the outside world; in such cases, the interviewer can only overcome these obstacles if she is perceived as being able to understand the world of the respondent, either because she has personal experience of it or because she knows something about it. For example, in a study on young drug addicts, an interviewer who has had some sort of contact with the world of drugs, who knows its jargon and can immediately understand its situations, is likely to have more success than one whose style is that of the psychologist.

The interviewer's role   From all that has been said so far, it will be obvious that the role of the interviewer in the qualitative interview is *crucial*, in that in determines the outcome of the conversation. In this regard, we should briefly recall what was said in Chapter 5, Section 2 about the *constructivist* approach to social research. Indeed, within the interpretive paradigm, the interview is *not* seen as a means of 'collecting data' or of simply recording the interviewee's opinions; rather, it is looked upon as a dynamic relationship in which the interview is 'constructed' by the interviewer and the respondent together, and its outcome will depend largely on the empathetic link that is forged between the two interlocutors.

In this perspective, the interviewer's role is complex and not without contradictions. On the one hand, the interviewer is called upon to play an active role in orienting the interview towards his own objectives: 'The interviewer consistently rewards full and complete responses, rewards responses focused on the objectives of the interview, and tends to discourage communications irrelevant to those objectives' (Kahn and Cannel, 1967: 59). On the other hand, care must be taken to ensure that these attempts to keep the interview on track do not alter the respondent's thought; by confining the respondent to issues that are in keeping with the research objectives, the interviewer risks drawing him away from his genuine feelings, and may even end up by directing his answers.

Clearly, then, the task of the qualitative interviewer is much more demanding than that of the interviewer who implements a questionnaire. What he is required to do goes well beyond simple diligence and the faithful execution of detailed instructions. He needs sensitivity, intuition, the ability to identify with his interlocutor, experience in human relations and, not least, a thorough knowledge of the issue under investigation. The more open and unstructured the technique, the greater the skill required of the interviewer. In the case of unstructured interviews, interviewing may well be carried out directly by the researcher(s), without the aid of interviewers. Alternatively, limited use may be made of interviewers, who will maintain close contact with the research team throughout the entire interviewing phase.

Some examples of this kind of organization can be seen in the studies quoted earlier. In the study by Alberoni et al. (1967) on party activists, the interviews (108 in all) were conducted by 12 researchers, who were all members of the research team (some of these were among the authors of the volume in which the research data were presented; others wrote essays on the study for various publications). In Barbagli's research (1995) on crime, the author interviewed the 28 key informants (magistrates, lawyers, police officers, etc.) personally, while the 65 interviews with criminals, in view of the sensitivity of the issue, were conducted by two interviewers who had had some previous experience of the criminal underworld. Nevertheless, these two interviewers maintained continuous close contact with the research director (who, for example, listened to the recordings of the interviews immediately after they had been conducted, discussed them with the interviewers and, together with the interviewers, decided whether further contact should be made and which points remained to be explored). In their study of adaptation to divorce, Wallerstein and Kelly (1980) interviewed 120 divorced wives and husbands and 136 children with the aid of five interviewers. By contrast, in her study of divorced women, Arendell (1986) interviewed all 60 women herself.

That interviews should be conducted personally by the researcher – or at most with the aid of a small number of interviewers who function almost as co-workers – is a rule that applies chiefly to unstructured or semi-structured interviews. In the case of structured interviews, this criterion is less binding, in that the standardization of the questions limits the interviewer's freedom; this means that outside interviewers can be used, thereby enabling large samples of subjects to be interviewed. For example, in the research on mother-child relationships (Newson and Newson, 1978) the authors used a fairly large number of interviewers, most of whom were health visitors from Nottingham City Health Department. However, even when conducting structured interviews, researchers sometimes prefer to work with a very small number of interviewers grouped into a close-knit team. In the research on children and school (Capecchi and Livolsi, 1973), which involved interviewing 144 children between the ages of 7 and 13 years, their parents and their teachers, all the interviews were conducted by only six interviewers. Among the examples quoted, the research conducted by Granovetter (1995) on strategies used to find a job is somewhat exceptional: although the sample was fairly large (282 subjects), all the interviews were conducted by the researcher himself.

By their very nature (and particularly on account of the need to establish a deep personal relationship between the interviewer and the respondent), qualitative interviews can only be carried out face-to-face (other types of interview – postal, telephone, computer-assisted and so on – can only be used to administer questionnaires). Moreover, as a general rule, qualitative interviews are taped. The temptation to write a summary while the interview is taking place should be avoided, as the result would be incomplete, dull, or even incomprehensible. By contrast, recording preserves the interviewee's account in its original and complete form. In transcribing recorded material, it is always advisable to write out the respondent's speech *in full*, including dialect forms, errors in syntax, unfinished sentences and so on, as it is these very features of the spoken language that make the interview lively and communicative.

Finally, it should be added that recording the interview enables the interviewer to concentrate solely on the conversation and to maintain a more natural relationship with the interviewee; this would be much more difficult if the interviewer had to take notes. In some cases, of course, the presence of the tape-recorder might inhibit free expression on the part of the respondent (especially if he holds an official position). In most cases, however, this does not happen and the presence of the tape-recorder, which may initially cause some embarrassment, is soon forgotten as the interview proceeds.

5. ANALYSIS OF EMPIRICAL MATERIAL

5.1 Qualitative analysis

Once the interviews have been conducted, recorded and transcribed, they have to be analysed and interpreted in order to write up the research report. The analysis of data from qualitative interviews was dealt with fairly amply in Chapter 2 (Section 3.3 and 3.4), in our comparison of the quantitative and qualitative approaches to the various phases of social research. In order to give the reader a clear picture of the differences between the quantitative interview (questionnaire) and the qualitative interview, the two techniques were often examined side by side. We will now return to the question of the *qualitative* analysis of interviews.

Analysis of the data is case-based, unlike the quantitative approach, in which it is variable-based. This point was reiterated at the beginning of the present chapter. The qualitative approach is holistic, in that the individual is observed and studied as a complete entity, in the conviction that each human being (like each social phenomenon) is more than the sum of a collection of parts (in this case, the variables). As we have said repeatedly, the objective of the analysis is to *understand people* and not to analyse the relationships among variables.

Results are presented in accordance with a narrative perspective; episodes are recounted and cases are described, often in the exact words used by the respondents so as to communicate to the reader the vividness of the situations studied without altering the material recorded. The standard procedure is as follows: an argument is put forward and an interview extract is reported in order to support and illustrate the point. For example, in the research on political party activists quoted

in Chapter 2, it is claimed that older Communist Party activists have a strictly dichotomic view of the world, in the sense that in every field it is guided by a basic distinction between 'us' and 'them', between friends and enemies and between proletariat and capitalists. To illustrate their point, the authors report interview extracts referring to international politics (US and USSR), political parties (Communist Party and Christian Democrats), sport and so on (a sample extract can be found in Chapter 2, Section 3.4).

Likewise, in a chapter of her study in which she looks at the financial condition of divorced women, Arendell writes: 'But even the women who had worried most about how they would manage financially without their husband's incomes had not imagined the kind of hardship they would face after divorce ... 90% of them (56 out of 60) found that divorce immediately pushed them below the poverty line, or close to it ... an experience not shared by their ex-husbands. Like women generally, they were "declassed" by divorce' (Arendell, 1986: 36–7). This analysis is followed by a series of interview extracts in which divorced women describe their living conditions, their disappointment, their sudden social demotion, the difficulties of everyday life, the disinterest of their ex-husbands and so on.

In this kind of presentation, the researcher's analysis is interwoven with illustrations, examples and empirical support in the form of interview extracts.

Syntheses and generalizations often take the form of classifications and typologies. This question was dealt with both in Chapter 2, Section 3.4, in which the procedures of quantitative and qualitative analysis were compared, and in our chapter on participant observation (Chapter 9, Section 6), in which we discussed classification and how the dimensions used for classifying are identified. With regard to this point – and also to the two previous points (data analysis and the presentation of results) – it should be pointed out that the way of using and analysing empirical material yielded by qualitative research is substantially unitary, and does not vary according to whether the material comes from participant observation, interviews, or documentary sources of other kinds (as we will see in the next chapter). For this reason, there is no point in returning to these issues here; the reader should refer to the sections in which they have already been dealt with.

5.2 Mixed analysis (quantitative and qualitative)

In Chapter 5, Box 5, we described the feature which typically distinguishes quantitative research from qualitative research – indeed, the major difference between them – i.e. the data-matrix. Indeed, the data-matrix constitutes a standardized organization of the information gathered and, as such, presupposes that human attitudes and behaviour can be classified and rendered uniform, a notion that is incompatible with the individualistic approach.

Nevertheless, there is a particular case in which the two approaches co-exist: the *structured interview*. In the structured interview, the questions are predetermined while the answers are open. This means that all respondents are asked for the same information, but that they are free to provide that information in whatever way they see fit. This common information base can be rendered uniform through a coding procedure.

By way of example, we will return to the research conducted on Nottingham mothers (Newson and Newson, 1978), and in particular to the questions reported in Table 10.1 on the subject of discipline and punishment. The interview contained various questions on smacking (e.g. 'How do you feel about smacking children of his age?'). Naturally, the answers varied considerably (from analytical descriptions of the problem to terse replies). As is customary, these answers were recorded and transcribed in their entirety, and were then classified according to the recurrent categories. In this case, the answers to questions 160–3 were coded together, thus giving rise to a single variable in three categories (ranging from agreement to disagreement with smacking, see Table 10.1). Likewise, the answers to

the question regarding the mothers' own emotional reactions to smacking were coded in three categories.

A similar procedure was followed in the research on children's attitudes to school, which is also reported in Table 10.1. In the interviews, various questions were asked in order to explore the child's relationship with school (for example, 'Do you like going to school?', 'What do you like most about school?, etc.). The interviews were recorded. Subsequently, the questions were coded not on the basis of the answers to the single questions, but by assigning an overall judgement to a block of questions. For example, with reference to the questions reported in Table 10.1, the child was classified on a four-point scale of 'acceptance/refusal of school', which ranged from complete refusal to motivated acceptance.

This procedure gives rise to a classic data-matrix, in which all the subjects are classifiable in terms of the same variables. It should be noted, however, that what is coded is only a part of the interview, the part which is, so to speak, common to all cases; it is a kind of lowest common denominator, which may even be very limited. Each interview also has a specific part, which varies from case to case and which is not discarded. Indeed, analysis of the empirical material proceeds along two tracks; the standardized data are analysed by means of classic statistical instruments (frequency distributions, tables of the relationships among the variables, multivariate analysis), while the complete texts of the transcriptions are analysed according to the typical modalities of qualitative research.

It should be added that this way of quantifying qualitative data is not restricted to the structured interview. Any type of qualitative interview may contain themes that are common to all cases, which can provide information on all interviewees. For instance, in their study of party activists, Alberoni et al. (1967) submitted the texts of the interviews – these were semi-structured interviews based on somewhat general guidelines – to a 'panel' of three adjudicators, who re-read the texts and, for each respondent, filled in a questionnaire with closed questions regarding those issues that were common to all interviews.

Of course, such qualification makes sense only if the sample is large, which is rarely the case in unstructured interviews. For this reason, we have associated this way of handling empirical material mainly with the structured interview, in which the use of a team of interviewers enables the researcher to deal with samples that are large enough to undergo quantitative analysis.

A crucial step in this procedure is the coding of the answers. Clearly, this is a task that can only be carried out by a small group of persons who are able to work together closely in order to establish common criteria for classification and judgement. In most cases, coding is carried out by the team of researchers themselves. Even when this is not possible (e.g. in a study conducted on a very large sample), very close coordination by the researcher(s) is indispensable. Moreover, in order to avoid ending up with some interviews that lack the information required for coding in the data-matrix, it is advisable to establish the coding scheme before interviewing begins, so that each interviewer is aware of what information to ask for.

6. A FINAL NOTE: INTERACTION AND LACK OF STANDARDIZATION

In qualitative interviews, the lack of standardization is both a strength and a weakness. Working under few constraints, the *interviewer* is able to pursue unforeseen leads and to work out and explore new hypotheses concerning the phenomenon under investigation, thereby going beyond the original formulation of the problem. Enjoying complete freedom of expression, the *respondent* is in a position to put forward his point of view using his own mental categories and his own language. The qualitative interview is therefore particularly suited to discovery and – as has already been said – *understanding*. At the same time, however, this lack of standardization makes both

comparison and quantitative assessment of the phenomena studied problematic. For example, while the qualitative interview is better able to pick out even the deep-seated reasons why people are in favour or against the expulsion of illegal immigrants, it is difficult to quantify the relative weights of the various reasons (how many of those in favour are motivated by racial prejudice, how many by economic considerations, how many by a sense of legality, etc.); moreover, it is equally difficult to make comparisons (is expulsion favoured more by men or women, by younger or older citizens, by the more educated or less educated, etc.?).

Thus, the lack of standardization not only makes comparison difficult (how can we compare two people if we do not ask them the same question?), it also makes synthesis difficult (how can we count the number of people opposed to immigration on grounds of racism if – once again – we have not asked them all the same question?). But even if we could count and compare, it would still remain difficult to make inferences on a larger population, on account of the small number of cases studied. As has been said, the qualitative interview, precisely because it is conducted in depth, cannot be conducted on very large samples. It is one thing to ask 'Do you agree or disagree with the expulsion of illegal immigrants?', or 'Which of the problems listed here led to the breakdown of your marriage?'; through succinct questions and a set of pre-established answers, dozens of people can be questioned in a short time, even by telephone. It is quite another thing, however, to go deeply into the issue of immigration, to uncover the hidden, and perhaps even unconscious, racist (or at least ethnocentric) vein that can be found in all of us, or to elicit a long and intricate conversation about the breakdown of the respondent's marriage. Such conversations require a great deal of time, which – assuming equal resources are allocated – limits the number of subjects that can be interviewed.

In addition, we need to consider how much preparation qualitative interviews require.

First, respondents have to be identified and tracked down; the purpose of the interview then has to be explained and the respondent's trust has to be gained through preliminary contacts or presentation by intermediaries, and appointments have to be arranged at times when the respondent is available for interview and in places where the conversation can take place without any disturbance. All these aspects are much more demanding in the qualitative interview than in an interview through a questionnaire, and therefore require much more time and organization. Moreover, the interview may be so sensitive that it can only be conducted by the researcher herself, in which case the number of respondents will have to be limited even further.

In sum, without standardization it is *more difficult to make comparisons, more difficult to count and more difficult to extrapolate findings* from a sample to a broader population. Naturally, these drawbacks are amply offset by the fact that the qualitative interview enables the researcher to investigate in depth, to bring out what is hidden or unforeseen.

Few scholars deny that the in-depth interview is useful in social research. However, the arguments put forward in support of this technique by those inspired by the positivist paradigm differ markedly from those used by the interpretivists. Even the staunchest advocates of the quantitative approach admit that the qualitative interview can make a valuable contribution to the exploratory phase of the research. This position was the norm in texts on social research methodology at least until the 1980s. For example, one of the most widely used manuals in the 1960s and 1970s states that 'Informal techniques will remain invaluable at the pilot stage of even formal surveys, to provide guidance on what are the important questions and how they should be asked. Where feasible they may sometimes also be usefully employed together with formal surveys in researching complex problems' (Moser and Kalton, 1971).

The qualitative interview may also be used in quantitative research in order to investigate a particular theme in greater depth, *after* the quantitative data have been collected. This serves not only to examine an issue that has been insufficiently explored by the questionnaire, but also to give substance and texture to the issue through the aid of interview extracts. For instance, if a survey reveals that voter turnout is particularly low among well-educated young people living in metropolitan areas, the researcher may decide to conduct unstructured interviews with subjects who are typical of these groups, in order to understand the reasons behind their behaviour. Or again, if analysis of the questionnaires reveals that an important issue has been neglected, this issue may be investigated through a new set of ad hoc interviews.

In all these cases, the qualitative interview plays a *supporting role* for the quantitative data collection. The main empirical base is made up of the questionnaires, and the qualitative phase only serves to pave the way for the quantitative procedure, to add illustrative support to its findings, or to clarify some aspects that the quantitative data have not brought to light.

By contrast, the scholars who subscribe to the interpretive paradigm claim that the qualitative interview is the only technique based on questioning that can lead to a genuine understanding of social reality. As we have seen, the interpretive paradigm rejects the objectivity of social phenomena as a misleading myth and embraces a 'constructivist' vision of research, according to which data are not 'gathered', but rather 'generated' by the interaction between the subject who studies and the subject who is studied. Thus, in order to produce knowledge, the interview must be the product of that particular social interaction between the interviewer and interviewee which is unique to each case. Rather than an *act of observation*, it is an *instance of interaction* through which the researcher gains direct access to the world of the interviewee, in much the same way as the participant observer does. It is this participation that enables him to reconstruct the reality of that world, thereby achieving that 'vision from within' which, according to the interpretive paradigm, constitutes the only true form of social knowledge.

As Schwartz and Jacobs write, with regard to the interpretive paradigm, 'The only "real" social reality is the reality from within … In order to understand social phenomena, the researcher needs to discover the actor's 'definition on the situation' – that is, his perception and interpretation of reality and how these relate to his behavior … From this perspective, social meanings (which direct human behavior) do not inhere in activities, institutions, or social objects themselves' (Schwartz and Jacobs, 1979: 7–8).

SUMMARY

1. The qualitative interview can be defined as a conversation that has the following characteristics: it is elicited by the interviewer; interviewees are selected on the basis of a data-gathering plan; a considerable number of subjects are interviewed; it has a cognitive objective; it is guided by the interviewer; it is based on a flexible, non-standardized pattern of questioning.

2. Questioning human beings in order to obtain knowledge of society can be done with qualitative approaches (such as qualitative interviews) and quantitative approaches (standardized questionnaires). Qualitative interviewing is distinguished by the following features: absence of standardization; comprehension is privileged over documentation (context of discovery versus context of justification); absence of a representative sample; a case-centered approach is preferred over a variable-centered approach.

3. Qualitative interviews can be classified in three types. In *structured interviews*, all respondents are asked the same questions with the same wording and in the same sequence (the questions are predetermined both in content and in form, as in a questionnaire with open questions). In

semi-structured interviews, the interviewer does not pose pre-written questions, but refers to an 'outline' of the topics to be covered during the course of the conversation (only the content, not the form, of the questions is predetermined). In *unstructured interviews*, the interviewer's only task is to make sure that predetermined topics that are dealt with during the conversation, according to forms and modes that he feels are most adequate in the particular interviewing situation (neither the content nor the form of the questions are predetermined). Some special cases of qualitative interviews are *non-directive and clinical interviews, interviews with key informants* and *focus groups*.

4. The qualitative interview does not simply involve recording information; it is a process of social interaction between two individuals. Conducting a good qualitative interview is a difficult art. This process can be described with reference to preliminary explanations, primary and secondary questions, probing, language and the interviewer's role.

5. Once the interviews have been conducted, they have to be analysed. *Data analysis* is case-based (and thus differs from the quantitative approach, in which it is variable-based), in that the individual is observed and studied as a complete entity. *Results* are presented in accordance with a narrative perspective. *Syntheses and generalizations* often take the form of classifications and typologies. In the case of structured interviews we can analyse the data according to a mixed approach, both qualitative and quantitative (and thus by resorting to a data matrix).

FURTHER READING

An exhaustive review of the state of the art of interviewing, regarding conceptual, methodological and practical issues, the history of its use, its various forms, its fields of application, analysis procedures, the role of new technologies and so on, is the massive collection of essays edited by J.F. Gubrium and J.A. Holstein, *Handbook of Interview Research: Context and Method* (Sage, 2002, pp. 981).

There are also many good monographs on interviews, including (for traditional interviews) the classic R.L. Kahn and C.F. Cannell, *Dynamics of Interviewing: Theory, Technique and Cases* (Krieger, 1983, pp. 368) and (for a critique of stimulus-response interview models, based on a perspective which sees the interview as a joint product of interviewer and interviewee) E.G. Mishler, *Research Interviewing: Context and Narrative* (Harvard University Press, 1986, pp. 189).

J.T. Chirban, *Interviewing in Depth: The Interactive-Relational Approach* (Sage, 1996, pp. 144) and G. McCracken, *The Long Interview* (Sage, 1988, pp. 88) deal with special kinds of unstructured interviews.

As regards focus groups, D.L. Morgan, 'Focus Groups', *Annual Review of Sociology 1996*, provides an introductory review; for a more detailed and applied treatment, see D.W. Stewart and P.N. Shamdasani, *Focus Groups: Theory and Practice* (Sage, 1990, pp. 153).

NOTES

1. None of the studies that we will present involves fewer than 50 cases; in most studies, about 100 subjects are interviewed.

2. In the text, the simple term 'interview' refers to the qualitative interview, while the term 'questionnaire' refers to the interview conducted according to the quantitative approach.

11   The Use of Documents

Every society produces a vast amount of documents, and this chapter explains how to use them as social research data. The chapter is divided into two parts. The first deals with personal documents, produced by individuals for private use (diaries, letters, autobiographies), and oral testimony and life histories, which resemble autobiographies. The second part deals with institutional documents, produced by public bodies; such documents are 'signs' left behind by the organisational life and cultures which produced them.

1.   READING SOCIAL TRACES

In the introduction to this part of the book, we said that the three fundamental actions underlying the techniques of qualitative research are *observing, asking* and *reading*. Chapters 9 and 10 deal with the first two of these. We will now discuss the third. This involves the reading of documents that individuals and institutions have produced and continue to produce. What do these documents consist of?

A *document* is any material that provides information on a given social phenomenon and which exists independently of the researcher's actions. Documents are produced by individuals or institutions for purposes other than social research, but can be utilized by the researcher for cognitive purposes. They may therefore include letters, newspaper articles, diaries, autobiographies, organization charts of companies, minutes of board meetings, acts of Parliament, court sentences, company balance-sheets, marriage certificates, commercial regulations and contracts, and so on. Normally, these documents exist in written form (hence the above reference to 'reading'). However, social documents also include 'material traces' (as in other disciplines, such as archaeology, history and anthropology). In addition, we will also deal with the personal testimony and memories of single individuals under this heading.

The fact that such documents[1] are produced independently of the actions of the researcher offers two clear advantages over the research techniques presented previously. In the first place, this information is 'non-reactive', in the sense that it is not subject to possible distortion due to the interaction between the researcher and the subject studied. In an interview, for instance, a respondent may be less than truthful or answer according to socially approved standards in order to make a good impression on the interviewer. The same person, however, is much more likely to be sincere when writing a personal diary or a letter to a family member. Similarly, a company balance-sheet, a patient's medical records, a tax return or the minutes of a meeting, though providing a particular view of social reality, are not liable to distortions caused by the act of recording itself. Of course, this characteristic has its negative aspect; when dealing with pre-existing documents, the researcher cannot 'ask further questions', but has to be content with the information provided, even if this proves to be incomplete with respect to the cognitive objectives proposed.

The second advantage stemming from the fact that documents exist independently of the researcher's activity is that they can also be used to study the past. In this case, the sociologist's work blends with that of the historian, and indeed their research techniques overlap (from this point of view, as well as from that of the content, it is difficult to distinguish between sociology and social history). In order to preserve the distinction between these two fields, we will restrict our discussion to the use of documents in the study of contemporary society.

This chapter deals with two profoundly different types of document. The first type is constituted by *personal documents* This term is used to underline the *private* nature of these documents – that is to say, the fact that they are produced by single individuals for strictly 'personal' use; they are also called 'expressive' documents, in that they express the feelings, the affairs and, more generally, the personality of the individuals who produce them. This category covers letters, autobiographies and diaries.

The second type is what we will call *institutional documents*, in that they are produced by institutions, or by single individuals within the context of their institutional roles. They include speeches, company documents, newspaper articles, the minutes of trials, etc. In contrast with the previous type, these documents generally have a *public* nature.

2. PERSONAL DOCUMENTS

Diaries, letters, memoirs and so on have always been important sources for the historian. Historical research, however, has traditionally utilized such material to shed light on famous personalities, the protagonists of history. In the social sciences, by contrast, attention is focused on documents produced by 'ordinary people', with a view to reconstructing social patterns and relationships on the basis of the experiences of the protagonists of everyday life. As Plummer points out, 'the world is crammed of personal documents. People keep diaries, send letters, take photos, write memos, tell biographies, scrawl graffiti, publish their memories, write letters to the papers …' (1983: 13). Though extremely diverse, all these documents are united by the fact that they are genuine expressions of the personalities of those who produce them. Such accounts of personal experiences spring from within the subject and are not intended for public use; as such, they display that 'vision from within' which characterizes the interpretive approach.

The history of this kind of sociological research parallels the fluctuating fortunes of qualitative research. Personal documents were first used by Thomas and Znaniecki in *The Polish Peasant in Europe and in America*, which was published between 1918 and 1920. In the wake of that imposing research, the 1920s and 30s saw widespread use of this type of material, especially among the researchers of the Chicago School. Subsequently, however, the popularity of this approach soon declined, as did the whole current of qualitative research in general. In later years – we might say from the 1980s onwards – the biographical approach to social research was revived; this revival was also spurred on by the development of the so-called 'oral history' in the field of historiography, which utilizes very similar recording techniques and empirical material.

2.1 Autobiographies

An autobiography is a *written* account of the *whole life* of a person, produced *by that person* in a limited time, and therefore within a *retrospective vision* (if it is written while the events are in progress, it is a diary). In its ideal form, the autobiography is *spontaneously* written by an *unselected* author.

In the social sciences, however, autobiographies are rarely encountered in this form, in that it will be a matter of sheer good fortune if the researcher comes across some sort of memoir while inspecting documents concerning the phenomenon under investigation. Therefore, in the social sciences, the autobiography is often elicited, in the sense that subjects who are thought to have an interesting contribution to make to the research are expressly asked to write their autobiography. For example, in the research mentioned above, Thomas and Znaniecki asked a Polish immigrant, a certain Wladek, to write his autobiography (which ended up being over 250 pages long) on payment of a sum of money. These two authors, nevertheless, claimed that 'ambition, literary interest and interest in his own life probably became at once the main motives' (Thomas and Znaniecki, 1919: 86).

In such cases, when the autobiography is commissioned for study purposes, the researcher may orient the account by asking questions or by providing a checklist of issues to be covered. A classic example of the use of the autobiographical account in social research is seen in *The Professional Thief* by Edwin Sutherland, published in 1937. Two-thirds of this autobiography was written by a professional thief on the basis of a list of subjects provided by the researcher (Sutherland himself); this account was then integrated with conversations between the thief and the researcher, who transcribed the contents of these talks after each meeting. The final product is a synthesis of these two inputs and is constituted by 200 pages of autobiographical account followed by 30 pages of interpretation by the researcher. In the earlier case of the Polish peasant, the final text was made up of about 250 pages of autobiography preceded by a 70-page introduction by the authors, who also included many other types of personal documents in their wide-ranging research design.

However, the classic case remains that of the autobiography written wholly by the author and published as a personal testimony without comment or interpretation.

Such is the case of *Pimp: the Story of My Life* (Iceberg, 1967). After serving a long prison sentence for living off the earnings of prostitution, the author wrote his life story, in which he described Chicago's criminal fraternity in the 1940s and 1950s, the world of gangsters, prostitutes, drug dealers, corruption and violence; this autobiography provides a 'vision from within' that is both lucid and richly informative. Another example is seen in *Quarantine Island*. The author of this autobiography left his village in the Italian Alps in 1891, at the age of 16, to look for work. After doing various labouring jobs in Austria, Hungary, Bohemia, Silesia, Galice and Saxony, he crossed the Atlantic at the age of 30 to work in Canadian mines, before ending up in New York City in 1922. At that time, aspiring immigrants were quarantined before being admitted to the United States, and it was during this period of enforced inactivity that the autobiography was written (Del Piero, 1994). This account provides fascinating sociological insight into the great waves of emigration that swept over the poorest areas of Europe in the late 1800s and early 1900s.

These 'pure' autobiographical accounts, which are written without mediation or interpretation by the researcher, cannot readily be assigned to the sphere of social research. First of all, someone who writes an autobiography is obviously not an ordinary person; the mere fact of deciding (or agreeing) to write one's own life story denotes a very particular kind of personality. Moreover, autobiographies often include only what their authors consider to be interesting, dramatic or worth telling, while omitting anything that might be deemed discrediting. Finally, the autobiography involves the risk – like all documents based on memory – that past events might be rationalized with hindsight. Conditioning by social roles that have, in the meantime, become customary and the inevitable fact that past experiences are viewed from the present standpoint, may provide a distorted picture of the true frame of mind in which certain past situations were faced at the time.

✳ 2.2 Diaries

The diary has been called 'the personal document *par excellence*'. What is special about diaries is that they are written for strictly personal use and at the same time as the events described take place. This means that diaries are not subject to the principle handicaps faced by autobiographies. In particular, the fact that the diary records the writer's actions, opinions, feelings and points of view at that specific moment in time makes this type of document a precious and unique testimony to the individual's inner life (as well as providing a precise description of the unfolding of the events in which he is involved). Nevertheless, although diaries figure prominently in literature, no major social research has ever been based exclusively on diaries. This is probably because – as in the case of autobiographies – documents of this kind rarely fall into the hands of researchers; moreover, such material frequently offers little scope for generalization.

In sociological research, greater use of diaries was made in the 1920s and 1930s, when the dominant research model was that of the Chicago School. Even at that time, however, their role was substantially limited to that of an adjunct to other types of documentation. In his methodology manual *Field Studies in Sociology*, Palmer (1928) quotes two studies involving the use of diaries: one by Cavan (1928) on suicide, in which the diaries of two suicide victims are analysed, and the other by Mowrer (1927) on family breakdown, which reports the diary of a young woman whose marriage was gradually failing. The Lynds also report using two diaries in their research on Middletown.

A particular case of the use of diaries in social research is that of daily accounts drawn up on the request of the researcher. In our chapter on surveys (Chapter 5), we mentioned the use of 'time budgets'; this technique involves asking subjects to fill in a detailed schedule of their daily activities for a certain period (perhaps a day or a week). Though typical of the quantitative approach, it is a technique that can also be applied to qualitative research. For example, in a longitudinal study of the mechanisms of adaptation to old age in a sample of 142 subjects of high social class, Maas and Kuypers (1974) asked a number of subjects to keep a diary for a week and to record, in addition to the basic chronological account of their activities, their thoughts, feelings and comments. Similarly, Zimmerman and Weider (1977) offered their subjects a modest reward for keeping a diary for a week, in which they were asked to describe each activity on the basis of the questions: Who? What? When? Where? How? What was original in this study was that the diaries were subsequently used not only in their own right, but also as the basis for in-depth interviews on the facts reported.

Clearly, diaries that are 'commissioned' by the researcher differ markedly from those that are produced spontaneously (strictly speaking, they are not documents, if we limit this term to material that already exists before the research). Nevertheless, they constitute an interesting and original form of empirical recording.

✳ 2.3 Letters

One of the earliest and best known sociological studies was based to a great extent on letters. This was *The Polish Peasant in Europe and in America* by William Thomas and Florian Znaniecki (1918–1920), which we mentioned earlier. These authors were able to obtain letters exchanged between Polish immigrants in the US and members of their families back in Poland by placing an advertisement in the newspaper of Chicago's Polish community and offering a reward for each letter. In this way, they built up an imposing body of correspondence, which they utilized as empirical material for their research (together with newspaper articles, the autobiography mentioned previously and other documentary material). Many of these letters were published (occupying over 600 printed pages) in the completed volumes of the research.

The letters shed light on the traditional lifestyles of rural Poland, the early social changes resulting from industrialization and urbanization at the end of the century, the breakdown of traditional peasant society and its reorganization into new forms, and the process of integration of Polish immigrants in the US. It was through these letters that the authors were able to focus on the subjective aspects of these social processes, the relationship between the individual and society, and in particular on the ways in which individuals adapt to a changing society.

We will briefly mention a few other cases in which research has been based on letters. A rather singular study, in that it utilized letters from only one correspondent, was conducted by Strauss. Over a period of 25 years, this author saved the letters that he received from an alcoholic friend, who recounted his vicissitudes in trying to break the drink habit, his periods of hospitalization, his fitful relationship with the world of work and his subjective experience of this precarious existence. To return to research designs involving numerous subjects united by a common experience, we can quote the research conducted by Salzinger (1958) on the basis of letters written by emotionally disturbed children to their parents and friends, and a study by Janowitz (1958) based on letters and diaries confiscated from German soldiers during the war.

A further category comprises letters sent to newspapers and magazines or to well-known personalities. Naturally, these documents differ from the above, in that spontaneity and personal revelation are likely to be diminished by the fact that such letters are destined to be read by the public (or at least by a public figure). Nevertheless, the availability of such ample homogeneous documentation makes for very interesting research material. Among the studies based on letters to political personalities, we can quote the research carried out by Sussman (1963) on the correspondence received by Franklin Delano Roosevelt. With regard to letters written to newspapers, an interesting example is provided by a study conducted by Boltanski (1990). This author studied the phenomenon of 'public denunciation' – the action of the citizen who publicly condemns some form of

perceived injustice – through the analysis of 275 letters received by the French daily newspaper *Le Monde* from 1979 to 1981 (only a small proportion of which were actually published).

Research based exclusively, or almost exclusively, on letters has always been rare, and has become increasingly so over the years. Indeed, letter-writing has declined as the telephone has become commonplace, and only returns to the fore as a means of communication in exceptional circumstances, such as wars or large-scale migration.

Letters provide precious insights into the thoughts and feelings of individuals; they are a pure expression of the subject's interpretation of situations. However, we might add that 'every letter speaks not just of the writer's world, but also of the writer's perceptions of the recipient' (Plummer 1983: 23). In this sense, the letter is not always an unadulterated manifestation of the writer's personality (as the diary presumably is), but should rather be interpreted as the product of the interaction between two persons.

2.4 Oral testimony

The personal documents that we have mentioned so far cannot easily be used for the purposes of social research. First of all, these are *rare documents*, produced by exceptional individuals or in unusual circumstances; moreover, they are difficult to obtain, as the owners of letters, diaries or other personal documents may well object to their being rendered public. Second, as it is not produced for research purposes, such material may be *fragmentary* and *incomplete*, thus depriving the researcher of information that is essential to the understanding of the situation studied. Finally, there is a serious problem of *representativeness*. Indeed, the researcher cannot choose which cases to study, but has to make do with those that are available – that is to say, the authors of the documents that are turned up. Such cases are normally sporadic, unsystematic and bereft of any selection criterion. To make matters worse, these subjects are nearly always unrepresentative of the wider population involved in the phenomenon under investigation. For instance, with regard to the earlies example, not many Polish peasants in those days would have been capable of writing letters, and those who were would surely constitute a particular sub set of the population. Apart from the problem of literacy, there is also the question of personality. As already mentioned, people who keep a diary or spontaneously write their autobiography are few and far between, and possess personal features that distinguish them from the rest of the population.

In an attempt to overcome these obstacles, social research has developed a new approach to the collection of personal documents. This consists of systematically gathering oral testimony from subjects. In other words, the researcher *elicits* what we might call 'oral autobiographies' – accounts of life experiences which should differ from written autobiographies only in terms of the recording medium.

This technique is common to various social disciplines. In anthropology, oral sources have always been called upon when studying societies that have no written documentation; in psychology, this approach has yielded celebrated 'case studies' in which the biographical component played a fundamental explanatory role in defining mental illnesses; in history, recent years have witnessed an increased use of 'oral history', which has made noteworthy contributions to several sectors of contemporary history (the workers' movement, the condition of women, industrialization, urban history, etc.).

Narrating one's own past to an interviewer bears a striking resemblance to the technique of the non-structured interview, which was discussed in the previous chapter. There are, however, at least three important differences.

First of all, in the present case, the subject provides a narrative of his own life (generally, the *whole* of his life). The attention is focused on the autobiographical dimension, which is absent from the qualitative interview, or at least is not necessarily present.

Second, in these life stories, the role of the interviewer is much more limited, essentially being one of simply recording, in much the same way as an author might speak into a tape-recorder or an illiterate peasant might dictate a letter to a scribe. An interview regarding the subject's own life often takes the form of an autobiographical account that flows autonomously, almost without questions being asked; rather than asking actual questions, the interviewer is more likely to encourage the narrator to explain his memories in greater detail or to connect events in sequence. The conversation does not, therefore, follow the pattern of an interview, but that of an *account* from memory.

Finally, the biographical method is not particularly concerned with the number of cases studied. As we saw in the previous chapter, qualitative interviews are generally conducted on a few dozen subjects. By contrast, studies that use the biographical technique often involve only a few cases, and sometimes even a single case (some examples of 'case studies' will be seen later), the supposition being that insight into the mind of even one individual can shed light on the entire phenomenon studied, not unlike the analysis of a single clinical case in psychological research.

Naturally, oral testimony does not strictly conform to our definition of what a 'document' is, in that it does not exist prior to the research nor is it produced independently of the cognitive purposes of the research. Since oral accounts are elicited by the researcher, that definition will need to be revised. Such revision, however, does not undermine its general sense. Often – though not necessarily, as we will see – the use of oral testimony involves recording the memories of older generations of subjects. As Evans puts it, in his study of East Anglia villages, 'this particular generation was living history, "books that walked"' (Evans, 1975: 16). In a sense, therefore, interviewing people about their past lives can be regarded as 'reading documents', the only difference being that these are 'living documents'. Again in the words of Evans, 'these old people had followed their jobs, kept up the customs, used the tools, exactly as their ancestors had done for centuries; and they could describe their activities accurately in all their detail in language possessing in itself countless reverberations from the past' (Evans, 1975: 16).

The use of this technique, however, does engender a risk of 'reactivity'; the interviewer's presence may elicit a reaction on the part of the subject, with the result that the account may lose its authentic flavour. It is therefore essential that the interviewer should interfere as little as possible in the narrative, in order to preserve its naturalistic, or spontaneous, character.

Another problem is that of possible memory lapses. However, as Paul Thompson, one of the founders of the modern oral history, points out, it seems that memory lapses primarily involve recent events; moreover, at more advanced ages 'you can find what is widely recognised by psychologists as the phenomenon of "life review": a sudden emergence of memories and a desire to bring these memories out, a special candour which goes with a feeling that active life is over'. Therefore, Thompson concludes, 'interviewing the old does not introduce major methodological issues separate from the normal problems of the interview' (Thompson, 1972: 13–14).

Compared with written documents, oral sources offer several advantages. First, as the researcher can choose which subjects to interview, she can construct a sample that is systematic, if not entirely representative. Second, she can ask questions in order to prompt the subject to fill in any gaps in the narrative. Finally, as the oral account does not require the informant to be literate, the researcher can extend her pool of information beyond the higher social classes. In this way, she can reconstruct the story 'from below', as it were, by gathering information on the living conditions, everyday life and religious culture of ordinary folk.

The technique of gathering documentary material through oral testimony can be applied in various ways. The two main categories into which this kind of material can be divided are, in our view, life stories and oral histories.

A *life story* is an account of the subject's own life as narrated to the interviewer. An *oral history* is the subject's account of some specific events that he/she has witnessed. The object of the life story is an *individual*, his biographical data, feelings, outlook and personal experiences. The object of the oral history is *society*, its customs and events. In the former case, the narrator stands at the centre of the account; in the latter case, the account focuses on the events that the narrator has lived through. We may add that life stories belong mainly to the sociological tradition of social research, while the oral history belongs to the historical tradition.

Life stories These are autobiographical accounts centred on the subject's own life. Sociological research is generally based on a limited number of these 'oral autobiographies'. A typical study is likely to comprise about 10 such accounts, though numerous studies have been based on a single autobiography. However, the most important criterion for classifying research of this kind is not the number of cases studied; rather, it is the way in which the material is handled by the researcher. A review of the research reveals three approaches.

The first of these might be defined as a *pre-scientific* use of the material. This takes the form of a simple *collection of autobiographies*; the accounts are collected and published in a single volume, accompanied by a brief introduction by the researcher (whose role, in this case, is more akin to that of a journalist than sociologist). Such 'slices of life' are undoubtedly fascinating, often evocative and sometimes of considerable literary worth. The fact remains, however, that life stories, as any social document, do not speak for themselves; they need to be 'interrogated'. This way of handling autobiographical material is sometimes justified on the grounds that it is 'naturalistic'; by reporting these accounts in their original form, without selection, comment or interpretation – in other words, 'without manipulation' – the researcher gives a voice to those who do not normally have an opportunity to speak, thereby enabling the downtrodden, the powerless and the marginalized to make themselves heard; moreover, it is a way of bringing to light the point of view of the lower classes which, if mediated by the researcher, would inevitably be distorted in that it is an expression of a different culture. However, these narratives are not only lively but also fragmentary. Placing accounts side by side without a common synthesis, or at least an attempt to tie their essential themes into an explanatory scheme, prevents these outputs from becoming genuine social research – that is, scientific products in the true sense.

By contrast, this explanatory scheme is found in the second way of handling autobiographical material. Accounts are again presented in their complete and autonomous form, but this time they are accompanied by a copious interpretative essay. This is the case of the study on Polish peasants conducted by Thomas and Znaniecki (1918–1920), which was quoted earlier. The first part of this research (contained in the first two of the five volumes of the original edition) consists of 754 letters[2] published in their entirety and covering more than 600 pages; these are preceded by an essay of almost 200 pages analysing Polish peasant society (the family, the class system, economic life and religious beliefs). This analysis – as indeed all the theoretical parts of the study – has always been widely acclaimed for the breadth of its theoretical scope and its truly illuminating insight into the effects of social change on the lives of individuals. At the same time, however, it has been claimed that their theoretical analysis is detached from the empirical side of the research, from which, on the contrary, it ought to have drawn inspiration. The best-known comment to this effect was made by Herbert Blumer on the occasion of the debate organized by the American Social Science Research Council in 1938 on Thomas and Znaniecki's research. Blumer maintained that:

The problem, then, which confronts us here is that of the relation between their materials and their theoretical analysis ... Supposedly

the theoretical analyses either arose out of (these materials) or were tested by them ... (But) it seems quite clear that Thomas and Znaniecki did not derive all of their theoretical conceptions from the materials which are contained in their volumes ... perhaps not even the major theoretical conceptions were derived from them. (Blumer, 1939: 73–74)

Blumer went on to suggest that the authors had already constructed their interpretative schemes, on the basis of their familiarity with Polish peasant society, before beginning their research. Indeed, 'The theoretical conceptions in *The Polish Peasant* far exceed the materials ... some interpretations, indeed, are born out of content of the documents and sometimes the interpretations do not seem to be verified adequately' (1939: 75).

This detachment between theoretical interpretations and empirical material, which is so evident in this albeit exceptional study, is a constant risk in research based on personal documents (and in qualitative research in general). Moreover, this risk is greater when the researcher does not conduct the analysis through continual comparison – statement after statement – with the empirical material, but instead treats the autobiographical accounts (or other personal documents) as a unitary corpus to be interpreted in a global and isolated manner.

The above objections lead on to the third method of analysing autobiographical documents. This involves systematic interaction between empirical material and theoretical interpretation through continual comparison. It is an approach that can be seen in the way in which the text is constructed; the treatise is guided by the theoretical issues, which constitute the unifying theme that links the empirical material. Socio-anthropological interpretations are integrated and intertwined with the autobiographical documents, the former acting as a guide, while the latter illustrate, support and demonstrate. In other words, the oral testimony is not presented in isolation, but is interpreted; episodes are taken out of their chronological order, linked together and placed in a broader context. The researcher's task is therefore to organize the material, to spot logical connections and to establish links among the facts (e.g. between a certain type of socialization and certain adult behaviours).

A fine example of research that implements this approach is *The Fence* by the American scholar Darrell Steffensmeier (1986). This study is based on the experience of a 60-year-old fence, named Sam Goodman, whom the author met in an American prison where Goodman was serving a three-year sentence for receiving stolen property. The book offers a lively and illuminating description of the criminal underworld, whose life runs in parallel with that of law-abiding society. This account reveals how the fence starts up in business and establishes contacts with thieves and customers, how the stolen goods market works, how prices are fixed and deals are made, how profitable the business is and what skills it requires – including the skills needed to avoid detection and arrest – and, in the event of arrest, how to get off as lightly as possible. The autobiographical material is not handled in chronological order, but arranged by subject (the receiver's 'profession', how to go into business, how to set up shop, how to buy, how to sell, how to handle relationships with the police, etc.). Every subject is dealt with by interweaving analysis with documents. For example, the chapter entitled *Buying stolen goods* contains a thorough discussion of the tacit rules governing prices (the basic criterion according to which one-third of the retail price is paid, variations in price according to market demand and the risk involved, competition with other fences, how payments are made, bargaining, etc.). Each theme is dealt with according to the same format: exposition and discussion of the issue by the author, followed by a statement and an interview extract to support and illustrate it. For instance, the statement 'Some thieves are more informed about the quality, the price and the market for the goods they have to sell than others, and thus fare much better in their price negotiations with the fence' (1986: 89) is

followed by an interview extract in which Sam talks about experienced thieves who know the price of everything, about beginners who do not know how to bargain, about the fence's ability to recognize a 'good' thief and to treat him well so as to ensure future business and so on.

Oral history In this case, oral testimony is used to gather information on society rather than to record the subject's personal life. While anthropology has always made use of oral sources, history has traditionally relied on written material. In recent years, this approach has been criticized and oral testimony has been increasingly utilized in historical research.

The technique that would later be called 'oral history' originated towards the end of the 1940s at Columbia University. By the 1960s, it was being implemented in the US by hundreds of researchers to record eye-witness accounts of historical events (not least with a view simply to recording for posterity documentary evidence that would otherwise be lost). Subsequently, the movement took on a more academic character with the emergence of the British school (the magazine *Oral History* was founded in Britain in 1972). One of the general objectives of this movement was to take a fresh look at history 'from below', as it were. Instead of focusing on battles and treaties, on the affairs of the élite and of the ruling classes, and on the endeavours of imperialism, this new perspective was centred on the history of peoples and their everyday life, the underprivileged classes and ethnic minorities, and the movements for national and racial liberation. Though sometimes shot through with populism, this approach made important contributions to the reconstruction of earlier societies and was able to exploit the mine of information contained in the memory of the older generations.

A classic example of social history based on oral sources is *The Edwardians* by Paul Thompson (1975), in which the author paints a portrait of British society at the beginning of the 1900s by describing the structure of social and economic inequalities, relationships between parents and children, the differences between city and country life, leisure activities, the role of religion, political movements, etc. The documentary base is constituted by a fairly systematic sample of subjects; about 500 men and women of various social levels born between 1872 and 1906 were interviewed in order to cover the main social and geographical areas of British society of the day. This material was also integrated by the life stories of 12 individuals who lived through that period.

It should be pointed out, however, that the samples used in studies of this kind are rarely so large or systematic; more often, the subjects are numbered in tens rather than in hundreds. As to the integration of such personal accounts into the text, most of the books are generally devoted to the author's descriptive and interpretative analysis, with interview extracts being inserted here and there to illustrate and support the statements made.

3. INSTITUTIONAL DOCUMENTS

So far, we have discussed documents produced by individuals within the context of their own lives. However, the public sphere of every society also produces a whole range of documents, which remain as a 'trace' of that culture and which constitute a source of information for the social researcher. Moreover, in addition to persons and institutions, even 'things' can instruct the researcher by providing 'physical traces' of the culture that has produced them.

For example, Michel Foucault (1975) has reconstructed the emergence and development, from the sixteenth to the nineteenth centuries, of what he calls 'disciplinary society', which came into being through the establishment of a whole set of procedures to classify, control, measure and train individuals in order to make them both docile and useful at the same time. This process is described on the basis both of written documents, such

as school and factory regulations, and of material documents, such as the architecture of buildings. For instance, he points out how the architecture of public buildings changed from serving purely aesthetic purposes (the pomp of palaces) or the requirements of external defence (the layout of forts) to facilitate close internal control; thus, schools, hospitals and workshops, as well as prisons and barracks, took on the features of surveillance structures, through the use of circular designs that enabled constant supervision to be exercised. The author discerns the same pattern in what could be called the 'company and administrative documents' of the period, such as the hierarchical regulations governing the workplace, and quotes the example, among others, of the regulations in force in a French factory in 1809, which illustrate in detail the disciplinary system with regard to work. On the basis of these documents, which codify the rules governing factories, schools, the army, hospitals and so on, Foucault reconstructs the disciplinary climate of the era, which regulates the life of the pupil, the patient, the worker or the soldier down to the last detail.

In the field of humanistic studies, the discipline that relies most heavily on the study of the documents that societies have produced over the centuries is history. Nevertheless, documents also provide sociology with a valid empirical base for the study of contemporary society. Every day, modern societies produce enormous amounts of documents of the most diverse kinds: contracts, job applications, railway timetables, telephone bills, identity cards, newspapers, television programmes, company balance-sheets, medical records, school registers, road signs, and so on and so forth.

These documents are the product of our institutionalized society, and it is for this reason that we have grouped them under the general heading of 'institutional documents'. These documents consist mostly of written texts, though there is no shortage of material documents. They do not only concern the memorable moments of a society or culture (such as peace treaties, laws or literary texts) but also, and especially, the daily lives of ordinary people. Institutional documents can therefore become research 'data'; they provide empirical material for the study of innumerable social phenomena: from the use of telephone directories to plot the geographical distribution of surnames, and hence the geographical and cultural roots of populations in different regions, to the study of the cultural 'consumption' of a population through sales of theatre or cinema tickets.

As we saw in Chapter 7, a whole range of documents generated by administrative acts are collected and systematized to produce official statistics. For such purposes, these documents are organized in such a way as to enable the information that they contain to be handled in a quantitative manner.

In this chapter, however, we will look at other types of documents, especially those of a less organic and uniform nature, which are more suited to qualitative analysis. In this regard, it should be noted that there is no clear-cut distinction between documents that are suitable for quantitative analysis and those that lend themselves to qualitative treatment; often, the same type of document can be handled in either way. This is especially true of written documents (or those that are transcribed from oral communications, such as the account of a fairy-tale or a television news reporter's summary), which constitute most of the documentary material that we will present. Indeed, a text can be analysed either from the qualitative standpoint, by 'interpreting' it in its totality and examining its 'meanings', or from the quantitative standpoint, by breaking it down into homogeneous components and relating these to one another. The quantitative approach has given rise to a branch of social research called *content analysis*, which involves dismantling texts in order to code them into a data-matrix that can undergo statistical analysis.

The difference between content analysis and the qualitative analysis of texts can be likened to the by now familiar distinction between questionnaires and qualitative interviews. Over the years, content analysis has taken on the form of an organic set of techniques. A complete discussion of these would require a separate section in our treatment of quantitative methods; for reasons of space, this has not been added.

In the remaining part of this chapter, we will not deal with textual documents from the point of view of the techniques of analysis, but from that of their sources. The intention here is to give the reader an idea of where documentary material can be found and how it can be used to study a diversity of social phenomena. In keeping with the location of this chapter within the volume as a whole, we will mainly quote examples of the *qualitative* analysis of documents. There is no easy way to classify these documents; we will begin by looking at texts, then move on to bureaucratic documents, and conclude with heterogeneous material.

3.1 Mass media

In modern societies, the greatest producers of documentary material on society itself are the mass media. The press systematically provides coverage of every factual and cultural aspect of our societies, ranging from the smallest news items to representations of dominant ideologies and values. Moreover, it is unequalled as a documentary source for the study of societies that have preceded ours in the twentieth century and in the last decades of the nineteenth century. Likewise, television today provides us with the most faithful mirror of society, by adding the power of images to the already rich documentation of written journalism.

A great deal of research has been carried out on the mass media and on the production, use and content of their texts. In this regard, we will briefly mention a few qualitative analyses conducted on newspaper articles and television programmes.

Social events described in the newspapers have been analysed by means of the categories of the cultural anthropologist. One such study was conducted by David Kertzer on political rites. Kertzer claims that politics expresses itself through symbolism and that, especially in contemporary societies, it makes much greater use of symbolic instruments than of force in order to affirm its power and gain the approval of the masses. He writes, 'to understand the political process, then, it is necessary to understand how the symbolic enters into politics' (Kertzer, 1988: 2).

The author analysed various political rites: some involving primitive societies (African tribal ceremonies of succession after the death of a chief, ritual conflict sublimation in Brazilian tribes) and others taken from modern societies (John Kennedy's funeral in 1963, President Reagan's 1985 visit to the German military cemetery in Bitburg, a pacifist demonstration in Manhattan in 1967 …). To document these episodes, he used newspaper accounts. Some extracts from the description of Kennedy's funeral are reported below:

> … A black draped caisson, pulled by six gray horses, drew up to the White House to receive the casket. It was the same caisson that had carried President Roosevelt's body less than two decades earlier … the drums draped in black bunting … at a slow melancholy cadence … A company of navy men … strode with the nation's flag. A minister, priest, and rabbi marched with them … Finally, moving slowly, came a black wrapped, riderless horse, the symbol of the fallen leader, with a black-handled sword in a silver scabbard hanging from the saddle … At this moment, just after noon, Americans throughout the country stopped their other activities … Times Square was silent, as cab drivers stopped their cars and got out to stand with bowed heads … At St. Matthew's cathedral, three-year-old John Kennedy Jr. joined soldiers and policemen in a final salute … At the burial site, 50 air force and navy planes – one for each state – boomed low overhead. They flew in inverted -V formations, with the point of the final V missing: the leader has gone. (Kertzer, 1988: 58–61)

Kertzer analyses each step in the ritual, draws out the symbolic elements and interprets them. He claims that the value of the ritual lies in its ability to promote social solidarity, and discusses the issue of American civil religion and the need for what he calls the typically American worship of the State: 'In polyreligious societies … religious rituals may be societally divisive … thus worship of the state gives people a way to express their unity' (1988: 65).

We will not dwell further on Kertzer's research, which clearly illustrates the use that can be made of newspapers in social research. The perspicacious researcher guided by theoretical hypotheses is able to construct a thoroughly convincing analysis out of the wealth of information provided by newspaper reports. We might also add that, apart from its descriptive aspect, as revealed in newspaper reports, the press is an inexhaustible mine of information on society in many other ways. We need mention only a few such sources: advertising (e.g. in studying changing social taboos regarding ways of attracting the consumer's attention), classified advertisements offering or requesting jobs (e.g. in studying trends in the labour market), obituaries (e.g. in studying changes in the social image of death), and readers' letters (e.g. in studying changes in citizens' concerns).

Our second example is to do with televised documents. Again, there is no need to dwell on the wealth of information that this material provides on the events and culture of every society. A great many studies have investigated the various types, or genres, of television programme: news coverage, sport, variety, action films, adventure, westerns, talk shows, soap operas, comedies, quizzes, cartoons, advertisements, etc. We will briefly mention a study conducted by two American researchers on soap operas, those stories broadcast in episodes, usually in the afternoon, largely involving sentimental relationships (Cantor and Pingree, 1983). These are what the authors call 'the only type of nationally televised dramatic entertainment specifically targeted … for the female audience', and as such are able to reveal society's female stereotype and the prevailing image of the 'average woman' in the world of advertising.

The most interesting aspect of this research is the authors' analysis of the serial *The Guiding Light*, the only soap opera to have been broadcast on the radio before being televised. This longest-running programme ever made in the US was first aired on the radio in 1947 and continually renewed its plots and characters over the years. The researchers analysed the characters involved, the style and the subjects of the dialogues, the settings, personal relationships, social issues, moral standards and sexual roles. As the material that they examined covered such a long period of time, it provided a faithful representation of how the condition and the image of women in American society had changed over the years. The authors regard the soap opera as a form of popular art that closely adheres to reality and follows its transformations. As they point out, 'the soap opera provides an ideal example of a popular art form that has evolved to meet the changing social conditions of its followers' (1983: 16).

3.2 Narratives, educational texts and folktales

First of all, it should be pointed out that the narrative may be an extraordinary source of social knowledge, though one that is not often exploited by social researchers. To illustrate the point, we might mention the brilliant anthology by Lewis Coser, *Sociology through Literature* (1963), in which the author presents a collection of extracts taken from classic authors (Dostoyevsky, Proust, Mark Twain, Ignazio Silone and others) on purely sociological themes, such as culture, socialization, social stratification, power and authority, bureaucracy, mass behaviour, deviance, etc. It is a book that clearly demonstrates the ability of literature to paint vivid pictures and provide insightful social analyses. This kind of material is, of course, most useful in the interpretive phase of the research, in which it can offer ideas, hints, inspiration and hypotheses. Nevertheless, we should not overlook its potential documentary value: e.g. the realistic descriptions of the living conditions of miners in northern France at the end of the 1800s in

Emile Zola's *Germinal* constitute a social document of great descriptive capacity.

Much can be learnt about the culture of a society from educational texts: school books and short stories designed to instil religious or moral precepts. As their purpose is to hand down the values and norms of the adult world to the new generations, these texts are probably the most faithful (and sometimes the most naïvely transparent) mirror of the culture and ideology of each period. A large amount of research has been done on such material, especially by analysts of educational processes. One such study compared primary school reading books used in Italy in three different periods: the fascist period, the immediate post-war period and the 1970s. The study clearly revealed the changes in values that had taken place over the years. For instance, the ideals of 'fatherland' and 'courage', which had occupied a dominant position in the 1930s, almost disappeared in the two subsequent periods; the importance of 'religion' was underlined in the 1950s Italy of the Christian Democrats, while the presence of 'family' values remained stable throughout (Livolsi et al., 1974: 265).

To conclude this section, we will briefly mention documents arising out of popular tradition. Folklore and the oral transmission of stories from one generation to the next have generated numerous such documents. *Morphology of the Folktale* by the Russian scholar Vladimir Propp (1928) is a well-known study of the structure of traditional Russian folktales. The author's analysis is based on the idea that the constituent units of the tale are not characters or events, but the 'functions' that these characters and events carry out – that is to say, the meaning that they take on in the unfolding of the plot. Every tale can be reduced to a succession of functions, which – and this is the most important finding of the study – follow one another according to recurrent patterns (even though the events, characters and settings may change). For instance, a great many tales begin with the following sequence of functions: estrangement (one of the family members leaves home), prohibition (imposed on the hero), disobedience (the prohibition is not respected), revelation (the villain elicits information from his victim), entrapment (the villain tries to deceive the victim), etc.

Propp's approach was very important insofar as it paved the way for structural analysis, from which modern structuralism was to emerge. However, our reference to Propp's work is intended merely to illustrate a particular form of document – the document generated by popular tradition – and how it can be used for the purposes of social research.

3.3 Judicial material

The judicial sphere provides a great deal of documentary material for social research. Judgments handed down by the courts, the minutes of trial proceedings, transcriptions of statements, reports of crimes, etc. provide a wealth of documentation for the study of numerous social phenomena, and particularly delinquency.

Ample use of this kind of documentation can be seen in the study conducted by Diego Gambetta (1992) on the Sicilian Mafia. This author examines the thesis that the Mafia, although brutal and secretive, belongs to a world that is not radically different from our own, in that it merely represents a particular kind of economic activity; it is an industry that produces, promotes and sells private protection. Starting out from this definition, the author analyses the activities of the Mafia, revealing its internal mechanisms, agreements between protector and protected, guarantees offered, services rendered, rewards agreed upon, territorial control, and relationships with officialdom and the police. In addition, he examines the structure of the organization, alliances, the power balance among groups, initiation rites, the career of the *mafioso*, internal rules and codes of conduct.

The documentary material on which the author bases his reconstruction is mostly taken from transcriptions of evidence given by Mafia 'turncoats' and recorded by investigating magistrates or during the trials held in Palermo and Agrigento in the second half of

the 1980s. These documents contain a wealth of detailed accounts, analyses of the motivations behind the protagonists' own actions, and attempts to interpret their own experience, all of which provide the researcher with precious information on the phenomenon of the Mafia. It should, however, be pointed out that the emergence of documentary material from the testimony of 'turncoats' is an exceptional occurrence within the sphere of delinquency studies. Nevertheless, the case quoted is a good example of how these documents (particularly statements made by the accused) can be used in social research.

Another source of judicial information is that of the so-called 'law reports', that is to say, the judgments handed down by the courts. These are generally very detailed; they report the facts, the various positions that emerge during the course of the trial and the reasons underlying the judges' decisions. They therefore constitute an excellent record of society and its dominant values. They are published regularly (we may quote, among others, the *Weekly Law Reports* and the *Court of Appeal Law Reports* in the UK) and widely consulted within the legal profession (especially by lawyers), since their decisions constitute precedents that may be invoked in future trials.

Such reports can also be used as documentary material for the purposes of social research. An example of this is provided by a study conducted in the UK by Paul Robertshaw (1985) on gender discrimination as revealed by the minutes of trials. The author examined 76 cases of trials held in the UK in the second half of the 1970s involving gender discrimination in employment. Chiefly by analyzing the language used in the judgments, he was able to uncover the cultural prejudices against women that pervaded the British judiciary at all levels from the Local Tribunals to the Court of Appeal and right up to the House of Lords.

In this case, law reports were not used to study unlawful behaviour, but to shed light on the ideology of society. In other cases, judgments have been used to investigate criminal phenomena. For example, Bourget et al. (2000) analyzed 387 cases of spousal homicide in Quebec between 1991 and 1998, in 55 of which homicidal spouses subsequently killed themselves. The judicial dossiers on each case were used as empirical material in this analysis. These revealed that the majority of such crimes were committed by men who were separated from their wives and often suffered from clinical depression.

3.4 Political documents

The world of politics offers the social researcher a rich source of documentary material, from acts of Parliament to political manifestos, and from politicians' speeches to election propaganda. Moreover, political documents were among the first to be used in social research; indeed, the earliest content analyses were conducted on political propaganda.

One of the first such studies was conducted by Lasswell and Leites (1949) on the slogans used in the Soviet Union between 1918 and 1943 in connection with the celebration of May Day. The authors classified these slogans into 11 categories on the basis of their content ('revolutionary' symbols, such as international communism, socialism and world revolution; 'national' symbols, such as the motherland, patriotism, defence, the enemy and aggression; 'personal' symbols, such as Lenin and Leninism, Marx, Engels, Luxembourg, Hitler, etc.). They subsequently analysed changes in the frequency of the use of the symbols over time (which revealed, for example, that, as the republic became progressively institutionalized over the years, the use of revolutionary symbols declined, while that of national symbols grew, and that 'moral' symbols, such as solidarity, discipline and honour, gave way to 'liberal' symbols, such as brotherhood, freedom and citizenship). Finally, party slogans were analysed as indicators of party policy and the political climate of the period.

A more recent study was conducted by Jeffrey Tulis (1987) on the evolution of 'presidential rhetoric' during the course of American history. The study was based on an analysis of presidential 'addresses to the nation', a method of communication whereby the President speaks directly to the people, without the mediation of any institution (such as the Congress). Tulis examined the speeches made by successive Presidents and noted that a profound transformation had taken place between the nineteenth and the twentieth centuries. The rhetorical appeal of the presidential address was seen to be a feature of the twentieth century; in the previous century, presidential speeches were mainly of a ceremonial nature, made little reference to patriotism and, especially, were never designed to mobilize public opinion with a view to influencing the legislative process. The author points out a marked change from one century to the next in terms of the number of presidential addresses, their format (which changed from written to oral) and their audience (mainly the Congress in the nineteenth century and the people in the twentieth). He maintains that this transformation can only be partly ascribed to the advent of new methods of communication, and particularly television (which obviously makes direct communication more efficacious); instead, he claims that it is mainly due to a transformation in the political culture of the country.

A great deal of documentation on the political life of a nation is, of course, produced at election time. Among the multitude of studies that have focused on electoral campaigns, political propaganda and party manifestos, we can quote the vast research conducted in the 1980s by three British scholars on the electoral programmes of political parties in 19 democracies from the end of the Second World War up to 1980 (Budge et al., 1987). Using election manifestos or, when these were not available, newspaper articles, the authors collected the electoral programmes of about 90 parties. They then analysed the content of the programmes, classified the issues mentioned into 54 categories (e.g. decolonization, peace, social justice, traditional morality, economic planning, etc.), and examined differences over time, among nations and among parties. For instance, they concluded that, in almost all countries, there was a left-right division which could be discerned in the content of the programmes. Further themes tackled by their research concerned the trend towards convergence/divergence of party programmes over time, the classification of parties into ideological families, and the changing similarities/differences among nations over time.

Among the studies conducted on electoral propaganda and political communication, we might mention the research carried out by Roderick Hart (2000) on electoral campaigns in the US. The author examines presidential elections over a long period of time (1948–1996) through documents such as transcriptions of speeches and debates, televised reports and propaganda broadcasts, newspaper articles and even citizens' letters to newspapers. The aim of this research was to investigate changes in the rhetoric of political communication in the US over the past 50 years.

3.5 Administrative and business documents

We will now look at the documents produced by work organizations. During the course of their institutional life, businesses, schools, hospitals, professional associations, companies, etc. produce a whole range of documents that are able to provide a complete representation of the slice of society to which they belong. Such documents include balance-sheets, letters, circulars, company organization charts, membership lists, stock inventories, tax returns, the minutes of meetings, annual reports, financial statements, etc.

This material is extremely heterogeneous. As Atkinson and Coffey (1997: 48) point out, 'certain document types constitute – to use a literary analogy – *genres*, with distinctive styles and conventions', in the sense that they use specialized forms of language that are associated with particular fragments of our daily lives. Just as there are literary genres, we might say that there are bureaucratic genres. We need only think of the language used to present an art exhibition or to describe the 'bouquet' of a wine, of the wording of a company balance-sheet, or of that prototype

of cryptic language that is accessible only to the initiated, medical language.

Many studies have been conducted on the basis of these documents. In accordance with our usual procedure, we will briefly illustrate a few of them in order to give the reader an idea of the potential of this kind of material.

We will begin with the world of business in the strict sense. An illustrious pioneer in this field was Max Weber. On observing the radical changes that the advent of large industry was exerting on society, Weber pondered what effect this might have 'on the personality, occupational destiny and leisure-time lifestyle of its workers' and wondered 'what physical and mental qualities it develops in them and how these are manifested in the overall life of the workers' (Weber, 1924). In order to investigate these questions, he conducted a study in 1908 on what he called 'the psychophysics of industrial work' in a Westfalia textile factory owned by relatives of his. He examined variations in worker productivity in relation to changes in the weather, how wages were paid (hourly or piece-rate), the personal features of the workers (differences between men and women, young and old, the married and the unmarried, etc.), working hours, the type of machinery used (different kinds of loom), etc. What interests us here is that he carried out this research on the basis of company documents, spending 'long weeks poring over account books and production registers', as we are told by his widow Marianne Weber (1924: 67).

The balance-sheets of public administrations are, of course, an important documentary source for the study of public policy. This kind of material, and particularly municipal balance-sheets, was used in a study conducted in Italy at the beginning of the 1980s (Felicori, 1984). In the administrative elections of 1975–1976, the left had won control of several large municipalities, such as Rome, Milan, Turin, Venice, and Florence. The question therefore arose as to the innovative scope of these new administrations, particularly with regard to expenditure on cultural events. This was a time in which mass cultural events were in vogue and local authorities financed and organized collective entertainment at public venues. One of the questions raised was whether this new cultural policy extended to all municipalities and was not limited to the large, more visible municipalities. A further query was whether this really was a policy of the new left-wing administrations, and not simply a general trend that involved the whole country.

The study was able to focus on these issues by analyzing local authority balance-sheets. These revealed how much of the total expenditure for cultural purposes had been channelled into the new 'mass events' as opposed to the traditional items (museums, libraries, theatres, etc.).

School archives also hold a quantity of documentary material that can be used in social research. For instance, the essays that educational institutes often keep for years may be used to study changes in youth culture over time. In the 1970s, the British sociologist Peter Woods carried out research in a secondary school in an industrial town in Britain. While his study was conducted mainly through participant observation, Woods also made ample use of documentary material from the school archives. For example, he studied the way in which teachers expressed their assessments of pupils and the mental categories that they used in order to do so. To this end, he examined the school reports that the teachers periodically filled in and sent to their pupils' parents; in addition to the marks awarded in each subject, these reports also contained a succinct judgement (such as 'works hard', 'could do better', etc.). Woods used these judgements to analyse the teachers' culture and the way in which they made their assessments. He maintains that 'nowhere teachers' categorization systems … are so clearly evident and so succinctly crystallized as in school reports' (Woods, 1979: 171). In his careful analysis of the content of these judgements, Woods picked out the most important concepts and 'ideal types'. He maintains that this process of rapid classification of pupils into rather coarse stereotypes is typical of

institutions, which are obliged to work out standard procedures in order to 'ensure mass treatment based on efficiency'.

Social research can also make use of the large amounts of documentary material generated by the world of health care. In 1977, Lindsay Prior conducted a study of the way in which the World Health Organization classifies diseases and the causes of death. The author maintains that every system of classification, rather than being an accurate representation of an external order inherent in objective reality, is an expression of the rules and themes that predominate in a given socio-cultural context. It is the qualitative researcher's task to identify what is a projection of the culture of that society rather than a reflection of an external reality. It is from this standpoint that Prior analyses the classification of the cause of death and its evolution over time (since it was first drawn up in 1903). He therefore asks when old age and decrepitude ceased to be regarded as causes of death. Today, diseases are viewed as 'somatic', a vision that is centred on the body as a biological system, on symptoms rather than on causes. But, he adds, has there ever been a time when 'poverty' was included among the causes of death?

3.6 Physical traces

So far, we have dealt with written documents. However, in the course of their activities, human beings also leave physical traces, *material documents* from which it is possible to trace the activities that have produced them. A detective carried out a similar task: if a body is found in a wood, the detective will observe the surrounding traces, the posture of the victim, the arrangement of the clothing, footprints on the ground and so on, in order to reconstruct how the murder was committed. Likewise, by analysing the scene of a party the morning after, we can work out how many guests attended, how old they were, what they drank, how long the party lasted, and what went on, even down to specific incidents such as a fight.

In a well-known volume published in the 1960s, which was the first to tackle this issue,

Webb and colleagues (1966) distinguished two broad categories of physical traces: traces of erosion and traces of accretion. *Traces of erosion* are encountered whenever a human activity causes the wear and tear of a given physical support. The degree of this wear and tear can be taken as an indicator of the activity that has produced it. For example, these authors point out that it is possible to estimate the number of people who frequent a certain place by observing the degree of wear of the floor, and suggest using this technique to gauge, for instance, the relative popularity of the various rooms in a museum. To illustrate their point, they report that in the Science Museum in Chicago the vinyl floor covering around an exhibit of live chicks had to be replaced every six months, while in other parts of the museum it lasted for years. Likewise the popularity of books in a library can be judged through signs of wear on the pages (tattered edges, marked, creased, yellowed) and they report that the most frequently consulted sections of the *International Encyclopedia of Social Sciences* in their university library were immediately distinguishable by the different colour of their pages (1966: 7–9).

By contrast, *traces of accretion* are left when the activity carried out causes material to be deposited. In this regard, we can quote the studies on refuse carried out by Rathje, who organized teams to collect, sort and classify household refuse from a sample population, thereby making interesting discoveries about the lifestyles of these families (Rathje and Murphy, 1992). Further examples include studies on the productivity and work practices of a machine maintenance department through the measurement of the amount of dust found on the parts to be overhauled, or again the operationalization of the condition of isolation (or otherwise) from the outside world of patients in a psychiatric hospital on the basis of the amount of mail that they received (Webb et al., 1966).

Various studies have examined graffiti. Though executed purely for amusement, graffiti may nevertheless reveal deep urges. In his monumental study of sexuality in America, Kinsey collected hundreds of examples of graffiti from the walls of public lavatories and found significant differences in the incidence of erotic graffiti between men's and women's lavatories (providing empirical corroboration for the thesis that there is a different sexual culture between males and females in contemporary society) (Kinsey et al., 1953). Studies that are in some respects similar have been conducted on the graffiti and wall-writings that have accompanied social protest movements, such as the student movements of the 1960s and 1970s.

Other physical signs, which are not classifiable as traces of erosion or accretion, include road signs and public notices in languages other than the official language, thus indicating the recognition and acceptance of different ethnic groups; or the seating arrangements of blacks and whites at a public meeting, as an indicator of racial integration (Bouchard, 1976: 283).

Finally, we will conclude this section by briefly mentioning visual documents (strictly speaking, these should be dealt with in a separate section devoted to *visual sociology*, as they cannot easily be classified as material documents). Photography, cinema and television, in addition to being the subjects of study as cultural products or forms of mass communication, can also be used as research instruments, as social documents of considerable cognitive importance. The history of the images of social reality encountered a major turning point with photography around 1830. For almost a century, this reality was depicted mostly in photographs: portraits, war photographs, photographs documenting the great cities of industrial civilizations or journeys to exotic lands, photographic souvenirs of everyday family life. Subsequently, the cinema came on the scene, and then television. More recently, the invention of the video-camera, which enables social phenomena to be filmed live, has placed a powerful new tool in the hands of the researcher. In reality, our reflection on this theme should take into account both the historical-documentary contribution of visual documents (photographs and footage of past events) and the new potential offered by the ability to record movements and sequences, and to do so 'in the field', thus providing the researcher with new ways of observing and analysing society.

4. A FINAL NOTE: AN ENDLESS SOURCE OF SOCIAL KNOWLEDGE

4.1 Reading individual documents

As has already been noted with regard to other qualitative techniques, there are essentially two ways of approaching personal documents. The first of these is substantially 'reductive'. The literary fascination and evocative power of these sources are acknowledged but, since they are accounts of unique and irreducible experiences of life, personal documents are relegated to a pre-scientific domain; at best, they are assigned an integrative (and, in the final analysis, 'illustrative') role in support of theoretical considerations acquired by other means.

Even Herbert Blumer, who was one of the theoreticians of the qualitative approach to social research, casts doubt on the contribution of personal documents. While they 'offer to the student the opportunity to increase his experience and to sharpen his sense of inquiry' and help the reader of a report to 'form a closer acquaintance with the kind of experience which is being studied and to form a judgement as to the reasonable nature of the interpretations proposed' (Blumer, 1939: 80–1), personal documents alone are not enough to validate a scientific theory. Indeed, 'the interpretive content of a human document depends markedly on the competence and theoretical framework with which the document is studied. One person, by virtue of his experience and his interests, may detect things that another person would not see ... Human documents seem to lend themselves readily to diverse interpretations. One can see this in the ease with which they can be analysed by different theories of motivation. Theories seem to order the data' (Blumer, 1939: 77).

A different position is adopted by the staunchest advocates of the interpretive approach. According to Schwartz and Jacobs, for example, 'there is the "objective" world ... and the individual's experience of that world' (1979: 61), both of which are worthy of interest. However, if the researcher decides to investigate the latter, then even the study of a single case becomes a significant source of empirical information:

> The *idiographic* approach[3] ... stresses the legitimacy of investigating and researching the life of a single individual ... This view contends that it is scientifically valid and methodologically correct to study the behavior of one human being and to perceive her not only as a representative of a group but also as an independent totality from which generalizations can be drawn. It further contends that the true goal of the social sciences is *understanding* behavior, not quantifying, classifying, or dissecting behavioral patterns. Idiographists feel that this is best accomplished through the use of the case-study method, since this allows one to study the totality of a single personality on a gestalt level (Schwartz and Jacobs, 1979: 69).

In other words, if our aim is not to *explain* facts, but to *understand* them, then even the study of single cases can shed light on the reality that we are studying, and therefore help us to understand. We may also say – in a way that is only slightly different – that, although personal documents are surely insufficient for the purposes of *describing*, and probably also for of those of *explaining*, social phenomena, they can nevertheless make a valuable contribution to our *interpretation* of these phenomena.

Finally, we should not lose sight of the fact that personal documents are so called because they concern the 'personal lives' of the individuals studied. Reconstructing the personal affairs of the subject also enables us to understand how that unique set of biographical circumstances has been able to produce certain behaviours. In this sense, personal documents – and particularly life stories – provide a diachronic view of the subjects' affairs that is not accessible through other instruments. The analysis of life stories may, in some cases, be the only way of understanding how certain persons have become what they are and why they behave as they do, and thus contributes in an original and unique manner to the interpretation of social phenomena.

4.2 Reading institutional documents

Every recognizable human activity in our society produces documents. Modern society is a society that documents itself continuously; there is no institutional act or socially organized activity that does not leave behind some documentary trace. This means that there is no phenomenon in the life of society that cannot be studied through the analysis of documents.

The most obvious advantages of using documents for the purposes of social research can be summarized under three headings: (a) non-reactivity; (b) the possibility of diachronic analysis; and (c) lower costs. The first two of these points were touched upon at the beginning of this chapter. As to the third, this feature chiefly concerns institutional documents. By definition, the use of documents does not involve the cost of producing the information (as, for example, in the case of an interview), in that the material has already been produced. We might also add that institutions produce large numbers of documents, which – when they are accessible – are often grouped together in specific locations; the additional cost of recording each single document is therefore modest, which means that very large samples can be constructed at low cost.

The disadvantages of using institutional documents are also obvious, and can be summarized as: (a) the incompleteness of the information, and (b) the official nature of what they represent. With regard to the first point, we need only refer back to what was said in the first section of this chapter (the information contained in the documents – which are produced for purposes other than those of research – is often scant and insufficient; nor can it be supplemented, as the document is 'found' and not produced by the researcher).

For what concerns the second problem (the official nature of the documents), it should be said that documents often are not objective representations of the institutional reality to which they refer, but instead provide an 'official' representation of it. Thus, the balance-sheets of a company or political party are drawn up in response to the regulations in force, and often provide a distorted image of the true financial situation of the organization. Similarly, it will not be possible to study the real distribution of power in a company only on the basis of the company organization chart, and schoolchildren's essays on what they think of their school or their country often reflect social conventions more than their true opinions.

In other words, institutional documents reflect exactly what their definition suggests – that is to say, the institutional dimension of the phenomena studied, which is certainly different from the personal dimension. Once again, we will draw the reader's attention to the different viewpoints from which social reality is seen in the two parts of this chapter, the first devoted to personal documents and the second to institutional documents. However, difference does not, of course, suggested inferiority of either one or the other perspective.

SUMMARY

1. Three fundamental actions underlie techniques of qualitative research: *observing, asking* and *reading*. This chapter involves the third element: reading documents produced by individuals and institutions. A document is any type of material that provides information on a given social phenomenon and which exists independently of the researcher's actions.

2. *Personal documents* have a private nature, being produced by single individuals for strictly personal use. They are also called 'expressive' documents, in that they express the feelings, the affairs and, more generally, the personality of the individuals who

produce them. They have been classified into autobiographies, diaries, letters and oral testimony.

2.1. Autobiographies are written accounts of the whole life of a person, produced by that person in a limited time, and therefore within a retrospective vision. In its ideal form, the autobiography is spontaneously written by an unselected author, even if in the social sciences autobiographies are rarely encountered in this form.

2.2. *Diaries and letters* These documents are written for strictly personal use and at the same time as the described events take place. Rarely are studies based entirely on diaries and letters, in that these sources are usually used along with other documentary material. Diaries and letters were used especially in the early historical phases of qualitative research, in the 1920s and 1930s: today other types of narrative material, such as oral testimony, are preferred.

2.3. *Oral testimony* This type of 'document' comprises accounts of life experiences elicited by the researcher. We can distinguish between life stories and oral histories. A *life story* is an account of the subject's own life as narrated to the interviewer; its object is an individual, his biographical data, feelings, outlook and personal experiences. An *oral history* is the subject's account of specific events that she has witnessed; the object of the oral history is *society*, its customs and events. In the former case, the narrator stands at the centre of the account; in the latter case, the account focuses on the events that the narrator has lived through.

3. *Institutional documents* are produced by institutions or single individuals within the context of their institutional roles.

Unlike personal documents, they generally have a public nature. These documents consist mostly of written texts; they do not only concern the memorable moments of a society or culture (such as peace treaties, laws or literary texts) but also, and especially, the daily lives of ordinary people. They have been classified, according to their sources, into mass media; narratives, educational texts and folktales; judicial material; political documents; administrative and business documents; and physical evidence. Such documents represent an irreplaceable source of empirical material for the study of contemporary society (much as documents of the past are precious for historical research).

FURTHER READING

A comprehensive introduction to the use of 'personal documents' in general, such as diaries, letters, autobiographies, oral histories, photographs, films, etc., can be found in K. Plummer, *Documents of life* (Allen & Unwin, 1983, pp. 175).

T.L. Orbuch's 'People's Accounts Count: The Sociology of Accounts', *Annual Review of Sociology 1997* is a brief review on the use of personal accounts in social research. For a comprehensive introduction to the use of biographical and family history, in a balanced treatment that addresses realist, neo-positivist and narrative methodological approaches, see R.L. Miller, *Researching Life Stories and Family Histories* (Sage, 2000, pp. 192).

An introduction to the use of documentary sources in social research is given by J. Scott, *A Matter of Record: Documentary Sources in Social Research* (Polity Press, 1990, pp. 233). For so-called 'unobtrusive measures' (including material culture, physical traces, audiovisual documents, etc.) we suggest a classic: E.J. Webb, D.T. Campbell, R.D. Schwartz and L. Sechrest, *Unobtrusive Measures* (Corwin Press, revised ed. 1999, pp. 240). A more recent book on the same subject is A. Kellehear, *The Unobtrusive Researcher* (Allen & Unwin,

1993, pp. 177). I also recommend a stimulating review article on 'sociology of place' (material forms of cities, natural physical environments, technology and transportation, and urban landscapes) by T.F. Gieryn, 'A Space for Place in Sociology', *Annual Review of Sociology 2000*).

NOTES

1. Except for the last case quoted (oral testimony), which will be dealt with later.

2. The fact that, in this case, the empirical material does not consist of life stories, but of letters, is of no relevance to the point that is being illustrated (considerations on how autobiographical material is handled are applicable to all personal documents).

3. 'Idiographic' means: relating to individual features (from the Greek ídios, 'one's own', and graphos, 'written').

References

Abbagnano, N. (1971) *Dizionario di filosofia*, Torino, Utet.

Adorno, T.W., Frenkel-Brunswik, E., Levinson, D.J. and Nevitt. R. (1950) *The Authoritarian Personality*, New York, J. Wiley; quotations from 1964 edition.

Alberoni, F., Capecchi, V., Manoukian, A., Olivetti, F. and Tosi, A. (1967) *L'attivista di partito*, Bologna, Il Mulino.

Anderson, N. (1923) *The Hobo*, Chicago, The University of Chicago Press.

Arendell, T. (1986) *Mothers and Divorce*, Berkeley, University of California Press.

Aronson, E., Brewer, M. and Carlsmith, J.M. (1985) 'Experimentation in Social Psychology', in G. Lindzey and E. Aronson (eds), *Handbook of Social Psychology*, New York, Random House.

Atkinson, P. (1995) *Medical Talk and Medical Work*, London, Sage.

Atkinson, P. and Coffey, A. (1997) 'Analyzing Documentary Realities', in D. Silverman (ed.), *Qualitative Research*, London, Sage.

Babbie, E.R. (1979) *The Practice of Social Research*, Belmont, Wadsworth.

Bales, R.F. (1951) *Interaction Process Analysis*, Reading, Addison-Wesley.

Bandura, A., Ross, D. and Ross, S.A. (1963) 'Imitation of Film Mediated Aggressive Models', *Journal of Abnormal and Social Psychology*, 66: 3–11.

Banfield, E.C. (1958) *The Moral Basis of a Backward Society*, Glencoe, The Free Press.

Barbagli, M. (1995) *L'occasione e l'uomo ladro*, Bologna, Il Mulino.

Bartolini, S. and Mair, P. (1990) *Identity, Competition and Electoral Availability*, Cambridge, Cambridge University Press.

Bastin, G. (1961) *Les techniques sociométriques*, Paris, Puf.

Bechhofer, F. (1974) 'Current Approaches to Empirical Research: Some Central Ideas', in J. Rex (ed.), *Approaches to Sociology: An Introduction to Major Trends in British Sociology*, London, Routledge & Kegan Paul.

Becker, H. (1963) *Outsiders. Studies in the Sociology of Deviance*, Glencoe, The Free Press.

Biemer, P.P., Groves, R.M., Lyberg, L.E., Mathiowetz, N.A. and Sudman, S. (eds) (1991) *Measurement Errors in Surveys*, New York, John Wiley.

Bishop, G.F., Tuchfarber, A.J. and Oldendick, R.W. (1986) 'Opinions in Fictious Issues: The Pressure to Answer Survey Questions', *Public Opinion Quarterly*, 50: 240–50.

Black, T.R. (1999) *Doing Quantitative Research in The Social Sciences: An Integrated Approach to Research Design, Measurement and Statistics*, London, Sage.

Blaikie, N. (1993) *Approaches to Social Inquiry*, Cambridge, Polity Press.

Blalock, H.M. (1961) *Causal Inferences in Nonexperimental Research*, Chapel Hill, The University of North Carolina Press.

Blalock, H.M. (1970) *An Introduction to Social Research*, Englewood Cliffs, Prentice Hall.

Blau, P. and Duncan, O.D. (1967) *The American Occupational Structure*, New York, Wiley.

Blumer, H. (1939) *An Appraisal of Thomas and Znaniecki's 'The Polish Peasant in Europe and America'*, New York, Social Science Research Council, Bulletin 44.

Blumer, H. (1969) *Symbolic Interactionism: Perspective and Method*, Englewood Cliffs, Prentice Hall.

Bogardus, E.S. (1925) 'Measuring Social Distance', *Journal of Applied Sociology*, 9: 299–308.

Boltanski, L. (1990) *L'Amour et la Justice comme compétences*, Paris, Métailié.

Borman, K.M., LeCompte, M.D. and Goetz, J.P. (1986) 'Ethnographic and Qualitative Research Design and Why It Doesn't Work', *American Behavioral Scientist*, 30: 42–57.

Bottomore T.B. and Rubel, M. (1956) *Karl Marx: Selected Writings in Sociology and Social Philosophy*, New York, McGraw Hill.

Bouchard, T.J. (1976) 'Unobtrusive Measures: An Inventory of Uses', *Sociological Methods and Research*, 4: 267–300.

Boudon, R. (1984) *La place du désordre*, Paris, Presses Universitaires de France; quotations from *Theories of Social Change*, Cambridge, Polity Press, 1986.

Bourget, D., Gagne, P. and Moamai, J. (2000) 'Spousal Homicide and Suicide in Quebec', *Journal of the American Academy of Psychiatry and the Law*, 28(2): 179–82.

Bryman, A. (1988) *Quantity and Quality in Social Research*, London, Routledge.

Bryman, A. and Burgess, R.G. (1994) *Analyzing Qualitative Data*, London, Routledge.

Budge, I., Robertson, D. and Hearl, D. (1987) *Ideology, Strategy and Party Change*, Cambridge, Cambridge University Press.

Bunge, M. (1959) *Causality*, Cambridge, Harvard University Press.

Burawoy, M. (1979) *Manufacturing Consent: Changes in the Labor Process under Monopoly Capitalism*, Chicago, University of Chicago Press.

Campbell, A., Gurin, G. and Miller, W.E. (1954) *The Voter Decides*, Evanston, Row and Peterson.

Campbell, D.T. and Stanley, J.C. (1963) *Experimental and Quasi-experimental Designs for Research*, Chicago, Rand McNally.

Cantor, M.G. and Pingree, S. (1983) *The Soap Opera*, Beverly Hills, Sage.

Cantril, H. and Free, L.A. (1962) 'Hopes and Fears for Self and Country: the Self-Anchoring Scale in Cross-Cultural Research', *American Behavioral Scientist*, 6, suppl. October: 1–30.

Capecchi, V. and Livolsi, M. (1973) *Televisione e bambini*, Roma, Rai – Servizio opinioni.

Caplow, T., Hicks, L. and Wattenberg, B.J. (2001) *The First Measured Century: An Illustrated Guide to Trends in America, 1900–2000*, Washington D.C., AEI Press.

Caplow, T., Bahr, H.M., Modell, J. and Chadwick, B.A. (1991) *Recent Social Trends in the United States 1960–1990*, Montreal & Kingston, McGill-Queen's University Press.

Carley, M. (1981) *Social Measurement and Social Indicators*, London, George Allen & Unwin.

Carmines, E.G. and Zeller, R.A. (1983) *Reliability and Validity Assessment*, Newbury Park, Sage.

Cartocci, R. (1993) 'Rilevare la secolarizzazione: indicatori a geometria variabile', *Rivista italiana di scienza politica*, 23: 119–52.

Cavan, R.S. (1928) *Suicide*, New York, Russell & Russell.

Chirban, J.T. (1996) *Interviewing in Depth: The Interactive-Relational Approach*, Newbury Park, Sage.

Cicourel, A.V. (1964) *Method and Measurement in Sociology*, New York, The Free Press.

Clayman, S.E. (1993) 'Booing: the Anatomy of a Disaffiliative Response', *American Sociological Review*, 58: 110–130.

Cochran, W.G. (1977) *Sampling Techniques*, 3rd ed., New York, Wiley.

Cole, R. (1979) *Work, Mobility and Participation*, Berkeley, University of California Press.

Collett, P. and Marsh, P. (1974) 'Patterns of Public Behaviour: Collision Avoidance on a Pedestrian Crossing', *Semiotica*, 12: 281–99.

Collins, R. (1988) *Theoretical Sociology*, Orlando, Harcourt Brace Jovanovich.

Collins, M., Sykes, W., Wilson, P. and Blackshaw, N. (1988) *Nonresponse: the UK Experience*, in Groves et al. (1988).

Converse, P.E. (1970) 'Attitudes and Non-attitudes: Continuation of a Dialog', in E.R. Tufte (ed.), *The Quantitative Analysis of Social Problems*, Reading, Mass, Addison-Wesley.

Converse, J.M. and Presser, S. (1986) *Survey Questions: Handcrafting the Standardized Questionnaire*, Thousands Oaks, Sage.

Cook, T.D. and Campbell D.T. (1979) *Quasi-experimentation: Design and Analysis Issues for Field Settings*, Boston, Houghton Mifflin.

Corbetta, P. and Parisi, A.M.L. (1987) 'Il calo della partecipazione elettorale: disaffezione delle istituzioni o crisi dei riferimenti partitici?', *Polis*, 1: 29–65.

Corsaro, W.A. and Rizzo, T.A. (1990) *Disputes in the Peer Culture of American and Italian Nursery School Children*, in Grimshaw (1990).

Coser, L. (ed.) (1963) *Sociology Through Literature*, Englewood Cliffs, Prentice Hall.

Costrich, N., Feinstein, J., Kidder, L., Marecek, J. and Pascale, L. (1975) 'When Stereotypes Hurt: Three Studies of Penalties for Sex-role Reversals', *Journal of Experimental Social Psychology*, 11: 520–30.

Coulon, A. (1995) *Ethnomethodology*, Thousands Oaks, Sage.

Creswell, J.W. (1994) *Qualitative and Quantitative Approaches*, Thousands Oaks, Sage.

Crook, S. (2001) *Social Theory and the Postmodern*, in Ritzer and Smart (2001).

Dahl, R.A. (1961) *Who Governs?*, New Haven, Yale University Press.

Davis, F. (1973) 'The Martian and the Covert: Ontological Polarities in Social Research', in *Urban Life*, 3: 333–43.

Del Piero, A. (1994), *L'isola della quarantina*, Firenze, Giunti.

Denzin, N.K. (1989) *The Research Act*, Englewood Cliffs, Prentice-Hall.

Denzin, N.K. (1997) *Interpretive Ethnography: Ethnographic Practices for the Twenty-first Century*, Thousand Oaks, Sage.

Denzin, N.K. and Lincoln, Y.S. (eds) (1994) *Handbook of Qualitative Research*, Newbury Park, Sage; 2nd ed. (2000).

De Vellis, R.F. (1991) *Scale Development: Theory and Applications*, Newbury Park, Sage.

Dillman, D. (1978) *Mail and Telephone Survey: The Total Design method*, New York, Wiley.

Dillman, D.A. (1991) 'The Design and Administration of Mail Surveys', *Annual Review of Sociology 1991*, 17: 225–49.

Dilthey, W. (1883) *Einleitung in die Geisteswissenschaften*, Leipzig.

Duncan, O.D. (1984) *Notes on Social Measurement: Historical and Critical*, New York, Russell Sage Foundation.

Durkheim, E. (1895) *Les règles de la méthode sociologique*, Paris, Alcan; quotations from *The Rules of Sociological Method*, New York, MacMillan, 1982.

Durkheim, E. (1897) *Le suicide: Étude de sociologie*, Paris, Alcan; quotations from *Suicide. A Study in Sociology*, New York, The Free Press, 1966.

Edwards, A.L. (1957) *Techniques of Attitude Scale Construction*, New York, Appleton.

Evans, G.E. (1975) *The Days that We Have Seen*, London, Faber and Faber.

Felicori, M. (1984) 'Feste d'estate: indagine sulla politica culturale dei comuni italiani', in A.M.L. Parisi (ed.), *Luoghi e misure della politica*, Bologna, Il Mulino.

Firebaugh, G. (1997) *Analyzing Repeated Surveys*, Thousand Oaks, Sage.

Fisher, R.A. (1935) *The Design of Experiments*, Edinburgh, Oliver & Boyd.

Foucault, M. (1975) *Surveiller et punir. Naissance de la prison*, Paris, Gallimard.

Fowler, F.J. Jr. (1995) *Improving Survey Questions: Design and Evaluation*, Thousand Oaks, Sage.

Friedrichs, R.W. (1970) *A Sociology of Sociology*, New York, The Free Press.

Gallino, L. (1978) *Dizionario di sociologia*, Torino, Utet.

Galtung, J. (1967) *Theory and Methods of Social Research*, Oslo, Universitetsforlaget.

Gambetta, D. (1987) *Were They Pushed or Did They Jump?*, Cambridge, Cambridge University Press.

Gambetta, D. (1992) *La mafia siciliana*, Torino, Einaudi.

Gane, M. (2001) *Durkheim's Project for a Sociological Science*, in Ritzer and Smart (2001).

Geertz, C. (1973) *The Interpretation of Cultures*, New York, Basic Books.

Genders, E. and Player, E. (1995) *Grendon: a Study of a Therapeutic Prison*, Oxford, Clarendon Press.

Gieryn, T.F. (2000) 'A Space for Place in Sociology', *Annual Review of Sociology 2000*, 26: 463–96.

Glaser, B.G. and Strauss, A.L. (1967) *The Discovery of Grounded Theory: Strategies for Qualitative Research*, New York, Aldine.

Glass, G.V. (1976) 'Primary, Secondary and Meta-analysis of Research', *Educational Researcher*, 5 (10): 3–8.

Glass, G.V., McGaw, B. and Smith, M.L. (1987) *Meta-analysis in Social Research*, Beverly Hills, Sage.

Glock, C.Y. (1959) 'There is a Religious Revival in the United States?', in J. Zahn (ed.), *Religion and the Face of America*, Berkeley, University Extension, University of California.

Glueck, S. and Glueck, E. (1950) *Unraveling Juvenile Delinquency*, New York, The Commonwealth Fund.

Goffman, E. (1959) *The Presentation of Self in Everyday Life*, New York, Doubleday.

Goffman, E. (1967) *Interaction Ritual*, New York, Doubleday.

Goldfarb, W. (1945) 'Psychological Privation in Infancy and Subsequent Adjustment', *American Journal of Orthopsychiatry*, 15: 247–53.

Goldthorpe, J.H. (2000) *On Sociology: Numbers, Narratives, and the Integration of Research and Theory*, Oxford, Oxford University Press.

Goode, W.J and Hatt, P.K. (1952) *Methods in Social Research*, New York, McGraw-Hill.

Gouldner, A.W. (1954a) *Patterns of Industrial Bureaucracy*, New York, The Free Press.

Gouldner, A.W. (1954b) *The Wildcat Strike*, New York, The Antioch Press.

Granovetter, M. (1995) *Getting a Job*, Chicago, The University of Chicago Press.

Grimshaw, A.D. (ed.) (1990) *Conflict Talk*, Cambridge, The University Press.

Groves, R.M. (ed.) (1988) *Telephone Survey Methodology*, New York, Wiley.

Groves, R.M. (1989) *Survey Errors and Survey Costs*, New York, Wiley.

Groves, R.M. (1990) 'Theories and Methods of Telephone Surveys', *Annual Review of Sociology 1990*, 16: 221–40.

Guba, E.G. and Lincoln, Y.S. (1994) *Competing Paradigms in Qualitative Research*, in Denzin and Lincoln (1994).

Gubrium, J.F. and Holstein J. (1997) *The New Language of Qualitative Method*, New York, Oxford University Press.

Gubrium, J.F. and Holstein, J.A. (eds) (2002) *Handbook of Interview Research: Context and Method*, Thousand Oaks, Sage.

Gurr, T.R. (1972) *Politimetrics*, Englewood Cliffs, Prentice Hall.

Guttman, L.A. (1944) 'A Basis for Scaling Qualitative Data', *American Sociological Review*, 9: 139–50.

Guttman, L.A. (1950) 'The Basis for Scalogram Analysis', in S. Stouffer (ed.), *Measurement and Prediction*, Princeton, Princeton University Press.

Hall, G. (1976) 'Workshop as a Ballerina: an Exercise in Professional Socialization', *Urban Life and Culture*, 6: 193–220.

Halfpenny, P. (2001) *Positivism in Twentieth Century*, in Ritzer and Smart (2001).

Halsey, A.H. and J. Webb (eds) (2000) *Twentieth-Century British Social Trends*, Houndmills, Palgrave Macmillan.

Hammersley, M. and Atkinson, P. (1983) *Ethnography: Principles in Practice*, London, Tavistock; 2nd ed. Routledge, 1995.

Hanson, N.R. (1958) *Patterns of Discovery*, Cambridge, Cambridge University Press.

Hart, R.P. (2000) *Campaign Talk: Why Elections are Good for Us*, Princeton, Princeton University Press.

Henry, G.T. (1990) *Practical Sampling*, Newbury Park, Sage.

Heritage, J. (1984) *Garfinkel and Ethnomethodology*, Cambridge, Polity Press.

Heritage, J. and Greatbatch, D. (1986) 'Generating Applause: a Study of Rhetoric and Response at Party Political Conferences', *American Journal of Sociology*, 92: 110–57.

Holland, P.W. (1986) 'Statistics and Causal Inference', *Journal of the American Statistical Association*, 81: 945–60.

Horn, R.V. (1993) *Statistical Indicators for the Economic & Social Sciences*, Cambridge, Cambridge University Press.

Houtkoop-Steenstra, H. (2000) *Interaction and the Standardized Survey Interview: The Living Questionnaire*, Cambridge, Cambridge University Press.

Hughes, J.A. (1980) *The Philosophy of Social Research*, New York, Longman.

Hyman, H. (ed.) (1954) *Interviewing in Social Research*, Chicago, The University of Chicago Press.

Iceberg, S. (1967) *Pimp: the Story of My Life*, Los Angeles, Holloway.

Inglehart, R. (1977) *The Silent Revolution*, Princeton, Princeton University Press.

Irwin, J. (1970) *The Felon*, Englewood Cliffs, Prentice Hall.

Irwin, J. (1980) *Prisons in Turmoil*, Boston, Little, Brown & Co.

ISR – Institute for Social Research (1976) *Interviewer's Manual*, Ann Arbor, University of Michigan.

Janowitz, M. (1958) 'Inferences about Propaganda Impact from Textual and Documentary Analysis', in W.E. Daugherty and M. Janowitz (eds), *A Psychological Warfare Casebook*, Baltimore, Johns Hopkins Press.

Jenkins, R. (1983) *Lads, Citizens and Ordinary Kids*, London, Routledge & Kegan.

Jorgensen, D.L. (1989) *Participant Observation*, Newbury Park, Sage.

Kahn, R.L. and Cannel, C.F. (1967), *The Dynamics of Interviewing*, New York, Wiley; new edition, *Dynamics of Interviewing: Theory, Technique and Cases*, Malabar, Krieger, 1983.

Kalton, G. (1983) *Introduction to Survey Sampling*, Beverly Hills, Sage.

Kasprzyk, D., Duncan, G., Kalton G. and Singh M.P. (eds) (1989) *Panel Surveys*, New York, John Wiley.

Kellehear, A. (1993) *The Unobtrusive Researcher*, St Leonards, Allen & Unwin.

Kendon, A. (1990) *Conducting Interaction*, Cambridge, Cambridge University Press.

Kertzer, D. (1980) *Comrades and Christia: Religion and Political Struggle in Communist Italy*, Cambridge, Cambridge University Press.

Kertzer, D. (1988) *Ritual, Politics and Power*, New Haven, Yale University Press.

Kiecolt, K.J. and Nathan, L.E. (1985) *Secondary Analysis of Survey Data*, Beverly Hills, Sage.

King, G., Keohane, R.O. and Verba, S. (1994) *Designing Social Inquiry*, Princeton, Princeton University Press.

Kinsey, A.C., Pomeroy, W.B., Martin, C.E. and Grebhard, P.H. (1953) *Sexual Behavior in the Human Female*, Philadelphia, Saunders.

Kish, L. (1959) 'Some Statistical Problems in Research Design', *American Sociological Review*, 2: 328–38.

Kish, L. (1965) *Survey Sampling*, New York, Wiley.

Klecka, W.R. and Tuchfarber, A.J (1978) 'Random Digit Dialing: A Comparison to Personal Surveys', *Public Opinion Quarterly*, 42: 105–14.

Knoke, D. and Kulinski, J.H (1982) *Network Analysis*, Newbury Park, Sage.

Krebs D. and Schmidt P. (eds) (1993) *New Directions in Attitude Measurement*, New York and Berlin, Walter de Gruyter.

Kruskal, J.B. and Wish, M. (1978) *Multidimensional Scaling*, Beverly Hills, Sage.

Kuhn, T.S. (1962) *The Structure of Scientific Revolutions*, Chicago, The University of Chicago Press; quotations from 1970 edition.

Kutchinsky, B. (1973) 'The Effect of Easy Availability of Pornography on the Incidence of Sex Crimes', *Journal of Social Issues*, 29: 163–81.

Lasswell, H.D. and Leites, N. (eds) (1949) *Language of Politics: Studies in Quantitative Semantics*, New York, Stewart.

Lavrakas, P.J. (1993) *Telephone Survey Methods: Sampling, Selection and Supervision*, 2nd ed., Thousand Oaks, Sage.

Layder D. (1998) *Sociological Practice: Linking Theory and Social Research*, London, Sage.

Lazarsfeld, P.F. (1948) 'The Use of Panels in Social Research', *Proceedings of the American Philosophical Society*, 42: 405–410.

Lazarsfeld, P.F. (1959) 'Problems in Methodology', in R.K. Merton, L. Broom, L.S. Cottrell (eds), *Sociology Today*, New York, Basic Books.

Lazarsfeld, P.F. and Oberschall, R. (1965) 'Max Weber and Empirical Research', *American Sociological Review*, 30: 185–99.

Lazarsfeld, P.F. and Rosenberg, M. (eds) (1955) *The Language of Social Research*, New York, The Free Press.

Likert, R. (1932) 'A Technique for the Measurement of Attitudes', *Archives of Psychology*, 140.

Livolsi, M., Schizzerotto, A., Porro, R. and Chiari, G. (1974) *La macchina del vuoto*, Bologna, Il Mulino.

Lofland, J. (1971) *Analyzing Social Settings*, Belmont, Wadsworth.

Lofland, J. and Lofland, L.H. (1995) *Analyzing Social Settings*, 2nd ed., Belmont, Wadsworth.

Lord, F.M. and Novick, M.R. (1968) *Statistical Theories of Mental Scores*, Reading, Addison-Wesley.

Lynd, R.S. and Lynd, H.M. (1929) *Middletown*, New York, Harcourt, Brace & World; quotations from 1957 edition.

Lynd, R.S. and Lynd, H.M. (1937) *Middletown in Transition*, New York, Harcourt, Brace & World.

Maas, S. and Kuypers, J.A. (1974) *From Thirty to Seventy: a 40 Year Longitudinal Study of Adult Life Styles and Personality*, San Francisco, Jossey Bass.

Madge, J. (1962) *The Origins of Scientific Sociology*, New York, The Free Press.

Malinowski, B. (1922) *Argonauts of the Western Pacific*, London, Routledge & Kegan Paul.

Mangione, T.W. (1995) *Mail Surveys: Improving the Quality*, Thousand Oaks, Sage.

Mann, L. (1969) 'Queue Culture: the Waiting Line as a Social System', *American Journal of Sociology*, 75: 340–54.

Mann, L. (1973) 'Learning to Live with Lines', in J. Helmer and N.A. Eddington (eds), *Urban Man: The Psychology of Urban Survival*, New York, The Free Press.

Maranell G.M. (ed.) (1974) *Scaling: A Sourcebook for Behavioral Scientists*, Chicago, Aldine.

Marradi, A. (1980) *Concetti e metodi per la ricerca sociale*, Firenze, Giuntina.

Marradi, A. (1981) 'Misurazione e scale: qualche riflessione ed una proposta', *Quaderni di sociologia*, 29: 595–639.

Marradi, A. (1996) 'Una lunga ricerca sui valori ed alcuni suoi strumenti', in A. Marradi and G.P. Prandstraller (eds), *L'etica dei ceti emergenti*, Milano, Angeli.

Marsh, C. (1982) *The Survey Method: The Contribution of Surveys to Sociological Explanation*, London, George Allen & Unwin.

Maxim, P.S. (1999) *Quantitative Research Methods in the Social Sciences*, Cambridge, Cambridge University Press.

Maynard, D.W. and Clayman, S.E. (1991) 'The Diversity of Ethnomethodology', in *Annual Review of Sociology, 1991*, 17: 385–418.

Mayo, E. (1966) *Human Problems of an industrial Civilization*, New York, Viking.

McCracken, G. (1988) *The Long Interview*, Newbury Park, Sage.

McIver, J.P. and Carmines, E.G. (1981) *Unidimensional Scaling*, Newbury Park, Sage.

Menard, S. (1991) *Longitudinal Resarch*, Newbury Park, Sage.

Merton, R.K. (1965) *On the Shoulders of Giants*, New York, The Free Press.

Merton, R.K. (1968) *Social Theory and Social Structure*, 2nd ed., New York, The Free Press.

Merton, R.K., Fiske, M.O. and Kendall, P.L. (1956) *The Focused Interview*, New York, The Free Press.

Milgram, S. (1974) *Obedience to Authority: An Experimental View*, New York, Harper & Row.

Mill, J.S. (1843) *A System of Logic Ratiocinative and Inductive*, London, Longmans; quotation from 1973 edition, London, Routledge & Kegan Paul.

Miller, R.L. (2000) *Researching Life Stories and Family Histories*, Thousand Oaks, Sage.

Mishler, E.G. (1986) *Research Interviewing: Context and Narrative*, Cambridge, Harvard University Press.

Moreno, J. (1970) *Barrios in Arms*, Pittsburgh, University of Pittsburgh Press.

Moreno, J.L. (1934) *Who Shall Survive?*, Washington D.C., Nervous and Mental Disease Publishing Co.

Morgan, D.L. (1996) 'Focus Groups', *Annual Review of Sociology, 1996*, 22: 129–52.

Moser, C.A. and Kalton, G. (1971) *Survey Methods in Social Investigation*. London, Heinemann.

Mowrer, E.R. (1927) *Family Disorganization*, Chicago, University of Chicago Press.

Newman I. and Benz C.R. (1988) *Qualitative-Quantitative Research Methodology: Exploring the Interactive Continuum*, Carbondale, Southern Illinois University Press.

Newson, J and Newson, E. (1978) *Seven Years Old in the Home Environment*, Harmondsworth, Penguin Books.

Nunnally, J.C. (1959) *Test and Measurement: Assessment and Prediction*, New York, McGraw Hill.

Nunnally, J.C. (1978) *Psychometric Theory*, New York, McGraw Hill.

Orbuch T.L. (1997) 'People's Accounts Count: The Sociology of Accounts', *Annual Review of Sociology 1997*, 23: 455–78.

Osgood, C.E. (1952) 'The Nature and Measurement of Meaning', *Psychological Bulletin*, 49: 197–237.

Osgood, C.E., Suci, G.J. and Tannenbaum, P.H. (1957) *The Measurement of Meaning*, Urbana, University of Illinois Press.

Palmer, V.M. (1928) *Field Studies in Sociology: a Student's Manual*, Chicago, University of Chicago Press.

Patton, M.Q. (1990) *Qualitative Evaluation and Research Methods*, Newbury Park, Sage, 1990.

Pawson, R. and Tilley, N. (1997) *Realistic Evaluation*, London, Sage.

Pedhazur, E.J. and Pedhazur Schmelkin L. (1991) *Measurement Design and Analysis: An Integrated Approach*, Hillsdale, Lawrence Erlbaum Associates.

Pheterson, G.I., Kiesler, S.B. and Goldberg, P.A. (1971) 'Evaluation of the Performance of Women as a Function of their Sex, Achievement, and Personal History', *Journal of Personality and Social Psychology*, 19: 114–118.

Plummer, K. (1983) *Documents of Life*, Boston, Allen & Unwin.

Polsby, N.W. (1963) *Community Power and Political Theory*, New Haven, Yale University Press.

Popper, K.R. (1934) *Logik der Forschung*, Vienna; quotations from *The Logic of Scientific Discovery*, London, Routledge, 1992.

Prior, L. (1997) *Following in Foucault's Footsteps: Text and Context in Qualitative Research*, in Silverman (1997).

Propp, V. (1928) *Morfologjia skazki*, Leningrad, Academia; *Morphology of the Folktale*, Austin, University of Texas Press, 1968.

Rathje, W. and Murphy, C. (1992) *Rubbish! The Archaeology of Garbage*, New York, Harper & Collins.

Reichenbach, H. (1951) *The Rise of Scientific Philosophy*, Berkeley, University of California Press.

Ricci, A. and Salierno, G. (1971) *Il carcere in Italia*, Torino, Einaudi.

Riessman, C.K. (1990) *Divorce Talk*, New Brunswick, Rutgers University Press.

Ritzer G. and Smart B. (2001) *Handbook of Social Theory*, London, Sage.

Robertshaw, P. (1985) 'Semantic and Linguistic Aspect of Sex Discrimination Decision. Dichotomised Woman', in D. Carzo and B.S. Jackson (eds), *Semiotics, Law and Social Science*, Roma, Gangemi.

Robinson, J.P., Shaver, P.R. and Wrightsman, L.S. (1991) *Measures of Personality and Social Psychological Attitudes*, San Diego, Academic Press.

Robinson, J.P., Shaver, P.R. and Wrightsman, L.S. (1999) *Measures of Political Attitudes*, San Diego, Academic Press.

Romero, M. (1992) *Maid in the USA*, New York, Routledge.

Rosenthal, R. (1966) *Experimenter Effects in Behavioral Research*, New York, Appleton Century Crofts.

Rosenthal, R. and Jacobson, L. (1968) 'Teacher Expectations for the Disadvantaged', *Scientific American*: 19–23.

Rossi, P.H., Wright, G.D. and Anderson, A.B. (1983) *Handbook of Survey Research*, San Diego, Academic Press.

Rothschild-Whitt, J. (1979) 'The Collectivistic Organisation: an Alternative to Rational-Bureaucratic Models', *American Sociological Review*, 44: 509–27.

Rotton, J. and Kelly, I.W. (1985) 'Much Ado About the Full Moon: A Meta-Analysis of Lunar-Lunacy Research', *Psychological Bulletin*, 97: 286–306.

Roy, D. (1952) 'Quota Restriction and Goldbricking in a Machine Shop', *The American Journal of Sociology*, 57: 427–42.

Rubin, D.B. (1974) 'Estimating Causal Effects of Treatments in Randomized and Nonrandomized Studies', *Journal of Educational Psychology*, 66: 688–701.

Rugg, D. (1941) 'Experiments in Wording Questions: II', *Public Opinion Quarterly*, 5: 91–2.

Runciman, W.G. (1966) *Relative Deprivation and Social Justice*, London, Routledge & Kegan.

Salzinger, K. (1958) 'A Method of Analysis of the Process of Verbal Communication between a Group of Emotionally Disturbed Adolescents, and their Friends and Relatives', *The Journal of Social Psychology*, 47: 39–53.

Sampson, R.J. and Laub, J.H. (1993) *Crime in the Making*: Pathways and Turning Points through Life, Cambridge, Harvard University Press.

Sánchez-Jankowski, M. (1991) *Islands in the Street*: Gangs and American Urban Society, Berkeley, University of California Press.

Sanstrom, K.L. Martin, D.D. and Fine, G.A. (2001) *Symbolic Interactionism as the End of the Century*, in Ritzer and Smart (2001).

Schuman, H. and Presser, S. (1981) *Questions and Answers in Attitude Surveys*, New York, Academic Press.

Schutz, A. (1932) *Der Dinnhafte Aufbander sozialen Welt; eine Einleitung in die Verstehende Soziologie*, Wien, Springer; quotations from *The Phenomenology of Social World*, Evanston, Northwestern University Press, 1967.

Schwartz, H. and Jacobs, J. (1979) *Qualitative Sociology*, New York, The Free Press.

Sciolla, L. and Ricolfi, L. (1989) *Vent'anni dopo*, Bologna, Il Mulino.

Scott, J. (1990) *A Matter of Record: Documentary Sources in Social Research*, Cambridge, Polity Press.

Scott, M. (1968) *The Racing Game*, Chicago, Aldine.

Selltiz C., Wrightsman, L.S. and Cook, S.W. (1976) *Research Methods in Social Relations*, New York, Holt, Rinehart and Winston.

Shaw, B. (1941) *The Doctor's Dilemma*, New York, Dodd, Mead & Co. (1st ed. 1911).

Sheatsley, P.B. (1983) *Questionnaire Construction and Item Writing*, in Rossi et al. (1983).

Sherif, M. (1967) *Group Conflict and Co-operation: Their Social Psychology*, London, Routledge & Kegan.

Siegfried, A. (1913) *Tableau Politique de la France de l'ovest sous la Troisiéme Republique*, Paris, Libraire Armand Colin.

Silverman, D. (ed.) (1997) *Qualitative Research*, London, Sage.

Smith, T.W. (1984) 'Nonattitudes: A Review and Evaluation', in C.F. Turner and E. Martin (eds), *Surveying Subjective Phenomena*, New York, Russell Sage Foundation.

Sniderman, P.M. and Grob, D.B. (1996) 'Innovations in Experimental Design in Attitude Surveys', *Annual Review of Sociology 1996*, 22: 377–99.

Spradley, J.P. (1979) *The Ethnographic Interview*, New York, Holt, Rinheart & Winston.

Spradley, J.P. (1980) *Participant Observation*, New York, Holt, Rinehart & Winston.

Steffensmeier D.J. (1986) *The Fence*, Totowa, Rowman & Littlefield.

Stevens, S.S. (1946) 'On the Theory of Scales of Measurement', *Science*, 103: 677–80.

Stewart, D.W. and Shamdasani, P.N. (1990) *Focus Groups: Theory and Practice*, Newbury Park, Sage.

Stinchcombe, A.L. (1968) *Constructing Social Theories*, New York, Harcourt, Brace & World.

Strauss, A.L. and Corbin, J. (1990) *Basics for Qualitative Research: Grounded Theory Procedures and Techniques*, Newbury Park, Sage.

Sudman, S. and Bradburn, N.R. (1982) *Asking Questions*, San Francisco, Jossey-Bass.

Sudman, S., Bradburn, N.M. and Schwarz, N. (1996) *Thinking About Answers: The Application of Cognitive Processes to Survey Methodology*, San Francisco, Jossey-Bass.

Sussman, L. (1963) *Dear F.D.R.*, New York, Bedminster.

Sutherland, E.H. (1937) *The Professional Thief*, Chicago, University of Chicago Press.

Tashakkori A. and Teddlie C. (1998) *Mixed Methodology: Combining Qualitative and Quantitative Approaches*, Thousand Oaks, Sage.

Thomas, W.I. and Znaniecki, F. (1918–1920) *The Polish Peasant in Europe and America,* Chicago, The University of Chicago Press.

Thomas, W.I. and Znaniecki, F. (1919) *The Polish Peasant in Europe and America, vol. III, Life record of an Immigrant*, Boston, The Gorham Press.

Thompson, P. (1972) 'Problems of Method in Oral History', *Oral History*, 4, 2: 1–47.

Thompson, P. (1975) *The Edwardians. The Remaking of British Society*, London, Weidenfeld.

Thurstone, L.L. (1927) 'A Law of Comparative Judgement', *Psychological Review*, 34: 273–86.

Thurstone, L.L. (1928) 'Attitudes Can Be Measured', *American Journal of Sociology*, 33: 529–54.

Thurstone, L.L. (1931) 'Rank Order as a Psychophysical Method', *Journal of Experimental Psychology*, 6: 187–201.

Thurstone, L.L and Chave, E.J. (1929) *The Measurement of Attitude*, Chicago, The University of Chicago Press.

Tingsten, H. (1937) *Political Behaviour: Studies in Election Statistics*, London and Stockholm, King & Son.

Tocqueville, A. de (1856) *L'Ancien régime et la révolution*; quotations from *The Old Régime and the French Revolution*, Garden City, N.Y., Doubleday Anchor Books, 1955.

Tulis, J. (1987) *The Rethorical Presidency*, Princeton, Princeton University Press.

Van Maanen, J. (1988) *Tales of the Field*, Chicago, The University of Chicago Press.

Van Maanen, J., Dabbs, J.M. and Faulkner, R.R. (1982) *Varieties of Qualitative Research*, Beverly Hills, Sage.

Vidich, A.J. and Stanford, M.L. (2000) *Qualitative Methods: Their History in Sociology and Anthropology*, in Denzin and Lincoln (2000).

Vuchinich, S. (1990) *The Sequential Organization of Closing in Verbal Family Conflict*, in Grimshaw (1990).

Wagenaar, A.C. (1981) 'Effect of the Raised Legal Drinking Age on Motor Vehicle Accidents in Michigan', *HSRI Research Review*, 11: 1–8.

Wallerstein, J.S. and Kelly, J.B. (1980) *Surviving the Breakup,* New York, Basic Books.

Walum, L.R. (1974) 'The Changing Door Ceremony', *Urban Life and Culture*, 2: 506–515.

Wasserman, S. and Faust, K. (1994) *Social Network Analysis*, Cambridge, Cambridge University Press.

Webb, E.J., Campbell, D.T., Schwartz, D. and Sechrest, L. (1966) *Unobtrusive Measures*,

Chicago, Rand Mcnally; 2nd ed., *Nonreactive measures in the Social Sciences*, Boston, Houghton & Mifflin, 1981; 3rd ed., Corwin Press, 1999.

Weber, M. (1904) *Über die 'Objectivität' sozial wissenshaftlicher und sozialpolitsher Erkenntins*; later reprinted in Weber (1922b).

Weber, M. (1922a) *Wirtschaft und Gesellshaft*, Tübingen, Mohr.

Weber, M. (1922b) *Gesammelte Aufsätze zur Wissenschaftslehre*, Tübingen, Mohr.

Weber, M. (1924) *Gesammelte Aufsätze zur Soziologie un Sozialpolitik*, Tübingen, Mohr.

Weisberg, H.F. and Rusk, J.G. (1970) 'Dimensions of Candidate Evaluation', *American Political Science Review*, 64: 1167–85.

Weiss, J. and Gruber, G. (1987) 'The Managed Irrelevance of Federal Education Statistics' in W. Alonso and P. Starr (eds), *The Politics of Numbers*, New York, Russell Sage Foundation.

Whimster, S. (2001) *Max Weber: Work and Inter Relation*, in Ritzer and Smart (2001).

Whyte, W.F. (1943) *Street Corner Society. The Social Structure of an Italian Slum*, Chicago, The University of Chicago Press; 2nd ed., 1950.

Whyte, W.F. (1984) *Learning from the Field*, Beverly Hills, Sage.

Winship, C. and Morgan, S. (1999) 'The Estimation of Causal Effects from Observational Data', *Annual Review of Sociology 1999*, 25: 659–707.

Wiseman, J. (1979) 'Close Encounters on the Quasi-Primary Kind: Sociability in Urban Second-Half Clothing Stores', *Urban Life*, 8: 23–51.

Wolfinger, R. (1973) *The Politics of Progress*, Englewood Cliffs, Prentice Hall.

Woods, P. (1979) *The Divided School*, London, Routledge & Kegan.

Zimmerman, D.H. and Wieder, D.L. (1977) 'The Diary-interview Method', *Urban Life*, 5: 479–97.

Index

Page references in italics indicate figures, tables or boxes.